ADULT NONFICTION   c.1

920.72 R196

Raven, Susan
Women of achievement :thirty-five c
enturies of history

8000031257

W9-BWO-850

Raven, S   920.72
                                  R196
Women of achievement   c.1

WITHDRAWN

ADULT DEPARTMENT

1. Fine Schedule
   each day overdue . . . . grace period, no fine
   6-10 days overdue . . . . 25¢ per item
   11-19 days overdue . . . . 75¢ per item
   20th day overdue . . . . $2.00 per item
2. Injury to books beyond reasonable wear and all
   losses shall be paid for.
3. Each borrower is held responsible for all books
   drawn on his card and for all fines accruing on
   the same.

FOND DU LAC PUBLIC LIBRARY
COUNTY LIBRARY DEPARTMENT

GC
FOND DU LAC, WISCONSIN

—WOMEN OF—
ACHIEVEMENT

Endpapers British suffragette Sylvia Pankhurst
addressing a crowd in 1912
(BBC Hulton Picture Library)

—WOMEN OF—
ACHIEVEMENT

Thirty-five Centuries of History

Susan Raven and Alison Weir

Foreword by Elizabeth Longford

HARMONY BOOKS   NEW YORK

Our thanks are due to the many friends and acquaintances
who gave us ideas and information with this book. For
particular help, we would like to thank David Doughan at
the Fawcett Library; Nicholas Mason of *The Sunday Times*
Sports Department; Jeff Franklin and Ray Smith of *The
Sunday Times* Library; Robert Thirkell of the BBC; Kikki
Mattei and Dr Jonathan Miller.
And especial thanks to Kate Dunning of Weidenfeld and
Nicolson, who nursed the project from the beginning and
encouraged us throughout; to Beatrice Phillpotts, without
whose brilliant editing our raw copy would never have
reached the printed page (any infelicities are, of course, our
responsibility); and finally to Brian stone, our agent, and
Colin Webb, then at Weidenfeld, who between them
asked us to write it.

Copyright © Susan Raven and Alison Weir, 1981

All rights reserved. No part of this publication may be
reproduced, stored in a retrieval system, or transmitted, in
any form or by any means, electronic, mechanical,
photocopying, recording or otherwise, without the prior
permission of the copyright owner.

First published in Great Britain under the title
Women in History by
George Weidenfeld and Nicolson Ltd
91 Clapham High Street, London SW4

First published in the United States by
Harmony Books, a division of Crown Publishers, Inc.
One Park Avenue, New York, New York 10016

Designed by Allison Waterhouse

Filmset in Great Britain by
BAS Printers Limited, Over Wallop, Hampshire
Printed in the United States of America

Library of Congress Cataloging in Publication Data
Raven, Susan.
Women of Achievement

1. Women—Biography, I. Weir, Alison, joint author.
II. Title.
HQ1123.R38 1980   920.72   80–24239
ISBN 0-517-53982-9

FOND DU LAC PUBLIC LIBRARY

- - -

COUNTY LIBRARY DEPARTMENT

920.72
R196
c.1

CONTENTS

FOREWORD

'LET US NOW PRAISE famous *women*.' It was not the fault of the biblical writer that he invited us to praise only the men. We must blame Civilization for its patriarchal bias. Now Susan Raven and Alison Weir have courageously set themselves the task of putting the record straight. The result is deeply impressive.

The Raven–Weir presentation has a cumulative effect and builds up a convincing and hopeful picture of women's progress. If you like, it is 'feminist'. Outstanding is the great nineteenth-century drive for women's equal opportunities, known as the Women's Movement. We see 'Women's Lib' as a twentieth-century case of the damped-down fires breaking out again. New claims are being made for the total personality and soul of woman, as well as those for her rights which are still unattained.

We all have our special interests. I might have pushed forward another mystic and sacrificed a body masseuse. But I applaud Raven and Weir's selection for its originality and comprehensiveness. The contribution of black women is particularly welcome. One of the touchstones of women's advance – motherhood – is brought to mind by the many black women on whom has been bestowed the time-honoured title of 'Ma'.

There are plenty of other landmarks in different fields: nursing, education, science, medicine, legal rights, the vote, the veil, temperance, anti-slavery, local government, peace and planned parenthood. These issues were or are either women's 'causes' or universal problems in which women have found the chance to distinguish themselves. Here are the 'first' women to do this or that, and many of the Nobel Prize-winners.

Businesslike and efficient as Raven and Weir are in the handling of their vast subject, they still find room for verbal fireworks: Dame Kathleen Lonsdale, required to enter her race on a visa-form and writing 'Human'; Susan B. Anthony adopting as her motto, 'Men, their rights and nothing more – Women, their rights and nothing less.' Or a favourite type of feminist joke, here made by a man, William Booth of the Salvation Army: 'Some of my best men are women.'

Coming to the end of these economical yet vivid pages, I am left with three thoughts. First, how parochial we all are, whatever nation we belong to, and how much we women need this fascinating book. Even in the English-speaking world, for example, how many of us can associate Amelia Bloomer with anything but knickers? Second, what a lot can be done by women of character, however dead-weight the opposition. Third, women's glory in these pages is not to have become mirror-men but to have become themselves – themselves fulfilled.

Elizabeth Longford.

INTRODUCTION

THIS BOOK IS NOT A HISTORY OF WOMEN; it is about just some of the women whose lives and work would have to be reckoned with in such a history – indeed, must be reckoned with in any history of human achievement.

When we began our research, we were immensely excited about the sheer numbers of women who, in the past, had managed to emerge from the conventional strait-jacket of wife-mother-mistress, and had made their mark in the wider world. We could well have written about ten or twenty times as many, and still only included a small fraction of the women of achievement whose names have survived. But we have decided to write in some detail about a few hundred of them, rather than too briefly about a few thousand – partly because we find them interesting in themselves, and partly to give a better idea of their individual histories, and of the disadvantages and difficulties they faced, and overcame.

Having to make a choice, we have confined ourselves, as our title suggests, to historical women. We have excluded – with regret – the heroines of myth and legend. There are no mother goddesses, no Amazons, none of the women of the Bible, no Dido. We felt, too, that women with no name had to be left out; we have not included the Delphic oracle and the Cumaean Sybil, and other anonymous priestesses of the ancient world. We have also omitted women whose societies left no written record. There is only Queen Boudicca, who led an army against the Roman occupation of Britain, to represent the warrior queens of Celtic Europe who briefly cross the pages of Greek and Roman historians or are remembered in the legends of early Ireland. Nor is this book about famous wives and mistresses (although some of the women we include may incidentally be famous wives or mistresses), muses, mothers, or even great ancestresses: so there is no Pocahontas, no Cornelia (mother of the Gracchi), Nell Gwynn or Madame du Barry, no Jacqueline Kennedy Onassis.

The women who remain span the whole range of human achievement and the whole range of human character. If Joan of Arc had never lived, what novelist would have dared to invent her – or even been able to imagine her? Who could have predicted that three little girls growing up in poverty in an isolated Yorkshire rectory would between them write several of the greatest novels of the nineteenth century? How did Wu Chao, a minor concubine in seventh-century China, break every taboo and become, in a male-dominated society, ruler both in name and in fact?

Many of the women we include are like the Brontë sisters, so familiar that perhaps we take their achievements for granted. But there was nothing in the background of Florence Nightingale to encourage her (indeed, everything to discourage her) to revolutionize the nursing profession virtually single-handed – and then, though bedridden for the remaining fifty years of her life, embark on a second career as an expert on the British Army, India, sanitation and Poor Law Reform. Madame Tussaud started her professional life as an art tutor to the sister of the king of France, switched during the French Revolution to making death masks of the victims of the guillotine, and emigrated to England where for thirty years she toured with her waxworks exhibition before founding in London what is still, more than a century later, one of the most successful 'museums' in the world. Marie Curie had great difficulty in getting to university, and once there had to study in a foreign language; she had many years of desperate poverty and illness before the discovery of radium – itself a triumph of persistence and back-breaking labour – won her the Nobel Prize.

We believe that however impressive, various, or important the achievements of our chosen women may be, those achievements are only part of their story; so where possible we have also tried to describe something of the background of our subjects, both their personal histories and the context of their lives. Often, the achievements shine all the more.

Of necessity we have concentrated on women from Europe and North America, and from recent centuries, not only because their lives are normally far better documented, but also because modern women in the Western world have had more opportunities for achievement than all but a handful of women in the ancient world or in today's developing world. Nevertheless, we have ranged as widely as possible: from Greece in the sixth century BC to modern India, from seventh-century Korea to modern Egypt. No continent is unrepresented; and few centuries in the last three thousand five hundred years.

We have divided the book into ten sections. Some are unavoidably modern. *Sport*, for instance, is a very recent phenomenon (indeed it is, substantially, for men also), as is *Travel*, which tends to be the privilege of comparative affluence – although nuns and other religious women have travelled far from home as pilgrims and missionaries since the days of the Roman Empire. *Education and Social Reform* – an area in which women's contribution, especially in the last century when they were still without civil rights, has been particularly impressive – is also overweighted towards modern times, and so is the section on *Money and Management* – not surprisingly, since the legal constraints on women's economic independence were formidable until at least a hundred years ago.

Since there were constraints, too, on women performing professionally on the stage, nearly all our entries in the *Performing Arts* date from the seventeenth century and later; though we are well aware that there have always been women singers and dancers (the seventh-century Byzantine Empress Theodora started life as a mime actress). But it has been a pleasure to be able to include so many women from the more distant past in our sections on the *Visual Arts* and the *Written Word* – not only from Europe, but from the Far East also. We have been particularly struck by the number of women artists we had to choose from, most of whom were unfamiliar names to us; fortunately this is a field of research in which feminist art historians are now hard at work. By contrast, we knew we should be faced with an immensely large number of women writers; all the same the number of women writers from previous centuries, though less surprising than the number of women artists, is gratifying. Choosing from among them has been difficult, and although the *Written Word* is by far our longest section we are painfully aware of the dozens of writers we have not had room to include.

In *Science and Medicine*, too, there are representatives not only from the modern world but from the Middle Ages and even the ancient world. There could have been more entries in this section also. The same is true of *Religion* – we could have included scores of names from practically every century of the Christian era. The Christian Church has been notably thorough in recording and handing down its own history, from the Acts of the Apostles and St Paul's Letters to the lives of its saints and the trials of its martyrs – women as well as men. Limited though their role in the Christian churches is, women have a more important place in the history of Christianity than in that of other religions in historic times – which has created another imbalance: this section is almost entirely Christian.

Politics and Power is the section which ranges most widely – from women at the top of society to women at the grassroots. It includes Cleopatra and Golda Meir, Rosa Luxemburg and Angela Davis – and a spectrum of women in between. It offers some of the most striking examples of women's worldly capabilities, and of their courage. It also offers striking examples of virtue – and of vice. In any catalogue of human villainy the Empress Wu, among the most brilliant of the rulers of China, would comfortably outclass the Borgias – let alone Catherine the Great or Ana Pauker.

However, there is an immense variety of background and character in all ten sections. There is also an obvious variation of 'importance' – some women have achieved far more, or been more influential, than others; the achievement of yet other women has been primarily of benefit to themselves. But our choice has been guided by a desire to include unfamiliar names as well as familiar; and some of the unfamiliar ones are, we believe, among the most interesting, and often 'important' too. Few people will have heard of Hypatia, who taught philosophy in Egypt in the early fifth century; or Aletta Jacobs, who opened the world's first birth control clinic in Holland; or Shirley Smith, an Australian aborigine who has spent her life working for her fellow aborigines.

Finally, women themselves are so various. Time and again we could have put individual women not into one category alone, but into two or even three. Hester Bateman: silversmith or businesswoman (she ran the family workshop)? Maria Sibylla Merian: artist, traveller, or botanist? Margery Kempe: mystic, writer, or traveller? Should fashion designers – who are also immensely successful business women – be under *Visual Arts* or *Money and Management*? Even ballet impresarios like Dame Ninette de Valois or Martha Graham, who founded great and famous companies and are certainly entrepreneurs as well as exponents of the performing arts, caused us problems. We have not solved them all satisfactorily. But we hope that part of the fun of a book like this is becoming involved and interested enough to quarrel with our judgement, to complain (occasionally) about our inclusions and above all bewail (often) our omissions. No one is more conscious of the names that are not here than we are – or of the millions of nameless women whose achievements are buried in the silence of prehistory or the anonymity of the crowd.

Susan Raven, Alison Weir, London 1981

POLITICS AND POWER

WOMEN IN POLITICS remain the exception rather than the rule, even in the most liberal societies. However, in spite of the relatively small number of women in public life in the late twentieth century, India, Sri Lanka, Israel, Iceland, Norway, Dominica, Britain, Portugal, Bolivia and Argentina all have, or have had, women presidents or prime ministers.

Yet a woman ruler is no new thing. By an anomaly of the European laws of inheritance it is easier for a woman to inherit a throne in her own right than for her to inherit a lesser title. (A crown descends to a daughter if the monarch has no sons; a coronet, with rare exceptions, descends only in the male line, and thus to a brother and his sons if there are only daughters.) So the history of Europe is rich in women rulers, many of them exceptionally able, notably Margaret of Scandinavia, Isabella of Spain, Elizabeth I of England, Christina of Sweden and Maria Theresa of Austria-Hungary. Other countries too – China, India and Egypt, for example – have had their women rulers, women regents, even women usurpers.

But politics is not only about established power, it is also about overturning that power, and in the revolutionary movements of the modern world – in France, Russia, Germany, China, Vietnam, Ireland, America and South Africa – women have played a vital role. Significantly, that role has been largely overlooked, principally because once a revolution has been won, women have not inherited their rightful share of the power. This was particularly true of the French Revolution in 1789 and the Russian Revolution in 1917. For every Furtseva who was to gain a place on the Politburo, there were three Kollontais who were either side-tracked away from the centre of power, as Kollontai herself was, or left to rot away their lives in prison.

Madame Binh at the Vietnamese Peace Conference in Paris, 1973.

Abigail Adams, first First Lady at the White House, engraved from a painting by Gilbert Stuart.

Abigail Adams
American (1744–1818)

As the wife and mother of two Presidents (the second, John Adams, and the sixth, John Quincy Adams), Abigail Adams had great influence in the early years of the United States. She was the first First Lady at the White House (which was built in 1800) and set the pattern for many First Ladies to come. Her marriage to John Adams was widely admired as a true partnership; she spoke up for the education of women and in 1777 urged her husband and the Founding Fathers of the new Republic of the United States not to 'put such unlimited power into the hands of the Husbands. Remember, all men would be tyrants if they could.'

She was born Abigail Smith in 1744, one of three daughters of a parson of Weymouth, Massachusetts.

At 19 she married John Adams, a young lawyer, and bore him five children. Together they played an important part in the fight against the British Crown which led to the Declaration of Independence in 1776. When John Adams became congressman in Philadelphia, she remained behind at Quincy to manage the family farm and wrote the many lively, intelligent letters – some 150 survive – for which modern Americans still honour her. In 1775, with Mrs Winthrop and Mrs Warren, she was given the task of interrogating those women who still supported the British monarchy and as 'judges' she won her political spurs. Her advice was eventually sought not only by her husband but by many others too.

From 1784 to 1788 Adams accompanied her husband to Europe, where he was the new U.S. representative, first in France and then in England. When her husband became Vice-President she was closely involved in much of his official work. When he became President in 1797, they led a simple and unostentatious official life. After his defeat in 1801 she returned to Quincy where she lived until her death from typhoid – still consulted on affairs of state, but now by her son John, who some years after her death was to become the sixth President of the United States.

Nancy Astor
American (1879–1964)

Although not British by birth, Lady Astor was the first woman (cf. Constance Markiewicz) to sit in the House of Commons at Westminster, and she gave the job a style and sparkle all her own.

She was one of the five beautiful Langhorne sisters from Virginia and at 18 married Robert Gould Shaw; they had one son. The Shaws were divorced in 1903 and in 1906 she married Waldorf Astor, later Viscount Astor, the son of an American multimillionaire living in England who had been raised to the peerage. They had four sons and one daughter. Waldorf Astor was Conservative Member of Parliament for the Sutton Division of Plymouth, but when his father died he inherited the peerage and had to resign his seat. Nancy Astor was elected in her husband's place.

Nancy Astor speaking out against McCarthyism at a Red Cross lunch in Washington, March 1953.

Her maiden speech against the Intoxicating Liquor Bill launched Lady Astor on 25 years of political battle for issues close to her heart. 'I hate wars – all wars – but I love fighting,' she said.

A controversial figure, she later said her first six months in Parliament were 'hell': in one famous exchange, she told Winston Churchill, 'If I were your wife I'd put poison in your coffee.' 'If I were your husband,' he replied, 'I'd drink it.' Other MPs said they felt as though she 'had come into their private bathroom.'

In 1931 Nancy Astor went to the Soviet Union with her friend George Bernard Shaw and asked Stalin 'when he was going to stop killing people.' Many influential people gathered at Cliveden, the Astors' country house; they were known as the 'Cliveden Set' and were accused of being 'a second Foreign Office' and pro-Nazi Germany in the thirties. During the Second World War Lady Astor bravely toured her bombed-out constituents in Plymouth and was still active in promoting teetotalism and Christian Science (cf. Mary Baker Eddy) when her husband requested her – much against her will – to retire from politics in 1945.

Lakshmi Bai, Rani of Jhansi
Indian (1835–1857)

The Rani of Jhansi, who died fighting the British in the Indian Mutiny, was one of the great heroines of modern India. She was born in Jhansi, lost her mother early and was brought up with adoptive brothers, with whom she received not only a basic education but also learnt the arts of riding, swordsmanship and archery.

Lakshmi became the second wife of the Raja of Jhansi, Srimanta Gengadhar Rao. When their only child died, the Raja adopted his nephew as his heir, with Lakshmi's full approval. However, when ten years later the Raja died, the British saw an opportunity to make the state of Jhansi dependent on the British Crown by declaring the adoption of the new heir illegal, thus depriving Jhansi of its independent status.

The Rani appealed to London, but in vain. Enraged, she bided her time, though keeping on good terms with the British. In 1857, when the sepoys at Jhansi joined the Indian mutiny against the British, the Rani was expected to side with the British in their attempts to recapture Jhansi. But she did not. For 13 days during the British assault she was on horseback among her own troops, in the thick of the fighting, until just before Jhansi fell, when she slipped away under cover of darkness to join the troops of her neighbour Tatya Tope. During Tatya's absence to raise fresh troops, the Rani defended the fort at Kalpi against the British.

When she was finally forced to retreat, the British moved to attack her. Wearing soldier's uniform and riding like one, 'using her sword with both hands and holding the reins of her horse in her mouth', the Rani once more rode among her troops, encouraging them. She was cut down by a British hussar.

Sirimavo Bandaranaike
Sri Lankan (b. 1916)

Sirimavo Bandaranaike became the first woman Prime Minister of modern times in 1960. She was born into an old aristocratic Sinhalese family; her father was a member of the Senate, and many of her ancestors had held high office under the ancient Sinhalese kings. She was educated at St Bridget's Convent, Colombo, 'the Roedean of Ceylon', where she finished a course in domestic science. She then lived at home until a marriage was arranged in 1940 between her and Solmon Bandaranaike, an aspiring politician in his mid-forties , who was in need of the power base her family could provide. For the next 19 years she devoted herself to her husband's political career and to raising a family, while supporting such causes as the All Ceylon Women's Institute, family planning, and women's rights.

Her husband became Prime Minister in 1956, but was assassinated in 1959. His party, the Sri Lanka Freedom Party, having no suitable figurehead for the forthcoming election, persuaded Mrs Bandaranaike to take over his progressive and nationalist policies. On August 5, 1960, she became Prime Minister from a nominated seat in the Senate, in a coalition with the Communists and Trotskyites. Unfortunately in a poor country with free medicine, education and rice, her progressive policies led to increasing poverty and unemployment, and this, combined with her discrimination against the Tamil minority, led to her defeat at the 1965 elections.

However the National Freedom Party fared little better, and in 1970 she won a landslide victory. In 1972 she changed the constitution, Ceylon became the Commonwealth republic of Sri Lanka, and at the same time she extended her term of office by two years. But a combination of the 1973 world recession, and the nationalization of the tea-estates and banks in 1975, led to increasingly high unemployment, soaring inflation, and the absence of many imported goods and basic necessities. This, combined with charges of corruption and nepotism (her nephew was Minister of Finance, her daughter Minister of Defence and Foreign Affairs) and the political tactlessness and interference of her son, Anura, led to her crushing defeat in the 1977 election, and the appointment of a judicial commission of investigation.

Gertrude Bell
British (1868–1926)

Gertrude Bell was a traveller, letter writer and Arabist who had great influence on Middle Eastern politics. She was the daughter of Sir Hugh Bell, an industrialist in the North of England, and the first woman to get a first-class degree in history at Oxford in 1888. Thereafter, she travelled extensively. She learnt Persian, Arabic and Turkish besides some of the languages spoken in India, China and Japan, and in 1897 she published her translation of the Persian poet Hafiz. Bell made her name in 1901 as a climber in the Swiss Alps, but returned to the Middle East where she felt she had heard what she described as 'the true call'. In 1905 she made an adventurous journey from Syria to Turkey where she worked on a Hittite archeological site, the basis of *The Palace and Mosque of Ukhaidir* (1914).

Determined to be the second woman in Central Arabia (cf. Lady Anne Blunt), Bell then embarked on her remarkable journeys eastwards from Damascus, which she described in voluminous letters. These expeditions gave her an unrivalled knowledge of the Bedouin, and in 1915, during the First World War, she was employed by the Arab Bureau in Cairo; Egypt was then a British protectorate. She was sent to India by the British Government in 1916 and, after the war, was made Oriental secretary in Baghdad, a post of considerable importance. Her influence resulted in the appointments of Faisal, Hussein and Ibn Saud as rulers of those regions of the former Ottoman Empire, which are now Iraq, Jordan and Saudi Arabia.

Bell's travel books include, notably, *The Desert and the Sown* (1907) and her administrative gifts can best be seen in her *Review of the Civil Administration of Mesopotamia* (1921). In 1918 she was made Director of Antiquities in Baghdad, where a wing of the museum commemorates her achievements.

16

Gertrude Bell, traveller and Arabist, who had great influence on Middle Eastern politics.

Nguyen Thi Binh
Vietnamese (b. 1927)

Madame Binh led North Vietnam's National Liberation Front delegation at the Vietnamese Peace Conference in Paris which began in 1968. It was she who, on January 27, 1973, signed the Paris accords on behalf of the NLF, which marked the end of the Vietnam War.

Nguyen Thi Binh, then Head of Foreign Affairs, was born in Saigon, South Vietnam, in 1927, daughter and granddaughter of militant nationalists in the fight against the French colonialists. Her grandfather was the famous patriot Phan Chau Trinh, her father was a civil servant, and after her mother's death, when her father was forced to go underground, she had to bring up her five younger

brothers and sisters. She was educated at a French lycée, and eventually became a teacher. In 1951 she was imprisoned for three years for organizing protests and distributing leaflets. On her release, after the signing of the Geneva Agreement which ended French rule in 1954, she married the son of a landowner in the Mekong Delta. But they both had to go underground – literally – during the dictatorship of President Diem, emerging only at night. Mme Binh had a son and a daughter, whom she has seen very little. Those were the long years of organizing the National Liberation Front against Diem and, later, the Americans. In 1969 Mme Binh was appointed Foreign Minister of the NLF's Provisional Revolutionary Government, and since the North Vietnamese victory has been one of the few South Vietnamese to hold government posts. She was appointed Minister of Education in 1976.

Other Vietnamese women played leading parts in the struggle against foreign domination; Mme Nguyen Thi Dinh was Deputy Commander of the liberation forces in South Vietnam, and there were two other women ministers in the Provisional Revolutionary Government. Vietnam has a long history of women leaders. In AD 40 the two Trung sisters led a rebellion against the Chinese overlords, and in AD 248 Trieu Thi Trinh, a peasant of 23, led thousands of her compatriots in a revolt against the Chinese; when it was unsuccessful, she committed suicide.

Clare Boothe Luce
American (b. 1903)

Clare Boothe Luce has been journalist, playwright, politician, ambassador, even a child actress: she once understudied for Mary Pickford (q.v.). But she is best known as the author of the play, *The Women*, which was produced in 1936 and had a very successful run, and as President Eisenhower's Ambassador to Italy from 1953 to 1957: the first American woman head of mission to a major posting. She was also the first woman elected to Congress by the state of Connecticut, and served from 1943 to 1947.

Clare Boothe Luce says she was born in 'genteel poverty'; she did not go to university, but was 'taken up' as a secretary by Mrs Belmont, a member of the New York society group known as 'the 400'. Through her she met and soon married the very rich, much older George Tuttle Brokaw. She had a daughter, but the marriage ended in divorce. In the early 1930s she was senior editor on *Vogue* and *Vanity Fair*, then switched to writing plays.

In 1935 Clare Boothe married Henry Luce, millionaire founder and proprietor of the *Time-Life* magazine empire. (He died in 1967.) In the Second World War she became a foreign correspondent for *Life*. An exceptionally able public speaker, she campaigned for the Republicans in the 1944 Presidential elections, and delivered the keynote address at the 1944 Republican National Convention. She became a convert to Roman Catholicism in 1946, after the death of her daughter in a car crash. She now lives in Hawaii.

Boudicca
British (d. AD 61)

Boudicca was the warrior Queen who defied the Roman conquerors of Britain. Her husband, King Prasutagus, ruled his tribe, the Iceni, under Britain's Roman governor in what is now the county of Norfolk, England. Before he died in AD 61 he willed half his territory to his daughters and half to the Emperor Nero, hoping to protect his family from the greed of the Roman governor, Suetonius Paullinus. Suetonius ignored the dead King's wishes; Queen Boudicca was ousted, the daughters raped and their lands expropriated. Boudicca then raised 80,000 soldiers from the tribes of Britain and, after sacking the Roman city of Colchester, defeated the Roman commander Petillius Cerealis before marching against London, which she also sacked and set on fire. The same fate befell Verulanium (St Albans). But the governor Paullinus, who had been putting down a rebellion in Anglesey, North Wales, was now moving south with the main Roman army. He met Boudicca's brave but disorganized troops somewhere in the Midlands. Boudicca is said to have driven her chariot round the battlefield shouting, 'Better masterless poverty than prosperous slavery! The

Romans are hares and foxes trying to rule over dogs and wolves!' However, the Romans routed Boudicca and her tribesmen; she took poison and died. But her rebellion had urged a change of heart among the Roman rulers. Suetonius Paullinus was recalled and a more humane policy was inaugurated.

Margaret Brent
British (c. 1600–1670)

Not quite a Founding Mother, but often looked on as one of America's first feminists because she asked for the 'vote', Margaret Brent was, with her sister, the first Maryland woman to own her own estate and also a powerful woman in the early government of Maryland.

Margaret Brent was born in Gloucestershire, England, one of 13 children of a lord of the manor and on her mother's side a descendant of Edward III. In 1638, along with a sister and two brothers, she emigrated to Maryland armed with an introduction from Lord Baltimore, then proprietor of the colony. Margaret and Mary Brent acquired about 70 acres which they called Sisters Freehold, and in 1642 Margaret acquired a further 1,000 acres from her brother, on which she raised livestock. Governor Calvert, who was the absent Lord Baltimore's brother, appointed her executor of his estate on his deathbed in 1647, and she became responsible for raising money from Lord Baltimore's properties to pay off the colony's troops, who were threatening mutiny because they had not been paid. She also received the right to act on behalf of Lord Baltimore.

The following year Margaret Brent asked for two votes in the Maryland Assembly, one for herself as a freeholder, and one on behalf of Lord Baltimore. When the Assembly refused, she protested against all their proceedings. However, when Lord Baltimore objected from England to her selling his property, the Maryland Assembly wrote to him: 'It was better for the Colony's safety at that time in her hands than in any man's else in the whole Province after your brother's death, for the soldiers would never have treated any others with that civility and respect.'

Thereafter she and the rest of her family moved to Virginia, where for 20 years she farmed a plantation called Peace.

Jane Byrne
American (b. 1934)

Jane Byrne is the Irish-American who took on the mighty machine of the Chicago mayor's office and won. She herself was elected Mayor of Chicago in February 1979.

Chicago born and bred, Jane Burke studied at Barat College, then married William Byrne, a Marine Corps pilot who was killed in a crash in 1959. They had a daughter, Katharine. In 1978 she married Jan McMullen, a political reporter on the *Chicago Sun-Times*.

Byrne joined John F. Kennedy's presidential campaign in 1960, and in 1964 was offered a job at City Hall by Chicago's famous Mayor Daley. She became Commissioner of Sales, Weights and Measures in 1968, and antagonized many of Daley's supporters because she actually enforced the rules.

When Daley died, Michael Bilandic became mayor. Shocked by the corruption that infected City Hall, Mrs Byrne called the Press in, and the mayor had to face a trial. The jury, however, did not find grounds for an indictment, and not surprisingly Mrs Byrne lost her job.

So many people urged her to keep on fighting that she decided to run against Bilandic. In spite of apparently having no chance, she won, backed by an extensive publicity campaign.

Empress Catherine the Great
German–Russian (1729–96)

The minor German princess, Sophia Augusta Frederika, who ruled Russia for 34 years as the Empress Catherine was born in Stettin, Germany, daughter of the Prince of Anhalt-Zerbst. She was well educated, and in 1744 her mother's intriguing secured for her an invitation to Russia as a possible bride for the nephew and heir of the formidable Empress Elizabeth, daughter of Peter the Great. In preparation, Sophia Augusta Frederika changed her name to Catherine, was converted to the Orthodox religion and learnt Russian. The wedding duly took place in 1745, but the young Archduke Peter was mentally subnormal and interested in little more than playing with toy soldiers. Catherine found consolation in a series of lovers and also in reading the French encyclopaedists: 'Voltaire,' she said, 'formed my mind'; she later had a famous correspondence with him.

For 15 years the young couple's lives were organized entirely by the Empress Elizabeth. When Catherine's son Paul was born in 1754 (the father was probably not Peter but her first lover, Sergei Saltikov), the baby was taken from her to be brought up by Elizabeth. Catherine consoled herself with a new love affair with the young diplomat Count Stanislas Poniatowski (who was to become King of Poland), by whom she had a daughter, Anna, who was also taken from her by the Empress, and died young.

In 1761 everything changed. The Empress died and Catherine's husband the Archduke Peter became Emperor. Within six months a *coup*, masterminded by Gregory Orlov, an artillery officer and Catherine's current lover, ousted Peter (who was subsequently murdered) and installed Catherine in his place. Thereafter she ruled for 35 years until her death.

Catherine was one of the 'enlightened despots' of the eighteenth century, like Maria Theresa of Austria (q.v.) and Frederick the Great of Prussia. Although she supported the rights of the peasants, she was successfully opposed by the nobility who had put her in power, and when there was a serious peasant rebellion in 1773 she condoned its brutal suppression, and gave away many estates and their serfs to her favourites.

Catherine believed in religious toleration, and discouraged torture and capital punishment. She hoped to lay the foundations of universal education, rightly recognizing that education was the key to genuine reform (she even experimented with boarding schools, being an admirer of Madame de Maintenon (q.v.)). She tried to codify the law, to

Constantinople

Russi

Catherine the Great bridging the gulf between Russia and Constantinople, from a 1792 cartoon.

rationalize the administration and promote public health (setting an example by having herself inoculated against smallpox), but most of these improvements were not effected until long after her death. She encouraged both arts and sciences, and set an example of good manners and refinement in what was still a barbaric society.

Catherine was hard-working and considerate. She was witty, a lively correspondent, and wrote plays, memoirs, children's books and even a 'manifesto' of her political beliefs, *Instruction*, a model of the enlightened thought which she failed to turn into reality. She edited Russia's first literary review, was herself a painter and sculptor, and an indefatigable collector: the famous Hermitage in St Petersburg (Leningrad) is her outstanding memorial.

Her most obvious successes, in an age which thought conquest proper to rulers, were in foreign policy. Her armies and her diplomacy won for Russia access to the Black Sea, and a large part of Poland (cf. Maria Theresa).

Catherine was notorious for her many lovers, in particular her gifted minister Potemkin who seized the Crimea from the Turks and whom she may have married secretly in 1774.

20

Shirley Chisholm: she became the first black woman Congressman in 1968.

Shirley Chisholm
American (b. 1924)

'The first black woman Congressman', as Shirley Chisholm calls herself, was born in Brooklyn but brought up by her grandmother in Barbados, West Indies. She was clever at school and went to Brooklyn College before taking a Master's degree at Columbia. In 1949 she married Conrad Chisholm, and ran a nursery school. The achievements of Harriet Tubman (q.v.) served as an inspiration to her, but Shirley Chisholm finally decided to go into politics when an old black woman brought a nine dollar campaign contribution to her door in an effort to persuade her. She was elected to the New York State Assembly in 1964, and to Congress for Brooklyn in 1969. She refused a back-seat appointment in the Department of Agriculture; as she explained: 'All they know is that *A Tree Grows in Brooklyn*.' In 1972 she ran unsuccessfully for the Democratic nomination for President: 'I had the nerve to dare to say that I'm going to run for the presidency of the U.S.,' she remarked to some disapproving fellow workers. In 1977 she divorced Conrad Chisholm and married Arthur Hardwick Jr.

'One thing the people in Washington and New York are afraid of in Shirley Chisholm is her mouth,' she says. Total racial and sexual equality is her ambition.

Ch'iu Chin
Chinese (1875?–1907)

In the long history of Chinese warrior heroines, Ch'iu Chin is the most extraordinary modern figure. She was responsible for organizing the rebellion of an entire province against the rule of the Empress Tzu Hsi (q.v.). The rebellion failed and she was executed, but her memory is revered in China still.

She was born into a middle-class family in Shao-hsing and, although she did not have her feet bound according to the ancient Chinese tradition, she was brought up conventionally and at 18 had an arranged marriage with Wang T'ing Chun, by whom she had a son and a daughter (who became China's first woman flyer).

In 1900, when she was 25, the family moved to Peking: there she was so horrified by the corrupt and effete Manchu elite who had ruled China for nearly 300 years that she became an ardent nationalist radical, and a feminist. She devoted herself to progressive literature and poetry. In 1903 she took the immense step for a dutiful wife of leaving her husband and children, and went to Tokyo to study. There Ch'iu Chin attached herself to a group led by Sun Yat-sen. Strikingly individual in dress and manner, she often wore men's clothes and carried a sword; drank like a soldier; wrote poetry; debated at public meetings; and preached revolution and the liberation of women. Back in China in 1906, she became an active revolutionary for the last year of her life. In the intervals of teaching she opened a branch of the Restoration Society (China's main revolutionary movement), made bombs, founded a feminist newspaper, and journeyed to her native province to organize an uprising there to coincide with a national

'Concubinage is truly a hell on earth which competes with the hell of the dead' Ch'iu Chin

Ch'iu Chin, who was executed in 1907 for organizing an uprising aimed at overthrowing the Manchu dynasty.

insurrection. In 1907 – an astonishing appointment for a woman – she became principal of the Ta-t'ung School of Physical Culture in Shao-hsing, which had 1,000 students. In her spare time she worked unremittingly to organize her secret army, drilling her own students as soldiers. She was herself an excellent horsewoman, and could both box and fence.

The nationwide rebellion misfired, however. The government were alerted, arms and ammunition were found in Ch'iu Chin's college, and she was arrested. She was tried and executed within a few days. She was only 32. But the reform movement was not to be halted and within four years the Manchu dynasty had been swept away. Ch'iu Chin's body was disinterred and given a hero's burial, and her name has since occupied an honoured place in Chinese history.

Queen Christina of Sweden
Swedish (1626–1689)

Christina was one of the most remarkable women of her own or indeed any age. She was the only child of the 'lion of the North', King Gustavus Adolphus of Sweden, who, before his death in battle in 1632, led his armies to many victories in Germany during the Thirty Years' War and made Sweden a European power. Christina inherited the throne before she was six, and as a young woman introduced the values of the European Renaissance to Sweden. Then, to universal astonishment, she abdicated in her late twenties in order to become a Roman Catholic and move to Italy.

Christina had a masculine upbringing. As a child she was given a prince's education, learnt to ride like a boy, and as a woman loved to dress as a man. After two traumatic childhood years in isolation with her grief-stricken widowed mother, the German princess Maria Eleonora, she was brought up with the son and daughters of her father's sister, and was always expected to marry the son, her cousin Charles Gustavus. But when she grew up she broke off the engagement and, although insisting that he be recognized as her heir, announced that she would never marry.

She was prodigiously clever. A keen linguist, she learnt German, French, Italian, Spanish, Latin and Greek, besides studying mathematics and astronomy. Such was her appetite for learning that she persuaded the most famous philosopher of the day, René Descartes, to come to Stockholm in 1649 – and insisted that he give her instruction at five in the morning, the only time she was free.

Scholars, artists and craftsmen came from all over Europe to Stockholm at the Queen's behest. French and German architects embellished the capital with magnificent new buildings (and the countryside with great mansions for the nobility); dancers, actors and musicians came to perform at court. Christina bought paintings, statues, art treasures and rare books from abroad, and imported carpets and furniture for her palace. During her reign further education expanded enormously.

Meanwhile she took her public duties seriously,

A contemporary print of Queen Christina of Sweden, also known as the 'Minerva of the North'.

CRISTINA REGINA SVECIÆ, ETC,

T v Merlen

1655. There she lived in immense style for the next 30 years, a great hostess and patron, occasionally angling unsuccessfully to return to power: in Sweden (when her cousin died in 1660), in Naples and in Poland. When her plans to gain the throne of Naples were betrayed in 1657 by her equerry, Monaldeschi, she had him put to death, virtually before her eyes. It was in Rome that Christina formed her most intimate relationship with a man – Cardinal Dezio Azzolini, who became the master of her household. He was at her side when she died, aged 62, and himself died two months later.

Cleopatra
Egyptian (69–30 BC)

The dazzling queen of Egypt, Shakespeare's 'lass unparalleled' and 'serpent of old Nile', belonged to the Macedonian dynasty which had ruled Egypt since the death of Alexander the Great in 323 BC. Her father, Ptolemy, was descended from one of the generals of Alexander the Great, and she was born in Alexandria, a city which had been founded by Alexander and was always more Greek than Egyptian. She survived a perilous childhood as Ptolemy and her elder sister Berenice struggled for the throne; and when, at 17, she inherited the throne with her younger brother, another Ptolemy, she was soon ousted herself. It was not until she was 21, with the help of Julius Caesar, that she became securely queen.

The relationship of Egypt to Rome, and Cleopatra's relationship with Rome's great leaders, first Julius Caesar and then Mark Antony, dominated her life. Egypt was rich; but Rome was powerful, and at this period was extending its rule all round the Mediterranean. Egypt had no hope of not being drawn into the power politics of the day. Yet Cleopatra lent to Egypt's inevitable destiny as client-kingdom a wonderful gloss of style. Everything about her life has become the stuff of legend, from her first meeting with Julius Caesar, when she was smuggled into his presence through enemy lines rolled up in some bedding, to her death nearly 20 years later from the bite of an asp which was smuggled to her in a bowl of fruit as she awaited the

from presiding at meetings of the Diet and extricating her country from the Thirty Years' War (which she regarded as a drain on her hard-pressed resources), to receiving ambassadors and inspecting warships. A shrewd politician, she was extremely adroit at using the complaints of the poor against the nobility as a lever to gain their co-operation in the furthering of her own schemes.

By this time Christina was increasingly drawn to the Roman Catholic religion, to which Descartes and the French ambassador had introduced her, and the idea of living in Italy, and in 1654 she abdicated. She took with her most of the contents of her palace and, having received the promise of a munificent annuity, slipped away, disguised as a nobleman. She rode out of her kingdom to Denmark, crying 'At last I am free!' Christina was received into the Roman Catholic faith at Innsbruck, and reached Rome in

advent of the victorious Roman enemy.

Cleopatra became Julius Caesar's mistress, bore him a son, Caesarion, in 47 BC and lived in Rome until Caesar's death in 44 BC. After Caesar's death, the Roman provinces were divided, and Mark Antony took those in the eastern Mediterranean; their meeting in 41 BC led to their nine-year love affair and eventual marriage (not recognized in Roman law, however). She bore him three children – twins, Alexander and Cleopatra, in 40 BC and another son, Ptolemy, four years later.

Together with Mark Antony, Cleopatra took her armies to war against Parthia, and her fleet into battle at Actium against the Roman, Octavian, in 31 BC. Both campaigns ended in disaster. Back in Egypt, having lost the fight for mastery of the Roman world, she and Antony both committed suicide. Cleopatra's son Caesarion, then 17, was put to death by Octavian, who shortly became Augustus Caesar, the first Roman Emperor. Her daughter survived to become the wife of the client-king Juba of Numidia, in North Africa. Cleopatra was the last of her line, but her reputation lived on. She remains the most famous and glamorous woman of the ancient world.

Angela Davis
American (b. 1944)

One of the most celebrated Black Power leaders, Angela Davis was a philosophy lecturer when she first hit the headlines in the University of California at Los Angeles disturbances of 1969. Her parents were school teachers in Birmingham, Alabama. She could read at four and made rapid progress at school. She went to Brandeis College in 1961, and spent her second university year in Paris. Davis' political views were formed by the frequent bombings of private houses owned by blacks in her middle-class suburban neighbourhood, then by the bus boycott of 1956 and the rise of the civil rights movement. When Martin Luther King was killed in 1968 she joined the Communist Party and completed her master's degree at UCLA with the Marxist philosopher, Herbert Marcuse, but her appointment to teach philosophy at UCLA was terminated when her connection with

Angela Davis in London in May 1975 to launch the British publication of her autobiography.

the Jackson brothers, the black activists then in jail, was discovered. Of their subsequent deaths she wrote, 'George's death [was like] a disc of steel deep inside me, magnetically drawing towards it all the elements I needed to stay strong and fight all the harder.' Davis was accused of having supplied the weapons with which the brothers tried to escape (dying in the attempt), and during 1970 she was on the run, one of America's most wanted people. Once caught, she spent two months in New York House of Detention, but was later acquitted after a 13-month trial in 1972. Her *Autobiography* was published in 1974. In 1977 she was the Communist Party's nominee for Vice President of the U.S. She now teaches ethnic studies at San Francisco State University, and married her fellow-teacher Hilton Braithwaite in 1980.

Bernadette Devlin
Irish (b. 1948)

When this passionate Irish activist was elected
Independent Unity Member of Parliament for Mid-
Ulster in 1969 by the Roman Catholics of Northern
Ireland, she became the youngest MP in British
history since the younger Pitt nearly two centuries
earlier. One of six fatherless children of a poor
Catholic family, she won a scholarship to Queens
University, Belfast, to read psychology, and emerged
into national politics by way of the student civil rights
organization, the People's Democracy. An impassioned public speaker, she made a powerful maiden
speech in the House of Commons attacking British
policy in Northern Ireland, but nine months later was
found guilty of inciting riots, and served four months
in jail. In August 1971 she gave birth to an illegitimate
daughter. She always said she would not stand for the
British Parliament again, and she ceased to be an MP
in 1974. She married a schoolmaster, Michael
McAliskey, in April 1973, and since then has lived in
Northern Ireland with him and her three children. In
1977 she stood for the European Parliament. She
remains active in Irish politics and in January 1981 she
and her husband were seriously wounded by unknown gunmen at their isolated home.

Queen Elizabeth I
English (1533–1603)

The greatest of Britain's sovereigns was a woman,
and an unmarried woman at that: Elizabeth Tudor.
Not only was she exceptionally able politically, but
she presided over and helped to inspire the flowering
of the English Renaissance.

Elizabeth had a perilous girlhood (at one point she
was imprisoned in the Tower of London by her own
sister), largely because of the fierce hostility between
Protestants and Catholics in England at that time. She
was the youngest daughter of Henry VIII, by his
second wife the Protestant Anne Boleyn, whom he
had married after defying the Pope and divorcing his
Catholic queen, Catherine of Aragon, who had failed
to produce a male heir.

Elizabeth I: a painting by an unknown artist circa 1560.

Elizabeth's mother was put to death for infidelity
when she was two, and Henry himself died – having
had four more wives and one son – when she was 13.
She was educated by some of the best scholars of
the day, and learnt French, Italian, Latin, Greek,
mathematics and science. (Later she learnt Spanish
and some German: foreigners did not then bother to
learn English.) She was an excellent horsewoman,
and a tireless dancer and follower of the hunt well
into her sixties.

Elizabeth came to the throne in 1558, following
the brief reigns of her younger half-brother, the
Protestant Edward, and her elder half-sister, the
devoutly Catholic Mary. The country was still
deeply divided in its religious allegiance; and because
many of her Catholic subjects believed that her
father's marriage to her mother was invalid, her title
to the throne remained uncertain. For the next 30

25

years there were plenty of enemies, at home and abroad, who were prepared to try to put her cousin and heir, the Catholic Mary Queen of Scots who was briefly Queen of France, on the throne in her place.

Elizabeth warded off Catholic hostility by not claiming to be 'Supreme Head of the Church' like her father and brother (tactfully using instead '&c' after her titles), and by not persecuting Roman Catholics – at least until she was excommunicated by the Pope in 1570. She was the true founder of the modern Church of England; her religious settlement based on the Book of Common Prayer was eventually accepted by the great majority of the English people.

Elizabeth was 25 when she became Queen. A council memorandum of the day read: 'The Queen poor; the realm exhausted; the nobility poor and decayed; good captains and soldiers wanting, the people out of order; justice not executed; all things dear; excesses in meat, diet and apparel; division among ourselves; war with France; the French King bestriding the realm; having one foot in Calais and the other in Scotland; steadfast enemies, but no steadfast friends.'

She was six months short of 70 when she died. In the intervening 45 years she and her great ministers, notably William Cecil and his son Robert Cecil, guided her kingdom into a prosperous, united nation state with a commanding position in the politics of the Atlantic. The war with France was ended; Mary Queen of Scots was defeated and eventually, reluctantly, executed in the wake of yet another plot (1587); a war with Spain was triumphantly concluded in the rout of the Spanish Armada (1588). At Tilbury, on the eve of the Armada, Elizabeth delivered the following stirring address: 'My loving people … I am come amongst you, as you see, at this time, not for my recreation and disport, but being resolved, in the midst and heat of the battle, to live or die amongst you all – to lay down for my God, and for my kingdom, and for my people, my honour and my blood, even in the dust. I know I have the body of a weak and feeble woman but I have the heart and stomach of a king, and of a king of England too, and think foul scorn that Parma or Spain or any prince of Europe should dare to invade the borders of my realm …'

Elizabeth's failure to marry caused great controversy. She used her single state as a bargaining counter in her constant diplomatic dealings with the powers of Europe. Many foreign princes were dangled before her, but she only truly loved Robert Dudley, whom she had known all her life. She was unable to marry him; he was married already and when his wife, Amy Robsart, died in 1560, it was in such suspicious circumstances that a marriage to the Queen would have seemed a confession of guilt. But she made him Earl of Leicester and they remained close until his death nearly 30 years later. Leicester was succeeded as her favourite by the young Robert Devereux, Earl of Essex, a foolish, vain young man who, aspiring to the throne, rebelled against her in 1601 and was executed.

When she died two years later, the succession passed peacefully to James VI of Scotland, the son of her old enemy Mary Queen of Scots.

Isabella d'Este
Italian (1474–1539)

Isabella d'Este presided over one of the richest and most brilliant courts of the Renaissance. The granddaughter of the King of Naples, she received a thorough education in the ancient languages, philosophy and poetry. At 16 she was married to Francisco Gonzaga, future Marquis of Mantua, who was more of a soldier than a scholar. Blessed with intelligence and a strong personality, Isabella d'Este attracted the great artists of the day to her palace – Leonardo da Vinci (who painted her portrait), Raphael, Titian and the author Castiglione. She adored display and commissioned brilliant extravaganzas for performance in her private theatre or at *fêtes champêtres*. Isabella's enthusiasms were boundless; she had apes and fools for amusement, she also gambled, wrote and painted. Like Webster's 'White Devil' she mixed her own face creams. She travelled ceaselessly, sometimes on pilgrimages. Far from being merely frivolous, Isabella d'Este formed an efficient spy network and her entertainments were the occasion of much political intrigue. She saved Mantua from invasion when her husband was taken prisoner in 1509 and ruled over it after his death in 1519.

Isabella d'Este, from an engraving after Titian's portrait.

Ekaterina Furtseva
Russian (1910–1974)

Furtseva was the only woman ever to rise to the inner circle of the Kremlin and was Minister of Culture when she died. She was born in Vyshniy Volochek to the north of Moscow, into a family of textile workers. She did well at school and was admitted into the Young Communists League at the early age of 14. At 27 she had graduated as a chemical engineer and was rising in the Party in the wake of Nikita Khrushchev. In 1952 she was elected on to the Central Committee to become one of the three women in a total membership of 133. In 1956 she became the first woman to be elected a member of the Praesidium. In 1960 she was made Minister of Culture, visiting other countries to promote cultural exchange, although she disapproved of modern art 'which does not serve the people'. She was married to Nikolai Firyubin, deputy Foreign Minister.

Indira Gandhi
Indian (b. 1917)

Mrs Gandhi was Prime Minister of India from 1966 to 1977, and after two years out of power made an astonishing comeback in January 1980 when she was re-elected Prime Minister.

The only child of Jawaharlal Nehru, himself Prime Minister from 1947 to 1964, and niece of Vijaya Lakshmi Pandit (q.v.), Indira was steeped in politics from an early age. As a child she played her part, including organizing an army of children to carry clandestine messages, in the Nehru family's involvement in the struggle against the British Raj, but was educated in England at Badminton and, briefly, Somerville College, Oxford. Back in India she spent part of 1942 in jail. The same year she married journalist Feroze Gandhi (no relation of Mahatma Gandhi), and they had two sons, Rajiv and Sanjay. Feroze Gandhi was eventually elected to Congress; but Indira Gandhi decided to live with her father, by now Prime Minister, and be his hostess rather than her husband's. Feroze Gandhi died in 1960.

Mrs Gandhi was apparently happy to stay in the

Indira Gandhi was elected Prime Minister of India in 1966 and 1980.

background, but she was her father's closest confidante and it seems likely that he groomed her to succeed him. She became President of the Congress Party in 1959–60, when no one else wanted the job, and chairman of the Citizens' Central Council in 1962. When her father died in 1964 she was elected to Congress in his place, and became Minister of Information and Broadcasting under Premier Lal Bahadur Shastri. When Shastri died in 1966 she became Prime Minister, supported by divided colleagues who expected her to be merely a front woman.

Instead, she proved a shrewd and masterful ruler, dispensed with her former patrons, and, with a landslide victory in the 1971 elections on an 'abolish poverty' ticket, had apparently achieved an impregnable position. Her success in 'liberating' Bangladesh from Pakistan did not, however, prevent massive popular opposition to her rule, which had failed to alleviate poverty (about 300 million Indians still live on an income of less than £60 a year), in 1974 and 1975. Since she had a huge majority in Parliament, the people took to the streets. Mrs Gandhi declared a state of emergency, had her political opponents put in jail – in all 110,000 people were detained without trial – censored the press, and brought her younger son Sanjay in to help her (and made the trains run on time). Sanjay was at that time her most obvious weakness: she indulged his desire to run an Indian car factory, a disastrous enterprise; he also caused immense hostility by attempting to clear the Delhi slums and by imposing a sterilization programme. In 1975 Mrs Gandhi had charges of corrupt election practices brought against her, and was found guilty.

In the 1977 elections the Congress Party lost resoundingly; Mrs Gandhi even lost her own seat. But the Janata party, now in power, lacked leadership; their quarrels and ineptitude, combined with inflation, drought, and a rising crime rate, were to give her a second chance. She outwitted the Shah Commission which had been set up in 1977 to investigate crimes committed during the emergency, and brilliantly exploited the divisions within both government and opposition parties, playing one faction against another. She stood for Congress again in a by-election in 1978 and won with a majority of 77,000; by late summer 1979 it was clear that no one could any longer count on a majority in Parliament, and new elections would have to be called.

During her election campaign this energetic and ambitious woman travelled 63,000 kilometres in 63 days; 240 million Indians heard her speak at her vast open-air meetings. An eight per cent swing in her favour increased her share of the seats in Congress from 153 to 351 – and she again became Prime Minister. Her son Sanjay was also elected to Parliament for the first time – but his death in an aircraft accident five months later has since robbed her of the associate she has most relied on.

Emma Goldman
American (1869–1940)

'Red Emma', as Emma Goldman became known,

was the most flamboyant and influential feminist and pacifist at the centre of twentieth-century American radicalism. The daughter of Russian-Jewish parents, she grew up in East Prussia with her grandmother, and emigrated to America in 1886 to escape an arranged marriage. She went to work in the sweatshops of Rochester, New York State, and found conditions so appalling that she became a labour agitator. She married Jacob Hersner that year and moved to New York City, now a convinced left-wing political radical following the hanging of the Chicago anarchists in 1887. In 1889 her lover, Alexander Berkman, was jailed for 14 years for the attempted murder of Henry Frick, the steel millionaire, during a strike in Pittsburg. In 1890 she went to the International Socialist Congress in Paris which established May Day as a worldwide workers' holiday.

In the U.S., Goldman became one of the most remarkable orators in the history of American politics. She urged unemployed men that it was their 'sacred right' to steal if they were starving; she told women to keep their mouths open and their wombs shut. She founded a newspaper, *Mother Earth*, which ran until she obstructed the draft of American soldiers in 1917 and was sent to prison for two years before being deported to Russia. There Goldman denounced Bolshevism as 'not revolutionary at all' and eventually settled in Western Europe. At a dinner in London in 1924 she deplored the 'tragic fate of the thousands of men and women in the prisons and concentration camps of Russia.' In 1926 she married a Welsh miner, James Colton, hoping to re-enter the States on a British passport; but the American authorities only allowed her back to the U.S. on a lecture tour in 1934, on condition that she did not talk politics.

'Anarchism is stronger than I am,' she said. 'I can't see people suffering without feeling I will die if I can't help them.' At 70 Goldman was raising money for the exiled Republicans who had fought in the Spanish Civil War. As she once said: 'Everyone is an anarchist who loves liberty and hates oppression. But not everyone wants liberty for the other fellow. That is my task.'

Emma Goldman addressing a crowd in Union Square, New York, in 1916.

Olympe de Gouges
French (1748–1793)

Olympe de Gouges struggled to have the rights of women represented in the councils of the French Revolution and was a brave forerunner of women's liberation in France.

She was born Marie Gouze in Montauban; her legal father was a butcher, although she claimed that her true father was a local aristocrat. She was married at 16 to an army officer, Louis Yvres Aubry. Soon after her son Pierre was born in 1766, Olympe de Gouges, as she now called herself, left for Paris with a rich lover. Her life in the capital was a round of pleasure until her looks began to fade and she turned to writing plays for the Comédie Française. The plays and the pamphlets she wrote were not distinguished, but were revolutionary in their subject-matter.

When the Revolution broke out in 1789, many women thought that they, too, would benefit from the call for Liberty, Equality, Fraternity. But by 1790 there was little sign of it. De Gouges thereupon founded a fraternal society and in 1791 she wrote a *Declaration of the Rights of the Woman and the Citizen.* She badgered the revolutionary leaders constantly, and freely expressed her hatred of Robespierre. In 1793 she was arrested and put on trial, partly for her opinions, partly for having defended Louis XVI in print, saying he was 'not wicked but weak'. As she mounted the scaffold she quoted the Revolution's battle hymn, *La Marseillaise*, saying, 'You will avenge my death, children of my native land.'

Ella Tambussi Grasso
American (1919–1981)

The first woman to become an American governor in her own right, Italian-American Ella Grasso has been a career politician most of her life. Her parents, Giacomo and Maria Tambussi, were working-class Italian immigrants; her father was a baker. Ella, their only child, did well at school in Windsor Locks, Connecticut, and majored in sociology and economics at Mount Holyoke College, Massachusetts. During the Second World War she was assistant director of research in Connecticut for the federal War Manpower Commission. In 1942 she married Thomas Grasso, and they had a son and daughter. She entered her first primary election when her younger child was 18 months old, and at 33 was elected to the Connecticut General Assembly. Three years later she was floor leader, and from 1959 to 1970 served as Secretary of State (an office filled by women since 1938). She represented Connecticut's Sixth District in Congress from 1970 to 1974, retiring in order to run for Governor.

Grasso was against the war in Vietnam, and against abortion, while recognizing and respecting its legality. Although her first political membership was with the League of Women Voters, she is not a member of the women's movement, but has said, 'It's done a great deal in a short time to provide equal opportunity for women, and I feel I've been a beneficiary.'

One of the few Egyptian sculptures of Hatshepsut to escape ritual defacement by her successors. This black marble head was auctioned at Sotheby's in 1924.

Hatshepsut
Egyptian (1560?–1482 BC)

The first woman Pharaoh ruled Egypt for more than 20 years. Her reign was peaceful in spite of opposition from generals and priests.

Hatshepsut married her half brother, Tuthmosis II, when he succeeded to the throne. She had two daughters, but a son was born to a concubine of Tuthmosis. When Tuthmosis died, the boy was only six, and Hatshepsut become first regent, then Queen – breaking a 2,000 year tradition of masculine rule. To consolidate her position further, Hatshepsut married her daughter Meritha to her stepson, Tuthmosis III. Hatshepsut then restored religious rites hitherto forgotten and erected two magnificent obelisks in the temple at Karnak; she encouraged agriculture; and inspired a voyage of exploration to the Land of Punt (Somalia). The royal ships came back laden with marvels: myrrh, green gold, ebony, ivory, cinnamon, incense, baboons, new species of fish and trees. Reliefs of the cargo are carved on the walls of her beautiful funerary temple, Deir el Bahri, near the Valley of the Kings, on the banks of the Nile. She always wore men's clothes and was addressed as His Majesty.

Hua Mu-Lan
Chinese (c. AD 400)

Most famous of the women warriors of China, much celebrated in poetry and plays, was Hua Mu-Lan, 'filial daughter' of a general who taught her to fence *à l'épée*. When her ageing father was called to the colours in a national emergency, Mu-Lan insisted on taking his place; legend has it that she challenged him to a sword-fight and made him promise that, if she won, he would allow her to go. She won; and disguising herself as a man – 'none knew her as a woman' – spent 12 years at the front in the thick of the fighting. Then she returned home, and put on women's clothing again. Mu-Lan's brief story is told in the ancient *Dictionary of Famous People*, but has been much embroidered since. She was said to have been struck in the shoulder by an arrow, and to have been so admired for her courage by the Commander-in-Chief that (not knowing she was a woman) he offered her his daughter in marriage.

Chinese history records other women warriors. Three centuries later Nie Yin-niang, daughter of General Nie Feng of the Tang dynasty, acted as a one-woman Robin Hood, travelling in wild country bringing help to the weak and taking vengeance on the criminal. She was taught swordsmanship by a nun from the age of ten, and married a young man of simple background who polished mirrors for a living. In the late seventeenth century, Chin Liang-Yu, wife of Ma Sian-cheng of the Ming dynasty, was not only a famous writer but also fought as an archer at her husband's side, then rose to command a Division. After his death she led an army to many victories in a civil war.

Dolores Ibarruri
Spanish (b. 1895)

'La Pasionaria' was one of the most vigorous fighters for the freedom of Spain, and has remained a legend ever since 1936, at the outbreak of the Civil War, when she broadcast on the Republican radio: 'It is better to die on our feet than live on our knees.' A great popular orator, her rallying cry to the anti-Franco forces was 'They shall not pass', and she led a women's brigade against the Fascists. After Franco's victory, Ibarruri went into exile in Russia, and remained there until 1977 when, after Franco's death, she returned, to a triumphant reception. That same year, aged 81, she was elected to the Spanish Parliament in the first elections since 1936, when she had been elected for the first time.

The daughter and wife of Basque miners, she started life in domestic service. Under her pen-name 'The Passionflower' she wrote for a socialist weekly, and in 1920 she was one of the founder members of the Spanish Communist Party. She and her husband were arrested several times, but she was released following her election to Parliament just before the Civil War.

Fusaye Ichikawa
Japanese (b. 1893)

Japan's most distinguished feminist and first woman member of the Japanese Diet started life as a village schoolteacher. Fusaye Ichikawa became a reporter, then a stockbroker's clerk, and finally a trade union worker. In 1918 she founded the New Women's Association with the aim of giving women the right to make political speeches, at a time when they were forbidden even to listen to them. Thereafter she was constantly in the vanguard of reform; she led the long fight for women's suffrage and in 1952 was elected to the Upper House of Councillors, where, apart from a three-year gap, she has served ever since. Ichikawa has led a successful campaign against licensed prostitution, fought corruption in elections, opposed pay raises for members of the Diet, and given part of her salary to women's causes.

Queen Isabella of Spain
Spanish (1451–1504)

Queen Isabella of Castile was the moving spirit in the unification of the kingdom of Spain in the fifteenth century under the joint rule of herself and her husband, King Ferdinand of Aragon. She led troops in the field, she brought order and justice to her realm, and, having at first refused to do so, eventually agreed to sponsor Christopher Columbus's wild scheme to reach the Indies by the Atlantic route – thus handing on to her successors the wealth of a vast American empire.

Isabella was born in 1451, the daughter of King Juan II of Castile and Isabella of Portugal. Her father died when she was young, leaving his throne to her elder brother Enrique IV, a degenerate, incompetent man at the head of a corrupt, intriguing court. She steered her way cleverly through plots to unseat Enrique, narrowly avoided being arrested by him, and insisted on marrying the man of her choice, Ferdinand, heir to the King of Aragon. When Enrique died in 1474, she moved fast and got herself crowned Queen of Castile in place of Princess Juana – Enrique's legal heir, but widely known not to be his child. When the King of Portugal invaded Castile to put Princess Juana on the throne, Isabella and Ferdinand (who had not yet inherited Aragon) raised an army and routed the invaders in 1475.

Isabella then set about reforming her kingdom. She persuaded the nobles to give up some of their privileges; she rid the country of brigands; she restored the currency, and codified the law. She introduced polyphonic music from Flanders and brought to her court painters of the Dutch School. Isabella always maintained her independence from Ferdinand, who became King of Aragon in 1479, but they worked closely together.

Isabella and Ferdinand's desire to achieve religious unity for Spain proved a more questionable enterprise. In 1480, Isabella allowed the Inquisition to start work in Spain to rid the country of heresy. During the 1480s the couple made war on the state of Granada, in southern Spain, where the Moslem Moors had ruled for centuries. Isabella played her part in the campaigns, wearing armour and riding among the soldiers, organizing supplies, taking her five children everywhere with her. The city of Granada finally fell in January 1492. The same year some 170,000 Jews were expelled. Spain, although now united save for Navarre on the French border, and with hopes of becoming united by marriage with Portugal, had lost some of its most valuable citizens.

'The Catholic Kings', as the Pope called Ferdinand and Isabella, had made Spain one of the most powerful countries in Europe, but had created other problems for their successors.

Isabella's youngest daughter Catherine became the ill-starred first wife of Henry VIII of England.

Mary Harris Jones
American (1830–1930)

A great character, popularly known as 'Mother', Mary Harris Jones was leader in America of the fight against low pay. Her family emigrated from County Cork, Ireland, to Canada where she went to school; she taught for a while in a convent in Michigan, then worked in the garment industry in Chicago before returning to teaching in Memphis, Tennessee. There

The photograph of Mary Harris Jones which appears in the radical weekly Mother Jones *named after her.*

she married a member of the Iron Moulders' Union in 1861, but six years later, in 1867, her husband and their four children died of yellow fever in the space of a week.

Jones went back to Chicago alone to earn her living as a dressmaker. She lost what little she had in the Chicago fire of 1871 and thereafter devoted herself to the struggle against long hours, low pay and poor working conditions. In 1877 she went to Pittsburgh during the railroad workers' strike and lived through the terrible riots that followed. From 1880 onwards she travelled all over the U.S. giving lectures and organizing strikes. The plight of coal miners became her particular concern and in the United Mine Workers strikes of 1900 and 1902 she led women armed with brooms and mops to deal with blacklegs. In 1903 'Mother' Jones marched children on strike from the textile mills in Pennsylvania to President Theodore Roosevelt's private house in Oyster Bay, New York. In 1913 she was sentenced to 20 years for 'conspiracy to commit murder' during the notorious West Virginia miners' strike; she was only freed after considerable public protest.

All management efforts to ban her failed. In her eighties, in 1915 and 1916, she directed New York City strikers, and in her nineties was urging on new generations of miners and their families. She was still campaigning at the age of 100. The radical weekly *Mother Jones* was named after her.

Alexandra Kollontai
Russian (1872–1952)

Alexandra Kollontai was one of the most important figures in the underground movement which eventually overthrew the Russian monarchy. She became a member of Lenin's government, and finally an ambassador for the new USSR. She was also an immensely vigorous campaigner in the fight for women's rights, both as a politician and as a writer, and in the 1970s became a heroine of the women's movement. Many of her writings explored economic and sexual difficulties women faced and still face. Her life exemplified them.

She was the daughter of a Russian aristocrat, Mikhail Domontovich, a career soldier who was to become a general, and a Finnish mother, Alexandra Masalina, who had left her first husband to marry him. Much younger than her two half sisters and brother, the young Alexandra was brought up by servants. At 16 she got her teaching diploma, and although not allowed to go abroad to study was taken on a 'grand tour'; while in Berlin she went to meetings of the German Socialist Party and read Marx and Engels. At 21 she married a distant cousin, Vladimir Kollontai, and had a son, Mikhail.

The new Mrs Kollontai hated her restricted married life ('Happy? And what am I going to do all day?'), and began writing, and teaching young factory workers. The turning point of her life came in 1896 when she accompanied her husband, who was a factory inspector, on a business trip to a textile factory on the Gulf of Finland. She was stunned by the appalling conditions and long hours, and quarrelled violently with her husband, who thought the answer lay in improved ventilation. So she joined the workers' movement, and soon after left her husband in order to study economics in Zurich, leaving her young son behind. Once back in St Petersburg, she witnessed the Tsar's soldiers killing hundreds of peaceful demonstrators on the Nevsky Prospect in 1905, and thereafter committed herself to the coming revolution, insisting always on the importance of women's rights. The experiences of those years inspired *On the Question of the Class Struggle* (1905) and *The Social Basis of the Women's Question* (1908).

Kollontai became a tireless speaker and propagandist for both women's rights and socialism, a delegate at international congresses, and eventually a member of the Bolshevik party. She was constantly under police surveillance and frequently called in for questioning. She was forced into exile in 1908 but continued to work for pacifism and international socialism (which included a lecture tour of America). She returned to Russia after the fall of the Czar in 1917, and was one of the party that welcomed Lenin when he, too, returned from exile. When Lenin formed the first Bolshevik government, Kollontai became commissar for Public Welfare. However, when Trotsky and Lenin showed that in governing

POLITICS AND POWER

Love of Worker Bees (1923). Both deal explicitly with the painful and apparently necessary choice between love and work.

Rosa Luxemburg
Polish (1870–1919)

The 1974 West German postage stamp issued in commemoration of Rosa Luxemburg's life's work.

Alexandra Kollontai: a photograph from the family archives taken in 1908.

they intended to bypass the trade unions for whose political voice she had fought for so long, Kollontai joined the Workers' Opposition. But the original principles of the revolution were defeated, and the Workers' Opposition was banned. By 1922, Kollontai, whose championship of sexual equality and whose own fairly public love affairs (notably with Pavel Dybenko and Alexander Shlyapnikov) made her vulnerable, had been sidetracked by the Party Secretary, Joseph Stalin, into leading a trade delegation to Norway. Thereafter her life was spent virtually in exile as a diplomat. She was Russia's minister in Norway, Mexico, Norway again, and finally Sweden (promoted to ambassador) for 15 years. While in Sweden she negotiated the end of the Soviet-Finnish war in 1944, and in her final years she was an adviser to the Russian Foreign Ministry.

Kollontai's books include *Autobiography of a Sexually Emancipated Woman* (1926) and the novel

'Red Rosa', as Rosa Luxemburg became known, was a socialist, feminist and pacifist of immense courage who profoundly influenced European and Russian revolutionary thinking at the beginning of the century. She was a Jewish girl born in Russian-occupied Poland. A socialist as a schoolgirl, she helped found the party that eventually became Poland's Communist Party, and had to leave home in 1889 to escape the Russian police. After studying for a law degree in Zurich in 1897, she married a German in order to become a German citizen and help set up a Socialist party in Berlin. She taught at the Communist Central Party school in Berlin and edited a workers' newspaper during the revolution of 1905; *The Mass Strike* is her account of that time. She was a thorn in the flesh of many governments in Eastern Europe during these years, and never wavered in her support of left-wing principles, in spite of her longing for an ordinary family life with her lover Leo Jogiches. At the outbreak of war in 1914 she founded, with Karl Liebknecht and Clara Zetkin

35

(q.v.), the Spartacus League for the pacifist extreme left. 'If they think we are going to lift the weapons of murder against our French and other brethren, then we shall shout, "We shall not do it"', she declared. She was in prison for her pacifism for most of the Great War but continued to write against war and in favour of revolution. She was released in 1918 and was co-founder of the German Communist Party before she was re-arrested early in 1919. She was 'rescued' from the police on the way to jail by a right-wing mob, beaten up and drowned in the Landwehr canal. In 1974 West Germany issued a postage stamp in commemoration of her life's work.

Lady Constance Lytton
British (1867–1923)

Lady Constance Lytton was a martyr to the suffragette cause in Britain. She was the daughter of Lord Lytton, Viceroy of India, and after his death in 1889 lived with her mother in the country. Although she would have liked to study music and journalism, her only outlet was to help her aunt write gardening books. In 1906 her life changed dramatically when she inherited a small sum of money which enabled her to embark on a life of working for others. She supported a club for working girls: 'I stumbled by chance on a piece of social radium,' she said. For through her work with the club she met Olive Schreiner (q.v.) and was drawn into the suffragette movement. The sight of Emmeline Pankhurst (q.v.) in prison and the humiliating failure of her own petition to the Home Secretary that suffragettes should not be treated as common criminals combined to turn the gentle Lady Constance into a militant, who like other militant feminists found herself on the wrong side of the law. But she was determined not to be given preferential treatment in jail because of her title. So, when she threw a stone at Lloyd George's car in 1909 she was disguised as 'Jane Wharton, seamstress'. In prison after her arrest and conviction, the doctor declared her 'perfectly fit' to undergo force-feeding; in fact it resulted in a stroke. Although partially paralysed, Lady Constance spent the rest of her life writing letters and articles in the cause of Votes for Women.

Lady Constance Lytton, the British suffragette and martyr.

Flora MacDonald
Canadian (b. 1926)

Foreign affairs, like the treasury, has remained largely a male preserve. Exceptions have been Ana Pauker in Romania (1944, q.v.), Golda Meir in Israel (1956, q.v.), Karin Söder in Sweden (1976, in a government which included six women in the cabinet), and most recently Flora MacDonald in Canada in 1979–80.

Flora MacDonald was born in North Sydney, Nova Scotia, the third of six children of a Western Union telegraph operator, who encouraged his children to take an interest in politics. Flora did well at school, went to business college and became a bank clerk. At 25 she left home to work her way around the world, and for several years led the kind of mind-broadening, nomadic lifestyle that was beginning to be possible for thousands of her own and later generations – women as well as men.

Back in Canada, she worked at the Progressive Conservative national headquarters from 1957 to 1966, starting as a typist and ending as its executive director. She was fired by Premier John Diefenbaker, with whom she did not get on, but from 1966 to 1969 was national secretary of the Progressive Conservative Association of Canada, and held a tutorial post in the Department of Political Studies at Queen's University from 1966 to 1972. She also became the first woman to graduate from Kingston's National Defence College.

In 1972 she was elected to Parliament for Kingston, Ontario, and was particularly concerned with Canadian Indian affairs and housing and urban affairs before being appointed Secretary of State for External Affairs in 1979. She tried for the leadership of the Progressive Conservatives in 1976, but was defeated by Joe Clark, being considered too progressive by many in her party.

MacDonald is a keen campaigner for many causes – the Third World, human rights, prison reform and the abolition of capital punishment – and has also supported abortion on demand. She is famous for her energy, her refreshing informality and accessibility. In early 1980 she approved the plans of the Canadian embassy in Iran to smuggle six American diplomats out of the country.

Winnie Mandela
South African (b. 1935)

Winnie Mandela is one of the heroines of the black activist movement against the apartheid policies of the South African Government. Since her marriage in 1958 to Nelson Mandela, one of South Africa's first black lawyers and a leading member of the African National Congress, she has suffered imprisonment (including solitary confinement for 491 days), preventive detention, banning orders, restrictions, searches and harassment of all kinds. Since 1977, she has been banished from her home in Soweto to a township in the Orange Free State, where her home is without electricity, running water, bath, stove or

main drainage. All these punishments, ostensibly for minor contraventions of the cruel laws enforced against her, are in reality due to the fact that she has become a black nationalist leader in her own right. Among other things, she was a founder member of Soweto's Black Parents Association.

Mandela was brought up in Pondoland, where her father was Minister of Agriculture in Transkei Bantustan. She trained as a social worker in Johannesburg, married Nelson Mandela when he was on trial, and after his acquittal enjoyed only a brief married life, which included the birth of two daughters, before her husband was arrested again in 1962. Since 1964, he has been an inmate on Robben Island, where she is allowed to visit him only once a month for an hour. Since 1969, Winnie Mandela has had exactly eight months free of imprisonment or banning orders; she used that time to speak out, fearlessly and tirelessly, for the justice she believes must one day come.

Queen Margaret of Scandinavia
Danish (1353–1412)

The union in 1397 of the three Scandinavian kingdoms of Norway, Denmark and Sweden was achieved by a remarkable Danish woman.

Earlier in the century, Norway and Sweden had briefly been united under King Magnus, but the difficulties proved insurmountable, and King Magnus's elder son subsequently took the Swedish throne and his younger son, Haakon, took the Norwegian throne. In 1363 King Haakon of Norway married the 10-year-old Princess Margaret of Denmark, who eventually bore him a son, Olaf. (The new Queen Margaret had a Swedish mistress of her household: a daughter of St Bridget, q.v.)

In 1375, when she was barely 22, Queen Margaret's father, King Valdemar III of Denmark, died; yet despite the fact that it had been agreed that the Danish throne should devolve on a nephew, Margaret managed to get the Danish Council to elect her own son, the five-year-old Prince Olaf, instead – with herself as Regent. Five years later, her husband Haakon died; once more Prince Olaf inherited a

POLITICS AND POWER

Winnie Mandela in detention in 1976, before her banishment from Soweto.

throne, and once more Queen Margaret became Regent: the beginning of a union between Norway and Denmark which was to last for more than 400 years.

The young King Olaf had also, through his grandfather Magnus, a claim to the throne of Sweden; but he died suddenly in 1387 at the age of 17. Such was Queen Margaret's personality and gift for rule, however, that within a week she had personally been acclaimed Denmark's 'sovereign lady, master and guardian', and soon after Norway's 'mighty lady and master' also, although her accession was contrary to the prevailing laws of succession. A month later the Swedish nobles, who were grappling with a usurper, accepted her as Sweden's 'sovereign lady and rightful master'. (The citizens of Lübeck addressed her as 'Lady King'.)

Margaret appointed her young great-nephew, Eric of Pomerania, to replace her as ruler, and he was eventually crowned king of the three kingdoms at Kalmar in Sweden in 1397. She appears to have had plans for the three kingdoms to be ruled in perpetuity as a single state, but the mysterious document which outlines a possible constitution seems not to have been formally ratified.

But the Queen continued to rule, even after King Eric came of age in 1401. She recovered both Finland and the large island of Gotland in the Baltic Sea for her great-nephew's crown; and she had some success winning Schleswig (her own mother had been a sister of the duke) in the southern part of Denmark. She was a born administrator, and attempted to give the kingdom a sound financial basis by improving the tax system and reforming the coinage. She appointed deputies from one country to rule over provinces in the others, as well as appointing Danish bishops to rule over Swedish and Norwegian bishoprics, in order to forestall regional rebellions. She encouraged her nobles to intermarry, and was instrumental in getting St Bridget of Sweden (q.v.) canonized. Her administration was based in Copenhagen, Denmark, where she instituted the beginnings of a national assembly, with representatives from both nobility and towns.

Unfortunately this far-sighted statesmanship was in the end partially undermined by the failure of Eric and his queen, Philippa of England, to produce an heir.

Empress Maria Theresa
Austrian (1717–1780)

The Archduchess Maria Theresa of Austria, also by inheritance Queen of Hungary and Bohemia, was the architect of the unified Austrian state, and one of the ablest rulers of eighteenth-century Europe, despite the fact that her father did not give her any formal training in statesmanship.

The Hapsburg domains comprised Hungary and part of Italy, as well as Austria and Bohemia which were then a major part of the Holy Roman Empire. Maria Theresa was the eldest of three daughters of the Hapsburg Archduke Charles VI, the Holy Roman Emperor, an office to which he had been elected by the German princes. In 1736 she married Francis, son of the Duke of Lorraine, who shortly became Duke of Tuscany. The marriage was on balance happy: Maria Theresa gave birth to five sons and 11 daughters (among them Marie Antoinette, wife of Louis XVI of France, who was guillotined in the French Revolution).

Maria Theresa's father died suddenly in 1740 when she was only 23 and expecting her fourth child. Almost at once she was faced with the War of the Austrian Succession (when her right to Bohemia was disputed by Frederick of Prussia and his allies), at a time when Austro-Hungary had been weakened by long wars against the Turks of the Ottoman Empire. Eventually in 1748 she had to yield to Frederick the rich province of Silesia, and was fortunate to lose little else.

Her husband Francis became co-ruler, and in 1745 was elected Holy Roman Emperor; Maria Theresa was thereafter called Empress-Queen. But the Emperor Francis was not, in practice, co-ruler; he left cares of state to his capable wife and her ministers.

The War of the Austrian Succession had exposed the alarming weakness of the divided Hapsburg Empire. For the next 30 years, apart from a failed attempt to retrieve Silesia during the Seven Years'

39

War in 1756, Maria Theresa devoted her energies to modernizing Austro-Hungary. She turned her feudalistic kingdoms, each with its separate constitution, into a modern, unified bureaucratic state, with a proper tax structure and educational system. She reformed the law, abolished torture and promoted trade. Many of the powerful nobles were lured into giving up their local powers by the attractions of elevated appointments as privy counsellors, diplomats or court officials in Imperial Vienna. They brought their wealth with them, and inspired by the Hapsburg example – Maria Theresa converted a former hunting lodge into the beautiful palace of Schönbrunn – helped create the elegant and sophisticated capital that Vienna became in the second half of the eighteenth century.

When the Emperor Francis died in 1765, their son Joseph became co-ruler and was elected Holy Roman Emperor. In 1772, not wishing to disadvantage Austria, she shared in the notorious partition of Poland with Russia and Prussia, and added Galicia to her empire. During her reign, Maria Theresa had transformed a poor, divided and ungovernable inheritance into a leading European power.

Constance Markiewiecz
Irish (1876–1923)

The 'Red Countess', as Constance Markiewiecz became known, was the first woman to be elected to the House of Commons (cf. Nancy Astor), and one of the few women to have fought like men in the cause of Irish nationalism. The eldest daughter of an Anglo-Irish landowner, Sir Henry Gore Booth, she was brought up with her sisters at Lissadell, a house in County Sligo celebrated by the poet W.B. Yeats. During the 'troubles' of the 1880s the sight of peasants being evicted from their cottages turned Constance into a Sinn Feiner and her sister Eva (cf. also Christabel Pankhurst) into a socialist.

Constance went to Paris in 1898 to study painting and married a Pole, Count Markiewiecz; they had a daughter, They were well enough off to divide their time between Poland and Ireland.

In Dublin Constance Markiewiecz worked for

Constance Markiewiecz, Irish Nationalist leader.

women's suffrage – and Irish freedom. She befriended many of the Irish Republican leaders. Nicknamed 'Madame', she drove a four-in-hand to a suffrage meeting in 1905; she organized a soup kitchen for the workers during the strikes of 1913; and in the Easter Rising of 1916, as second in command, she marched at the head of 120 Irish Republican soldiers to defend St Stephen's Green against the British. When they had to surrender after three days' fighting, she kissed her revolver a fond farewell. She and 15 others were sentenced to death by the British authorities, but in her case the sentence was commuted to 20 years' penal servitude.

Her popularity was such that while in prison in England she was elected to the British Parliament in 1918 by a Dublin constituency. But, like other Sinn Feiners, she never took her seat at Westminster as a matter of principle, even though she was released in the 1919 amnesty.

Golda Meir, Prime Minister of Israel from 1969–1974.

During the 1920s she formed the Irish Boy Scouts, toured the states to raise money for Sinn Fein and was arrested for distributing leaflets for Republican hunger strikers not long before she died. Enormous crowds filed past her coffin.

Golda Meir
Israeli (1898–1978)

Golda Meir became stop-gap Prime Minister of Israel in 1969, at the age of 70 – and remained Prime Minister for five years. Her predecessor, Ben Gurion, called her 'the only man in my Cabinet' – not her idea of a compliment, especially since she particularly enjoyed cooking and domestic life. None the less she proved a natural leader.

She was born Goldie Mabowehz in a Jewish ghetto in Kiev, Russia, daughter of a carpenter, who, in 1903, emigrated to America; his wife and children followed in 1906, and the family settled in Milwaukee. Golda trained as a teacher, and became active in the Zionist movement. She married another Russian immigrant, Morris Myerson, and in 1921 they emigrated to Israel. They lived on a kibbutz, where Golda looked after poultry, but left after two years because of Morris's health. Golda Myerson took in washing to make ends meet on her husband's salary as a bookkeeper. A son and daughter were born. Meanwhile she began working in the labour movement and the World Zionist Movement, and by 1948 was a sufficiently important figure to be one of the signatories of Israel's Declaration of Independence and to become, for a year, Israel's representative in Russia.

In 1949, after she was elected to the first Knesset, Prime Minister David Ben Gurion appointed her Minister of Labour. In 1956 (the year that, now a widow, she hebraicized her name to Meir) she took the job of Foreign Minister, which she held for nine years. Meir acted as chairman of Israel's delegation to the United Nations from 1953 to 1966 and was Secretary General of the Israeli Labour Party from 1965 until she retired in 1968. When Levi Eshkol died in office in 1969, however, she was summoned from retirement to become Prime Minister.

Meir handled her premiership with great adroitness, combining efficiency with a warm heart. There was never any threat to her leadership from either of the two young lions, Moshe Dayan or Yigael Allon, even during the Yom Kippur War. A determined Zionist, she once said: 'We live in a very dangerous part of the world. We intend to stay there.'

Nur Jahan
Indian (c. 1571–1634)

One of the legendary women of Moghul India, Nur Jahan, wife of the Emperor Jahangir, ruled in all but name for 16 years. She was the daughter of a Persian, Itimad-ud-daulah, who had risen to high office under Akbar, greatest of the Moghul emperors, and she married another Persian, Sher Afghan, by whom she had a daughter. They lived for many years in Burdwan, Bengal, and Nur Jahan only moved to the court after her husband was killed resisting arrest. She was 40 when in 1611 she married the Emperor Jahangir, who, it was said, had loved her for many years.

Thereafter her Persian relatives were all given advancement; her brother became Prime Minister, her niece Mumtaz (whose mausoleum is the Taj Mahal) married the heir to the throne, her daughter married the Emperor's second son. Nur Jahan's influence over her husband, who was overfond of drink and opium, was such that, as Jahangir said, it looked as if he had given her the Empire 'in return for a cup of wine and a few morsels of food'. Coins were minted in her name, she sat in the Hall of Audience, she issued *firmans* in the Emperor's name. She played polo and shot tigers, and together with her husband led a lavish life and attracted a circle of scholars, connoisseurs, poets, architects and painters. In tribute

to his wife, Jahangir wrote: 'In the whole empire there is scarcely a city in which the princess has not left some lofty structure, some spacious garden', though it was Jahangir himself who designed the famous gardens of Shalimar in Kashmir.

Nur Jahan tried to promote the claim to the throne of her daughter's husband, the Emperor's second son, which caused the heir (married to her niece) to rebel; eventually, however, the heir was reconciled, and when Jahangir died in 1626 Nur Jahan's son-in-law was captured and blinded, and Nur Jahan herself retired to lead a completely private life until her death 16 years later.

Vijaya Lakshmi Pandit
Indian (b. 1900)

Representing her country with great distinction, Vijaya Lakshmi Pandit held important posts as an ambassador and became the first woman to be elected President of the United Nations, in 1953–4.

Her father was Motilal Nehru, a distinguished westernized lawyer who belonged to an upper-class Brahmin family in Allahabad. Her brother Jawaharlal Nehru, who was to become Prime Minister of India, was sent to Harrow and Cambridge, while she and her sister were educated by an English governess, Miss Hooper, and not sent to university. In 1921 she married a Hindu scholar and lawyer, Ranjit Pandit.

The Nehrus' anglicized lives were totally changed by the Amritsar massacre in 1919, in which hundreds of Indian demonstrators were killed by the British Army and thousands wounded. Motilal Nehru gave up his legal career to join Mahatma Gandhi in the struggle to free India from the Raj, and the whole family dedicated itself to the cause. Mrs Pandit joined the campaign as soon as her three daughters were old enough to be left on their own, and was imprisoned three times for a total of 27 months. Her husband was to die in 1943 from the effects of such imprisonment.

Mrs Pandit reached national government by way of local government in her home state of Uttar Pradesh. In 1946, on the eve of Indian independence, the then Viceroy, Lord Wavell, insisted that she should lead the Indian delegation to the United Nations, where her fighting speech about the racialist politics of South Africa ensured an important vote against that country. Thereafter she was successively Ambassador to Moscow (1947–9), and to the U.S. and Mexico (1949–51); a member of the Indian Parliament (1952–4) and President of the United Nations Assembly (1953–4); High Commissioner in London and ambassador to Ireland (1954–61) and to Spain (1958–61); and Governor of the province of Maharashtra (1962–4).

In her seventies Pandit has emerged from retirement to oppose the policies of Indira Gandhi (q.v.), daughter of her brother Jawaharlal.

Dame Christabel Pankhurst
British (1880–1958)

Christabel Pankhurst was the strategist behind the increasing militancy of the campaign for votes for women in Britain – and as much of a celebrity as her mother Emmeline (q.v.). 'Queen Christabel' became perhaps the first non-royal, non-theatrical pin-up, for she was still in her early twenties when she achieved fame as a speaker of exceptional charisma, and only 25 when, with the ex-mill girl Annie Kenney, she became Britain's first woman political prisoner of modern times. Like her younger sisters Sylvia (q.v.) and Adela, Christabel learnt her radical politics from her parents. She read law at Manchester University, the only girl then to do so, at the suggestion of Eva Gore Booth (cf. Constance Markiewicz), a feminist friend of her mother's. The same friend recruited her to awaken interest in women's suffrage among local textile workers; and Christabel – who certainly had a great deal of the actress in her – discovered her métier as a speaker. By the time she was 21 she was speaking regularly – and already her platform was the activist view that women could not wait for their 'friends' in the Liberal or Labour parties to 'give' them the vote. In 1903 she was one of the founder-members of the Women's Social and Political Union (WSPU); two years later, after demanding an answer from Sir Edward Grey and Winston Churchill to the question 'Will the Liberal Party give women the vote?' at a big

Mrs Pandit at the United Nations Organization in 1954.

public meeting in Manchester, she was convicted of assaulting a policeman, while Annie Kenney was convicted of obstruction. The outcry was immense. it was to be the first of three prison sentences. Soon afterwards Christabel achieved a first-class degree in law – an exceptional achievement when she was so much in demand as a speaker – and went to work in the WSPU headquarters as Chief Organizer.

Christabel Pankhurst's main contribution to the women's movement was her impeccable flair for publicity, and the splendid slogan: 'Do not beg, do not grovel.' Like her mother, she was in some ways unnervingly conventional: she was not particularly interested in votes for working women, believing that votes for middle-class women was the necessary first step, and concerned above all that even at their most militant the suffragettes should be sexually and morally above reproach. This conservatism led

43

Mrs Emmeline Pankhurst campaigning for women's suffrage in Trafalgar Square, London, in 1908.

directly to the split with her sister Sylvia – just as the militancy which she encouraged and orchestrated was to cause a split in the WSPU itself.

Christabel went to prison three times; when the fourth arrest was imminent, in the wake of the first window-smashing campaign in 1912, she retreated to Paris to organize the campaign from a safe distance. But even from Paris she continued to write trenchant editorials for the WSPU's magazine, *The Suffragette*, organizing teams of couriers across the English channel, and offering her mother a haven – much appreciated by Mrs Pankhurst – whenever she was released from prison. After the outbreak of the 1914 war, she, like her mother, became an ardent patriot (re-christening *The Suffragette Britannia*). After the war she failed to become the first woman Member of Parliament by a narrow margin, and thereafter virtually disappeared.

When she did re-emerge from obscurity, it was with a new campaign: Second Adventism. She continued to write, and to lecture, and in 1936 was made a Dame of the British Empire; but spent the last 20 years of her life in California, an eccentric combination of evangelical Christian and perfect lady. She adopted a daughter in 1930. Dame Christabel refused to publish her history of the suffragette movement during her lifetime. *Unshackled: The Story of How We Won the Vote* was finally published in 1959.

Emmeline Pankhurst
British (1858–1928)

Mrs Pankhurst was the most famous of the suffragettes who fought to secure the vote for British women. With her daughter Christabel (q.v.) she led the militant wing of the movement until limited franchise was granted to women over 30 in 1918.

Emmeline Goulden was the eldest of five daughters of a well-to-do Manchester cotton manufacturer, who intersted himself in the Liberal Party and radical causes. Emmeline went to private school, and was 'finished' in Paris; and at 20 she married Manchester's most celebrated radical, the 40-year-old Dr Richard Pankhurst. It was a love match – Dr Pankhurst was too radical and his earning power too erratic to please his father-in-law – and Emmeline had three daughters and a son (who died as a baby) in the space of five years. She had a second son, who died as a young man, but all three daughters grew up to be doughty campaigners like their parents (cf. also Sylvia Pankhurst).

Emmeline Pankhurst won her political spurs at her husband's side. Dr Pankhurst stood three times as a Parliamentary candidate (without success); Mrs Pankhurst learnt to speak in public, to face hecklers, and even to brave being stoned. She urged him to live in London, where his voice would be better heard, and there, for seven years, she presided over gatherings which attracted socialists and progressives, including Annie Besant and Elizabeth Cady Stanton (qq.v); together, she and her husband founded the Women's Franchise League. Shortage of funds – made worse by Mrs Pankhurst's ill-starred attempts to retrieve their finances by opening a fancy goods shop in the West End – drove them back to Manchester. There she organized free canteens for the poor, was elected to a Board of Poor Law Guardians (of a workhouse) and, after Dr Pankhurst's death in 1898, took paid employment as a Registrar of Births and Deaths. She also opened her shop in Manchester.

In 1903, with her daughters and others, Pankhurst founded the Women's Social and Political Union. It was to be the irresistible combination of her evangelical oratory and her daughter Christabel's remarkable political sense and youthful magnetism which made of women's suffrage a force to be reckoned with. The WSPU, with its clarion call to action and its members' readiness to face prison and worse, soon quite outclassed the rival wing of the British women's movement, which for 40 years had waited for the Liberal Party to honour its professed allegiance to the cause of women's suffrage. In 1905 Christabel and Annie Kenney became Britain's first women political prisoners, and in the space of ten years 1800 other women followed them there – including, on several occasions, Mrs Pankhurst herself. She eventually resigned her post as a Registrar and took a suffragette salary of four guineas a week from the rapidly expanding WSPU funds. The famous sequence of events in the suffrage cause began: lobbying Parliament, torchlight processions, rallies – one in Leeds was said to have numbered 100,000 – heckling, demonstrations, and eventually brick-throwing, arson at grandstands and cricket pavilions, the cutting of golf and bowling greens, and other attacks on property by the most enthusiastic members of the movement. The damage was done, as Mrs Pankhurst said, 'Not at all in a spirit of wanton mischief, but with the direct and practical object of reminding the dull and self-satisfied English public that when the liberties of English women were being stolen from them it was no time to think of sport.'

In 1914 the Great War overtook the campaign. By now Mrs Pankhurst was emaciated and ill after her hunger strikes in prison, and was released from three years' penal servitude imposed for an attempt, for which she claimed responsibility, to blow up the Prime Minister's (unoccupied) new house. She called off her own hostilities for the duration of the war. When the vote was finally granted at the end of 1918, she at once went to campaign for Christabel, who stood for Smethwick, and only failed to win a seat in Parliament by 775 votes. In 1919 she went to the U.S., and for several years earned a good living on the lecture circuit – inveighing in particular against the evils of venereal disease. But she was still restless. In 1925 she briefly opened the Teashop of Good Hope at Juan-les-Pins in the South of France – which was a commercial fiasco – before returning to England where she was adopted as a Conservative parliamentary candidate in the East End of London.

But before she could fight an election on her own account, she died of the medical complications from which she had suffered ever since her hunger-strikes.

Sylvia Pankhurst
British (1882–1960)

Sylvia Pankhurst was the third member of the Pankhurst family to fight for votes for women. But for her 'votes for women' did not mean votes for middle-class women alone – the tactical stepping-stone adopted by her mother and sister – but votes for all women; and her belief in equality and justice eventually led her to become an ardent socialist and pacifist, and a fighter for the rights of the Third World.

Sylvia Pankhurst's first love was painting; she won a much-coveted scholarship to the Royal Academy in London in 1902. However, she was soon drawn into the WSPU campaign as a speaker, and she, too, went to prison and like her mother endured the indignity of force-feeding when she went on hunger strike. But she deeply disliked the increasing militancy of the WSPU, and in 1914 founded the East London Federation of Suffragettes, which included in its programme both socialism and pacifism. She also started a paper, *Woman's Dreadnought*. In 1919, having become a Communist, she was sentenced to six months in jail for incitement to sedition. She declared: 'I am going to fight capitalism even if it kills me.'

The British Communist Party however eventually expelled her for not toeing the Party line, and she retired to a cottage outside London with her lover, Silvio Corio, an Italian radical. In 1927 she had a son, Richard, whose father she always refused to identify.

In 1936 Sylvia Pankhurst founded a paper called *New Times*, which she intended to be a voice for the oppressed of all nations. With the encouragement of Silvio Corio, she adopted Ethiopia, which had recently been invaded by Mussolini and his Italian troops, as her particular cause. She raised funds for a hospital in Addis Ababa, and made her first long-awaited visit in 1944. After Corio's death in 1954, she emigrated to Ethiopia, where her son Richard became a teacher at the university.

Her books include *The Suffragette Movement* (1931), a major, highly critical source for the history of the campaign, *Save the Mothers* (1930), about the need for proper obstetric care for women, *The Ethiopian People* (1946), *Cultural History of Ethiopia* (1955), and even a very well researched book about India, a country she never visited.

Rosa Parks
American (b. 1914)

Rosa Parks earned fame as the black woman who, going home laden with shopping just before Christmas, 1955, refused to give up her seat to a white man on a bus in Montgomery, Alabama. Her action inspired a general black boycott of the buses and a widespread demand for courtesy from the drivers, for seats on a first-come-first-served basis and for the employment of black drivers in black districts. 'A miracle has taken place,' said Dr Martin Luther King Jr., as the progress of a peaceful Civil Rights movement gathered momentum in the wake of Parks' action. The United States Supreme Court affirmed the following April that laws requiring segregated buses were unconstitutional.

Ana Pauker
Romanian (1893–1956)

The modern world's first woman foreign minister was the Communist Ana Pauker. She was also deputy premier and in effective control of Romania until she was 'purged' in 1952.

Ana Pauker was born in Bucharest, the daughter of Zvi Rabinsohn, a Jewish ritual butcher, in a country where anti-Semitism was strong. She taught Hebrew briefly, and became a socialist under the influence of a young lawyer called Steinberg. She studied medicine at Zurich, where she met and married Marcel Pauker, son of a Romanian newspaper proprietor; they had three children. Thereafter her life was devoted to politics, and she was first imprisoned for her beliefs in 1918. In 1921 she joined the 100-strong Romanian

Communist Party and was soon on its Central Committee. After helping to organize a railway strike in 1933 which ended in bloodshed she was arrested and eventually sentenced to 10 years. She was released in 1940 and spent the war in Moscow, where her husband was killed – some say at her instigation. She organized Romanian prisoners of war into a division of the Red Army and became a friend of Stalin. When Russia 'liberated' Romania she returned as a colonel and played a key role in turning her native country into a Russian satellite. King Michael of Romania was forced to make her Foreign Minister in 1947. The most feared woman in Romania, she wielded immense power. Even after her fall from power in 1952, Pauker remained active in Romania's Communist Party.

Alice Paul
American (1885–1977)

Alice Paul led the militant wing in the last years of the fight for women's suffrage in America. She founded the Congressional Union for Women's Suffrage in 1913, and the National Woman's Party shortly afterwards, and secured a great deal of publicity for the feminist cause. Alice Paul was born into a Quaker family in Moorstown, New Jersey, and was educated privately before graduating from Swarthmore College, Pennsylvania in 1905. She did settlement work both in America and England where she was actively involved in the British struggle for the vote and was jailed three times.

In New York in 1913, Paul set up the Congressional Union and led a protest march of 10,000 women past the White House the day before President Wilson's inauguration. In 1913 she seceded from Carrie Chapman Catt's (q.v.) National American Women's Suffrage Association; she had no faith in Catt's gradualist approach. She founded her own National Woman's Party (which still exists) in 1916, and campaigned against the re-election of President Wilson. Congress finally passed the Nineteenth Amendment, giving women the vote, in 1919.

For the next 10 years Alice Paul continued with her legal work and became chairperson of the Women's Research Foundation in 1927. Later, in Geneva, Switzerland, she worked for world peace and campaigned to get women more say in world affairs. 'This world crisis came about without women having anything to do with it,' she said in 1941.

Frances Perkins
American (1880–1965)

'Ma' Perkins was a pioneer in the political reform of working conditions, and the first woman member of a U.S. Cabinet. The daughter of Republican New Englanders, she graduated from Mount Holyoke and taught chemistry in Chicago. She soon gravitated towards settlement work at Hull House (cf. Jane Addams). In 1910 she took her Master's degree at Columbia and founded a Consumers' League. Three years later, she witnessed the Triangle Shirtwaist Factory fire in which nearly 150 women and girls died unnecessarily. Thereafter 'Ma' Perkins worked tirelessly to improve safety standards at places of work and became an inspector in New York in 1912.

In 1913 she married Paul Wilson and had a daughter, Susanna, in 1916. In 1919 she became the first woman to be appointed to the New York State Industrial Commission and became chairman in 1926. As head of the Department of Labour in 1933 she became the first U.S. woman Cabinet Member.

Eva Perón
Argentinian (1919–1952)

The blonde and beautiful 'Evita' is the most striking twentieth-century example of the woman who charms a soldier, and rises at his side to charm – and rule – an entire nation. The 'Queen of the Shirtless Ones', she became the first ever Presidenta of Argentina.

She was born Eva Maria Duarte in Los Toldos, a dusty, provincial town, where her unmarried mother took in lodgers. She escaped to Buenos Aires at 15 to earn a living in the entertainment business. She was 'Senorita Radio' when she married the middle-aged

Eva Perón making her election address for vice president in August 1951. She died of cancer in 1952.

Colonel Juan Domingo Perón in 1945 and became the most ardent Peronista – fighter for the rights of the workers – of them all. In 1946 an army *coup* put General Perón in prison, whereupon Eva mobilized the masses and he was set free. He became President and she – in a total departure from tradition – Presidenta.

Both of them were bitterly opposed to the oligarchy of the *ancien régime*. 'La Presidenta' spent her working day at the Ministry of Labour, interviewing people with problems and administering the enormous sums donated to the Eva Perón Foundation. No army officer or politician was a match for her. She took over the best hotels for the aged, founded schools and hospitals, and nationalized large estates to be turned into parks and swimming pools. Twice a

week she broadcast to women all over the country; in 1948 she got them the vote, instituted the legalization of an eight-hour day and the payment of sickness benefit. Wrapped in furs and glittering with jewels, she made speeches to the workers; she was the idol of the trade union movement and, indeed, the working class all over the the country. In 1951 she published *My Life's Work*. The following year she died – aged 33 – of cancer; thousands of mourners filed past her open coffin. 'Women have created happy homes,' she said, 'why cannot they make the world and all its peoples happier?'

Maria de Lourdes Pintassilgo
Portuguese (b. 1930)

Maria de Lourdes Pintassilgo became Europe's second woman prime minister as caretaker Prime Minister of Portugal on 1 August 1979. Like Britain's Prime

Minister, Mrs Thatcher (q.v.), she comes from a middle-class background, and is also a fully qualified industrial chemist. At university she became president first of the Catholic women students and then of the progressive international Catholic students' organization, Pax Romana.

Pintassilgo became a consultant to one of Portugal's largest chemical companies, representing Portugal at the first Organization for Economic Cooperation and Development Seminar on 'The Rational Organization of Scientific Research', and was a member of the Portuguese mission to the United Nations in 1972 and 1973. Her reputation as chemist, left-wing feminist and militant Catholic won her office after the Portuguese revolution of 1974; she became Secretary of State for Social Security and Minister for Social Affairs in the first two post-revolutionary governments. She promptly set up a committee to look into the status of women, and pushed a new women's rights bill through Parliament.

From 1975 Pintassilgo was Portugal's ambassador at UNESCO before being asked to form a government of her own in July 1979. She resigned the following December to make way for a government to be formed by the leader of the Social Democratic Party, the largest group in the Democratic Alliance which won the elections held that month. The new Prime Minister would not permit her to return to her UNESCO post, because her belief in non-alignment was incompatible with Portugal's association with NATO and the EEC.

Manon Roland
French (1754–1793)

Madame Roland was one of the heroines of the French Revolution – she welcomed it, fought for it and yet, like many others, was sent to the guillotine. It was on the scaffold itself that she uttered the words for which she has achieved immortality: 'Oh Liberty! What crimes are committed in thy name!'

The only child of a Paris watchmaker called Philipon, the young Marie Jeanne early saw the injustice of the times in 'the contrast between this Asiatic luxury and the poverty of the besotted people'. In 1780 she married Jean-Marie Roland, a middle-aged factory inspector, and helped him win a seat in the Assembly in 1791 by writing his speeches. 'I loved my country, I was enthusiastic for liberty,' she declared. Her husband was made Minister of the Interior to the Crown in 1792, when the King had not yet been executed, and for a few months after the overthrow of the monarchy Roland was again Minister of the Interior. But the Terror was almost upon them; there was no hope that the moderate policies supported by the Rolands and the Girondin party would prevail. The masses accused the Girondins of negotiating with the King, and 22 Girondins, including Madame Roland, were arrested. She languished in jail for over a year, but bravely decorated her cell with flowers, played the harpsichord and wrote her autobiography. In November 1793 she was executed. She sang the *Marseillaise* all the way to the guillotine. Roland himself had escaped arrest; but when he heard the news of his wife's death he killed himself.

Eleanor Roosevelt
American (1884–1962)

The niece and wife of Presidents of the U.S., Eleanor Roosevelt was also the classic example of an ugly duckling who turned not into a swan but certainly into a bird of a very different feather. She was born a Roosevelt, but her mother died young and she was brought up by unsympathetic relatives. Shy and plain all through her youth, she married her distant cousin Franklin when she was 19, and they had a daughter and four sons. Eleanor Roosevelt did social work and taught part-time, but her early married life was dominated by her formidable mother-in-law, who chose and decorated the young couple's houses and even hired (and paid) their servants. However, when Franklin D. Roosevelt was paralysed by polio in 1921 and his mother wanted him to retire completely from politics, it was Eleanor – determined that he should live as active a life as he wanted – who prevailed. With great courage she turned herself into the supporting helpmeet the future President needed,

Eleanor Roosevelt arriving in London to launch her autobiography in 1959.

Helen Suzman, leader of South Africa's Progressive Party photographed in 1975.

and after Roosevelt's death in 1945 President Truman appointed her U.S. delegate to the United Nations – calling her First Lady of the World. She wrote more than a dozen extremely readable books, including an autobiography; her newspaper column *My Day* ensured that she remained the best-known woman in America during her lifetime.

Queen Sonduk
Korean (c. AD 625)

Queen Sonduk ruled Korea from 632 to 647, because the male line of the Silla dynasty had died out. She was responsible for the building of the first known observatory in the Far East, Ch'omsong-dae (Tower of the Moon and Stars), the tower of which still survives as a tourist attraction at Kyong-ju, South Korea, ancient capital of the Silla kings. Sonduk lived

in violent times, but she tried to improve the lives of ordinary people, and encouraged education and learning. During her reign, scholars were sent to China for training.

At the age of seven, when her father the king received as a present from China a peony seed and several paintings of the flower, she is said to have exclaimed, 'What a pity it has no smell!' When her father asked how she could tell, she replied, 'If it had a smell, the paintings would show bees and butterflies on the flowers.' The seed was planted, and sure enough the peony flowers had no smell. 'My wise little daughter!' he said. 'She shall reign when I am gone.'

Helen Suzman
South African (b. 1917)

For 12 years Helen Suzman was the only member of the anti-apartheid Progressive Party in the South

African Parliament in Cape Town, a lone voice raised on behalf of justice for black people in South Africa. Since 1974, however, further Progressive candidates have been elected.

Suzman entered Parliament in 1953 as a member of the United Party, and with a number of other United Party members formed the Progressive Party in 1959. The rich white constituency of Houghton, Johannesburg, continued to elect her, while the others lost their seats.

The daughter of a first generation South African from Lithuania – Sam Gavronsky, an entrepreneur – Suzman was born into the privileged world of white Johannesburg. She became a university lecturer in economics at Witwatersrand University, a social worker and a hostess. She is married to a distinguished neurologist, and has two daughters.

Suzman has been saved from anything approaching the fate of Winnie Mandela (q.v.) by her colour, her social position and her parliamentary privilege, but her 12 year lone stand – constantly speaking, constantly forcing divisions – in an atmosphere of hostility and anti-Semitism has rightly brought her tributes from black people as well as white liberals: 'The one flickering flame of liberty', in Chief Buthelezi's words.

Margaret Thatcher
British (b. 1925)

Margaret Thatcher became Western Europe's first woman Prime Minister in May 1979, although she was followed within a few months by Maria Pintassilgo (q.v.) in Portugal.

She was born Margaret Roberts in Grantham, Lincolnshire, the younger of two daughters of a retail grocer, himself an unusual man, however – a Methodist lay preacher who twice became Mayor of Grantham. 'We were good *Daily Telegraph* people,' says his elder daughter. Margaret – her father's favourite – went to the local grammar school, where she was made head girl and vice-captain of the hockey team. Having learnt enough Latin in three months to pass her Oxford entrance exam, she won

Mrs Thatcher announcing the Conservative Party's Manifesto for Europe in 1979.

an academic award to Somerville College, Oxford, where she studied chemistry under Dorothy Hodgkin (q.v.). She then too a further degree and won the Somerville Natural Science Prize for a scientific essay, but work was already taking second place to politics. A member of the University Conservative Association, she was eventually elected its president, at a time when such an appointment was unusual for women. After Oxford she worked as a research chemist for BX Plastics near Colchester and J. Lyons & Co. but by 1949 she had been adopted as Conservative candidate for Dartford, Kent. It was a Socialist stronghold, but she reduced the Labour majority and met her husband Denis Thatcher, whom she married seven seeks after the 1951 election. He ran a family chemical and paint firm, and was well enough off for his wife to give up earning a living. The new Mrs Thatcher began reading for the Bar, and passed her Finals in 1953, the same year she gave birth to twins. She practised as a tax lawyer, and was elected Member of Parliament for Finchley, London, in the election of 1959. Two years later she achieved government office as Joint Parliamentary Secretary to the Ministry of Pensions and National Insurance, and in 1970, joined the Cabinet as Minister of Education. In 1979 she became Prime Minister. On the way she had had some experience of social security, housing, power and transport, but not the Treasury or Home and Foreign Offices, hitherto regarded as indispensable stepping stones. In February 1975, after the Conservative leader Edward Heath had lost two elections in a row, she stood against him (and others) for the leadership, and won decisively. Mrs Thatcher became Prime Minister when she led her party to a resounding victory over Labour in May 1979.

Since then she has made headlines all over the world. Many people, including fellow party members, dislike her hardline Conservative policies, but no one can deny that she has brains, ability, energy, and the courage of her convictions. Her integrity can be taken for granted, and she would be incapable of the pettiness of some of her predecessors. Mrs Thatcher is not a feminist; she believes she has got to the top entirely through her own efforts. But it is hard to believe that those efforts would have been enough if the new outspokenness of the women's movement had not softened public and political opinion at just the right moment.

Empress Theodora
Byzantium (c. 497–548)

Co-ruler for 20 years of the East Roman Empire with her husband the Emperor Justinian, Theodora rose from the poorest class of Constantinople by dint of her beauty, cleverness and charm. She was the second of three daughters of a bear-keeper, Akakios, who died when she was very young. She followed her elder sister on to the stage as a dancer and mime-artist, and a scurrilous account of her life-style was recorded in his *Secret History* by the historian Procopius. Even if much of this can be disregarded as malicious exaggeration, it seems likely that Theodora did not lead a sheltered life, for she bore one illegitimate child, and perhaps another, prior to her marriage. There can be no doubt of her beauty, charm, wit and self-confidence.

Theodora became the mistress of Hecebolus, a provincial governor, and she accompanied him to North Africa. However, she soon left him, and after

probably spending some time in Alexandria, where she appears to have met leading members of the Monophysite sect, she eventually returned to Constantinople. There she met the nephew of the Emperor Justin, Justinian, who fell passionately in love with her. From that day each appears to have been faithful to the other; certainly Procopius has no further gossip to retail. Although Theodora had a daughter by Justinian, who died young, they were unable to marry until 523 when the law was changed to allow leading citizens to marry women of servile origin. In 527 they were jointly crowned as rulers of the East Roman Empire.

Justinian was one of the ablest of Roman emperors, and his reign a brilliant one: he was responsible for the building of the great basilicas of Santa Sophia in Constantinople and San Vitale in Ravenna; for the codification of Roman law; for overhauling the administration of the empire; and for recovering, if only briefly, the lost provinces of the Western Mediterranean. Theodora had immense influence over her husband, which was not always exercised for the best; her support for the Monophysites made it difficult for Justinian to preserve the unity of the Church, and she obliged him to get rid of some of his best administrators and generals.

But of her spirit and courage there was no question, and during a dangerous popular uprising in 532 Justinian owed her his throne. As he was preparing to flee from his palace, she said: 'Every man born to see the light of day must die. But that one who has been emperor should become an exile I cannot bear. May I never be without the purple I wear ... I like the old saying, that the purple is the noblest shroud.' Justinian stayed, and ruled for another 33 years. Theodora herself died 17 years before him.

Empress Tz'u-hsi
Chinese (1835–1908)

'The Old Buddha', as the Chinese called the famous Empress Dowager Tz'u-hsi, effectively ruled China for the last half-century of the Manchu dynasty. An

Tz'u-hsi, Dowager Empress of China, also known as 'The Old Buddha'.

ultra-conservative ruler, she presided unwillingly over the first changes which the impact of the modern world forced on the ancient Chinese monarchy; at her death that monarchy was to disappear for good.

Like the Empress Wu (q.v.), Tz'u-Hsi started her career as an imperial concubine. She was one of several children of a minor mandarin called Hui-cheng, and appears to have been raised in poverty in south China. But her family belonged to the ruling elite, the Manchus (originally conquerors from Manchuria who displaced the Ming dynasty in the seventeenth century), so she was eligible for the concubinate, which was forbidden to Chinese women; and in 1851 she went to the Forbidden City in Peking as a concubine of the Emperor, who was the only man in a world of 6,000 women and eunuchs.

Although given no formal education, Tz'u-hsi taught herself to read and write. She studied Confucianism and calligraphy, and became a gifted amateur painter – a fact of which she was always very proud. In 1856 she gave birth to the Emperor's only surviving male child, and was appointed concubine of the second rank. It was then that she began to play a part in Manchu politics, at that time concerned with the suppression of the Taiping rebellion.

When the Emperor died in 1861 she was out of favour, but she managed to secure the succession for her son Tung Chih, and have herself appointed co-regent with the Emperor's widow. Their role was known as 'Listening Behind Screens to Reports on Government Affairs', and was not thought to be particularly important by the men who really ruled the Empire. But Tz'u-hsi's intelligence and personality soon brought her effective political control, which she did not relinquish even when her son Tung Chih came of age. When he died in 1875 she had her sister's son, another minor, appointed Emperor Kuang Hsu in his place, and ruled in his name also until 1889. Thereafter for a few years she concentrated on building herself a magnificent summer palace outside Peking, expropriating moneys earmarked for modernization of the Navy. All her life she lived in extraordinary luxury and isolation.

Her nephew the new Emperor, an intelligent young man, was meanwhile trying to bring China up to date. This was Tz'u-Hsi's opportunity to intrigue to unseat him with those ministers who disliked the new regime; and after the famous 100 days reform in 1898, she was back on the throne, six of the reformers having been executed and the Emperor Kuang Hsu ousted.

But the Empress Dowager was no fool. When the 'Boxer' rebellions of 1900, in which the Chinese people rose up and attacked the foreigners who were infiltrating the coastal cities, brought foreign reprisals and she herself had to flee from Peking disguised as a peasant, for the first time she saw the conditions in which her subjects lived. She changed her mind about reform: and in 1901, when she was in her late sixties, she instituted the reforms which she had resisted three years earlier. In January 1902, having consulted her horoscope, she re-entered Peking with the Emperor and Empress by train.

Tz'u-hsi decreed that Manchus and Chinese could marry; she abolished the binding of feet, a custom that had crippled generations of noble Chinese women; she introduced history, geography and sciences into the civil service exams; she opened state schools to girls, and modernized an examination system which had remained unchanged since AD622. She established a Ministry of Commerce; she 'nationalized' the Customs Service, which had been run by Europeans for generations; she abolished torture and outlandish methods of execution; and she began to suppress the growing of opium. She even introduced electric lighting. Finally, she sent a commission of enquiry to Europe, and in 1906 announced that the monarchy would have a constitution.

But China was bankrupt. The Emperor Kuang Hsu and the Empress Dowager died within a day of each other, on 14 and 15 November 1908 (some say she had him murdered when they were both dying, so that he should not be able to tell tales). The Chinese monarchy ended three years later.

Tz'u-hsi lived into the twentieth century, in a lifestyle that the Empress Wu (q.v.) would have recognized without difficulty, and which is today almost unimaginable. Tz'u-hsi had heard of Queen Victoria, and kept a portrait of her in her bedroom, saying: 'Do you know, I have often thought that I am the cleverest woman who ever lived and that others cannot compare with me. Although I have heard much about Queen Victoria and read a part of her life . . . still I don't think her life is half as interesting as mine. Now look at me, I have 400 million people all dependent on my judgment.'

Simone Veil
French (b. 1927)

Simone Veil has achieved the seemingly impossible and persuaded France, an ostensibly Roman Catholic country, to reform its restrictive law on abortion. She was born Simone Jacob in Nice, the youngest daughter of a Jewish architect. In 1944, the day after she had taken her *baccalauréat*, the family was deported to Auschwitz. Her father, mother and brother were never heard of again. She herself

survived Auschwitz, and back in France after the war she studied law. She married Antoine Veil, a fellow student whose sister had been with her in Auschwitz; and had three sons.

Veil became a magistrate at the age of 29, and an assistant public prosecutor at the Ministry of Justice in 1969. She then became a civil servant, drafted a new law on adoption and helped to write a book on the subject. In 1970 she was promoted to a job in charge of nearly 3,000 magistrates. Simon Veil became Minister of Health in 1974, a post she held for four years, during which she saw the implementation of her reform on abortion law. In 1979 she became President of the European Parliament.

Queen Victoria
British (1819–1901)

The modern style of British monarchy – domesticated, dutiful and revered, but with very little political influence – is recognizably the creation of Queen Victoria. Before her day the Hanoverian dynasty was openly reviled for its foreignness, its foibles, its morals and its politics.

Victoria herself was the daughter of King George III's fourth son, the Duke of Kent, who had given up a liaison of 27 years to marry the widowed daughter of the Duke of Saxe-Coburg and ensure the succession. He died a year after his only child, Victoria, was born.

In 1838, at the age of 18, Victoria succeeded her uncle William IV to the throne, and immediately shrugged off the restraining hands of her mother and governess. Two years later, deeply in love, she married a maternal cousin, Albert of Saxe-Coburg-Gotha, by whom, over the next 17 years, she had four sons and five daughters. Her descendants eventually succeeded to the thrones of Germany, Russia, Sweden, Denmark, Norway, Spain, Greece, Rumania and Yugoslavia, besides Great Britain.

Queen Victoria had little personally to do with the acquisition of the second British Empire (she became

Simone Veil, President of the European Parliament, photographed in July 1979.

Empress of India in 1876), nor with the industrialization of Britain (she left science and technology to Prince Albert), or the extension of the franchise in 1867 and 1884 (which she disliked). She had great dignity and immense personal influence, but presided none the less over the British crown's loss of effective political power.

Her family life was immensely important to her, and Albert's early death in 1861 led to years of grief-stricken seclusion, which eventually caused public criticism. She lived mostly at Windsor, Osborne (in the Isle of Wight) and Balmoral in Scotland, where she became extremely dependent on her ghillie John Brown, a relationship which has intrigued posterity but about which any surviving curiosity has not been satisified.

Victoria was a wonderful and happily prolific letter-writer (her letters were greatly admired by Gertrude Stein, q.v.), particularly to her prime ministers and to her daughters, and she kept a voluminous diary from which she published two selections during her lifetime, *Leaves from the Journal of our Life in the Highlands* (1868) and *More Leaves* (1884). She was also an extremely gifted amateur artist, and 50-odd sketchbooks of her drawings and watercolours survive in the Queen's collection.

Empress Wu Chao
Chinese (625–705)

There have been many women rulers, sometimes in their own right, sometimes as regents, sometimes as powers behind the throne. None has been more dramatically successful than the Empress Wu, who ruled China in fact if not always in name for half a century. She even usurped her own son – although a woman as sovereign flouted the deepest religious beliefs of her subjects – and ruled *de jure* as well as *de facto* for 15 of those 50 years. As ruler, the Empress Wu consolidated the work of her great predecessor the Emperor T'ai Tsung, and left a united and contented China as a legacy for her grandson, the Emperor Hsuan Tsung, whose reign was to be the high peak of T'ang poetry and art.

Wu Chao was the daughter of a general who had

Queen Victoria, from an 1897 print by Sir William Nicholson.

served the first T'an Emperor and had died when she was a child. Hearing of her beauty, the T'ang Emperor T'ai Tsung summoned her to court to be one of his many concubines. Once there, she succeeded in catching the Crown Prince's eye; so when, on the Emperor's death, she and her fellow concubines were forcibly retired for life into a convent (as was the custom), it was not long before she was back in the palace as concubine to the new Emperor, Kao Tsung, and had borne him a son. By the time she was 30, she had displaced both the Empress, who was childless (by allowing the Emperor to believe that, from jealousy, the Empress had murdered her second child), and the chief concubine. Once on the throne Wu Chao had the other concubines killed, and gradually proceeded to eliminate all opposition, including many members of her own family. She bore Kao Tsung two more sons and a daughter.

Thereafter Wu Chao took over the administration from the Emperor, who was a weak and doting husband and who in 660 contracted the paralytic illness from which he eventually died. In that year

Clara Zetkin in Red Square, Moscow, in September 1924.

excesses were in the end too much for her, and she had him killed in 696. He was replaced the following year by two young brothers called Chang – foppish, artistic and amusing – who were also reputed to be her lovers, and were certainly her most intimate companions until the year of her death. At court, the brothers Chang were hated and feared. Their scheming in the battle for the succession inspired the only *coup* which the Empress, now 80, did not foresee and could not suppress. Her most dependable ministers had the Changs killed and put the Crown Prince (whom the Empress Wu had usurped in 690) back on the throne. Wu Chao accepted this *fait accompli* calmly, retired to her summer palace, and died – in her bed – a few months later. The China which she had ruled for so long survived the court intrigues which broke out after her departure from the throne and, under her grandson Hsuan Tsung, enjoyed a golden age.

Wu Chao probably took over the direction of China's long-standing war with Korea by ordering an invasion by sea, and shortly achieved victory.

Wu Chao was responsible for a great improvement in government. She lowered taxes, picked good ministers, and made the work of lesser officials a good deal less arduous. Although there were constant plots against her (which she suppressed with a savagery from which the innocent suffered as much as the guilty), the army always remained loyal and the people themselves never rebelled. The Empire as a whole enjoyed several decades of peace and prosperity, and Wu Chao was able to embellish her capital with magnificent buildings.

Wu Chao was notorious for her favourites. First was the extraordinary Hsueh Huai-i, a peddler of cosmetics, whom she took up in 685 when she was 60, shortly after her husband's death, and who was believed by the historians of the dynasty to have been her lover. She made him an abbot, and then commander-in-chief against the tribes who were invading along the northern frontier; but although he had considerable talents, his extravagance and

Clara Zetkin
German (1857–1933)

'The last of the men,' Rosa Luxemburg (q.v.) called Clara Zetkin, the celebrated Marxist law reformer, pacifist and political activist. Her father was a village schoolmaster and she was one of the first women to train as a teacher in Leipzig (cf. Luise Otto-Peters). There Clara met various foreign revolutionaries, including Ossip Zetkin, a Russian socialist, who was expelled from Germany in 1880. She married him in Paris in 1882 and they had two children. Clara Zetkin launched a campaign to reform the law for women and families. In 1889 she went back to Germany to organize a social democratic women's movement, and found a paper, *Gleicheit* (Equality). Vehemently anti-war in 1914 she was put in jail for her activities. She co-founded the Spartacus League with Karl Liebknecht and Rosa Luxemburg (q.v.), and in 1918 the German Communist Party. She became a member of the German Reichstag in 1919. Although she spent much of her time thereafter in Russia, Zetkin remained a member until her death just before Hitler led the National Socialists to power.

EDUCATION AND SOCIAL REFORM

UNTIL MODERN TIMES, REFORM OF ANY KIND was the prerogative of the ruler, and it was a rare ruler who looked much beyond the defence of the realm, law and order, and the raising of taxes. The Church, which might have been expected to play a more charitable social role, has largely confined itself to the foundation of schools and hospitals and avoided involvement with such controversial issues as the slave trade, the death sentence or the grotesque exploitation of child labour. In general, the fight for better social conditions has been left to private individuals – working alone or in groups – to campaign for the rights of man, of woman, and of child.

From the end of the eighteenth century there was an unprecedented upsurge of reforming zeal in the western world, and in this social movement women, although virtually without rights and without votes, played a part out of all proportion to their power. Elizabeth Fry and Dorothea Dix devoted their lives to the much-needed reform of prisons and mental hospitals. Lucretia Mott and the Grimké sisters were to the fore in the fight against slavery, while a former slave, Harriet Tubman, known as the 'Moses of her people', for decades ran a notoriously successful slave escape line from the southern U.S. Prominent campaigners for peace like Jane Addams and Bertha von Suttner were awarded the Nobel Peace Prize for their efforts. In the controversial area of birth control, the foundations of planned parenthood were laid by such pioneering figures as Margaret Sanger, Marie Stopes and Dr Aletta Jacobs, while Josephine Butler, flying in the face of public opinion, courageously fought for the rights of prostitutes and Maria Montessori revolutionized the teaching of young children. The women's emancipation movement was probably the greatest single victory of the period, headed by such active campaigners as Susan B. Anthony and Elizabeth Cady Stanton. Individually and collectively in the nineteenth and twentieth centuries women were making themselves heard, as labour organizers, suffragettes, pacifists, educators, divorce law reformers, freethinkers and philanthropists.

Helen Keller (left) with her teacher Anne Sullivan Macy.

Jane Addams
American (1860–1935)

Jane Addams was the best known and best loved American woman of her time, for by bringing the concept of the 'settlement' to the U.S. she opened up the whole field of social work there. She was born in Cedarville, Illinois, in 1860, daughter of a prosperous timber merchant, and educated at nearby Rockford College. In 1889 she and a friend bought Hull House and founded a settlement in the slums of Chicago.

A 1933 Turkish postage stamp commemmorating Jane Addams' life's work.

They and their fellow volunteers made reports on neighbourhood conditions so as to campaign for better housing, sewage, schools and roads. Following a principle learned at Toynbee Hall, London, they also gave readings of *Romola* and lectures on art. By 1911 some 400 'Hull Houses' had been established.

Jane Addams' particular strength was a calm, peaceful presence; her skill in labour relations was such that she was appointed secretary of an Industrial Arbitration Committee in 1893. In 1910 she helped win a collective bargaining clause during a garment workers' dispute which proved valuable in keeping industrial peace. In 1912 she ran as a Progressive candidate, but lost.

In 1915 Addams became president of the Women's International League for Peace and Freedom and went on a peace mission to Europe. She discovered that soldiers on both sides in the First World War had to be given intoxicants before bayonet charges. When she revealed this back home she was accused of being 'unpatriotic' and a 'red', and headed a Daughters of the American Revolution black list. All her life she wrote, travelled and gave lectures. Her best books are *Democracy and Social Ethics* (1902), *Twenty Years at Hull House* (1910), and *Memory* (1916). In 1931 she became the second woman to receive the Nobel Peace Prize (Bertha von Suttner, q.v., had been the first, a quarter of a century earlier).

Susan B. Anthony
American (1820–1906)

Most famous of American feminists, Susan B. Anthony pioneered women's suffrage in the U.S. She was the second daughter of a cotton mill owner and his wife, both Quakers, of Battonville, New York. She learned the high cost of principles at an early age, when the family business failed and her father refused to buy slave-produced cotton. Anthony was taken away from her boarding school to work on the factory floor. 'Every girl should be trained for self support,' said her father.

For eight years she taught in upstate New York, where in 1848 she formed a society, the Daughters of Temperance, to combat the evils of drink (cf.

Elizabeth Cady Stanton). That same year the famous Women's Rights convention was held at Seneca Falls, New York, but it was not until after a series of humiliating disappointments in attempting to speak at all-male temperance meetings that Anthony began to campaign actively for women's rights herself. She attended her first Women's Rights convention in 1852 and was soon a friend of the leading feminists Elizabeth Blackwell and Margaret Fuller (qq.v.).

After the Civil War, in 1868, she launched her own paper, *Revolution*; its motto was the famous 'Men, their rights and nothing more. Women, their rights and nothing less.' The paper went bankrupt after two years, but by then it had made Anthony's name. She went on lecture tours all over the United States. In 1872 she cast her vote in Rochester, New York, for which she was put on trial. She refused to pay the 100 dollar fine, declaring 'Resistance to tyranny is obedience to God.'

In 1880 Susan B. Anthony and Elizabeth Cady Stanton began writing *A History of Woman Suffrage*. Continually active, she travelled and lectured until she died; asked once why she never married, she said, 'I never had the time.' Fourteen years after her death, women got the vote in America. In recognition of Anthony's achievements one of the new dollar coins bears her head.

Aspasia of Miletus
Greek (c. 400 BC)

Aspasia, probably the daughter of Axiochus of Miletus, lived with the great Athenian statesman Pericles from the mid-440s BC until his death in 429, and bore him a son. In an age when the women of Athens were expected to lead virtuous lives out of the public eye, a 'foreign' woman like Aspasia was exceptional – one of the great *hetairai* of the Greek world, highly educated and the intellectual equal of men. She is mentioned as a teacher of rhetoric in Plato's dialogue the *Menexenus*, and Socrates certainly knew and admired her. She was passionately interested in politics, excited much jealousy, and was the target of many insults in the comedies of the time. Plutarch, in his *Life of Pericles* (written, however, 600 years later), claims that 'she carried on a trade that was anything but honourable or even respectable, since it consisted of keeping a house of young courtesans.' Aspasia was prosecuted for impiety but was acquitted after Pericles made a personal appeal to the jurors. Six months after Pericles' death she married Lysicles, a cattle-dealer, and had a second son by him.

The U.S. 1979 dollar piece with the head of Susan B. Anthony.

Aspasia of Miletus, companion of Pericles and teacher of rhetoric.

Dorothy Beale
(see Frances Mary Buss)

Isabella Beeton
British (1836–1865)

Mrs Beeton is the most famous of the long and distinguished line of Britain's women cookery writers which stretches from the great Hannah Glasse by way of Elizabeth Raffald, Mrs Rundell and Eliza Acton right down to the generation of our own day, whose best known representative is Elizabeth David. *Beeton's Book of Household Management*, edited by Mrs Isabella Beeton when she was only 23, was published in book form in 1861, having been first published as a serial by her husband, Sam Beeton, in 30 monthly parts in 1859. It was an immense work, containing more than 3,000 recipes as well as advice on instructing servants, nursing, legal matters, etiquette and bringing up babies. As the title implies, it was *Beeton's* book, and the inspiration was undoubtedly Sam Beeton's. Many of the recipes were contributed by the readers of his successful weekly, *The Englishwoman's Domestic Magazine*, and others, as Mrs Beeton herself admitted, were simply taken from previous cookery writers (usually without acknowledging her sources) – in particular from Eliza Acton. Certain of the specialist chapters were written anonymously by experts – 'those on medical subjects by an experienced surgeon, and the legal matter by a solicitor'. No doubt Mrs Beeton also received help from the staff and resources of her husband's publishing firm. But even though she was not herself a creative cook, as a work of editing it is an immense achievement for someone so young.

Isabella Mayson was born in London, and, with an immense number of step, half and full brothers and sisters, spent much of her childhood in the Grand Stand at Epsom racecourse, where her stepfather was Clerk of the Racecourse. She was well educated, and 'finished' in Heidelberg, where she learnt French and German. She married Sam Beeton, an extremely able and enterprising young publisher, in 1856, and the following year began contributing a column on

Mrs Beeton, the most famous of a long line of women cookery writers.

various household matters to his *Englishwoman's Domestic Magazine*. The first of the cheap women's magazines, it pioneered the problem page and medical columns; the Beetons also introduced paper patterns from France to British readers. The death of the first of her four sons gave her the time to start what was to be her life's work. She lost her second son in 1862, and died herself of puerperal fever at the age of 28, after the birth of her fourth.

Annie Besant
British (1847–1927)

Annie Besant was a vigorous speaker and energetic reformer in a variety of causes, most notably birth control at a time when it was scandalous even to mention the subject.

Annie Wood was born in London of Irish parentage and married the Reverend Frank Besant in 1863; she had a son and daughter. Initially deeply religious, she gradually lost her faith when her son fell seriously ill. 'All my heart rose up against this Person [Christ] in whom . . . I saw my baby's agony, my own misery, all the bitter suffering of the poor … I could no longer kneel.' She left home and began to speak in public on the subject of religious doubt. She lived by writing, translating and teaching science.

In 1872 Besant began to write for *The National Reformer*, Charles Bradlaugh's free-thinking newspaper, and published a free-thinking pamphlet of her own. In 1877 she and Bradlaugh were charged with obscenity for publishing a pamphlet on birth control, *The Fruits of Philosophy or the Law of Population*. Their trial was one of the most sensational of the nineteenth century. Besant's daughter was taken away from her; 'If you are legally your husband's wife, you can have no legal claim to your children,' she said bitterly. 'If legally you are your husband's mistress, your rights as a mother are secure.'

She was converted to Fabianism when she met George Bernard Shaw in 1885, and was soon a popular speaker for the Fabian Society (which promoted gradual social and political reform, cf. Beatrice Webb). In 1887 she founded a newspaper, *The Link*, with a regular column called 'The Lion's Mouth' which publicized bad working conditions. Her most famous revelation was the scandal of 'phossy jaw', a cancer of the jaw caused by phosphorus which was common among girls working at Bryant and May's London match factory. Besant instigated a successful strike at the works, a distinctive figure there in her workman's boots, red neckerchief and close-cropped hair.

In 1889 Besant returned to religion, but of a very different nature. Having read *The Secret Doctrine* by Madame Blavatsky (q.v.), founder of the Theosophical Society, she became a convert to its belief in universal brotherhood. Angrily Shaw tried to dissuade her; 'I met my match,' he said. 'She listened to me with complete kindness and genuine amusement and then said she had become a vegetarian (as I

was) and that perhaps it had enfeebled her mind.' Thereafter Besant dedicated herself to the theosophical movement, which also flourished in the U.S. and India, and became its leader in 1907.

Besant eventually settled in India, where she set up schools for Hindu girls. She was briefly interned for her Indian nationalist activities but in 1917 chaired the Indian National Congress – an incredible achievement for a foreign woman.

She was certain she had lived many times before, as she declared in her *Autobiography* (1893); that had not prevented her from fitting in enough experience for several lifetimes in the space of one.

Mary McLeod Bethune
American (1875–1955)

Born the fifteenth child of freed slaves in South Carolina, Mary McLeod Bethune became one of America's most famous educators and the only black woman adviser to President Roosevelt, when she became director of the Division of Negro Affairs at the National Youth Administration.

Bethune taught for several years in mission schools, and then (in 1904) founded and raised funds for the Daytona Literary and Industrial School for Training Negro Girls in Daytona Beach, Florida. When it was merged with a boy's school 20 years later, it was Mary Bethune who became president of the new Bethune-Cookman Institute. She established a world-wide reputation for her hard work on behalf of young people.

Amelia Bloomer
American (1818–1894)

The first woman to own and publish a newspaper, Amelia Bloomer is probably best known for the pantaloons which took her name. She was born in Homer, New York, and founded the *Lily*, a Ladies' Temperance Society newspaper. In 1849 when Elizabeth Smith Miller was pilloried for wearing Turkish pantaloons in Seneca Falls, New York, the *Lily* leapt to her defence in what became a nationwide debate. The 'bloomers', as the pantaloons were

dubbed, were attributed to Bloomer herself, and although she was not the first to wear them (cf. Frances Wright), she adopted them for several years. 'There is nothing in the book of Genesis,' she said, 'to suggest that Adam's apron of fig leaves was bifurcated.' A highly convenient form of dress, bloomers became widespread as bicycling grew in popularity towards the end of the century.

Barbara Bodichon
British (1827–1891)

Few women in Victorian England gave so generously of their time and money to women's causes, education in particular, as Barbara Bodichon. Her grandfather had been a prominent anti-slavery Member of Parliament, and her father, Leigh Smith, also an MP, was deeply critical of the kind of education then available. He founded a 'Ragged School' in their London neighbourhood, to which he sent Barbara and her sisters. It was an experience she treasured all her life. Leigh Smith believed that girls should enjoy the same financial independence as boys, and at the age of 21 Barbara was given an income of her own – a rare privilege for women then. In 1849 she enrolled at Bedford College, London, to attend lectures.

Thereafter her life was largely spent supporting good causes. In 1852 she opened a primary school along free-thinking lines. In 1856 she collected 24,000 signatures in support of the Married Woman's Property Bill. In 1858 she gave money to launch the new women's suffrage paper, *The Englishwoman's Journal*, which soon became very influential.

Bodichon was extremely active in the campaign to set up a women's college at Cambridge (cf. Emily Davies); Girton College opened in 1874 thanks largely to her generosity. She founded scholarships for students there and also helped to finance individuals privately.

She married in 1857 a French doctor, Eugène Bodichon, whom she met when she was on a trip to Algiers. Thereafter she spent the winters with him

Although 'bloomers' were attributed to Amelia Bloomer, she was not the first to wear them.

and the summers in London. A woman of great character and charm, she was the model for George Eliot's (q.v.) novel *Romola*.

Frances Mary Buss (*British, 1827–1894*) *and Dorothy Beale* (*British, 1831–1906*)

Frances Buss and Dorothy Beale were the first headmistresses of British schools to provide a full education for girls. Buss's father was an unsuccessful engraver; she and her mother ran a school at home in London when she was 14 and her only education came from attending free lectures at Queen's College, London. By the age of 23, she was running the North London Collegiate school, which she and her mother had started. 'The terrible sufferings of women of my own class for want of good elementary training, have more than ever intensified my desire to lighten the misery of women brought up to be married and taken care of, but left alone in the world destitute.' She continued as headmistress until her death; and saw some of her pupils at last admitted to universities.

Dorothy Beale was 27 when she was appointed Lady Principal of Cheltenham Ladies' College; before that she had been head of a church school in Cumberland. She, too, was largely self-educated, although she came from a more prosperous family than Buss and had spent a year at school in Paris. Calm and determined, Beale disapproved of 'an institution in which government is entirely by punishment', and campaigned for more liberal methods of education.

Both headmistresses insisted on giving evidence to the Parliamentary Schools Commission of 1865. Beale supported her case for the education of girls by presenting as evidence more than 100 successful examination papers completed by her pupils. Through their vigorous efforts girls' schools were then officially recognized. On a lighter level, their singlemindedness inspired the popular rhyme:

> Miss Buss and Miss Beale
> Cupid's darts do not feel.
> How different from us,
> Miss Beale and Miss Buss.

Josephine Butler, a painting by G. F. Watts.

Josephine Butler British (1828–1906)

It required immense courage to champion the plight of fallen women in the Victorian age; but Josephine Butler campaigned vigorously on behalf of prostitutes and against the discriminatory Contagious Diseases Act.

Josephine Grey was born into an influential landowning family (one of whom, Lord Grey of Falloden, was Foreign Secretary in the early twentieth century) and married Canon Butler in 1852. She was a passionate advocate of women's rights, and even when her husband became a headmaster she welcomed 'fallen women' into their Liverpool home. Mrs Butler's charitable efforts redoubled after her small daughter was accidentally killed. She defended the female camp followers who lived near the Army barracks in Colchester from humiliating treatment by the police, and in 1869 took a page of

The Times to publish a protest against the Contagious Diseases Act signed by hundreds of sympathizers, including Florence Nightingale (q.v.). The Act was eventually repealed in 1886. In 1885 she led a demonstration against the proposed Criminal Law Amendment Bill – publicly praying on her knees in the Strand Palace Hotel that it should not pass – for if passed, the Bill would have lowered the age of consent for girls and done nothing to stop the notorious 'white slave' traffic. She inspired the influential editor W.T. Stead to publicize the unsavoury facts in the *Pall Mall Gazette*. His report, *The Story of a Modern Babylon*, in which he described how he had been able to buy a 12-year-old girl for £5, caused an outcry and helped ensure the defeat of the Bill. She wrote her autobiography, *Personal Reminiscences of a Great Crusade*, in 1896.

Dr Mary Calderone
American (b. 1904)

Pioneer of sex education in U.S. schools, Mary Calderone helped found the Sex Information and Education Council of the United States, believing that bigotry and ignorance are the enemies of happy sex lives. She faced a lot of hostility in her campaign to bring the subject of sex into the open.

Calderone was born in New York City, the daughter of the celebrated photographer Edward Steichen, and niece of the novelist Carl Sandburg. She originally studied chemistry, then drama, before deciding to become a doctor in her thirties. She married Frank Calderone in 1941 and has three daughters. In 1950 she became medical director of Planned Parenthood World Population, and her experience of the extent of sexual problems led her and some of her colleagues to found the Sex Education Council. Dr Calderone has lectured and written extensively and has received many awards.

Mary Carpenter
British (1807–1877)

Mary Carpenter did more than anyone else in nineteenth-century England to establish schools and reformatories for young offenders; hitherto children had been sent to adult prisons. Her father was a Unitarian minister, Lant Carpenter, in Bristol. Carpenter worked as a governess initially, then became superintendent of a Sunday school in 1831. A cholera epidemic in 1833 made her aware of the appalling conditions in her native city; in 1835 she formed a Working and Visiting Society, which she called a 'Domestic Mission'. Britain had no compulsory free education before 1871, and Carpenter encouraged the foundation of 'Ragged Schools' which served to keep poor and homeless children off the streets. Her aim was 'to love, instruct and feed' these 'semi-criminals', as the police called them. 'I consider,' she said, 'the condition they are in as one of *extreme neglect*.' She gave lectures and badgered government officials on behalf of poor children, and in 1854 she opened the first residential reformatory school for girls at Red Lodge, Bristol.

Carpenter became famous after her visits to India, which began in 1866; she wanted to bring education to the 10 and eleven-year-old brides immured in purdah. Queen Victoria (q.v.) invited her to Buckingham Palace and supported her life's work of establishing schools and aid for young offenders. Carpenter's autobiography, *Woman's Work in the Reformation of Women Convicts*, was published in 1872. Well ahead of her time, she believed that repentance and improvement come through love, not punishment.

Carrie Chapman Catt
American (1859–1947)

American women owe the vote to Carrie Chapman Catt as much as to anyone. She worked long and steadily to win public acceptance of women's suffrage – always determined that the franchise should be established by constitutional means.

At the age of 22 Carrie Lane was already head of a school in her home town, Mason City, Iowa; in 1883 she became one of the first women superintendents. She was widowed in 1886 after a brief marriage to Leo Chapman, an editor; thereafter she worked for

Carrie Chapman Catt, president of the National American Suffrage Association from 1915.

the Iowa Women's Suffrage Association for 13 years. In 1890, she married George Catt, an engineer, having signed a marital contract allowing her four months annually to work for the cause. His death in 1905 left her financially independent, and over the next 15 years Catt organized the National American Woman Suffrage Association. When she took over the Presidency in 1915, its membership was only 100,000. Two years later, by her efforts, it had a membership of more than two million.

As the judiciary committee of the House of Representatives continued to reject Susan B. Anthony's (q.v.) federal amendment on franchise, Catt determined to convert individual states singly. 'That vote has been costly,' she wrote in 1920 when the battle was finally won. 'Prize it.' Her party now disbanded, and for the rest of her life Catt worked for

peace and disarmament; well into her eighties, she was campaigning for the appointment of women to United Nations commissions after the Second World War.

Caroline Chisholm
Australian (1808–1877)

Caroline Chisholm, the 'Emigrants' Friend', helped thousands of homeless emigrants on their arrival in Australia. Caroline Wootton was the daughter of a well-to-do farmer in Nottingham, England, and went to India when she married Archibald Chisholm, an officer in the East India Company. The Chisholms subsequently moved to Australia and settled near Sydney with their three sons.

In Sydney Chisholm was appalled by the numbers of homeless girls in the streets, dumped by bounty-hunting ships' captains who received a bonus for every woman they brought out to Australia. Most of the girls came from the workhouses and orphanages and were penniless; a life in the 'bush' or a brothel was their only future. At first she took her protégées home with her, but soon there were too many; when she petitioned the Governor to arrange alternative housing she had little success. Chisholm then took the girls upcountry in bullock carts and settled them as servants in homesteads or inns. Ceaselessly vigilant on their behalf, she rode everywhere to visit them on her famous white horse, safe from attack even during the 'Roaring Forties'.

In 1846 Chisholm visited England where she founded the Family Colonization Loan Society and wrote the *ABC of Colonization* and *Meat Three Times A Day*, which encouraged thousands of emigrants to settle in Australia (she warned them to pack their belongings in barrels they could roll off the quay, as there were no porters 'down under'). In 1854, following the Gold Rush, there was a tremendous shortage of places to live, and the government of Victoria gave Chisholm £7,000 to build the shelters which became known as 'Chisholm Shakedowns'.

By 1862 the Chisholms' largely self-financed efforts – they had brought 11,000 emigrants over – had brought the couple close to financial ruin. Mrs

A 1968 Australian postage stamp honouring Caroline Chisholm's achievements.

Chisholm earned a living teaching Chinese immigrants English in Sydney until a public subscription was raised for her to open a girls' school. She spent the last 10 years of her life on a government pension in England. In recognition of her public service, the 1967 Australian five dollar bill bears her head.

Emma Cons
British (1837–1912)

Emma Cons devoted her life to housing reform and was also responsible for the foundation of one of Britain's most famous theatres. She was the second daughter of a poor piano maker and at 14 she studied at Mrs Hill's Ladies' Guild of Art, a charitable institution which had been founded to help poor girls. Like her friend Octavia Hill (q.v.), Cons determined to bring beauty to the London slums. In 1857 she apprenticed herself to a watchmaker, but the prejudice of the other craftsmen made her work impossible. She moved to a stained glass workshop and this time won recognition from the men by 'quiet persistence'. (Some of the windows in Merton College, Oxford, are her work.)

In 1874 Cons began her lifework of improving slum dwellings. She took over some disease-ridden, overcrowded 'courts' in Drury Lane, raising the necessary money from wealthy friends. 'I can only give my life,' she said, 'having no money.' Part of her scheme was to provide an alternative to the pub and she started 'coffee palaces' with entertainments such as brass band concerts on Saturdays and outings to the country on Sundays. Cons' next project was to raise money for 'model' housing in South London; she also took over the lease of the nearby Victoria Theatre for the entertainment of her tenants. She enforced strict temperance and gradually the gin drinkers disappeared from the audiences, and the shows became respectable. Eventually, under the management of her niece Lilian Baylis (q.v.), the theatre was to become the famous Old Vic.

An ardent feminist, Cons was on the executive of the Women's Liberal Federation, and in 1889 she was the first woman to be made an Alderman on the London County Council (now the Greater London Council). But her activities ranged even wider: at the age of 55 she enrolled at Swanley Horticultural College to encourage women to work as gardeners; and in 1895 the *Daily Mail* sent her to investigate the Armenian massacres.

Mairead Corrigan
(see Betty Williams)

Emily Davies
British (1830–1921)

Emily Davies pioneered higher education for women in Britain and was the first head of a British women's college. She was the fourth child of a clergyman and was educated at home, near Newcastle. When her brothers left for Cambridge University, Emily Davies resolved to open a college for women there, too; however, as an unmarried daughter she was expected to live at home. In her twenties she made friends with the feminists Millicent Fawcett and Barbara Bodichon (qq.v.); and together they began to make plans for such a college.

When Davies's father died in 1861 she was at last free to move to London; there she became editor of the new feminist paper, *The Englishwoman's Journal*, in 1862. By 1865 she and other feminists had

Emily Davies, pioneer of higher education for women in Britain.

convened an education committee, which lobbied for the right for girls to sit the preliminary college entrance examinations, previously open only to boys. In 1866 the committee bought a house for the proposed college in Hitchin. It was 30 miles from Cambridge itself, for Davies wanted to keep her handful of carefully selected young ladies well away from male undergraduates in conditions of the utmost propriety. As it was, a clergyman called them 'infidel ladies' when he saw them in a train.

To Davies 'education was a means to an end: that end was the admission of women to full equality'. Her students did well; they moved to a house three miles from Cambridge, and Girton College was opened in 1873 – the first of its kind in Britain. Davies herself was first Mistress (as the Principal of Girton is still known) until 1875 and then devoted herself to college finances and women's suffrage. She success-fully campaigned for women to be given degrees at London University in 1874, although Cambridge did not admit women for full degree courses until 1948.

Dorothea Dix
American (1802–1887)

Dorothea Dix campaigned for proper treatment of the insane at a time when they were still locked away in ordinary prisons. At the age of 12 she left her parents to live with her doctor grandfather in Boston, and at 14 opened a school which she ran along the disciplined lines advocated by the Englishwoman Hannah More (q.v.); she was later forced to close it owing to ill health.

In 1841, in East Cambridge, Massachusetts, Dix discovered a lunatic locked away in a shed, chained by a collar round his neck; the discovery led to her lifelong campaign for more humane treatment for the insane. She travelled all over North America, from Nova Scotia to the Gulf of Mexico, visiting State penitentiaries, houses of correction and alms-houses – the usual places in which the mad were to be found – gathering sufficient facts to persuade the authorities to build asylums. She even persuaded a Japanese diplomat in Washington to have two asylums opened in Japan.

Dix was in charge of the nurses during the Civil War and ruled the hospitals with a rod of iron – her nurses had to be 'plain looking' and of unimpeachable morals. Louisa May Alcott (q.v.) was one of her recruits. Dix was not popular, but her persistence and courage brought about much-needed changes in the treatment of the mentally ill in the U.S.

Maria Edgeworth
Irish (1767–1849)

Maria Edgeworth was the author of *Practical Education*, one of the best known schoolbooks of the Victorian age. She was the third of 22 children and had therefore had plenty of first-hand experience of the subject. When the Edgeworth family settled in 1782 at Castle Edgeworth, a large estate in Ireland, Maria helped her father to run it.

Maria Edgeworth, the author of Practical Education, *one of the best known Victorian school books.*

Her first book, *Letters to Literary Ladies* (1795), was a plea for education for women. *Practical Education* (1798), her best known book, was in part a translation of *Le Théâtre d'Education* by Madame de Genlis (q.v.). In 1802 father and daughter wrote their popular book, *An Essay on Irish Bulls*. Her two comic novels, *Castle Rackrent* and *The Absentee*, are based on her life in Ireland. Thackeray modelled his rogue-hero Barry Lyndon on her blarney-tongued steward. A prolific writer, Edgeworth said that once she had tasted ink there was no stopping her.

Fannie Farmer
American (1857–1917)

Fannie Farmer brought method to housewifery. Her father was a printer and the family was poor; Fannie went to work as a mother's help soon after leaving school in Medford, Massachusetts in 1873. In 1887 she

enrolled at the Boston Cooking School and subsequently became Assistant Principal and then Head in 1894.

So little did her publishers believe in the likelihood of success that she herself had to pay for the first edition of the *Boston Cooking School Cook Book*. This pioneering work, published in 1896, consisted of nothing but carefully tested, clearly explained recipes and has since sold more than four million copies.

For the last 15 years of her life – in spite of strokes and other illness – Farmer presided over the Miss Farmer School of Cookery and gave demonstrations and lectures. Work on diets for the Harvard Medical School strengthened her belief that sensible eating is the key to good health.

Millicent Garrett Fawcett
British (1847–1929)

For 50 years Millicent Fawcett led that section of the British women's movement which campaigned for the vote by strictly non-violent means. She was one of nine children of a prosperous grain-merchant of Aldeburgh, Suffolk. Her younger sister, Elizabeth Garrett Anderson (q.v.), was the first woman in Britain to qualify as a doctor; 'You, Millie,' said her friend Emily Davies (q.v.), 'must see about getting the vote.' At 20 she married the blind Member of Parliament, Henry Fawcett, and had a daughter Philippa (who later as a student mathematician outshone the Senior Wrangler – the top undergraduate mathematician – in the 1890 Cambridge Tripos Examinations). She spent the rest of her life campaigning, always within the law, to secure the vote for women.

In 1877 Fawcett was horrified to discover, having been robbed at Waterloo station, that the police listed her purse as 'property of Henry Fawcett'; thereafter she became an impassioned advocate of the necessity of changes to the Married Woman's Property Act. She also joined Josephine Butler (q.v.) in her campaign against the Contagious Diseases Act.

When Emmeline Pankhurst (q.v.), leader of the rival Women's Union for Parliamentary Suffrage, resorted to violence, Fawcett continued to lead her

Millicent Garrett Fawcett, leader of the non-militant section of the British women's suffrage movement.

Betty Friedan, feminist author and founder of the National Organization for Women.

National Union of Women's Suffrage Societies peacefully, with 'quiet persuasion and argument'. The vote was not won until 1918 but when Nancy Astor (q.v.) was elected the first woman MP she publicly declared that she felt 'almost ashamed she was not Millicent Fawcett.' Fawcett wrote eight books, including *Political Economy for Beginners* and *What I Remember* (1924).

Betty Friedan
American (b. 1921)

Betty Friedan is the author of the bible of modern American feminism, *The Feminine Mystique*. In it she pinpointed 'the problem that has no name' – the frustration and boredom of under-employed suburban housewives – an action which was to 'raise the consciousness' of women everywhere. Since the year of its publication, 1963, Friedan has worked tirelessly

for the improvement of opportunities for women. In 1966 she founded and became first president (until 1970) of the National Organization for Women, which remains, in spite of more militant competitors, and radical opponents within the organization, the most substantial and influential of all U.S. women's movements.

Friedan was born in Peoria, Illinois, daughter of an immigrant Jewish father and a mother who was formerly editor of the woman's page of the Peoria newspaper. She studied psychology and social science at Smith College and Berkeley, California, and became a labor journalist in New York in 1942. She lost her job when she became pregnant a second time after her marriage in 1947 to Carl Friedan, then a theatre producer, but confesses that at the time – 1949 – she too 'embraced and lived that feminine mystique'. Friedan had three children and lived in a New York suburb where she 'chauffeured, and did the PTA and buffet dinners' like her neighbours.

Elizabeth Fry, nineteenth-century Quaker pioneer of prison reform.

The *Feminine Mystique* catapulted her into the limelight. *It Changed My Life* is the title of her second book, a collection of articles on the women's movement published in 1977. Divorced from her husband in 1969, Friedan lives in New York City, and has been an active participant in all the feminist struggles of the 1970s, from the Women's Strike for Equality in 1970 to the fight for the Equal Rights Amendment.

Elizabeth Fry
British (1780–1845)

Elizabeth Fry was a pioneer of prison reform in Britain. She was born into one of England's great Quaker families, the Gurneys. She was the third daughter of a Norfolk merchant, and although converted to evangelical Anglicanism at the age of

18, married Joseph Fry, member of another great Quaker family. They had 10 children over the next 16 years.

Elizabeth Fry became a preacher and first visited Newgate Prison, London, in 1813. She was appalled by the conditions: 'The filth, the closeness of the rooms, the ferocious manners and expressions towards each other are quite indescribable.' Four years later, following the death of a beloved daughter, prison visits became the centre of her life. She would sit with the women and read the Bible, although the evidence she gave to a parliamentary committee in 1818 shows that she recognized that proper beds, good food and clothes were as vital as the prisoners' spiritual welfare. As the wife of an influential merchant Fry commanded attention – and she raised her voice constantly against overcrowding, flogging, hanging. Whereas women on their way to deportation were formerly chained together in open carts, Fry helped to ensure that they travelled with her in closed carriages and were accompanied by matrons on the long sea journey to Australia. She formed an Association for the Improvement of Female Prisoners and started schools for their children; she insisted that the prisoners should be consulted about their welfare. Fry and her brother toured prisons all over Britain and Europe. The information they collected led eventually to major reforms, not only of prisons but also of hospitals and asylums.

Margaret Fuller
American (1810–1850)

Margaret Fuller was the author of the influential *Woman in the Nineteenth Century* (1845), and the first woman foreign correspondent for the U.S.

She was the eldest of nine children of Timothy Fuller, a New England lawyer. After two years at boarding school she taught at the school run by Louisa May Alcott's (q.v.) father. When the school closed she taught German in Providence, Rhode Island. In 1840, at the age of 30, she became editor of *The Dial*, the paper founded by Ralph Waldo Emerson and other transcendentalist philosophers.

She wrote articles on economics and literary criticism for the *New York Tribune* in 1844, and made a study of prostitutes in prison. Her brilliant educational lectures on art and society, for women only, were published as *Woman in the Nineteenth Century* (1845). The liberating message of this pioneer feminist work was the inspiration behind the first Women's Rights Convention held at Seneca Falls in 1848 (cf. Elizabeth Cady Stanton).

In 1846 Fuller went to Europe as a foreign correspondent for the *New York Tribune*, whose editor greatly admired her. She met Wordsworth and Mazzini in London, and George Sand (q.v.) and Chopin in Paris, before reaching Rome in time for the Revolution of 1848. She was fascinated by the Italian struggle. She fell in love with the young Marchese d'Ossoli, and during the fighting she ran a hospital and nursed the wounded. But when the old régime defeated the new Roman republic, the couple married and set sail for America with their baby Angelo in 1850. Within 50 yards of New York harbour the little family, together with Fuller's manuscript of the *History of the Roman Revolution*, were lost in a shipwreck.

Stéphanie de Genlis
French (1746–1830)

Madame de Genlis was both an exceptional governess, far ahead of her time in teaching methods, and author of many popular novels. Stéphanie-Félicité du Crest de Saint Aubin came of a noble family with very little money. At six she went into a convent near Lyons. When she came to Paris in 1758 she soon became famous for her wit. She married Colonel le Comte de Genlis, had two children, and in 1770 was appointed lady-in-waiting to the Duchess of Chartres. Soon afterwards she became simultaneously the mistress of the Duke, who was the King's cousin, and governess to his children.

De Genlis used lantern slides to teach history and took her pupils on country walks to learn botany. Her zest for instruction was tremendous. She and the children were installed in an isolated building where she could supervize their every move, and it was there that she wrote her famous *Théâtre d'Education*, which

was subsequently translated into many languages. (Maria Edgeworth (q.v.) drew on it for her *Practical Education*.) In 1785 the royal princes' tutors were dismissed and de Genlis was put in charge of all the royal children – the first woman ever to be given such an honour.

In 1789, the year of the French Revolution, when her royal charges' father (later Louis XVI) secured his safety by calling himself Philippe Egalité, Madame de Genlis, although in sympathy with the new régime, escaped with Mademoiselle d'Orléans, the eldest daughter. Both her husband and her lover were guillotined. She herself earned her living in Germany by painting and writing, until Napoleon gave her a pension and she returned to Paris.

The best known of de Genlis's hundred or so novels is the romantic *Mademoiselle de Clermont* (1802). Her satirical book *Dîners du Baron à'Holbach* (1804) was so malicious that it cost her her government pension. However, all her books sold well and she prospered even in old age.

Agelina Grimké (American, 1805–1879)
and Sarah Grimké (American, 1793–1873)

The Grimké sisters were two wealthy Southerners who led the fight for the abolition of slavery. They were the daughters of a reactionary slave-owning judge in Charleston, Carolina. When she was four Sarah saw a female slave savagely beaten and never forgot it. She was still a little girl when she actively protested against the law which forbade anyone to teach slaves to read and write, and taught her personal slave to read, for which she in turn was beaten.

The two sisters renounced their cosseted lifestyle when Sarah persuaded Angelina to join her in Philadelphia and become a Quaker. In 1832 anti-slavery agitation had begun in earnest, and both sisters spoke in the abolitionist cause, in spite of police threats and general harassment. They settled in New York in 1836; there the open hostility towards the idea of women speakers turned Sarah into an active campaigner for women's rights: 'I ask no favours for my sex . . . all I ask is that they take their feet from off our necks.'

Stéphanie de Genlis, author of the influential Theatre d'Education.

In 1838 Angelina married a fellow abolitionist, Theodore T. Weld, at a non-religious ceremony witnessed by other abolitionists and two liberated Grimké slaves. The Welds and Sarah settled on the Hudson River and lived on a 'Graham' diet (vegetables and very little cooking) to leave more time for writing and campaigning. With the birth of their children, the Welds opened the progressive Belleville School in 1852. Liberated in dress, the sisters wore the controversial Bloomers (q.v.) for a time in 1861.

The chance discovery of three black Grimké nephews in 1868, all immediately acknowledged as relations by the sisters (one went on to become a minister in Washington, another a lawyer in Boston), was a painful reminder of the double standards they had spent their lives opposing.

74

Kageyama Hideko
Japanese (1865–1927)

Kageyama Hideko devoted her life to the plight of women in near-feudal Japan. She was the daughter of a lower ranking samurai, and at the age of 17, after hearing a speech made by another feminist, Kishida Toshiko, she determined to work for the women's movement.

In 1883 Kageyama Hideko and her mother opened a school for women, only to have it shut down a year later because of its liberal policies. Thereafter she became involved in left-wing politics in Tokyo, for which she served a prison sentence. On her release she became the common-law wife of Oi Kentara, a fellow activist, and founded a technical school for women. She left Oi Kentara when he fell in love with her young maid whom she herself had freed, and in 1892 she married Fukuda Tomosaku. Her three children all died young, and her husband died in 1900.

Kageyama Hideko founded *Sekai Fujin*, a socialist women's magazine in which she campaigned against the exploitation of workers and poor farmers. Her autobiography, *Half a Life as a Common-Law Wife*, was published in 1904, and her life story was later made into a film, *My Love Has Been Burning* (1949).

Octavia Hill
British (1838–1912)

Octavia Hill and her sister Miranda (1836–1910) pioneered housing reform and the preservation of open spaces in London. Their grandfather, Southwood Smith, was a pioneer in social health; he exposed the inadequacies of the London water system which was largely responsible for the cholera epidemics earlier in the century.

In 1864 John Ruskin, the art historian and socialist, entrusted Octavia Hill with five slum dwellings he owned and a £3,500 loan. She took a room for herself in the buildings. Most of the windows were broken, the stairs had collapsed and the roof leaked. The necessary repairs were financed from the rent (never allowed to be overdue) and gradually she restored order. 'My only notion of

Octavia Hill, founder of the Kyrle Society, which later became the National Trust.

reform is that of living side by side with people, till all that one believes becomes livingly clear to them,' she said of her methods. They were so successful that they were adopted by other 'lady visitors'.

Hill's articles on social reform appeared in the *Fortnightly Review* and *Macmillans*. She felt the planting of trees and preservation of open spaces was essential to the improvement of life for city dwellers, and in 1877 she and her sister Miranda founded the Kyrle Society: it eventually became Britain's admirable National Trust for the Preservation of Places of Historical Interest and National Beauty. Her ideas for housing schemes were embodied in an Act of Parliament in 1909.

Elly Jansen
Dutch (b. 1929)

Founder of the Richmond Fellowship, Elly Jansen is a pioneer in the creation and development of

75

Elly Jansen, who founded her first 'halfway house' in 1959.

therapeutic communities for people who have had a mental breakdown or are suffering from strain – not only in Britain, where she founded the first 'halfway house' in 1959, but all over the world. The Richmond Fellowship now has 30 houses in Britain, and others in America, Australia, New Zealand and Austria.

One of nine children of a company director in Holland, Jansen studied psychology, then trained as a nurse, and finally moved to England in 1955 to learn the language and to study theology, as she planned to become a missionary. She also worked part-time in mental nursing and social work, and saw the need for a new kind of therapeutic community independent of the official mental hospital umbrella: she believes strongly that people suffering from mental disorder can and must be helped to lead independent lives. With £100 of her own savings, she rented a house in Richmond, near London, advertised for residents, and found herself not with an experimental project, as she expected, but with a life's work.

Jansen married a fellow worker, George White-house, in 1969, and has three daughters.

Helen Keller
American (1880–1968)
Anne Sullivan Macy
American (1866–1936)

Helen Keller's life story is an astonishing example of triumph over adversity. Although a mysterious illness (possibly scarlet fever) at the age of 19 months completely destroyed both her sight and her hearing, she learnt to read, write and speak, and went on to study Greek, Latin, German, French and English at Radcliffe. She graduated *cum laude*, and devoted the rest of her long life to writing and travelling to raise money for the blind and other good causes.

Helen was born into a family of Southern landowners, the elder of two sisters. Her father had been a captain in the Confederate Army and was related to General Robert E. Lee. Her achievement would have been impossible without the remarkable teacher her parents found for her, Anne Sullivan. Miss Sullivan had been blind as a child, and had trained at the Perkins Institution for the Blind in Boston, where another blind deaf-mute, Laura Bridgeman, had been helped to communicate through the finger alphabet 50 years earlier.

Within a month of Sullivan's arrival, when Keller was not yet seven, she had already grasped that the signs Sullivan was spelling into her hand had meanings. Both she and her teacher have written of the joy and excitement of her understanding of 'w-a-t-e-r'. The wild, tormented little girl was being released from her prison. She was also taught manners and self-control.

Keller insisted on being taught to speak, a feat hitherto believed impossible for those both blind and deaf. The first of her many books was *The Story of My Life*, published when she was 23.

Sullivan's achievement was almost as remarkable as Keller's. She was a woman of spirit and character, and had to face considerable criticism from the educational world for making Keller apparently too dependent on her. Indeed Sullivan lived with her pupil for 50 years, including the years of her marriage to John Macy. After her death, however, Keller enjoyed an equally full life for a further 32 years with her new teacher, Polly Thomson, whom Sullivan had herself trained to take her place.

Anne Sullivan Macy
(see Helen Keller)

Françoise de Maintenon
French (1635–1719)

Françoise d'Aubigné, Marquise de Maintenon, who became Louis XIV's second wife in 1683, occupies a particular place in the history of women's education. With a friend, Madame de Brinon, she founded a school for poor girls of good family at Reuil, which moved to a specially built house at St Cyr in 1686. The school went beyond the training normally thought suitable for girls at that time, being emphatically a school and not a convent. The girls – some 250 of them, between the ages of six and 19 – were taught to converse and to write in excellent French, besides receiving instruction in history, literature, economics, geography and music. The informal, sympathetic régime became famous all over Europe, and was to inspire the educational schemes of Catherine the Great (q.v.) in Russia. It was for a performance by the girls of St Cyr that, at the request of Mme de Maintenon, the great playwright Racine broke a silence of 12 years to write *Esther* (1689) and *Athalie* (1691). Both Mme de Maintenon – who supervised every detail – and the King himself took a great interest in the school.

However, the girls and the *dames* who taught them became so conceited with all the attention they received that Mme de Maintenon decided to turn the school into a convent. The staff were obliged to become nuns, and conversation, literature, poetry and education itself were given up in favour of silence and household duties.

Mme de Maintenon was the daughter of a Huguenot of good family who was briefly imprisoned, and who on his release took his family to Martinique. After her father's death in 1645 the young Françoise returned to France and at the age of 16 became a Roman Catholic. She was too poor to make a good match; in 1652 she married the elderly poet Scarron, and through him got to know many powerful people. Scarron died eight years later, leaving her very poor; she survived on a tiny pension from the Queen Mother.

In 1669 Madame de Montespan, reigning mistress of Louis XIV, employed Madame Scarron as governess to her children by the King; he ennobled her as Marquise de Maintenon in 1675. When Madame de Montespan fell out of favour, it was to this beautiful, clever woman that Louis turned. Their marriage was secret, but so far as is known he remained faithful to her until he died in 1715. She retired to St Cyr for her last years.

Harriet Martineau
British (1802–1876)

Harriet Martineau became, most unusually for her time, an expert on politics and economics. Her parents were Dissenters and lived in Norwich, East Anglia. As a child she was given the same school education as her brother James, who became a well-known theologian, but was still made to sew for hours on end. Her articles on divinity and a plea for female education were published in a local paper when she was only a girl.

Martineau learnt about Malthus' theories of population control from *Conversations on Political Economy* by Jane Marcet (q.v.), a book which taught her the virtues of putting serious ideas in a readable form. Her own *Illustrations of Political Economy* (1832) took the form of a series of tales exposing errors in running the economy; they were so popular that the postmaster at Norwich asked her to fetch her fan mail in a special barrow.

The year 1829 had brought financial ruin to the family but Martineau's new success meant that their worries were over. She moved to London where she soon became well enough known to be invited to visit the U.S.A.; once there, she was socially lionized. In 1837 she published *Society in America* and

Harriet Martineau, author of Illustrations of Political Economy, *which ran into 25 volumes.*

two years later her first novel, *Deerbook*. When her health broke down, she claimed to be cured by Mesmerism. *Laws of Man's Social Nature* was published in 1851 and she also wrote her *Autobiography*. Strong-minded and well-informed, she continued to give her opinion on all important public matters; her newspaper articles were always eagerly read. In 1853 she retired to the Lake District and wrote a guide book about it. Active to the last, she supported the campaign to repeal the Contagious Diseases Act led by Josephine Butler (q.v.).

Jessica Mitford
British (b. 1917)

Jessica Mitford is an investigative journalist whose exposés regularly hit the headlines. Yet she did not become a journalist until she was 40. One of six children of the 2nd Lord Redesdale, her eccentric

upbringing, which omitted formal education, has been described by her sister Nancy Mitford in her novels.

At 20 Jessica Mitford eloped with another upper-class rebel, Giles Romilly; they joined the Communist Party and went to Spain – which Mitford describes in *Hons and Rebels* (1960). In 1939 the Romillys went to the U.S. where their daughter was born. Giles Romilly was killed in the Second World War, and Jessica Mitford then married an American lawyer, Robert Treuhaft. They have one son.

Mitford's most celebrated exposé is her first, *The American Way of Death* (1963), a blistering attack on the funeral business. When it was published, funeral parlour profits slumped and two large firms of undertakers introduced a code of practice. The cheapest hardboard coffins were nicknamed 'Mitford-style'.

Her account of *The Trial of Dr Spock* (following his protest against the draft) was published in 1969, and in *The American Prison Business* (1974, also entitled *Kind and Usual Punishment*) Mitford raised awkward questions about the use of prisoners as medical guinea pigs. A second volume of autobiography, *A Fine Old Conflict*, was published in 1977, and her collected articles, *The Making of a Muckraker*, were published in 1979.

Maria Montessori
Italian (1870–1952)

Maria Montessori was one of the most gifted of modern educationalists, for she revolutionized the teaching of young children.

The daughter of a soldier, she grew up determined to be not a teacher, but a doctor, and was the first woman to qualify as an MD in Italy. Her first job, as assistant doctor at a psychiatric clinic in Rome, brought her in contact with mentally defective children. She developed a method of teaching such children with teaching aids she herself invented, such as her famous sandpaper alphabet, which enabled many of them to do as well in public examinations as normal children. Montessori's success was widely praised, but it caused her to search 'for the reasons

Maria Montessori with a pupil from the Gatehouse School, London, which is run on Montessori lines.

79

which could keep back the healthy and happy children of the ordinary schools on so low a plane that they could be equalled in tests of intelligence by my unfortunate pupils.'

In 1906 she was appointed to run a *Casa dei Bambini* in a poor quarter of Rome. She believed that young children did not need to be dragooned to learn or to be taught by rote, and that they instinctively, given the right help and encouragement, preferred work to play. Soon her pupils were able to read, write and count by the time they were six or even younger.

Montessori's work was welcomed in Britain, Holland and elsewhere in Europe, and she became an inspector of schools in Italy in 1922. She was an excellent public speaker, and travelled as far afield as the U.S. and the Indian sub-continent (where she spent the Second World War with her son Mario, who worked closely with her), as well as writing books about her method. She herself preferred not to call her discoveries a method of education. She would say only, 'I simply gave some little children a chance to live.'

Hannah More
British (1745–1833)

Hannah More was a teacher and writer whose educational books were used by generations of English-speaking children. She was the fourth daughter of a schoolmaster from Stapleton, near Bristol, and went at the age of 12 to a boarding school run by her sisters. More's literary output began with a series of inoffensive pastoral plays for her fellow-pupils to act in. She moved to London in 1772 and had a great success with her play *Percy* in 1777. Her growing friendship with anti-slavery evangelicals turned her into a serious religious writer; among other works, she published *Sacred Dramas* in 1782 and a poem, *Slavery*, in 1788. In general More's writings were sympathetic to the British constitution, critical of the French and Tom Paine, and involved with the happiness of 'knowing one's place' in society. Her best known book, *Caelebs in Search of a Wife* (1808), was more of a religious tract than a novel. Her

Hannah More, a silhouette by A. Edouart, 1827.

Strictures on Female Education (1799) was greatly admired and used as a teaching guide by nineteenth-century governesses both in Britain and America.

Lucretia Mott
American (1793–1880)

Lucretia Mott was a pioneer in the anti-slavery campaign and an active supporter of women's rights. The second daughter of a Boston preacher, Lucretia Coffin was sent to boarding school when she was 13; she later taught there and her discovery that she was paid only half as much as male teachers turned her into a feminist. She settled in Philadelphia in 1811 with her husband, James Mott, a Quaker merchant, and had three children. She was made an official Quaker minister in 1821; in 1833 she formed a Female Anti-Slavery Society and another for the Relief and Employment of the Poor. As the abolition debate attracted increasing hostility, the public halls where Mott was engaged to speak were burnt down, and even her own house was threatened.

In 1840 Mott was one of the eight women delegates sent to the British and Foreign Anti-Slavery Society World Conference in London, but because they were women the Conference – otherwise all male – refused to let them take their seats; she and Elizabeth Cady Stanton (q.v.) were so incensed that they organized a protest meeting back home. That was the start of the first ever Women's Rights Convention at Seneca Falls, New York, in 1848, and the inspiration of the Declaration of 20th July, which launched the struggle for women's rights in the U.S. 'We hold these truths to be self-evident: that all men and women are created equal ...'

As a Quaker, Mott was not a militant, although she bravely travelled to the South on behalf of the abolitionist cause; she publicly declared that all war was wrong, even a war to end slavery. Her husband died after 57 years of marriage; she lived on, lecturing and writing into her mid-eighties.

Alva Myrdal
Swedish (b. 1902)

Alva Myrdal has had an immensely valuable public career, not only in her native country but internationally, in the fields of education, child care, diplomacy and nuclear disarmament.

Alva Reimer trained as a social psychologist, and went to university in Stockholm, Uppsala, the U.S. and Geneva. In 1936 she founded, and for the next 12 years directed, a training college for pre-school teachers in Stockholm, while campaigning for, among other things, educational reform, family allowances and free school meals. Notably, Myrdal was one of the moving spirits behind the post-war development of adventure playgrounds.

When her husband, the economist Gunnar Myrdal, was appointed executive secretary of the UN Economic Commission for Europe, she joined him briefly in Geneva, but soon became Principal Director of the United Nations Department of Social Affairs in New York and then – nearer home – Director of the Department of Social Sciences at Unesco in Paris. From 1955 she spent six years in India, first as Sweden's minister, and then as Ambassador. In 1961 she was back in Sweden as a member of the Senate and Ambassador at large, and for nine years she was chief Swedish delegate to the United Nations Disarmament Committee in Geneva. Active well into her seventies, Alva Myrdal's publications, visiting fellowships, chairmanships and contributions to both

public and academic spheres are too numerous to mention.

She and Gunnar Myrdal have three children. One of their two daughters is Sissela Bok, the Harvard author and philosopher.

Carry Nation
American (1846–1911)

The most active temperance worker of them all, the formidable Carry Nation waged war against alcohol. The brief experience of being married to Dr Charles Gloyd, who was an alcoholic, inspired her lifelong opposition to drink. Dressed in black and white, she would lead a band of ladies in what she called the 'hatchetation of joints' (bars), insulting the 'rummies' (drunks) they found there. 'A woman is stripped of everything by them,' she said of saloons, 'her husband is torn from her; she is robbed of her sons, her home, her food and her virtue.' She also campaigned against tobacco, foreign foods, corsets and short skirts. In 1877 she married David Nation, a lawyer, journalist and minister, but he sued her for desertion and divorced her in 1901.

The Prohibition Nation had worked for finally came about in 1919, but was not successful in stamping out drinking, and the Act was repealed in 1933.

Caroline Norton
British (1808–1877)

Caroline Norton was responsible, single-handed, for two important changes in English law concerning the custody of children and the rights of married women.

Caroline Sheridan was one of the three beautiful daughters of Thomas Sheridan, a Member of Parliament, and no doubt inherited her wit and literary talent from her grandfather, the playwright Richard Brinsley Sheridan. In 1827 she married a lawyer, Richard Norton, and they had three children who, under the prevailing laws, were the 'property' of their father. Norton left her husband in 1836, and earned her living by writing, but she was thereafter engaged in a continual struggle to gain legal access to her sons (one of whom died in 1842, aged eight,

War between Rum and Religion, a cartoon of temperance worker, Carrie Nation published in March 1901.

Caroline Norton, who fought for the legal rights of married women.

without her having seen him again). Vigorous lobbying of MPs – she was a friend of the Prime Minister, Lord Melbourne – and the publication of her pamphlet, *A Plain Letter to the Lord Chancellor* (1838), resulted in the passing of the Infant Custody Act in 1839.

Norton finally reached a financial settlement with her husband in 1848, but that did not prevent him from claiming for himself her earnings as a writer, on the grounds that any income of hers belonged to him; he even acquired a legacy she had inherited from her mother. Divorce proceedings were instituted in 1853: 'I do not ask for my rights. I have no rights. I have only wrongs,' she said bitterly. She wrote *English Laws for Women in the Nineteenth Century*, published in 1854, besides a strongly worded and widely circulated letter on the subject addressed to Queen Victoria. In 1857 the Marriage and Divorce Act was passed by Parliament, largely due to Norton's ceaseless efforts, although this legislation was only a beginning in improving the inferior legal position of married women.

Alive to all social problems, Norton also exposed the evils of child labour in *Voices from the Factories* (1836), besides writing many poems and novels. In the last year of her life she married Sir William Stirling Maxwell.

Luise Otto-Peters
German (1819–1895)

Luise Otto-Peters was the founder of the women's movement in Germany. Both her parents died when she was 16 and Luise Otto began to write novels about social problems. *Ludwig der Kellner* (1843) concerned class prejudice, and her most famous novel, *Kathinka* (1844), urged the need for the emancipation of women. The struggle for women's rights in Germany was launched in 1848 with her *Address to a Young Girl*; she campaigned for the rights of women workers to be recognized under state law, and in 1849 founded a newspaper for women. In 1851 she met the poet and freedom fighter, August Peters, then in jail, and married him in 1858, linking his name to hers. Well in advance of her time, Otto-Peters argued for equal pay, equal opportunity, equal rights, and the freedom for a woman to spend her own money according to her own wishes. In 1865 she formed an association for the education of women which became a nationwide women's movement, the General German Women's Association. The association campaigned for the employment of more women in teaching and the civil service, and for married women's property rights. A vigorous campaigner, Otto-Peters led the fight for more than 20 years.

Emily Post
American (1873–1960)

In a socially mobile age, those who are moving upwards usually feel the need to emulate the behaviour of those to whom they no longer wish to feel inferior. Mrs Post catered for that fundamental

Emily Post at a Liberty Loan Drive in 1918.

need in her famous *Etiquette: The Blue Book of Social Usage*. Born into a socially prominent Baltimore family – her father was an architect – she went to all the right schools, including finishing school in New York. In 1892 she married Edwin Main Post, a banker, and had two children but the marriage ended in divorce. Later she said it was vulgar to mention money; but initially she began to write because her husband lost his fortune and she needed it. By 1903 she was publishing articles on the bizarre behaviour of European aristrocrats and 'confession' stories.

The Blue Book of Social Usage came out in 1922 and rapidly sold 30,000 copies: it is still in print. Post concentrated on a simple formula, namely that 'no-one should do anything that can either annoy or offend the sensibilities of others'. Asked once how far a girl may run after a man, she answered, 'She may do a little stalking. But, run? Not a step!' Mostly she advised on social niceties, such as how to eat asparagus (with a fork) or a boiled egg (the American way) or corn on the cob ('Attack it with as little ferocity as possible'). From 1931 there was an Emily Post radio programme, and an Emily Post column was syndicated to 200 newspapers. Once America knew how to sit in a taxi, eat properly and organize a wedding, she turned to 'motor manners', architecture and interior decoration. From 1946 she taught 'gracious living' in the Emily Post Institute. In 1960 her immensely profitable business went to her son, Edwin, who continued the family motto: 'Etiquette embraces everything. It is the code of sportsmanship and honour. It is ethics.'

Catherine de Rambouillet
French (1588–1665)

Catherine de Vivonne, who married Charles d'Angennes, Marquis de Rambouillet, in 1600, was one of the most original and sophisticated women in French history; no beauty, but charming and amusing, she transformed the rough, boorish manners of the French nobility virtually single-handed and made *la politesse* fashionable.

Madame de Rambouillet was the first of the great French *salonnières*, setting a certain tone which was soon copied by others (for instance, Mademoiselle de Scudéry (q.v.) with her *samedis*), and which eventually percolated through to both the Court and the provinces. (The poorer imitations were to be mocked by Molière in *Les Précieuses Ridicules*.)

She was the daughter of the French ambassador to Rome, Jean de Vivonne, and an Italian mother; and found the French society to which her husband introduced her very unattractive after what she was used to in Rome. From about 1610 Mme de Rambouillet began to invite friends to her house once a week, not for gambling or drinking or political debate, but for conversation and amusement. A brilliant hostess, she mixed nobility and royalty with poets and other literary men, to the benefit of all. The conversation ran to books and plays, gossip and love; there might be reading aloud (Corneille is said to have read *Polyeucte* at the Hôtel Rambouillet) or epigrams and specially composed poems, maybe visits to the Château de Rambouillet in the summer; and many picnics, amateur dramatics, practical jokes and general fun.

Mme de Rambouillet designed her house in Paris herself. She was the first person to decorate her main room in blue, not the ubiquitous red or buff then in favour; she had the staircase built to one side, so that the salons could open into each other, and adopted the notion of alcoves from Spain, so that she might be spared the direct heat of the fire: in her thirties she developed a pathological dislike of heat.

Mme de Rambouillet had six daughters and a son; one daughter in particular, Julie d'Angennes, shared her gifts as a hostess.

Sue Ryder
British (b. 1923)

Sue Ryder, youngest of nine children of a rich English landowner, has devoted her life and energies to the relief of suffering, particularly that of the survivors of the Nazi concentration camps and, more recently, of the physically and mentally ill or handicapped and old people. She has founded 16 Homes in Britain and others in Poland, Yugoslavia and India, and, to raise funds for them, has opened more than 80 Sue Ryder shops. Her life, like that of Elly Jansen (q.v.), shows what can be done by one determined woman able to persuade hundreds of others to help her.

A devout Catholic, Ryder joined the First Aid Nursing Yeomanry during the Second World War, and found herself working with the Special Operations Executive whose agents were dropped into occupied Europe to work with the Resistance. She went to Algiers, Tunis and Italy with the Allied Armies. That led to relief work and prison visiting in a newly liberated Europe, and the discovery of her vocation. Her first Home was founded in Cavendish, Suffolk, in 1953. In 1959, she married Group Captain Leonard Cheshire, one of Britain's most famous war heroes and the founder of the Cheshire Homes for the disabled, and has two children.

Huda Sharawi
Egyptian (1882–1947)

Huda Sharawi was the founder of the women's movement in Egypt. Born into an upper class family, she was educated at home in Turkish and French and only learnt Arabic, then disdained by the upper classes, by listening to her brother's tutor. Married to a cousin at 14, Sharawi lived the customary life of seclusion and child bearing, but her wide reading in economics and philosophy made her determined to fight for the education of girls. In 1910 she succeeded in getting girls' schools opened, which led to the establishment of the first secondary schools for girls and their admission to university classes during the following decade. In 1919 she protested to the British authorities – Egypt was then still under British control – over the killing of civilians, including women, during anti-British demonstrations. She led more than 300 women to the British High Commission, an act which at that time required great courage. 'Here I am standing in front of you,' she said to the soldiers, 'Why don't you shoot me as you shot our other Egyptian women?' When Zaghul, the nationalist, was put under house arrest, she organized thousands of women to write 'Remember him' on bank notes.

In 1920 Sharawi became head of an association of women teachers and established a Women's Union with a school, workshop, club and magazine. But her most important action was to take off her veil; thousands eventually followed her example. It was the most revolutionary gesture she made. It caused her husband to divorce her, but they remarried in 1929. She founded the All-Arab Federation of Women in 1944. Just before her death she appealed for the abolition of all nuclear weapons.

Shirley Smith
Australian (b. 1927)

'Mum Shirl', as Shirley Smith has become popularly known, is an Aborigine woman known as 'soul mother' to thousands of her people in New South Wales, Australia. Born an epileptic, she never went to school; but her grandfather gave her a sound Aborigine traditional education. 'Never hate anybody and love yourself,' he would say. In 1970, with the help of 25 volunteer doctors, she set up a farm clinic for Aborigine alcoholics. In 1971 she co-founded a legal service for the Aborigines and became a counsellor in the prisons and corrective institutions in New South Wales because of her skill in bridging the racial gap. In 1977 she stood for Parliament (unsuccessfully) for the Uniting Party, declaring: 'Someone has to show young blacks and migrants how to do it, how to become leaders, because they haven't the confidence.'

'Mum Shirl' now lives in the yard of St Vincent's Catholic Church, Redfern, a shanty town near Sydney, where she cares for unmarried mothers who have won legal custody of their babies.

Elizabeth Cady Stanton
American (1815–1902)

Elizabeth Cady Stanton was, together with Susan B. Anthony (q.v.), one of the two most important figures in the American women's movement. The daughter of a judge in Johnstown, New York, she learnt of the harshness of the law towards women and children at her father's knee. She was educated at the famous Troy Female Seminary (cf. Emma Willard) and married Henry Brewster Stanton, an abolitionist lawyer, in 1840. They spent part of their honeymoon at the world's first Anti-Slavery Convention in London, where she was outraged that women delegates were not allowed to sit in the hall, and joined forces with Lucretia Mott (q.v.) to protest. Together they became the prime movers of the 1848 Seneca Falls Women's Rights Convention which was the launching pad of the American women's movement. Cady Stanton drafted their famous Declaration of Sentiments along the lines of the Declaration of Independence.

Cady Stanton had seven children and frequently addressed the New York State Legislature on the reform of family law. She was an energetic speaker and writer, contributed to the *Woman's Journal* (cf. Lucy Stone), and founded the newspaper *Revolution* with Susan B. Anthony in 1868. She was co-author of *The History of Woman Suffrage* with Anthony; she wrote her autobiography, *Eighty Years and More* (1898); she was president of the National Woman Suffrage Association for 20 years and in 1890 became first president of the National American Woman Suffrage Association, which was a merger between her NWSA and the American Woman Suffrage Association led by Lucy Stone (q.v.). 'I shall not grow conservative with age,' she once said, 'I am always busy, which is perhaps the chief reason why I am always well.'

Lucy Stone
American (1818–1893)

The first woman in the U.S. to keep her own name after marriage, Lucy Stone inspired what is now a commonplace practice for women in public life. A leading nineteenth-century reformer, she was the eighth of nine children of a well-to-do farmer and graduated in 1847 from Oberlin – the only college then open to women and black people. She was the first woman in Massachusetts to do so. She became a lecturer for the Massachusetts Anti-Slavery Society and persuaded them to allow a plea for women's rights to be part of her platform. 'I was a woman before I was an abolitionist,' she said, 'I must speak for the women.' An inspiring speaker, it was she who converted Susan B. Anthony to the feminist cause.

In 1855 Stone married an abolitionist lawyer, Henry Blackwell, brother of Elizabeth Blackwell (q.v.), in a ceremony that included a protest against existing marriage laws. Husband and wife worked together for female suffrage through State legislation and founded the weekly, *Woman's Journal*, in 1872. But Stone, like Julia Ward Howe (q.v.) was not a root and branch reformer; in the struggle for women's franchise she refused to be sidetracked into trade unionism or the growing movement for birth control; she disliked advanced views on sex. This attitude caused a split in the women's movement between the National Woman Suffrage Association led by Elizabeth Cady Stanton and Susan B. Anthony (qq.v.), and the American Woman Suffrage Associ-

ation under the leadership of Stone and her friend Julia Ward Howe. But the two factions eventually united as the National American Woman Suffrage Society for the final 30 years of the fight. 'Make the world better,' were Stone's last words to her only child, Alice Stone Blackwell. Alice, who was born in 1857, was the only original member of the Society to see the arrival of the vote for American women in 1919.

Bertha von Suttner
Austrian (1843–1914)

Bertha von Suttner was the architect of a European peace movement and winner of the Nobel Peace Prize. As an aristocratic but impoverished girl, Bertha Kinsky initially trained as a singer. In 1868, her voice having come to nothing, she went to Sweden as secretary-housekeeper to the millionaire inventor of dynamite, Alfred Nobel, who became a lifelong friend. In 1876 she married Baron Arthur von Suttner and settled in a little three-roomed wooden peasants' house in the Crimea, where they both wrote novels. In 1885 they went to Paris, where the atmosphere was heavy with the threat of an outbreak of war between France and Germany. There they met Alfred Nobel again; and Bertha von Suttner suggested to him that he should found a Prize for Peace. When the London International Peace Association met the following year, Suttner gave a series of lectures which were subsequently published in 1889 as *The Age of Machines* and *Lay Down Your Arms*. Thereafter she devoted herself to anti-war campaigns, writing books and making speeches. She herself was the first woman to be awarded the Nobel Peace Prize in 1905 in recognition of her tireless work in the pacifist cause.

Sojourner Truth
American (1797–1883)

Isabella van Wagener was a slave, the child and mother of slaves, but survived her wretched childhood to become an evangelist and champion of the abolition of slavery. She was born on a rich Dutchman's estate in New York, and as a child was sold from owner to owner. She bore several children by a fellow slave, four of whom survived; two of her daughters were sold away, but she was able to rescue her son Peter and daughter Sophia from a similar fate.

After slavery was abolished in New York State in 1828, she settled with Peter and Sophia in New York City. She earned her living in domestic employment, but she was already a visionary and joined first a preaching mission, then an evangelical community.

In 1843, when she was 46, she was 'summoned' to take the name 'Sojourner Truth' and to 'travel up and down the land'. She took to the road, preaching God's message and, later, the abolition of slavery, women's rights and temperance. Her great gifts as a speaker soon drew crowds wherever she went; Harriet Beecher Stowe (q.v.), whom she met in 1852–3, called her 'the Libyan Sybil'. She dictated *The Narrative of Sojourner Truth* to help earn her keep. In the mid-1850s she settled in Battle Creek, Michigan, and during the Civil War raised supplies for Negro volunteer regiments. After the war she briefly became a 'counsellor to the freed people', and was soon petitioning President Grant – unsuccessfully – for land in the Midwest for a Negro state. But thereafter many blacks from the South – including her own daughters – moved in hope to Kansas and Missouri. Sojourner Truth remained a popular figure until the end of her life.

Harriet Tubman
American (1815?–1913)

Born a Negro slave, Harriet Tubman later led thousands of slaves to freedom as the 'Moses of her people'. She married John Tubman, a free Negro, in 1844 and her one consuming passion, when it was still almost impossible, was to escape from the South. She eventually managed to do so in 1850. 'When I crossed that line,' [the Mason-Dixon Line] she said afterwards, 'I looked at my hands to see if I was the same person.' Exhilarated by her success, she went back to fetch her whole family.

For the next 10 years Harriet Tubman lived the dangerous life of a 'conductor' on the 500 miles of the 'Underground Railway' to Canada for escaped slaves:

yet she never once lost a 'passenger'. Tubman would sing to warn of her arrival, guided at night by the North Star. Armed with a gun she urged on weaklings with the caution, 'Brother, you go on, or die.' A reward of 40,000 dollars was put on her head. In 1860 she rescued a slave, Charles Nalle, from a mob who wanted to return him to the South. Anxious that the slave culture should not disappear, Tubman would dance and sing old Maryland songs at her rallies to raise money for the Anti-Slavery Society. During the Civil War she dressed in the dark blue Union uniform and in 1863, armed with a rifle, she and Colonel Montgomery led 300 soldiers on a raid to free more than 700 slaves on the banks of the Combakee River.

Worn out with nursing and fighting 'General' Tubman settled after the war with her parents in Auburn, New York. Unable to read or write, she dictated her autobiography in 1868 and spent the rest of her long life making speeches and fund-raising. Tubman only got her government pension when she was 80. 'There were two things I had a right to, liberty and death,' she once said when still a slave, 'If I could not have one, I would have the other, for no man should take me alive.' Tens of thousands of Negro slaves owed their emancipation to her.

Louisa Twining
British (1820–1911)

Louisa Twining worked to reform workhouses and hospitals for the destitute and dying in England. The youngest daughter of a prosperous London barrister, Richard Twining, Louisa began visiting an old woman who had been taken to the workhouse in the Strand, London, and was appalled at what she saw – the insolent porters who limited visits, the young chronically sick kept year in and year out in the dark, the filth, the drunken warders and nurses.

Twining initiated a campaign of protest letters to the newspapers and set up a Workhouse Visiting Society in the face of much opposition from the administrators. In 1855 she published *A Few Words about the Inmates of our Union Workhouses* in *Macmillan's* magazine and by 1856 had become a regular, unpaid inspector. Recognizing the desperate need for 'pauper' nurses, Twining attended a course herself in the Great Ormond Street Hospital in 1858. Annual Social Science Congresses – devoted to the airing of any matters in need of reform – were set up in Birmingham in 1857 and gave her a platform for her lectures on *Conditions in Workhouses*. In 1861 she enlisted help from Angela Burdett-Coutts (q.v.) to found homes for girls from workhouses to save them from drinking and prostitution. In 1867 she succeeded in getting the sick isolated in the workhouses and in 1879 she formed an association for trained nurses in workhouses. In 1886 she set up a home for epileptic girls and old women; she furnished it with her own family furniture and ran it herself until she was well into her seventies.

Speaking of her life's work in exposing and reforming workhouse conditions, Twining said, 'Patience, perseverance and faith ... such have been abundantly granted to me and I have endeavoured to use them.'

Beatrice Webb
British (1858–1943)

Beatrice and Sidney Webb played a leading role in the social reforms of early twentieth-century Britain. Beatrice Potter was born into a rich provincial family (of which Beatrix Potter, q.v., was a member) and lived at home, almost uneducated, until well into her twenties. However, as the result of a new interest which drew her away from her 'life of womanly love and self-devotion,' as she described it, she wrote *A Lady's View of the Unemployed in the East End* (1880) for the *Pall Mall Gazette*. She then wrote a study of the Co-operative Movement, and savagely attacked 'sweated labour' in industry. In 1889 she contributed to Charles Booth's painstaking social survey, *The Life and Labour of the People of London*.

Beatrice had for many years loved Joseph Chamberlain (a Member of Parliament and later Prime Minister) but finally, after much hesitation, agreed in 1892 to marry Sidney Webb, a lecturer – later professor – at London University and fellow member of the recently founded Fabian Society. She was 'confident that our marriage will not interfere

with our work.' Together the Webbs wrote on the Trade Union Movement, the absurdity of war, and the decay of capitalist civilization. They set up the now famous London School of Economics. In 1913 they founded the left-wing weekly, the *New Statesman*, and their gradualist, reformist policies had great influence on the infant Labour Party. After the 1914–18 war they expressed great enthusiasm for Soviet Russia and travelled there several times. In 1922 Sidney won the constituency of Durham for Labour; his wife vigorously campaigned for him.

In *My Apprenticeship* Beatrice Webb describes the long years of hard work – compiling statistics, public speaking and writing – which made them both such useful contributors to Britain's modern welfare state.

Emma Willard
American (1787–1870)

Emma Willard did more for the education of girls in America than anyone else in the early nineteenth century. Born Emma Hart, she was the sixteenth of 17 children from a respectable family in Berlin, Connecticut. In 1805 she went to a boarding school in Hartford, Connecticut, then taught there and in 1809 married the middle-aged school doctor, John Willard. When her son John was only four, her husband lost all his money and she opened the Middlebury Female Seminary in her own house in 1814. Willard considered geometry to be particularly important and would imaginatively demonstrate cones and pyramids cut out of turnips and potatoes. In 1821 the Governor of New York granted her a charter to open the Troy Female Seminary, later to become famous as the school which Elizabeth Cady Stanton (q.v.) attended. A Professor Eaton was specially hired to teach science, for although Willard agreed with the British educationalist, Hannah More (q.v.), that 'men and women are different like oak trees and apple trees,' she firmly believed that justice 'demanded equality with respect to privilege of education.'

After a brief visit to Europe in 1830, Willard translated books on education, brought American history books up to date and continued to promote the teaching of mathematics – activities only in-

Emma Willard, American poet and educationalist.

several years teaching, and became the first American woman college president at Evanston College, Illinois. Her fiancé, Charles Fowler, was president of the equivalent men's college and they quarrelled bitterly about combining the two colleges. She left him and devoted her energies to becoming president of the Chicago Branch of the Women's Christian Temperance Union in 1874. Although many members objected to her support of women's suffrage, she was elected National President in 1879. 'When an idea comes, I shall pull the string of the mental shower bath and take the consequences,' Willard once said, referring to the style in which she led the progressives of the Temperance Union. For the next 20 years she wrote and campaigned against 'the wicked spirit'. 'Falter who must, follow who dare' was her motto. The World's Temperance Convention held in Toronto in 1897 was her crowning triumph, and when she died in 1898 every railwayman in Chicago lined the processional route of her coffin. In 1905 the State of Illinois commemorated her achievements with a statue – the only one of a woman – in the Capitol.

terrupted by a brief and disastrous second marriage in 1838 to a gambler, Dr Yates. In 1845 she travelled 8,000 miles round the States to advocate education for women. In 1864 she published her poems; two of them have since become famous – *Rocked in the Cradle of the Deep* and *God Save America*. Willard refused to become actively involved in anti-slavery or women's rights campaigns; she reserved all her energies for the education of girls.

Frances Willard
American (1839–1898)

Frances Willard used the Temperance Movement in America as a platform to campaign for feminism and socialism. 'Frank', as she called herself, was the middle child of a Middle Western farming family and was brought up to be generally self-sufficient. There was no local school until she was 16, and only then did she receive any formal education. After graduating from North Western University she spent

Betty Williams (British, b. 1943) and Mairead Corrigan (British, b. 1944)

Betty Williams and Mairead Corrigan are the two Roman Catholic Irishwomen who founded the Ulster Peace Movement in August 1976 and, a year later, were jointly awarded the Nobel Peace Prize, the youngest people ever to receive it.

The atrocity which inspired the movement was the death of the three young children of Mrs Anne Maguire, Mairead Corrigan's sister, one of them a baby of only four weeks, all killed in a collision with a runaway car whose IRA driver had been shot by soldiers. Sickened by the news, Mrs Williams, wife of a merchant seaman and mother of a boy and girl, began knocking at doors asking women to join her in standing up for peace. Within a week she was leading a 10,000 strong demonstration – composed of both Protestants and Catholics – and together with Mairead Corrigan, a private secretary, had embarked on organizing and raising money for this most

Northern Ireland peace campaigners, Betty Williams (left) and Mairead Corrigan (right) in 1976.

hopeful of Northern Ireland's movements for peace. Both women had to face insults, intimidation, even death threats and assault, but within three months there were more than 150 local groups, and there had been rallies not only all over the province but in London's Trafalgar Square. Since then the two women have become extremely effective speakers and raised money on both sides of the Atlantic for a variety of community projects in Ulster. But each has continued to meet hostility at home. There was considerable criticism when their £80,000 Nobel Prize money was not given to the Peace Movement, but used to finance their lecture tours ('Join the Peace People and see the world' said cynics) and help for the Third World.

Their movement has been no more successful than any other. Betty Williams has since resigned and Mrs Maguire committed suicide early in 1980. Undoubtedly however the women helped focus world attention on the desire for peace in Northern Ireland.

Mary Wollstonecraft
British (1759–1797)

The greatest and most original of British feminist pioneers, Mary Wollstonecraft wrote the celebrated

A Vindication of the Rights of Woman. Her life was hard. She was born in London but her father – who had lost his family fortune and turned to drink – tried his luck as a farmer in Essex, Yorkshire and Wales. Wollstonecraft left home to be the companion of a rich lady in Bath and, when her mother died in 1782, went to live with a friend, Fanny Blood, while supporting herself as a seamstress. They later ran a school together in north London until Fanny married. Wollstonecraft then went to Ireland as a governess but was dismissed because the children were said to love her more than their mother. Back in London, she was befriended by the publisher Joseph Johnson, who gave her work to do. Her first book, *Original Stories from Real Life* (1788), was written for children.

Her masterpiece was largely written in response to a speech made by Edmund Burke, the right-wing Member of Parliament. *A Vindication of the Rights of Woman* was published in 1792 and immediately made her name. A fiery feminist polemic, it attacked the very foundations of contemporary society: 'Let us first consider women in the broad light of human creatures, who, in common with men, are placed on earth to unfold their faculties ... Who made man the exclusive judge, if woman partakes with him in the gift of reason? Do you not act a tyrant's part when you force *all* women by denying them civil and political rights to remain immured in their families, groping in the dark? It is time to effect a revolution in female manners, time to restore women to their lost dignity and to make them labour by reforming themselves to reform the world.'

In 1792 Wollstonecraft went to Paris – excited, as so many were, by the hopes raised by the foundation of the new Republic in France. Her account of that time, *An Historical and Moral View of the Origin and Progress of the French Revolution* (1794), was used as the basis for Carlyle's *French Revolution* forty years later. In Paris she had a child, Fanny, by Gilbert Imlay, who later sent her to Scandinavia on business for him. Her *Letters Written in Sweden* (1976) shows the great interest she always took in her surroundings and the people she met on her travels. The philosopher, William Godwin, whom she had met through her publisher, said that it was these letters that made him

Mary Wollstonecraft, eighteenth-century feminist author and mother of Mary Shelley.

fall in love with her. They subsequently married just before her daughter Mary was born in 1797. She died a few days after the birth of a child who was to become, in a very different way, as remarkable as her mother (cf. Mary Shelley).

Frances Wright
British (1794–1852)

One of the earliest campaigners for human rights in America, Frances Wright was born in Scotland, daughter of a wealthy merchant in Dundee. She and her sister Camilla were orphaned young and were brought up in England. When she was 16 Frances was fascinated by Botta's *History of the American Revolution*: 'There existed a country consecrated to freedom in which man might wake to the full knowledge and full exercise of his powers.' At 18 she escaped to a congenial great-uncle in Glasgow –

where she saw families evicted by their landlords under the Highland Clearances leaving sadly for the New World. Wright swore then 'to wear ever in her heart the cause of the poor and helpless.' A friend, Mrs Miller, who had spent a year in the states, urged her to go and see the New World for herself.

In 1818, she and her sister Camilla went to America on a long visit, and eventually decided to stay there. Frances was horrified to see chained Negroes and in 1824, after a visit to Robert Owen's New Harmony Commune in Indiana, she bought 2,000 acres of swamp at Nashoba on which to establish a community with 26 freed slaves. Nashoba did not turn out to be the 'Great Experiment' she had hoped and the slaves she had freed were eventually shipped to the new Negro republic of Haiti at her expense. Half her fortune was lost in the enterprise.

Nothing daunted, Frances Wright lectured on abolition, education for women, and the reform of the law of inheritance. She was a spell-binding speaker. Tall and beautiful, often dressed in Turkish trousers, she would stand in front of a map of America with a copy of the Declaration of Independence in her hand. In 1831 she married a French doctor, Phiquepal d'Arusmont, and had a daughter, Sylvia. But once back in New York, she founded the *Free Inquirer* with Robert Dale Owen (son of Robert Owen) in 1834; it gave her a platform for her campaigns against capital punishment and for more liberal divorce laws. Wright also became a leading figure in the infant Labour movement, which was known at one point as the Fanny Wright party.

Mary Slessor photographed in Nigeria with her adopted children.

RELIGION

OUR PREHISTORIC ANCESTORS worshipped female gods, and in the classical world, too, goddesses had their devotees. The worship of Isis and Diana survived into the Christian era, and echoes of the ancient Mother Goddess still linger in the devotion with which millions of Christians pray to the Virgin Mary. But no religion of historic times has given women an equal place with men. The Godhead is always male, whether Buddha, Jehovah or Allah. In the western world, the Judaeo-Christian patriarchal tradition within which the disciplines of archaeology and anthropology have developed, has been so powerful that the worship of a goddess is rarely dignified with the name of religion, but slightingly referred to as a cult (for example: 'cult of Isis', 'nature cult').

In its earliest years, however, women occupied an important place in the Christian Church. There is some evidence from early religious records in Gaul, Rome and North Africa, that women prophesied, taught, preached, proselytized, led congregations and perhaps acted as priests and even bishops: St Paul himself praised the work of women in the Church. But by the end of the second century attitudes began to change and women played a less active role in religion. The mysterious Pope Joan, reputed to have been a brilliant Englishwoman who lived her life as a man and was elected Pope John VIII in 855, has been virtually erased from the papal records, and the antipathy of the Roman Catholic Church, the Church of England and the Orthodox churches to women priests still appears to be insurmountable.

Historically, though, the Christian Church has adopted a more liberal attitude to women than for example Islam or Judaism. Its congregations are not segregated and women are regarded as equal in the sight of God. And within the Christian fold, women have been able to pursue religious vocations and careers – for many centuries the only serious alternative to marriage. They have founded their own sects and churches – for instance the Church of Christ, Scientist and the community of Shakers – and have been immensely influential in the development of rules of life and new religious sects. Women have been canonized and have become mystics, they have become scholars, writers, artists, they have served as missionaries, teachers, abbesses and mother superiors, the leaders of other women and sometimes of men.

Madame Acarie
French (1566–1618)

Barbe Avrillot Acarie was among the first of the upper-class women whose influence was to help transform French morals and manners in the seventeenth century. Where Madame de Rambouillet (q.v.), setting her face against the vulgarity and philistinism of the Court, made wit, civility and intellectual conversation fashionable and heralded the famous *salonnières* of the future, Madame Acarie, a mystic who founded the Carmelite Order in France, headed the wave of religious reformers and innovators who founded the new religious orders and great private charities which were to proliferate during the century.

It was in the Hôtel Acarie that the first private charitable works among the sick and the poor of Paris were organized. Madame Acarie – like many deeply religious women – combined mystical fervour with excellent practical sense, and divided her time between good works and bringing up her children. When her husband Jean-Pierre Acarie went into a monastery, she went into a convent. In 1604 she introduced the Carmelite Order into France, and was a leading spirit in the movement which reformed the houses of religion. She was beatified as Marie de l'Incarnation in 1791.

In 1608 Jeanne de Lestonnac (niece of the philosopher Montaigne) founded the Compagnie de Notre Dame; in 1610 St Jeanne de Chantal (grandmother of Madame de Sévigné, q.v.) founded, with St François de Sales, Bishop of Geneva, the Order of the Visitation; while in 1612 the Ursulines were established in Paris by Cardinal Bérulle and Madame de Sainte-Beuve. Many other women – Madame de Gondi, Madame de Lamoignon, St Louise de Marillac (q.v.), and Queen Anne of Austria – were drawn into good works by the example of St Vincent de Paul.

Jacqueline Marie Angélique Arnauld
French (1591–1661)

Mère Angélique was the most celebrated of a generation of reforming mother superiors of early seventeenth-century France. She was one of 20 children of Antoine Arnauld, advocate general to Queen Catherine de Médicis, and thus a member of the huge Arnauld clan which played a leading part in the development of Jansenism.

Religious institutions generally had become very lax by the end of the sixteenth century: vows were ignored, as were sermons and confession, while mother superiors, frequently appointed solely for their family connections (sometimes even as children), lived the life of great ladies, often taking lovers or having children.

Jacqueline Arnauld was just such a well-connected girl. She entered a convent as a child, and became abbess of Port Royal des Champs (near Versailles) at 11. By the time she was 18 she had found that religion was her true vocation; she summoned her younger sister Mère Agnès – already abbess of St Cyr since the age of six – to join her, and imposed an enclosed life on her fellow nuns. In 1609 she introduced the *guichet*, or little grill, and on one famous day, which became known as *la journée du guichet*, refused even to talk to her own father except through a little grill. Her nuns took a vow of poverty, and gave all their possessions to the convent. Thereafter she and her sister were invited to reform other convents. The convent of Port Royal moved to Paris in 1626, leaving the old premises to a group of devout men; together the two religious houses became the headquarters of the Jansenist movement. Mère Angélique was also involved in the Jansenist protest against Pope Innocent X's attack on Jansenism in 1653.

Gladys Aylward
British (1903–1970)

'The small woman', as Gladys Aylward became known, was a maid-of-all-work who, determined to be a missionary, saved for the fare to China for years out of her meagre earnings. In 1932 she was at last able to buy a train ticket from London to Vladivostok, the first leg of the cheapest route to the mountain town of Yangcheng in China, where she was to help an elderly Scottish widow who had been preaching the Christian gospel in China for 50 years. Gladys

Gladys Aylward's certificate of Chinese naturalization, issued in 1936.

Aylward then had to travel for three weeks by boat and cart to the 'Inn of the Sixth Happiness', which was how the mission house was described. Within a few months the elderly missionary had died and Aylward was alone – in a land threatened by approaching civil war and by Japanese invaders. She was soon known as Ai-weh-deh, 'the virtuous one'. The local mandarin trusted her and made her a 'foot' inspector to put an end to the cruel tradition of binding the feet of young girls; and it was a good way for her to make new converts. In 1936, having learnt the Shansi dialect, she became a Chinese citizen – an unprecedented step for a foreign missionary.

In 1938 Yangcheng was bombed by the Japanese and Aylward worked for months among the victims of the Japanese invasion. She became a wanted woman – the Japanese offered $100 for her capture – and in 1940 she left Yangcheng on her famous journey over the mountains leading more than 100 homeless children out of the war zone to safety. (Her dramatic story was made into a film, *The Inn of the Sixth Happiness*.)

Aylward was remarkable for the total devotion with which she identified with the people whom she felt she had been chosen to serve. Although very ill after her epic journey, she remained to work in China for another nine years before returning to England – where her story became known through the BBC, and she was much in demand as a speaker. But in 1957 she returned to the East – not to China, now Communist, but to the offshore islands, Hong Kong and Taiwan; there she worked with destitute refugees, and ran a mission and an orphanage, which she financed by fund-raising tours in the U.S. and the Far East.

St Bernadette of Lourdes
French (1844–1879)

As a direct result of the remarkable series of visions which the young Bernadette saw in 1858, her native village of Lourdes is now the largest place of pilgrimage in the Roman Catholic world. She was the eldest of six children, daughter of a very poor miller, François Soubirous. At the age of 14, on the rock at Massabielle, Lourdes, she had 18 separate visions of the Blessed Virgin Mary, who described herself as being of 'immaculate conception' (Pope Pius IV had made this an item of faith in 1854). The vision told Bernadette to drink from a hidden spring, and asked for a church to be built, prayers to be said and penances to be observed. An uneducated, asthmatic girl, Bernadette never wavered as she faced endless questioning by church officials. She spent the last 13 years of her life in a convent at Nevers, too ill to be present at the consecration of the newly-built basilica in 1876, three years before her death. She was canonized in 1933, and the healing spring now yields 4,000 gallons a day.

Helena Blavatsky
Russian (1839–1891)

Helena Blavatsky was a pioneer in the modern Western interest in Oriental religions. She had a great influence as a spiritualist, and was co-founder of the Theosophical Society, which drew on Tibetan mystical traditions.

Helena Petrovna Blavatsky was probably born in Ekaterinoslav in Russia. At 16 she married a man of 73, but soon left him and went to Tibet, where she later claimed to have been under spiritual instruction for seven years. Certainly she was very successful as a spiritualist and medium when she went back to Russia in 1858. On the strength of her gift she toured Canada, Mexico, Texas and India before returning to Tibet. Madame Blavatsky later claimed that two Tibetan 'mahatmas', or spirit guides, could appear to her at any time in their 'astral' bodies. She went to the States in 1870, became a naturalized citizen and stayed for six years. Her own 'real' birth happened, according to her, when she met an American lawyer, Colonel Olcott, with whom in 1875 she formed the Theosophical Society, which was to lead to the brotherhood of man. Her book, *Isis Unveiled*, appeared in 1877. She married a Unitarian minister but soon declared, 'To Hades with this thing called sex love. It is a beastly appetite that should be starved into submission.' She continued to travel widely, even offering her services as a spy to Russia, but established the headquarters of the Theosophical Society in London. 'Oh, my dear, if only you would come among us!' she exclaimed to the then socialist Annie Besant (q.v.) when Mrs Besant reviewed Blavatsky's last book, *The Secret Doctrine*, in 1888; Mrs Besant became Theosophy's most enthusiastic convert.

Blavatsky was an enormous woman who weighed over 16 stone. W.B. Yeats, himself no stranger to spiritualist circles, described her as 'a sort of peasant Irish woman with an air of humour and audacity.' Nevertheless at the time of her death there were at least 100,000 members and the Theosophists' paper, *Lucifer*, was sold in New York, Paris and London.

Madame Blavatsky, co-founder of the Theosophical Society in 1875.

Catherine Booth
British (1829–1890)

Catherine Booth was co-founder with her husband William of the Salvation Army: the greatest organized effort made to redeem the Victorian urban poor, and an organization which is still flourishing today.

Catherine Mumford was a delicate child brought up by a widowed mother in Brixton, South London. When she met her future husband at a prayer meeting, she wrote, 'It seemed as though we had

*Catherine Booth, who founded the
Salvation Army with her husband William.*

intimately known and loved each other for years, and suddenly, after some temporary absence, had been brought together again.' She encouraged him to leave the Methodist sect to which he belonged and to pursue his idea of finding a more effective way to reach the inhabitants of the newly industrialized cities of Britain. This ambition they achieved together, for Mrs Booth, although frail, insisted on doing her share. They started by preaching at street corners, but in 1864 they formed a 'Hallelujah Band' from a number of converted criminals, and called themselves the East London Revival Society. By 1878 the group had become known as the Salvation Army; they held open air meetings, visited public houses, prisons and private houses, held meetings in theatres and factories, and called upon converts to give daily witness.

Mrs Booth helped to draw up the regulations which stated, "The Army refuses to make any difference between men and women as to rank, authority and duties but opens the highest positions to women as well as men; the words 'woman', 'she', 'her', are scarcely ever used, even in orders, 'man', 'he', 'his' being always understood to mean a person of either sex unless it is obviously impossible." (Cf. G. B. Shaw's play, *Major Barbara*.) As William Booth, the Army's first General, once said, 'Some of my best men are women.' The 'Sally Army', as it became popularly known, was founded in the U.S. in 1880 and in Australia in 1881. By 1897 the Army had 50,000 officers, and in 1901 King Edward VII invited General Booth to his coronation. The Salvation Army is now one of the most respected of all lay religious movements.

Seven of the Booths' eight children became prominent salvationists. Sergeant Eva Cory Booth (1865–1960) sold the *War Cry*, the Army's newspaper, at 15 and became head of the Salvation Army in the U.S. She founded Evangeline Residences, became a U.S. citizen in 1923 and opened the Army's headquarters in New York City in 1930. She was elected General in 1934.

St Bridget of Sweden
Swedish (1303–1373)

The patron saint of Sweden was Scandinavia's most prolific writer during the Middle Ages, as well as the foundress of a religious order, the Birgittines, which is still active today.

Bridget was the daughter of Berger, governor of the province of Upland, and at 14 married a nobleman, also a governor, called Ulf Gudmarrson, by whom she had eight children. She became a lady-in-waiting to the Queen of Sweden about 1335, and soon after began to have visions and revelations; these prompted her to attempt to reform the customs of the court, and eventually the Papacy itself. Meanwhile she became a pilgrim, travelling first to St Olaf's shrine in Norway, then to St James Compostella in Spain (where her husband, who had accompanied her, died in 1344). Back in Sweden after a period of retreat, Bridget founded a monastery for 60 nuns and 25 monks at Vadstena, where the abbess was to be supreme in temporal matters, the monks in spiritual. It was dedicated to plain living and high thinking; the inhabitants were allowed as many books as they wished but luxury was forbidden. The first abbess at

Vadstena was Bridget's daughter Catherine, and the order eventually numbered some 80 houses throughout Europe. There are now 12, for nuns only.

In 1349 St Bridget left Sweden for Rome, to gain the Pope's acceptance of her new order. She eventually succeeded, and spent the rest of her life in Rome, devoting herself to work for the poor and sick, except for several other pilgrimages; she died shortly after her return from a journey to Jerusalem.

A person of immense energy, St Bridget, who was canonized in 1391, was an authority not only on morals but also on politics and military matters. She recorded her 700 visions and other religious compositions in her native Swedish; all but two have survived only in Latin or Norwegian translations. Her plea that the peoples of Scandinavia should speak and write a single language went unheeded.

St Brigid of Ireland
Irish (c. 450–523)

St Brigid is Ireland's second saint after St Patrick, so loved and admired in her day that she was held by some to be the personification of the Mother of Christ: Mary of the Gael. Her cult spread to Wales, Scotland and England (where many churches were dedicated to St Bride), and to this day she is also venerated in Portugal, parts of Italy and France and even Australia.

Brigid's great achievement was the founding of Ireland's first women's religious community at Kildare, of which she was abbess. Little is known about this community, but the many stories and miracles associated with her suggest not only that she was full of good works but that she occupied an immensely important place in the Irish-Christian life of her day. She may have been born at Uinmeras, to poor parents who had been baptized by St Patrick, and probably became a nun at a very early age.

St Catherine of Siena
Italian (1347–1380)

St Catherine was the nun who urged the word of God on popes and politicians in a series of powerful letters.

popes, cardinals, princes and captains.

Catherine was a vigorous leader: 'We are put here in this life like a battlefield and we must fight the good fight,' she declared in her *Dialogue with Divine Providence*, completed in 1378. Much of her time was spent attempting to make peace between the city state of Florence and the papacy, and in urging the need for a new Crusade in the East. She was appalled at Pope Gregory XI's rival papacy in Avignon and implored him to return to Rome; he did so, but died in 1378, and his successor Urban VI was immediately opposed by another rival pope. Urban had welcomed Catherine to Rome for her support of him, and it was there that she died, worn out by her efforts, 18 months later. She was canonized in 1461 and became patron saint of Italy in 1939.

St Clare
Italian (1194–1253)

St Clare was a contemplative and the founder of the great order of nuns known as the Poor Clares. Born to wealth, she was to follow the humblest of rules.

Clara Schiffi was the daughter of a noble family in Assisi, and was drawn to a life of poverty and penitence by St Francis. It was he who, to test her vocation, told her to put on sackcloth and beg. Her family were extremely hostile but eventually, on Palm Sunday 1212, Clara escaped and, dressed as a bride, had her head shaved by St Francis himself, who heard her vows of eternal poverty, chastity and obedience. Her sister – and later her mother – followed her into the tiny community for which St Francis had drawn up a 'Way of Life'. They lived strictly on alms for 40 years. It was once said that, when St Clare and St Francis had a rare meal together, a 'fire' was seen rising from the table; it was declared to be a holy nimbus. The church authorities tried to make St Clare's new order a branch of the Benedictines, but just before she died in 1253 a papal decree established the Sisters of Poor Clare as the second order of Franciscans. She was canonized two years after her death, and because she miraculously witnessed a Christmas Midnight Mass on the far side of Assisi during her last illness, she is now the patron saint of television.

St Catherine of Siena. A fourteenth-century painting by Andrea Vanni in San Dominico's, Siena.

She was the youngest of 20 children, the daughter of a wool-dyer of Siena called Giacomo Benincasa, and her praying and insistence on acts of penance were a constant irritation at home. Catherine was 16 when she entered the Dominican Third Order. She spent a year in total solitude in her desire to emulate the anchorites of the early Church before being sent to work in a hospital. She became celebrated for her asceticism and her ecstatic experiences, which began when she was a child, and her simple faith and personality were so strong that she rapidly attracted a group of disciples – dubbed the 'Caterinati' – who accompanied her everywhere. They took down hundreds of letters at her dictation (she never learnt to read or write) addressed to different influential figures:

Vittoria Colonna
Italian (1490–1547)

One of the great noblewomen of Renaissance Italy, Vittoria Colonna was a poet and a religious reformer. The daughter of an aristocratic family – her father was Fabrizio Colonna and her mother Anna di Montefeltro – she was betrothed at the age of four and in 1509 married Francesco d'Avalos, Marquis of Pescara. War separated them after only two years of marriage; they exchanged passionate letters, which still exist, and he died of wounds in Milan in 1525. Overcome with grief, Vittoria Colonna isolated herself on the island of Ischia, abandoned all worldly pleasures and wrote *Rime Spirituali* (religious verses). Friendship with Juan de Valdes, a Spanish humanist, inspired her interest in church reform; in 1537 she visited a Capuchin monastery run by a father who later became a Protestant. Colonna did not take her zeal for reform as far as conversion to Lutheranism, but she greatly helped those who wished to fight corruption within the Church. In 1538 her poems were published and in 1539 she became an intimate friend of Michelangelo, who made many drawings of her and wrote some of his finest sonnets in her honour. In 1544 she entered a convent in Rome where she died.

Dorothy Day
American (1897–1980)

Dorothy Day was a founder member of the Catholic Worker movement and is best known for her part in setting up the St Joseph Houses of Hospitality for the urban poor. She was the third of five children of a journalist who moved about the States, but she spent most of her adolescence in California. She won a scholarship to Urbana College, Illinois. There she became a socialist, and worked as a journalist on two socialist papers: *The Call* until 1917 and then *The Masses*. During the 1920s she entered into a common

Dorothy Day, founder member of the Catholic Worker movement and editor of the radical Catholic Worker *magazine.*

law marriage with Foster Bannerman; they had a daughter in 1927. But the same year she was received into the Catholic Church and supported herself and her daughter thereafter by writing.

In 1933, with Peter Maurin, a French Canadian priest, Day founded *The Catholic Worker*, a paper that fought against social evils such as the build-up of armaments and the visible material wealth of the Catholic Church. From championing the poor in the depression years in print, they turned to charity work and started setting up Houses of Hospitality. Soon there were 30 Houses in major cities across the States, serving meals and finding accommodation. A vigorous opponent of nuclear weapons in the fifties, Day fought all her life for peace and for the oppressed. She wrote two volumes of autobiography.

Mary Baker Eddy
American (1821–1910)

Mary Baker Eddy founded the Church of Christ, Scientist. In the process she became a multimillionaire and the publisher of a great daily newspaper, the *Christian Science Monitor*.

Mary Baker was the youngest child of a Calvinist New England farmer. As a child she was frequently ill with back trouble, which kept her from school. At 22 she married a Southerner, George Washington Glover of Charleston, who died a year later, leaving her pregnant. After freeing his slaves, she returned to her family and gave birth to a son in 1844.

In spite of constant pain from back trouble, she managed to earn a living by teaching and writing, and in 1853 married Daniel Patterson, an itinerant dentist, who eventually abandoned her. In 1862, in her forties, she was dramatically cured of her back ailments – if only temporarily – by the healer, Phineas B. Quimby. By 1866 she had come to the conclusion – central to her future life's work – that 'the mind governed the whole question of recovery'. Her new belief that 'disease was a failure of faith' was confirmed when she cured herself of the results of a fall by prayer. Her career as the originator of Christian Science had begun, and from 1867 onwards she preached the role of faith and prayer in healing.

In 1875 Mary Baker published *Science and Health*, which was to become the textbook of Christian Science, and by 1879 the mother Church of Christ, Scientist, was established in Boston. She lectured on the dangers of drink and tobacco and the idea that pain and disease are enemies. 'Anyone with the least understanding of God does not cough', she once said. She soon had an immense following.

Mary Baker was married for the third time in 1877, to Dr Asa Gilbert Eddy. As Mary Baker Eddy, she founded various journals, and in 1908 a daily newspaper, *The Christian Science Monitor*, which was 'to injure no man, but to bless all mankind'. She insisted the paper should never exploit crime and always take the broad view – still qualities of the paper today. Many can testify to the good done by Mary Baker Eddy's system of healing. At one time there were more than a quarter of a million Christian Scientists, and today there are more than 3,300 churches. Lady Astor (q.v.) and the British actress Joyce Grenfell were among the better known Christian Scientists.

St Elizabeth of Hungary
Hungarian (1207–1231)

Elizabeth of Hungary was the queen who gave up her title to become the humblest of nuns. She is one of the most popular German saints. She was the daughter of King Andrew II of Hungary and was educated from the age of four by the parents of the Landgrave Ludwig IV of Thuringia, whom she married in 1221; they had three children. Elizabeth, who had always been religious, was much influenced by the Franciscan brothers who had begun to arrive in Germany, and when famine struck, in her husband's absence, she ordered the granaries throughout his domains to be emptied for the poor. Previously Ludwig had been deeply critical of her extravagant charities, but now he became a convert. He embarked on a crusade to the Holy Land in 1227 but died of disease on the journey. The grief-stricken Queen Elizabeth entered the Tertiary Order of the Franciscans at Marburg in Hesse to do the most menial work for the sick and poor. She renounced everything to live in poverty

but died aged 24. In 1235 she was canonized and the convent at Marburg became an extremely popular shrine until 1539 when a Lutheran prince made off with the relics, which have never been recovered.

Marie Guyart
French (1599–1672)

Mère Marie de l'Incarnation, born Marie Guyart, was the first superior of the Ursuline Order of nuns in Canada and one of the 'founding mothers' of La Nouvelle France in North America. Her writings, particularly her wonderfully lively letters home, are an immensely important source for the early history of French Canada. Marie was also a leading mystic of the Roman Catholic Church, a good and much-loved woman and, like many mystics, extremely efficient in the day-to-day affairs of a life which was both hard-working and adventurous.

She was one of seven children of Florent Guyart, a master baker of Tours, and received a good education. She married a master silk worker, Claude Martin, and had one son. Widowed at the age of 20, she went to live with her sister. Marie already intended to become a nun, and secretly took the triple vow of poverty, chastity and obedience. Meanwhile, she brought up her son, worked in her sister's household and was finally, such was her obvious competence, entrusted by her brother-in-law Paul Buisson with the running of his carrier business, which involved working and negotiating on the wharfs on the banks of the Loire.

In 1631, the call from God was so imperative that she left her 12-year-old son to be brought up by her sister, and entered the Ursuline convent at Tours. There she began her mystical writings, and in 1639, again in response to a revelation, sailed for Canada with three other women.

In Canada she founded a convent (and rebuilt it when it was burnt down) and a boarding school for the daughters of settlers and Indian girls. She organized the garden, a farm, the digging of wells and all building work, and even did the baking. She survived raids from the Iroquois Indians and led missionary work among them, and learnt both

Iroquois and Algonquin in order to prepare dictionaries. Her advice was soon sought after by both merchants and the administrators of the province, and when she died Bishop Laval wrote to her son – who was by this time himself a Jesuit superior: 'She was a perfect Superior, an excellent mistress of novices; she was capable of carrying out all the works of religion. Her life, ordinary on the outside but very regular and animated by a completely divine inner nature, was a living rule for her entire community.'

Mère Marie is thought to have written some 33,000 letters, of which only 221 survive to attest to her humour and keen powers of observation, as well as other writings, including the *Relations* of 1633 and 1653. She was declared Venerable by Leo XIII, only lacking the necessary miracles associated with her to achieve sainthood.

Carter Heyward
American (b. 1945)

Isabel Carter Heyward is the best known of America's women priests. She was one of 11 women ordained by four Episcopalian bishops amid considerable controversy in July 1974; as she said, 'Priestess implies mumbo jumbo. Those who oppose us would love to call us that.' The ordination of the 11 women, although vigorously opposed by the majority of the House of Bishops, has begun to challenge the age-old view of the 'uncleanness' of women, as Carter Heyward put it: 'They can't strip us of the power of the Holy Spirit, and that scares them.' Many clergymen are very hostile to women priests. A young priest who took communion wine from Carter Heyward in a Manhattan church scratched deep into the back of her hand, saying 'I hope you burn in hell.'

Carter Heyward wanted to be a priest from the age of six and is now a professor of theology, after some years of parish work. In 1971 she had to decide between ordination as a deacon and living with the man she loved, 'but with whom I had never been able to be myself'. She chose the church. A firm believer in the 'sexlessness of persons' in religion, she says, 'The God I believe in is calling women to the full ministry right now.' Defending the sensational nature of her ordination she says, 'Sufficient legislation follows only after dramatic action.'

St Hilda of Whitby
British (614–680)

The life of St Hilda strikingly reveals the kind of opportunities open to women within the framework of the early Christian Church, despite the fact that the Church has never considered women equal except in the sight of God. No doubt Hilda was helped by the fact that she was well-connected: she was the great-niece of King Edwin of Northumbria, and with him was converted to Christianity when she was 13.

Hilda decided to become a nun when she was 33, having spent the interval 'most nobly in secular occupations', according to England's eighth-century historian, the Venerable Bede. At first she intended to join her sister (whose son was the King of the East Angles) at a monastery in Gaul, but her destiny lay in Northumbria, where she was shortly appointed abbess at Hartlepool. There she quickly established a reputation for both wisdom and good organization, and after a few years, in 657, founded a monastery for both men and women at the port of Whitby in Yorkshire. Her monastery became famous as a centre of learning – five bishops were trained there – and even of literature: for it was St Hilda who took in and encouraged an unlettered cowherd called Caedmon who was England's first Christian poet. The Synod of Whitby was held in 663/4 – a key conference in the history of English Christianity, for it decided that England should follow Roman forms rather than the Irish (which Hilda herself favoured).

The Venerable Bede, who was born in St Hilda's lifetime, is full of praise both for her and her abbey: 'No one there was rich, no one was needy, for everything was held in common, and nothing was considered to be anyone's personal property. So great was her prudence that not only ordinary folk, but kings and princes used to come and ask her advice in their difficulties and take it.' He claimed that all her acquaintances called her Mother 'because of her wonderful devotion and grace'.

Hildegard of Bingen
German (1098–1174)

Hildegard of Bingen is one of the great figures of German mysticism, 'the Sybil of the Rhine'. As a little girl in her aristocratic home in Bokelheim, Germany, she began to have visions, and at the age of eight she was taken into the household of Jutta, a recluse, who taught her reading, writing and Latin. Hildegard became a nun at 15 and, when Jutta died in 1136, was made the leader of their little community. About 10 years later she founded an independent Benedictine monastery at Bingen, and a second one in 1165.

Hildegard was held in high regard as a preacher and seer. At the age of 43 she began to write down her visions in *Scivias*: a compelling work, reminiscent in style of the Old Testament prophets. She was a prolific writer on a variety of subjects – she wrote letters to rulers, hymns, morality plays, lives of the saints and – very unusual for that period – observations on all aspects of the natural world, including a treatise on the circulation of the blood, which showed considerable scientific gifts. She also painted and played musical instruments.

Hildegard's genius and integrity were championed by St Bernard of Clairvaux, but the church authorities objected to the fact that she had allowed an excommunicate to be buried in sacred ground and, despite the miracles attributed to her, Hildegard has never been formally canonized.

Selina, Countess of Huntingdon
British (1707–1791)

The Countess of Huntingdon was the benefactor of a largely working-class sect of Calvinist Methodists which became known as the Countess of Huntingdon's Connection. Her father was Lord Ferrers and she married the Earl of Huntingdon in 1728. Thereafter she devoted her time and money to caring for the poor. In 1739 she put her money at the disposal of the famous preachers John Wesley and George Whitfield, preachers who urgently felt the need to spread the Gospel in practical ways – by

Selina, Countess of Huntingdon, benefactress of the Methodist movement.

visiting prisons, impromptu prayers and open prayer meetings.

After the deaths of her husband and two of her sons, Lady Huntingdon became even more dedicated to good works. She invited fashionable ladies to prayer meetings, although one lady of rank complained 'It is monstrous to be told that you have a heart as sinful as the common wretches that crawl upon the earth.' The evangelical ministers drew enormous crowds, however, and she offered them her house as a centre. Subsequently she built chapels all over England for the Methodists – as they came to be called – who were finally expelled from the Church of England. Many of the buildings put up at her expense are still standing. When six Methodist students were expelled from Oxford in 1768 for being 'too religious' she founded a training college for them (and others) in South Wales (since transferred to Cheshunt, Cambridge). A committed benefactress, she donated £100,000 to the sect.

St Joan at the stake in the market-place at Rouen. A late fifteenth-century French manuscript.

Anne Hutchinson
American (1591–1643)

Anne Hutchinson had the courage to defend the claims of individuals, including women, to communicate directly with God. By doing so, she offended the Puritans of Massachusetts and was banished from their community.

Anne Marbury was the daughter of a clergyman in Lincolnshire, England, and married William Hutchinson, a merchant, in 1612. In 1634 they went with their children to America and settled in Boston. There, Anne Hutchinson started weekly meetings of women to discuss the sermons they heard, meetings which became so popular that men were soon attending them. She gradually developed – and expressed – the view that believers could be saved by faith alone, a view not shared by the Puritan hierarchy. She was eventually banished from the community – or 'delivered up to Satan' in the words of the community leaders. In 1638 she and her family and a few followers moved to Rhode Island – the first people to settle there – and later, after her husband's death in 1642, to Long Island Sound. In 1643 she and all but one of her children were killed by Indians.

St Joan of Arc
French (1412–1431)

Joan of Arc had a brief, dramatic life as a warrior and king-maker which would have been totally astonishing even for a young man of her age and background. She was 19 when she was burned at the stake but in fact her active life was over when she was barely 18. By then she had halted the English for good in their attempts to conquer the whole of France, and had personally escorted Charles VII to conquer enemy-occupied Rheims. There she had supervised his coronation according to the ancient rites of France – 'thus showing that you are true king, and he to whom the Kingdom of France shall belong.'

Even that is not all. Joan's voices, her assumption of masculine dress, her famous 60-foot jump from her prison window at Beaurevoir, her trial, are all powerful components of her continuing hold on the imagination of posterity.

She was born at Domrémy in eastern France into a family of well-to-do peasants during the Anglo-French 100 Years War. She grew up immensely capable and sensible, but never learnt to read. At the age of 13 she began hearing voices which told her that she would go to the aid of the King of France in his fight against the English, and would raise the siege of Orléans. When she was 16 she went to the local army captain and, such was her belief in her mission, eventually persuaded him to send her with an escort to the Dauphin (the future Charles VII). She soon persuaded the Dauphin, too, of her divinely ordained mission, and, wearing a suit of armour and accompanied by a 'household', she joined the army which was to relieve Orléans. Joan's reputation had gone before her, and her presence and leadership undoubtedly invigorated the French troops. The siege of Orléans was duly raised, and the English army was defeated in the summer of 1429.

On 16 July Charles entered Rheims, and the following day he was crowned king, with Joan at his side, holding – alone of all those present – her personal banner: 'It had borne the burden', she later told her accusers, 'and it was right that it should have the honour'. Her mission was over, and she was still only 17. Thereafter Joan's luck gradually gave out. She failed to seize Paris, and she was captured at Compiègne in May 1430.

Early in 1431 the English put her on trial for heresy and witchcraft. After a spirited defence she was put to death in the market place on 30 May. Charles VII had made no attempt to rescue her. In the 1450s, the evidence was examined again, in a trial of rehabilitation; together with the record of the original trial, it makes her life the best-documented of the fifteenth century. But the essential mystery of her personality remains. Joan's achievement has been recreated dozens of times in novels and plays, of which perhaps the best-known are Shaw's *St Joan* and Anouilh's *L'Alouette*. She was canonized in 1920, and is the second patron saint of France.

Julian of Norwich
British (c. 1342–1414)

The mystic known as Julian of Norwich was the first English woman of letters; she was the author of *Revelations of Divine Love*. (Julian was not then an uncommon name for girls.) Little is known of her life but she may have been the widow of Roger Haubayn, who was killed in a duel. On his death Julian appears to have retired into a tiny cell attached to a church at Conisford, near Norwich. At the age of 30 she was severely ill and nearly died. When the curate held the crucifix out to her, she had the first of a series of visions; 'All that was beside the cross was of horror to me as if it had been greatly occupied by the fiends,' she wrote, 'I saw red blood trickle down from under the garland [the crown of thorns] hot and freshly and right plenteously.'

Gloom and sloth were the enemies of the solitary life, she said, and made her companions laugh at her visions of Christ triumphing over 'malice'. Cheerful and devout, Julian believed in simplicity: 'I understood no higher stature in this life than childhood.' She hoped to encourage a franker, more straightforward religious attitude. 'For our Lord Himself is sovereign homeliness, and as homely as He is, so courteous He is. It is the most worship to Him of anything that we do, that we live gladly and merrily,' she wrote. 'All shall be well and all shall be well and all manner of thing shall be well.'

She also wrote: 'As truly as God is our father, so just as truly is he our mother,' and compared God's love to that of a mother – even referring to 'our beloved mother Jesus' – a text that has been taken up by Britain's movement for the ordination of women.

Margery Kempe
British (1373–1438)

A mystic like Julian of Norwich (q.v.) and the second English woman of letters, Margery Kempe was the author of *The Book of Margery Kempe* – partly a description of her visions, partly a lively account of her life and many travels – which is the earliest known English autobiography.

Margery Brunham was the daughter of John Brunham, mayor of King's Lynn, Norfolk. She married John Kempe and had several children; the family traded as brewers and millers. Margery Kempe's visions caused people to suspect her of heresy, but her husband was a great support and accompanied her on several pilgrimages round England. In 1413 she went on a two-year pilgrimage to the Holy Land. An indefatigable traveller, Kempe also went to Compostella in Spain, and just before her death to Norway and Danzig. She dictated her memoirs to a priest, and the only known copy did not emerge from obscurity until 1934.

Komyo
Japanese (701–760)

Many of the famous temples of the Buddhist city of Nara, an early capital of Japan, were originally founded by Komyo, wife of the Emperor Shomu, who reigned from 724 until he abdicated in 749 in

Todaiji, Daibutsu-den, one of the temples at Nara founded by Komyo in the eighth century.

favour of his daughter, their only surviving child. Komyo was herself a native of Nara, a member of the powerful Fujiwara family, and a devout Buddhist. She used her position to urge the Emperor to establish temples and nunneries all over Japan. In Nara she founded charitable institutions to help the sick and starving, where she encouraged the use of Chinese medicine rather than the charms and talismans hitherto relied on, and personally washed – it is said – a thousand poor people. After the Emperor's death in AD 756, Komyo is believed to have ruled on behalf of her daughter, the Empress Koken.

Ann Lee
British (1736–1784)

'Mother Ann' brought the fervent beliefs of a breakaway Quaker sect across the Atlantic and founded the community of Shakers. She was the daughter of an illiterate blacksmith in Manchester, England, and as a girl worked in the Lancashire cotton mills. She was unable to read or write, but became an ardent follower and then leading spirit of the 'United Society of Believers in Christ's Second Appearing'. In 1762 she married Abraham Stanley, a blacksmith, and had four children, all of whom died in infancy. Believing she was guilty of their deaths, she denied herself food and sleep, and thereafter had frequent visions. Her fervour was such that in 1770 she was locked up. While in prison she saw in a vision that God was both male and female, whereupon she was elected 'Mother in spiritual things'. A further revelation in 1774 'instructed' her to take the group to America.

Once in New York, Lee earned her living as a washerwoman for two years, and then moved with her group to Watervliet near Albany, New York State. Within a few years the Shakers numbered several thousand.

Lee believed that she was the female Christ, and after her death her followers believed she was still among them. She ordained community of property, the duty of labour, the equality of men and women, and celibacy. The Shakers were to perpetuate themselves by conversion and adoption. Ten communities were founded – one of which survived into the twentieth century. They remained strictly attached to a pre-industrial way of life.

St Louise de Marillac
French (1591–1660)

One of a remarkable generation of Frenchwomen which included Mère Angélique and Mère Marie Guyart (qq.v.), Louise de Marillac was, unlike them, a lay woman, and the co-founder with St Vincent de Paul of what is still the largest lay order of the Roman Catholic Church, the Sisters of Charity.

She was the daughter of Louis de Marillac, a member of the French Parlement, and in 1613 married Antoine le Gras, *Secrétaire des Commandements* at the court of Queen Marie de Médici, wife of Henri IV. After her husband's death in 1625 she

joined St Vincent in his work of nursing the sick and feeding the poor. When they founded the Sisters of Charity in 1633, it was left to 'Mademoiselle Le Gras' to train the applicants, draw up their rule of life, and administer the affairs of the rapidly growing order. St Vincent de Paul wrote: 'Your convent is the home of the sick ... your chapel the parish church, your cloister the streets of the city.' In 1638 abandoned children – whose numbers probably ran into tens of thousands annually – began to be cared for.

In spite of poor health, Louise spent much of her time touring France visiting the various foundations, and by the time she died there were more than 40 houses. Many of her female aristocratic contemporaries also devoted their lives to good works; it was clear, as she herself wrote, 'that in this century Divine Providence has been pleased to make use of the female sex to help the afflicted'. Louise was canonized in 1934.

St Radegund
French (518–587)

Radegund, the daughter and wife of kings, managed to lead a life of exemplary piety in an age as violent as any in the history of Europe. She founded the monastery of the Holy Cross at Poitiers for some 200 nuns, and was its first abbess.

She was born at Erfurt, daughter of King Berthar of Thuringia; when she was 12 the Thuringians were defeated by the Franks, and she was brought up in the Frankish court, which was only nominally Christian. Radegund was obliged to marry the Frankish King Clotaire, whose cruelty and viciousness were legendary. When, after several years of childless marriage, Clotaire murdered her brother, Queen Radegund left him and took the veil, then the only way of escape for women.

Radegund founded a monastery which became a centre of learning. The chaplain was the poet Fortunatus, whose writings reveal her holy character: 'She led always an austere life, as far as her health permitted, sleeping on ashes and wearing a hair-shirt, rising to chant hymns before the community was up. In the work of the monastery she was never content unless she was the first to give her service. . . . Who shall tell the zeal with which she hastened to the kitchen when her week came round? . . . Human eloquence is struck almost dumb by the piety, self-denial, charity, sweetness, humility, uprightness, faith, and fervour in which she lived.' After her death miracles were reported at her tomb.

Elizabeth von Schönau
German (1129–1164)

Elizabeth von Schönau was the author of several powerful mystical writings which were widely read in the Middle Ages, notably *Visions* and a *Liberarium Dei*. She was brought up in a convent and became a nun in 1152. Soon afterwards she had visions of St Ursula and the 11,000 virgins martyred with her in Cologne on their way back from a pilgrimage to Rome. Her voices were said to come to her in many different languages, which her brother Egbert transcribed into Latin.

Despite ill health, von Schönau founded a convent which flourished until the seventeenth century.

Elizabeth Seton
American (1774–1821)

Elizabeth Seton was the first American saint. Her father was the first health officer of New York, and Elizabeth Bayley was brought up a devout Episcopalian. In 1794 she married William Seton, a wealthy merchant, and had five children. A visit to Italy in 1802 – during which her husband died – prompted her conversion to the Roman Catholic faith. In 1809 she took her vows and started a convent devoted to the poor in Emitsburg, near Baltimore. She also founded parish schools. Seton was canonized in 1975 for her strenuous efforts to combat mat-materialism.

Mary Slessor
British (1848–1915)

Mary Slessor was one of Protestantism's great missionaries – so close to her African charges that they called her Ma Akamba, the 'Great Mother'.

She was born into a poor family in Aberdeen, Scotland, went to school briefly and became a 'half-timer' in a factory at the age of 11. She worked ten hours a day at a loom yet managed to read as she did so. Determined to spread the Gospel, Mary Slessor finally set sail for West Africa in 1876 on a boat loaded with 'scores of casks [of alcohol] and only one missionary'. Uneasy in the main mission station at Calabar, Mary begged to be allowed to live alone up-river, among the Africans she had come to serve.

Once there, she set her face against all superstitious practices, especially the custom of crushing new-born twins into jars as objects of horror. She joined the village council as one of the men, and made a home for the many twin babies she rescued. She was one of the few Europeans approved of by **Mary Kingsley** (q.v.) for her courage and her practical view of the role of traders in Africa. Mary Slessor was forced to return home in 1883 because of ill-health, but soon returned to her hut on the Ohoyong River, where she remained for the rest of her life. 'I am ready', she used to say, 'to go anywhere provided it be forward'.

Mother Teresa
Yugoslavian (b. 1910)

In 1979 the Nobel Peace Prize was awarded to Mother Teresa, the Roman Catholic nun who has devoted her life to the care of the destitute and dying in the Calcutta slums.

Born Agnes Gouxha Bejaxhu, her parents were Albanian peasants living in Yugoslavia. She became a nun in 1927 and was sent to the sisters of Loreto Abbey, Rathfarnham, near Dublin, in 1928. She particularly wanted to go to India after reading letters from Jesuits working in the Bengal Mission in Calcutta, and after teaching for nearly 20 years there she was made head of a girls' school in Calcutta and put in charge of the Daughters of St Anne, the sisterhood attached to the school. One day, while travelling in a tram, she heard the voice of God tell her that she must devote herself to the people in the slums and in 1948, with only a few months' medical training behind her, she left the convent and together

Mother Teresa receiving the Nobel Peace Prize in May 1980.

with two other nuns, set about caring for the sick and poor in the streets of Calcutta. As Mother Teresa once said, 'The biggest disease today is not leprosy or tuberculosis, but rather the feeling of being unwanted, uncared for, deserted by everybody.' In 1950 she opened a Mother House of the Missionary Sisters of Charity and in 1970 a novitiate for Europeans and Americans. The Order now has over a thousand sisters and brothers with Homes all over the world.

St Teresa of Avila
Spanish (1515–1582)

Like many of the greatest saints, St Teresa combined a deeply mystical nature with great practical sense. She was the author of one of the greatest mystical works, *The Interior Castle*, and founded more than 20 religious houses. She braved both the Inquisition and house arrest to reform the Carmelite order.

St Teresa was born Teresa de Cepeda y Ahumada in a large family of the minor nobility in Avila. At 16 she was sent to be educated in an Augustinian convent

and two years later, much to her father's displeasure for she was his favourite daughter, she joined the local Carmelite nuns, initially more 'in fear of hell', as she later said, than for love of God. Significantly, for she was often in great physical pain, her religious vocation came to her during an illness. Over the next three years she was almost paralysed by illness until St Joseph, she believed, cured her. Thereafter she devoted herself to learning the joy of prayer.

In 1556 Teresa experienced the Mystical Betrothal – an almost intoxicating sense of the presence of Jesus: 'Oh what torment it is in this state to have to return to the company of men.' She levitated at mass and had to hang on to the altar rails in her efforts to hide the fact. 'I am only fit for talk', she once beseeched God, 'you have not been willing to put me to the test by deeds'.

The action that she craved came in middle age with a divine command to reform the Carmelites, who had become increasingly lax. Teresa moved to a tiny house in Avila with four other nuns to celebrate their first mass as 'Barefoot Carmelites' in 1562; they slept on straw, ate no meat and lived on alms. Although bitterly opposed by the Church, the group flourished; the sisters' only anxiety being if their Mother Superior went into a trance while cooking the food they got from begging.

St Teresa wrote her *Life; The Way of Perfection* which was written at the request of her superiors to instruct her nuns, and was never intended for publication; the *Book of Foundations*, which was the story of her reforms; and finally *The Interior Castle*, for which the Roman Catholic Church has recently made her a doctor of the spiritual life. She was also an exceptional and prolific letter writer, and her gaiety, good sense and candour make her one of the most attractive of all saints.

Between 1568 and 1580 she founded 17 convents and four monasteries in the face of continual opposition from the Church (she was even under arrest from 1577 to 1579) and in spite of increasingly poor health St Teresa supervised her religious houses untiringly, until she died. In 1622 she was canonized by Pope Gregory XV in recognition of her asceticism and for the visions which gave her such strength and joy.

The mystic St Teresa of Avila, author of The Interior Castle. *She was canonized in 1622.*

Simone Weil
French (1909–1943)

'Sergeant-Major Angel', as her brother André called Simone Weil, was a writer, philosopher and mystic. She was the daughter of free-thinking Jewish parents and even as a child her moral authority was marked. All her life she showed a profound sympathy for the poor and the afflicted, which at times seemed almost an inclination to become one of them.

Both she and her brother were exceptionally clever – each took the *baccalauréat* at 14 – and Simone went on to study philosophy under the great teacher Alain at the Ecole Normale. When she later became a teacher, at the higher salary her qualifications entitled her to, she deliberately chose not to spend the amount by which it exceeded an ordinary schoolteacher's salary. She never stayed long in any one school as her natural intransigence, her extra-curricular trade union activities and left-wing writings tended to cause disagreement with school authorities. For a year she worked as a power press operator in the Renault factory outside Paris. 'I received forever the mark of a slave', she wrote of the experience. 'Even today, when any human being speaks to me without brutality, I cannot help having the impression that there must be a mistake.' Later she worked as a farm labourer on a farm near Marseilles. She also joined the Republicans in the Spanish Civil War, but her life as a soldier did not last long either, and she returned to France soon after.

Weil never ceased to think and study. Friendship with a priest, her first mystical experience of the presence of Christ in her thirtieth year, and a poem, *Love*, by the seventeenth-century religious poet George Herbert, brought her to the brink of conversion to Christianity. But the Church itself always proved an obstacle.

In 1941 her parents persuaded her to leave Vichy France with them for New York, to escape the German occupation and the Nazi persecution of the Jews, but Weil's longing to be more active soon brought her back to Europe to serve with the Free French in London. There she drove herself to work so relentlessly, denying herself any food but the minimum available at that time in Occupied France, that she contracted tuberculosis, which proved fatal. Most of her work was published after her death – most notably *Waiting for God* (1951) and *The Need for Roots* (1952). Weil is now recognized as one of the most important religious philosophers of the twentieth century.

Simone de Beauvoir photographed in 1978

THE WRITTEN WORD

WHEN CHARLOTTE BRONTË, some ten years before the publication of *Jane Eyre*, sent some of her poems to the poet Robert Southey for an opinion, he replied: 'Literature cannot be the business of a woman's life, and it ought not to be. The more she is engaged in her proper duties, the less leisure she will have for it . . . To these duties you have not been called and when you are you will be less eager for celebrity.' Charlotte Brontë thanked Southey for the 'wise and friendly tone' of his letter but fortunately did not act on his advice.

The nineteenth century was the great age of the novel, and women writers such as the Brontës, Jane Austen, George Eliot, Harriet Beecher Stowe, Kate Chopin and George Sand shared in that achievement. Indeed, women writers have played a key role in the historical development of the novel. In mediaeval Japan, the Lady Murasaki was the author of the world's earliest surviving full-length novel, while the earliest exponents of the 'psychological' novel in seventeenth-century France were also women – Madeleine de Scudéry and Marie de La Fayette. Mary Shelley created *Frankenstein*, the first science fiction novel, and Agatha Christie has proved supreme in the detective puzzle. Women writers have also been major contributors in the area of children's fiction, from Louisa May Alcott, author of *Little Women*, to Beatrix Potter and Enid Blyton. There have been fewer women poets, but the genius of such poets as Sappho, whom the Greeks called the tenth muse, Emily Dickinson, Sylvia Plath and Anna Akhmatova have done much to restore the balance. Women have undoubtedly been more active in the field of literature than in almost any other sphere. But how many aspiring women authors, lacking the necessary courage of their convictions, have been silenced by the Southeys of their world?

The 'Voice of Russia', Anna Akhmatova, photographed in her study.

Anna Akhmatova
Russian (1889–1966)

The greatest poet of her day lived through the horrors of Stalin's Russia and became known as the Voice of Russia. Anna Akhmatova trained as a lawyer and married the poet Nikolai Gumilev; in 1912 she had a son, Lev. When her husband left her she began to write herself. Although her marriage ended in divorce in 1918, her former husband's execution as a spy in 1921 put her and her son in disgrace with Russia's new Communist government. However, she decided that it was her 'mission to endure and bear witness' instead of leaving for Western Europe. She published another book of poems in 1922, but her work was banned and she was only able to do translations for many years. She was exiled to the Black Sea. Both her son and her lover, Punin, were arrested during the Great Purge in 1935,

but in 1937 she wrote a long poem in tribute to Boris Pasternak, which showed that great poetry can be written even in disaster. When the Second World War broke out her son was sent into the army and she was allowed to publish again. She was greeted by a standing ovation at a reading in Moscow in 1944. Thereafter two secret service men followed her everywhere, and she was denounced as a mixture of a 'nun and a whore'. In 1949 her son was re-arrested and, in order not to incriminate him, she burnt all her papers, including a play about a woman poet on trial. After Stalin's death in 1953 she could publish once again – having kept Russian speech 'pure and free' and having borne witness through times of terror.

Louisa May Alcott
American (1832–1888)

Louisa May Alcott was the author of *Little Women* and its sequels, best-loved of all American family sagas. She was born in Boston, Massachusetts, second daughter of a high-minded, impractical teacher, Bronson Alcott, and his wife Abba. Bronson Alcott's school failed in 1840 when the family went to live near Concord in the Massachusetts countryside. The girls' education was more moral and practical than academic: both parents would write letters to them about their behaviour, leaving them round the house to be read and re-read at leisure. Always a scribbler and play-writer, Louisa kept an 'imagination book' as a child, and when she grew up she began selling her stories. Although very poor because of Mr Alcott's inability to provide, the family shared what they had with waifs and strays. Louisa and her sister taught and sewed for a living; in 1852 Louisa even took a domestic job, which she hated.

When the Civil War broke out she volunteered as a army nurse; but she became ill and depressed and the calomel used to cure her eventually poisoned her system. In 1863 the publication of *Hospital Sketches* increased her reputation as a writer and encouraged her to publish *Moods*, which she had written some time before. Left to herself with no parents to support, she would have preferred to concentrate on

Louisa May Alcott, author of Little Women.

that kind of lurid, introspective story. But her drive to make the family 'cosy' resulted in her being tied to the immensely successful *Little Women* sequence from 1868 onwards.

Little Women was begun after she had come back from Europe as a paid companion. The story of that family of girls and their 'Marmee' was written so effortlessly that the author thought it must be dull. On the contrary, it was so popular that a further seven volumes were requested and duly appeared over the next ten years. Alcott's last years were plagued by ill-health, and she died only a few days after her father.

Sibilla Aleramo
Italian (1876–1966)

Sibilla Aleramo was the author of a novel, *Una Donna*, which scandalized Italy in 1906. It was a semi-autobiographical account of a woman who had left her husband and child, like Nora in Ibsen's *A Doll's House*.

Rina Pierangeli Faccio was born in Northern Italy and brought up in a remote, provincial town on the Adriatic. One of her father's factory employees seduced her when she was 15; she married him, only to find herself, at 16, trapped with a baby in a narrow-minded and superstitious family. Somehow, however, she managed to educate herself by wide and enterprising reading.

By the time she was 24 Aleramo had published articles and short stories and even edited a magazine. At 26 she finally struck out for an independent life, leaving her much-loved son behind. She wrote and taught, and worked in medical centres on working-class housing estates in Rome. *Una Donna (A Woman)* was published in 1906. It was her most successful work and was translated into several languages, an encouragement to the then emerging 'New Woman' everywhere. She had to accommodate herself to various Italian regimes during her long life, but remained a feminist and socialist.

Hannah Arendt
German (1906–1975)

Hannah Arendt was one of the most powerful and controversial political philosophers of the twentieth century. She was born of Jewish parents in Germany. In 1933 she fled to Paris where she took up social work for Jewish youth for four years before she had to flee again, this time to New York. While working as an editor she wrote *The Origins of Totalitarianism* (1951), which argues that Nazism and Communism both derive from nineteenth-century anti-Semitism and Imperialism. She made the launching of an 'earth-born satellite' in 1957 the occasion for serious consideration of the human condition, declaring that scientists 'did not understand that once those weapons are developed, they would be the last to be consulted about their use ... speech has lost its power.' Arendt was sent to Israel by the *New Yorker* to cover the trial of Eichmann, and in *Eichmann in Jerusalem* (1963) she expressed the view that hounding individuals was worse than useless and that totalitarian states were

German philosopher and author Hannah Arendt, photographed in 1963.

German family and educated in a convent. She married a fellow writer and poet, and had seven children. She published another exchange of letters, this time with a woman poet, called *Gunderode*. After the death of her husband, her house became a centre for music and intellectual conversation. In 1848, a year of revolution in Europe, she wrote a *Letter to the King* (Frederick William IV of Prussia) in favour of such liberal ideas as human rights, the emancipation of the Jews, and the repeal of capital punishment.

Mary Astell
British (1668–1731)

Mary Astell was one of the first women in England to suggest that her sex ought to be educated. She tried to found a college for women two centuries before the foundation of Girton College (cf. Emily Davies).

She was the daughter of a Newcastle merchant and so clever that her clergyman uncle decided to tutor her in French, Latin, logic, philosophy and mathematics. At 20 she left for London to continue her studies. Astell's *Serious Proposal to the Ladies, for the Advancement of True and Greatest Interest* was published in 1696. It was welcomed enthusiastically by an anonymous rich woman (possibly Queen Anne) who was prepared to donate £10,000 for the foundation of 'a seminary, or college for the education of young women.' The scheme however was opposed by such leading Church figures as Bishop Burnett, who felt that an institution so like a (Popish) convent would reflect 'scandal on the Reformation'. Thwarted in her chief ambition Astell nevertheless went on studying science and the classics and became celebrated as a learned woman. If people interrupted her when she was working she would put her head out of the window and say, 'Mrs Astell is not at home.'

Although she never married, she wrote on the position of wives in *Reflections on Marriage* in 1700. In 1704 she published an article defending the memory of the 'Royal martyr', King Charles I. She became very severe and rigid in her habits as she grew older. Astell braved a mastectomy without a murmur before she died, probably of cancer.

guilty of a pervasive 'banality of evil' that colours all moral thought. She was the first woman to become a full professor at Princeton University and left at her death a three-volume *Life of the Mind* to be edited by her friend Mary McCarthy (q.v.).

Bettina von Arnim
German (1785–1859)

Bettina von Arnim was only 12 when she fell in love with the poet Goethe, then 60, and began writing to him the passionate letters for which she became famous. No one knows how Goethe responded to her highly romantic letters, but she published *Goethe's Correspondence with a Child* in 1835 after both the poet and her own husband had died.

Bettina von Brentano was born into a noble

Jane Austen
British (1775–1817)

No books in the English language can have given so much pleasure as Jane Austen's six novels. 'Two or three families in a country village', in her own words, supplied her with enough material to display all the workings of the human heart.

Jane Austen was the second youngest of a family of five brothers and two sisters born to a country clergyman, George Austen, and his wife, Cassandra Leigh. The family grew up happily in Hampshire. When she was 22 her father sent off her first novel, *First Impressions*, to a publisher with the claim that it 'was much the same length' as *Evelina* (cf. Fanny Burney), which had recently enjoyed great success. The publisher turned it down, although it later became her most-loved book, *Pride and Prejudice*.

In 1801 the Austens moved with their two daughters to Bath, which provided Jane with a wider experience of the comfortable upper-middle-class world. At Bath and London were the great centres for meeting suitable marriage partners. Neither sister ever married although Jane seems twice to have considered doing so. Her sister Cassandra was her lifelong confidante and friend. Jane disliked Bath as noisy and distracting and she therefore wrote little during their five year stay. When George Austen died in 1805, the family returned to Hampshire.

Back in her beloved countryside at Chawton, Jane Austen at least had the leisure to write. She worked in a room with a squeaky door, which meant that she had time to hide what she was doing when anyone approached. Early in 1811 *Sense and Sensibility* was published, followed by *Pride and Prejudice* ('my darling child'), in 1813. *Mansfield Park* (1814) her third novel, made Austen famous; so much so that the Prince Regent asked that her next book, which was *Emma* (1815), be dedicated to him. *Persuasion* (1818), her last novel, has a melancholy quality that almost suggests that she was aware of the onset of Addison's disease, which killed her at the age of 41. Along with the earlier *Northanger Abbey* (1818), it was published only after her death. Brave, self-controlled and witty, she was the embodiment in life of all the qualities she most admired in her characters.

Joanna Baillie
British (1762–1851)

Joanna Baillie was a poet and dramatist much admired in her day. After the death of her father, a professor of Divinity at Glasgow University, she and her sister moved to London to join their brother, a successful doctor. Baillie wrote rather conventional poems, but they earned her a great reputation. Their success encouraged her to write a series of plays intended to show the 'passions of the human mind'. Her play in the Gothic style, *De Montford*, was very popular and played to packed houses with Fanny Kemble and Mrs Siddons (qq.v.) in the leading parts. She and her sister never married, but for the rest of her long life it was the fashion in literary circles to call on her in her cottage in Hampstead.

Marie Bashkirtseff
Russian (1859–1884)

Marie Bashkirtseff was a brilliant and ambitious girl who achieved work of considerable distinction in her short life. She was the daughter of a Russian landowner, but when she was 11 her mother left him, taking her son and daughter with her to Nice on the French Riviera. Here Marie started her famous *Journals of Marie Bashkirtseff*; written in a mixture of French, Russian and English, the young girl's writings revealed a passionate if untutored adolescent. The *Journals* were published posthumously in 1889. The British Prime Minister Gladstone rightly claimed an 'audacious sincerity' for them.

Bashkirtseff also had aspirations as a singer and a painter. When tuberculosis put an end to her hopes as a singer, she went to the Académie Julien in Paris and became an extremely promising painter, although hampered by the inevitable restrictions due to her sex. Despite an active social life she produced much good work before her early death. Nearly a hundred paintings and numerous other works were given to the Russian Museum at St Petersburg and three of her paintings hang in the Musée de l'Art Moderne in Paris. The feverish activity characteristic of consumptives filled the 84 volumes of diaries, not all of them published even now. Bashkirtseff insisted on dying in a drawing-room draped with white silks and furs: 'I shall find something gay and delightful even in death.'

Simone de Beauvoir
French (b. 1908)

De Beauvoir's *The Second Sex* (1949), the most comprehensive and far-reaching study of women of modern times, is virtually the bible of the modern women's movement.

Simone de Beauvoir describes in the first volume of her autobiography, *A Dutiful Daughter* (1959), her rigid bourgeois upbringing in Paris. In the philosophy examinations at the Sorbonne in 1929 she came second only to the existentialist philosopher, Jean-Paul Sartre, who was to become her companion for life. They never married, on principle, but were united in their political views and shared a deep sense of the responsibility of the writer. Her professional life combined writing with philosophy. Her works include her first novel *L'Invitée (She Came to Stay)* (1943); *Les Mandarins (The Mandarins)* (1954), a semi-autobiographical novel about her love affair with the American novelist Nelson Algren; *The Long March* (1957), about China; besides essays on the question of women in society, *Brigitte Bardot and the Lolita Syndrome* and *Must We Burn de Sade?*; four volumes of autobiography (1958–74); and *A Very Easy Death* (1964), a moving account of her mother's long illness.

Along with many other well-known women, to help the cause of abortion law reform in France Simone de Beauvoir has admitted to having had an abortion, the abortion laws are one of many public issues in which she still plays an active part.

Aphra Behn
British (1640–1689)

Aphra Behn was the first woman in England to make a living by her pen. She wrote more than 20 successful plays during the Restoration period, and was much admired by the poet and playwright John Dryden.

Born in Kent, she went to Surinam, South America, with her parents and married a Dutchman in 1658, about whom little is known. When she came back to England she wrote a novel about a black prince of noble disposition, *Oroonoko*. Her tale of a 'noble savage' was translated into French and German and helped to awaken her readers to the horrors of slavery.

When her husband died Mrs Behn had very little money but, because of her knowledge of Dutch, Charles II sent her to Antwerp, Holland, as a spy. She found out that the Dutch planned to sail up the Thames and set fire to the English fleet – which they did in 1667. But she received neither credit nor money for her information; instead she was thrown into jail for debt. She only managed to discharge her debts and get out of prison by writing for the stage. Some of Behn's plays antedate modern feminism; *The Rover* (1688) concerns an adventurous woman very like Nell Gwynn, Charles II's mistress, and *The Forced Marriage* (1670) is an attack on a common social evil. The Victorians thought her coarse and unwomanly, and the most successful woman playwright of the English stage is only now receiving the recognition which is her due.

Elizabeth Bishop
American (1911–1979)

Elizabeth Bishop is widely regarded as one of this century's great poets in spite of her quiet style and small output. She was the daughter of a builder who died the year she was born and of a mother who went mad. She was brought up by grandparents in Nova Scotia, and went to Vassar College. Thereafter she lived partly in Brazil, partly in California. Her first book of poems, *North and South* (1946), expresses the pull she felt between hot and cold climates, the puritanical and the abandoned in temperament, tensions manifest in all her writing. In 1956 she published Alice Brent's fictional *Diary of Helen Morley*, an account of a very young girl growing up in South America at the end of the last century, which she translated from the Portuguese. She also published short stories in the *New Yorker*. Bishop taught

Nellie Bly in 1890. Her round-the-world trip took 72 days, 6 hours and 11 minutes.

when in 1890 she went round the world by boat, train and horse in just over 72 days, thus beating the fictional record set by Phileas Fogg in Jules Verne's *Around the World in Eighty Days.*

'Nellie Bly' was born in Cochrane's Mills, Pennsylvania, and got a job on the *Pittsburgh Dispatch* when she wrote a furious letter complaining about an editorial that claimed that women were good for little but housework. She covered social questions such as divorce, slum life, and conditions in Mexico for the paper. In 1887 she moved to Joseph Pulitzer's *New York World,* for which she exposed the conditions in which the insane lived by pretending to be mad and getting herself committed to the asylum on Blackwell's Island. She also investigated sweatshops, tenements, the world of petty crime and a *corps de ballet* by the same methods.

The high point in her life, however, was the round-the-world trip, which she made in 72 days, 6 hours, 11 minutes and 14 seconds. Joseph Pulitzer sent a special train to meet her on her return to San Francisco, and she was greeted by fireworks, gun salutes, brass bands and a parade on Broadway.

In 1895 Nellie Bly married a millionaire, Robert Seaman, 50 years older than herself, and retired. She lost most of his money after he died and in 1919 tried unsuccessfully to make a comeback.

and lectured as well, although she said she was 'opposed to making poetry monstrous or boring and proceeding to talk the very life out of it.' She drew images from nature, describing the sea as 'What we imagine knowledge to be/Dark, salt, clear, moving, utterly free/drawn from the hard cold mouth of the world.' *Geography II* (1976) was her last work.

Nellie Bly
American (1865?–1922)

One of the most adventurous journalists in nineteenth-century America was Elizabeth Cochrane Seaman, who adopted the name Nellie Bly from the Stephen Foster song. She became world-famous

Enid Blyton
British (1897–1968)

The creator of Noddy, the Famous Five and Mr Plod, Enid Blyton is the most successful, in terms of sales, of all British writers for children. Her books have been loved by generations of children but are despised by many literary critics and librarians who feel that her characters are unimaginative and commonplace. Children, however, like the stories for their very ordinariness and predictability; their plainness also makes them easy for beginners to read. Enid Blyton is the most frequently translated British writer after Agatha Christie (q.v.) and Shakespeare – her books have been translated into 165 languages.

Blyton had a suburban childhood near London and won a prize for children's poetry in 1912. She became a kindergarten teacher in 1915. She published her first story in 1920 and began to contribute stories and poems to magazines. She was married twice, first in 1924 to Hugh Pollock, by whom she had two daughters, then in 1943 to Kenneth Darrell Walters. She once said, 'My hands go down on the typewriter and I begin.' She produced 400 books over a period of 30 years.

Anne Bradstreet
British (1612–1672)

America's first woman poet was born in England, the daughter of a Puritan, Thomas Dudley. Anne educated herself by reading in a local landowner's library. She was 18, and already married, when the whole family sailed to Massachusetts where her father served four terms as governor.

Bradstreet was always determined to write: 'I am obnoxious to each carping tongue/ Who says my hand a needle better fits.' Although life was far from easy for the early settlers and she had eight children to care for, a collection of her poems was published in 1650 as *The Tenth Muse Lately Sprung up in America*. Her poetry is treasured for the charming, if submissive, pictures it gives of her happy marriage and New England home. At an early stage she seems to have opted for domesticity, for she asks in one poem for a 'Thyme or Parsley wreath' as her reward, not 'bays'.

Anne Brontë
British (1820–1848)

Anne Brontë was the youngest of the extraordinary Brontë sisters (cf. Charlotte and Emily Brontë), co-author of *The Poems of Currer, Ellis and Acton Bell*, and author of two novels – *Agnes Grey* (1847), based on her unhappy experiences as a governess, and *The Tenant of Wildfell Hall* (1848), which includes drink, drugs, debauchery, adultery and a wife who runs away and earns her own living as an artist. Always considered the most delicate of the sisters, and much cosseted when young because of her asthma attacks, Anne Brontë none the less had the firmness of purpose to stick at the governess work she hated

for a total of nearly five years of her short life. She spent more than four years in North Yorkshire with the Robinson family, the last two accompanied by her brother Branwell, who was appointed tutor to the Robinsons' son. With her sister Emily she shared the horrors of coping with Branwell's disintegration into opium addiction and delirium.

Anne's novels, like those of her sisters, were vilified by reviewers at the time of publication, but *The Tenant of Wildfell Hall* was second only to *Jane Eyre* as a best-seller both in America and Britain. Since then Anne's achievements have been somewhat over-shadowed by her sisters' but she expressed more forcibly the injustices under which women laboured, tackled the issues of sex and marriage and the power of good and evil with a robust integrity and moral perception that are entirely her own. Her illness, apparently like Emily's precipitated by the death of Branwell, took longer to run its course, but she died no less heroically, with calm acceptance in spite of feeling she had 'lived to so little purpose'. Her last words to the grief-stricken Charlotte were 'Take courage, Charlotte, take courage.'

Charlotte Brontë
British (1816–1855)

Author of one of the greatest and most famous of all novels in the English language, *Jane Eyre* (1847), Charlotte Brontë was the third of six children born in Yorkshire, England, to the Reverend Patrick Brontë and his wife Maria Branwell. Her mother died when Charlotte was five, and her two much-loved elder sisters, Maria and Elizabeth, when she was nine. Their deaths, from consumption brought on by the harsh conditions and harsher discipline of the boarding school to which they were sent, were to be immortalized by Charlotte in *Jane Eyre*.

For the next five years the four surviving children – Charlotte, Branwell, Emily and Anne – were educated by their father, by their mother's sister Aunt Branwell, but above all by each other. The small, spartan parsonage on the edge of the moors at Haworth was a forcing-house for the most precocious family of children in the history of

Branwell Brontë's portrait of himself and his sisters, painted about 1834.
He later obliterated himself from the group.

literature. Allowed to read any newspaper, magazine or book that came to the house, they were steeped in the Romantic Movement – from the poems of Byron to the melodramatic engravings of John Martin. Inspired by such works, the young Brontës, unknown to their elders, spent their childhood and even their early adulthood writing and illustrating sagas about fantasy worlds of their own. These apprentice works, written in minute handwriting on tiny pages, were unsuspected until long after their deaths.

At 14 Charlotte went to Roe Head School, Mirfield, where she received her first formal education and for the first time made friends outside her family. At 25 she went for two years to the Pensionnat Héger in Brussels, where she fell deeply in love with Monsieur Héger, a married man who did not return her feelings. This experience, which marked her for life, was the inspiration of two of her four novels, and of her first adult poems.

Neither she nor her sisters thought of writing for a living at the outset of their adult lives. As young women they had a succession of unsuitable positions as teachers and governesses and made an abortive attempt to set up their own school. Charlotte and Emily spent longer and longer intervals at home, looking after their father and watching over the tragic collapse of their brother Branwell.

In late 1845 Charlotte discovered some poems written by Emily, and recognized their quality at once. The discovery prompted her to persuade her sisters that they should publish a collection of their poetry, which was eventually published pseudonymously (at Emily's insistence) as *Poems by Currer, Ellis and Acton Bell* in 1846. Only two copies were sold, but by that time all three sisters had completed novels: *Wuthering Heights* (Emily), *Agnes Grey* (Anne), and *The Professor* (Charlotte). The first two found a publisher, at the fifth attempt; *The Professor* was rejected, but the sixth publisher expressed interest in anything more suitable that Charlotte might write. *Jane Eyre*, which she had begun in 1846, was finished and sent to him within three weeks. The publisher read it in one sitting, and published it two months later, in October 1847 – and 'Currer Bell' was famous.

So, shortly, were 'Acton' and 'Ellis'; but within 18 months Emily and Anne were both dead of consumption, and Branwell was dead of drink and drugs. Charlotte herself wrote two more novels, *Shirley* (1849) and *Villette* (1853) (*The Professor* was published posthumously), and lived to enjoy a little of her success. In 1854, after an 18-month courtship, she married the Reverend Arthur Nicholls, who had been her father's curate since 1845, before she herself succumbed to consumption in March 1855.

Compared with Emily, Charlotte was a less talented poet (as she well knew); as a novelist, her gifts were of a totally different order, but she was Emily's equal. She also inspired one of the great English biographies, Elizabeth Gaskell's (q.v.) *Charlotte Brontë*.

Emily Brontë
British (1818–1847)

Emily Brontë (cf. Charlotte Brontë) was the author of some of the finest poems in the English language, and of one novel, *Wuthering Heights* – a masterpiece about love and hatred in the small, minor-gentry world of the Pennine moors, which caused a sensation when it appeared in 1847.

Very little is known of Emily Brontë's private life, because Charlotte – in deference to her sister's passion for secrecy – destroyed all her letters and papers after her death. She was profoundly attached to the moors round Haworth parsonage, and devoted to animals, particularly her dog Keeper. She hated being away from home, and, apart from six months at Roe Head and another six in Brussels, was virtually unschooled. Emily almost certainly had mystical experiences, but was also, like many mystics, very domesticated: she was an excellent cook and housekeeper, looked after the sisters' financial affairs, and would fetch her brother Branwell from the local pub during the terrible months when he was drinking himself to death.

Emily was immensely courageous: when she was dying of tuberculosis, she refused to see the doctor until the day she died, and on the last day, although desperately weak, she got up as usual and fed her animals.

Elizabeth Barrett Browning
British (1806–1861)

By the mid-nineteenth century, Elizabeth Barrett was even more famous as a poet than Robert Browning, her husband.

She was the daughter of a rich West Indian planter; her mother died young. She was brought up with her eight brothers in the countryside near Malvern. She was 'inconsolable for not being born a man' and read voraciously, including *A Vindication of the Rights of Woman* by Mary Wollstonecraft (q.v.) at the age of 12. At 15 she developed tuberculosis and had to stay in bed; she spent the time turning herself into an excellent classical scholar. Even so, she longed 'to exchange some of this lumbering, ponderous, helpless knowledge of books for some experience of life and man.' Her first book of poems was published before she was 20; but *Seraphim*, her next collection, did not appear for another 13 years, in 1838. By that time a decline in the family fortunes had taken the Barretts to the famous house in Wimpole Street.

Elizabeth Barrett, like other notable upper middle-class Victorians such as Charles Darwin, Florence Nightingale and Harriet Martineau (qq.v.), made a habit of being an invalid. She kept to her room for several years after her favourite brother was drowned, in 'a thoroughly morbid and desolate state'. On a rare sortie from home in search of her lapdog, Flush, she first saw for herself the untold misery of the London slums, which inspired her influential poem, *The Cry of the Children* (1843). In 1846 Robert Browning, having written her many letters and at last been invited for tea, persuaded her to defy her father and elope to Italy with him. Once there, they lived happily in Florence; their son, Pen, was born in 1849.

Elizabeth Barrett Browning wrote her popular *Sonnets from the Portuguese* soon after her marriage, although they were not published until 1850. In 1856 her longest and most important poem, *Aurora Leigh*, was published, an immensely popular verse novel about the choices open to women of her class and the debate between the rightness of developing one's talents or devoting oneself to the reform of social evils. 'Many at this hour are dying from want. Can we tell them to think of their souls?' she cried in

Elizabeth Barrett Browning: a painting by Michele Gordigiani, 1858.

anguish to Victorian England.

During her last years she became interested in spiritualism. She died, comparatively young, and was deeply mourned by Robert Browning whose long narrative poem, *The Ring and the Book* (1869), is a homage to their love.

Frances Hodgson Burnett
British (1849–1924)

Frances Hodgson Burnett was the author of one of the most popular children's books ever written: *Little Lord Fauntleroy*. She was born in Manchester but emigrated with her family to Tennessee when she was 16. She began to write stories for magazines, and travelled to England on the strength of their success. In 1873 she married Dr Swan Burnett in Tennessee and had a son, Vivian. Her first novels, *That Lass of*

Lowrie's (1877) and *Haworth's* (1879), used the Lancashire factory background she knew as a child; *Little Lord Fauntleroy* was published in 1886 and has never stopped selling despite its uncomfortable sentimentality. Her insight into a child's outlook on the world is the strength of *The Secret Garden* (1911), a much finer book about an invalid child.

Hodgson Burnett was a compulsive traveller. Her second husband was an English surgeon and writer, Stephen Townsend, and she finally settled in London.

Fanny Burney
British (1752–1840)

Fanny Burney was one of the most spirited of diarists and the first Englishwoman to write a novel. Her father was Dr Burney, a well-known musician. Fanny educated herself through her own reading in his library and by meeting the many actors and writers who came to their house in London. She was Dr Johnson's 'pet, his dear love, his little Burney'. When she was 14 her mother died and her father married again; her stepmother did not approve of her constant scribbling and made her burn all her papers on her fifteenth birthday. In an attempt to be 'good' she tried to stop but could not manage more than six days without writing: 'I cannot resist what I find to be irresistible, the pleasure of popping down my thoughts on paper.' She started her diary when she was 16 and continued it for more than 70 years. Burney's novel, *Evelina*, published in 1778, was based on an early work which had been destroyed. The tale of a young girl's adventures in society, it was an immediate success and a great encouragement to subsequent women writers, including Jane Austen (q.v.). Burney's dialogue was so good she was encouraged to write plays – although they were not very successful. Her second novel, *Cecilia*, was published in 1782 and she became quite a celebrity in London society. In 1785 she was made Keeper of the Robes to Queen Charlotte, wife of George III. The court circle was dull and strict in the extreme, according to Fanny's diary, and she was constantly tired and bored. After six years she retired with a pension of £100 a year.

Fanny Burney, the first Englishwoman to write a popular novel.

In 1793, when she was over 40, Fanny Burney married General d'Arblay, a refugee from the French Revolution. They had a son in 1797. Her next novel, *Camilla*, was published in 1796 and earned her the princely sum of £3,000. In 1808 the d'Arblays were able to go back to France, where the General died 10 years later. His widow returned to England for the rest of her long life – keeping up her diary to the end.

Jane Welsh Carlyle
British (1801–1866)

Jane Welsh Carlyle was one of the liveliest letter writers in the English language, and the wife of one of Britain's most distinguished historians, Thomas Carlyle. Her father was a doctor in Haddington, near

Jane Welsh Carlyle: a drawing by Samuel Laurence, 1838.

Elizabeth Carter: a painting by Thomas Lawrence.

Edinburgh. She first met Carlyle when her father provided her with a tutor who brought his friend to the house. Thomas Carlyle was an extremely clever, although impoverished young man. 'I married for ambition,' she later explained in her forthright way, 'Carlyle has exceeded all that my wildest hopes ever imagined of him, and I am miserable.' Married life was a torment of indigestion, insomnia and irritability for both of them, although Jane Carlyle did her best to protect her husband from noise and other interruptions: 'To be sure,' she wrote, 'if I were to leave you today for good and all, I should need absolutely to go back tomorrow to see how you were taking it.' She was an excellent hostess in their Chelsea house and their many friends included Guiseppe Mazzini, Charles Dickens and John Stuart Mill. Forced to countenance her husband's obsession

with Lady Ashburton, she remarked tartly, 'People who are so dreadfully devoted to their wives are so apt, from mere habit, to get devoted to other people's wives as well.' Clear, cool and honest, she spared nothing and no one in the hundreds of sparkling letters, spanning more than 30 years, that she wrote to her mother, her mother-in-law and her husband.

Elizabeth Carter
British (1717–1806)

Most famous of the English eighteenth-century 'blue stockings' was Elizabeth Carter – called 'Mrs' as a social courtesy according to the custom of the day, although in fact she never married. She was born in Deal, Kent, and educated by her clergyman father. She was so eager to learn Hebrew, French, German,

Italian, Spanish, Portuguese and Arabic that she would keep herself awake at night to study, by taking snuff and chewing green tea. In 1734 some of her poems were published in the *Gentleman's Magazine*. Well read in science, she translated Algarotti's *Sir Isaac Newton's Philosophy explained for the Use of the Ladies* in 1739. Her translation of *Epictetus* (1758) earned her the approval of Dr Johnson, Walpole and other men of letters.

Willa Cather
American (1873–1947)

Willa Cather was one of America's most distinguished novelists. A brave and independent spirit, she wrote about the struggle of creative individuals in isolated communities. Her longer novels were the first to chronicle the American South West and its religious and racial problems.

Cather was born on a farm in Virginia but grew up in Nebraska. Impatient of convention, she cut her hair short and called herself William when she was a student at the University of Nebraska. In 1895 she became a journalist on the *Daily Reader* in Pittsburgh but turned to teaching in 1901 in order to have more time for writing. A book of her poems was published in 1903 and a collection of short stories in 1905; she became an editor of *McClure's* magazine in 1906. Cather lived with other women, from choice; 'She filled the whole space between door and window to brimming, as a man might do,' was how one friend described her. A compassionate writer, she sided with the misunderstood in narrow-minded, small communities; but her range was considerably wider in her best seller *Death Comes for the Archbishop* (1927), a novel about two priests in the South Western States of America. Her many other novels include *O Pioneers* (1913), *My Antonia* (1918) and *One of Ours* (1922).

Kate Chopin
American (1850–1904)

It has taken more than half a century for Kate Chopin to be valued at her real worth. The author of *The*

Awakening was born of an Irish father and a French-speaking Creole mother in St Louis, Missouri, society. She had a thorough education, read widely in several languages, sang and danced well and was also very pretty. She married another Creole, Oscar Chopin, and moved to Louisiana, where she had six children. In 1882 her much loved husband died of swamp fever; she turned to writing to support her family and to pay off his debts. Short stories about the poor Southerners she knew so well became the material for her collections *Bayou Folk* (1894) and *A Night in Acadie* (1897). She was greatly influenced by the French masters of the short story, Daudet, Flaubert and Maupassant.

Chopin's finest achievement was her last, astonishing work *The Awakening*, published in 1896, set in the soporific but highly charged atmosphere of the islands of the Gulf of Mexico, where she had once spent summers with her family. It was a story of multiple adulteries and suicide which greatly upset the general public, especially since it was written by a respectable woman. Chopin lost heart at the public outcry, she wrote little else and died within a few years.

Agatha Christie
British (1890–1976)

Nicolas Bentley's cartoon of detective novelist Agatha Christie published in The Sunday Telegraph *in 1964.*

The detective stories written by this remarkable innovator have been outsold only by the Bible and Shakespeare. Agatha Christie's success is richly deserved; no one has played fairer by her millions of readers, yet kept them guessing to the last page. *The Murder of Roger Ackroyd* has never been improved upon by herself, let alone any of her imitators.

Her father, Frederick Miller, was a rich American who lived in England and she had a happy childhood in Devon. She was first married to Archie Christie, a handsome Flying Corps officer, who was a financially irresponsible alcoholic. They had a daughter, Rosalind, but the marriage broke up, a tragedy she describes in *A Daughter's a Daughter* (1952) one of the novels she wrote under the pseudonym of Mary Westmacott. She had a mysterious breakdown and temporarily disappeared in 1926, an incident which has never been fully explained. In 1930 she married Professor Max Mallowan, later Sir Max, the archaeologist, and spent a few months every year on 'digs' in Iraq where she wrote at a simple wooden table in *Beit Agata* (Agatha's House). It was a life she loved.

The complicated but perfectly calculated plots and uncomplicated dialogue help to account for the tremendous popularity of her detective stories. Her two detectives were her egg-shaped Belgian gourmet with moustachios, Hercule Poirot, and her village spinster Miss Marple. Christie's mystery play, *The Mousetrap*, holds the record for the longest-ever run in London's West End. It opened in 1952 and is still playing nearly 30 years later.

Chu Shu-chen
Chinese (c. 1100–1200)

Almost nothing is known of the poet Chu Shu-chen's life, but her name is synonymous in China with a kind of refined misery. She was plainly, from her writing, a delicate spirit, and her husband, according to her, was *ts'u jen*, 'not clever'. Although not apparently either poor or ill-treated, she was wretchedly unhappy, and mourned her condition in *tz'u* poems of great delicacy. These poems were collected together under the title *Cutting Bowels Verses*, which refers to the Chinese belief that feelings spring from the bowels.

Chu Shu-chen's husband's name is not known, and she appears to have had no children.

Colette
French (1873–1954)

Perhaps the most admired French writer of this century, Colette was an extraordinary mixture of the earthy and the delicate, a countrywoman whose sophistication never allowed her to forget the natural world. She was the youngest daughter of devoted parents and had a wonderfully happy childhood in Burgundy. She was barely 22 when she married Monsieur 'Willy' – Henri Gauthier-Villars, a middle-aged Parisian journalist – and joined his 'factory' of writers, whose work he shamelessly published under his own name. Colette served a rigorous apprenticeship with him, but he recognized her literary talent and even locked her up to write the immensely successful *Claudine at School* series.

In 1906, after 13 unhappy years of marriage, Colette left Willy and began to earn her living on the music hall stage – a period of her life described in *La Vagabonde* (1912). Meanwhile she was also sending weekly stories to *Le Matin*. She married one of the editors, Henri de Jouvenel, in 1912 and in 1913 her only child, a daughter, was born. Her husband begged her not to write so much about love – to no avail. All relationships fascinated Colette, particularly the strange affinity between human beings and animals. Cats were a 'poignant necessity' to her, always. Indeed in *Chéri* (1929) and *The Last of Chéri* (1932) she creates a character, the young lover of an ageing tart, who is so feline and self-contained he appears to bridge the gap between man and cat.

Colette brilliantly expressed all the sensuous delights of living in her meticulous and yet spontaneous manner. 'I have always come halfway to meet you,' she said, and it is this loving quality that distinguishes her prose. Her second husband became French High Commissioner in Syria; Colette had meanwhile met the young Maurice Goudeket, whom she married in 1935. Her reputation was at its height after the Second World War; honours and prizes followed. Crippled with arthritis in old age, she none the less continued to write. She was 71 when she published *Gigi* (1944), perhaps her most famous novel. When she died people of all kinds filed past the coffin of 'Notre Grande Colette' for two days to pay their last respects.

Anna Comnena
Byzantine (1083–1148)

Anna Comnena, privileged princess of the Byzantine Empire, is best known for her history of her father's reign, the *Alexiad*. It is an essential source for modern historians of the period of the First Crusade; but she also wrote on medical matters (including a book on gout), inspired by her war work running the enormous hospital which her father had founded in Constantinople.

Anna Comnena, long awaited and much loved daughter of the Emperor Alexius Comnenus, grew up not merely clever, but learned. She knew the Scriptures, the classical authors, and studied geometry, arithmetic, music, astronomy, geography, history, medicine, and even military affairs. At eight she was betrothed to the charming Constantine Ducas, the heir apparent, and her future on the throne of Byzantium was apparently assured. But in 1091 her brother John was born and took her fiancé's place as heir; and in 1094 young Constantine died.

In 1097 Comnena married Nicephorus Bryennius, by whom she had two sons, and spent half her life intriguing to get her father to make him heir apparent in place of her brother John; even after her father's death in 1118 she was still intriguing to get him the throne. She failed, and resented the failure; the remainder of her life was devoted to writing.

Ivy Compton-Burnett
British (1884–1969)

Ivy Compton-Burnett is one of the most idiosyncratic English novelists of the twentieth century. The sixth child of a homeopathic doctor, she was brought up in Hove, a British coastal resort. She was educated at home and locally before going to Royal Holloway College for women in London, where she took a degree in classics. She began to write seriously in 1925 when she set up house with Margaret Jourdain, an expert in Regency furniture. Thereafter her life appears to have been uneventful. The claustrophobic conditions in the upper middle classes of that time provided her with all the material she needed for her 16 novels, which treat murderous events within the family behind a screen of extreme propriety, mostly in formal, cryptic dialogue. Memories of childhood and adolescence stalk her writing with the intensity of Greek myth. 'No,' she said, when challenged on the split between subject and manner in her work, 'I will not have comedy pushed into a back place, I think comedy and tragedy are a greater, wider thing than tragedy by itself. And comedy is so often seen to have tragedy behind it.'

Compton-Burnett rarely moved outside the upper-class life of English villages set rather indeterminately in late-Victorian times, saying, 'I do not feel I have any real or organic knowledge of life later than about 1910.' She refused to describe landscape or scenery in her novels; the characters are simply etched in the acid of their own voices.

Emily Dickinson
American (1839–1886)

Emily Dickinson is America's most famous nineteenth-century woman poet. She was the daughter of a lawyer and lived quietly all her life in Amherst, New England, in the house where she was born, scarcely leaving it except for one year spent at Mount Holyoke Female Seminary, Hartford (cf. Emma Willard). In 1861 she sent off her poems to a man of letters, Thomas Wentworth Higginson, to ask him if they 'breathed'. His answer was that they were 'too delicate'; and in fact only seven out of a total of nearly 2,000 poems were published in her lifetime.

Often hymn-like in their simplicity, Dickinson's poems are as strong and original as poems by William Blake. Eccentrically punctuated by dashes and exclamation marks, their short lines bolt across the manuscript page. Startling metaphors are compressed into the narrow verse: 'There is no Frigate like a

Book/To take us Lands away/Nor any Coursers like a Page/Of prancing Poetry –'. Some are spiritual and addressed to Death, others concern the lives of neighbours and everyday events. Dickinson loved music and gardening, country walks and parties. 'I am small, like the wren, and my hair is bold like the chestnut burr, and my eyes like the sherry in the glass the guest leaves.' When their parents died she lived with her sister Lavinia. Dressed in white and known as the 'moth of Amherst', she withdrew further and further into herself, still writing, but a social recluse. Dickinson is now perhaps America's most widely read poet.

Isak Dinesen
Danish (1885–1963)

Isak Dinesen, the pseudonym adopted by Karen Blixen, was the author of a masterly book about the coffee planters and colonials of East Africa, *Out of Africa*, and some fine short stories.

Blixen was born into an upper-class Danish family, learnt several languages as a girl and spent long periods in France and Italy studying art. In 1914 she married a cousin, Baron Blixen-Finecke, and they settled on a coffee farm near Nairobi in Kenya. The Blixen-Fineckes divorced in 1921 and the most important relationship of her life was with an Englishman, Denis Finch-Hatton, who died in an aircrash in 1930. She struggled unsuccessfully to run the farm alone and in 1931 she went back to Denmark and wrote *Out of Africa* (1938), a marvellous account of the people and the landscape she missed so much. 'The greatest passion of my life has become my love for my black brother and the depth of the wonders of this great wild countryside of ancient times.' The book is a unique testimony comparable only to *The Story of an African Farm* by Olive Schreiner (q.v.). Isak Dinesen also brought out *Seven Gothic Tales* (1934), and she went on to write other short stories, some of which were almost fairy tales, as well as more in her Gothic style. During the Nazi occupation she managed to publish her nationalist *Ways of Retribution*, later known as *The Angelic Avengers* (1947).

Isak Dinesen photographed by Cecil Beaton in 1959.

Marguerite Duras
French (b. 1914)

Marguerite Duras is a highly original writer and film maker. Born Marguerite Donadieu, her parents were school teachers in Indo-China. When her father died, her mother made an attempt to farm there, a bitter experience which left her daughter with a lifelong passion against injustice and colonialism. At the age of 16 she went to Paris to study law. In 1943, after six years' work at the Colonial Office, she became a full-time novelist in order to explore the quest 'on the deeper level for the impossible love', as she put it. The film *Hiroshima, Mon Amour* made her name in 1959; it sets a story of intense private passion against a background of indiscriminate mass death. In her search for a good way to live, Marguerite Duras has rejected religion and Communism in turn, although unshaken in her egalitarianism. 'I think we're all the same ... you simply have to convince yourself of that right down to the bone.' Neither institutions nor anarchy provide a social answer in her view. She explores these themes in her films, *Moderato Cantabile* (1960), *La Musica* (1965) and *The Vice Consul* (1966); *Détruire, dit-elle* (1968) concerns the students riots of 1968. Duras continues to make experimental films.

George Eliot
British (1819–1880)

The most morally forceful of all English novelists was brought up in a narrow Nonconformist country community in Warwickshire, a landscape which inspired her best-loved book, *The Mill on the Floss*. Her seven major novels firmly established her among the half dozen finest British novelists of any period. George Eliot was born Mary Ann Evans (later she changed her first names to Marian), one of three children of Robert Evans, a land agent to an estate owner; her family, which included many conservative aunts and uncles, revered 'whatever was customary and respectable'.

George Eliot was a clever child, and was given a good education at a boarding school. In adolescence she became deeply religious but when, after her mother's death and her elder sister's marriage, she kept house for her father, she found she was unable to go to church 'without vile hypocrisy'.

While still at home she made a reputation as a translator from the German and when her father died she eventually moved to London where she earned her living as a journalist. In 1851 she became assistant editor of the *Westminster Review*, a serious critical journal, and shortly became editor. But it was not until she met and decided to live with the writer George Henry Lewes that she had the idea, with Lewes's encouragement, of writing fiction.

A series of sketches, *Scenes of Clerical Life* (1856), was the modest beginning, and she began to sign herself with a combination of letters taken from 'To George I owe a lot'. *Adam Bede* was published in 1859,

George Eliot: a drawing by Lowes Cato Dickinson, 1872.

the partly autobiographical *Mill on the Floss* in 1860, *Silas Marner* in 1861. *Romola* (1862–3), although set in fourteenth-century Italy (the result of much research), is a portrait of her feminist friend, Barbara Bodichon (q.v.). *Felix Holt* was published in 1866. George Eliot's masterpiece, *Middlemarch* (1871), one of the greatest of all tragic novels, is a masterly account of high intentions and the ways in which they fail.

Deeply serious herself (the more so because she had put herself outside the Church), George Eliot wanted to change society as well as to depict it. 'The selfish instincts are not subdued by the sight of buttercups,' she wrote; 'to make men moral something more is requisite than to turn them out to grass.' Her sympathy with Jewish life inspired *Daniel Deronda* (1876).

Lewes, on whom she was so happily dependent and who helped her through her constant depression over her ability as a novelist, died in 1878. Although she was not a beautiful woman, Henry James once declared that 'one fell in love' with her after 15 minutes of conversation. A few months after Lewes' death, shortly before she died, she married a much younger man, John Cross, who had long been a friend.

Marie de France
French (c. AD 1150)

Little is known of the delightful poet known as Marie de France who became a minstrel at the English court; she may well have been a nobleman's illegitimate daughter. What is certain is that her long romances were much loved – *'mult l'aiment'*, as a contemporary wrote. The stories she used were not original. Every troubadour told the same tales. What was different was that she showed a true psychological insight into her characters. She breathed life into the stock figures that peopled the popular tales from the Orient, animal fables or stories of knights and squires. Marie de France even encouraged women to take the first step in love making, a pursuit which she firmly regarded as calling for an equal effort on the part of man and woman. In her own lifetime her work was translated into Norse, Middle English and High German.

Anne Frank
Dutch (1930–1945)

The diary Anne Frank kept during the last two years of her short life has become a symbol of the tragedy of the Jews under the Nazis. Her family fled from Germany to Amsterdam in 1933. During the Nazi occupation the Franks sheltered in a concealed part of Herr Frank's office, but in 1944 they were discovered and deported to Belsen; Anne Frank died there of typhus.

The notebooks which became *Diary of a Young Girl* were found in the attic of 'the House Behind',

where the Franks had hidden, and were handed to her father, who had survived, after the war. The *Diary*, now world-famous, describes with wonderful candour the developing loves and aspirations of an adolescent girl, despite her almost unbelievably restricted life. 'I want to go on living even after my death,' she wrote in her diary, 'and therefore I am grateful to God for giving me this gift, this possibility of developing myself and of writing, or expressing all that is in me.' The diary of this 15-year-old girl has been read by an estimated 60 million people. A statue to her stands near the house in Amsterdam, which has now become the Anne Frank Museum.

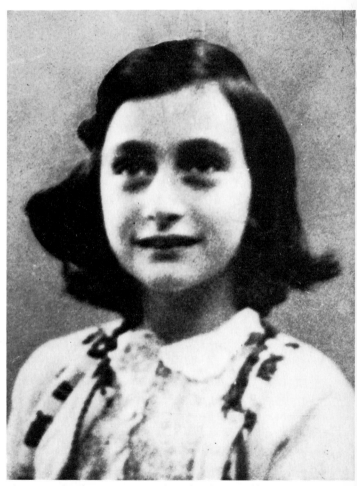

Anne Frank whose courageous diary has been read by an estimated 60 million people.

Hrosvitha von Gandersheim
German (930–973)

The first German woman writer, Hrosvitha von Gandersheim, entered a Benedictine convent for Saxon and German women of high birth in AD 959. The abbess encouraged her to write dramatizations of lives of the saints, both comic and tragic, for the nuns to act, besides religious narrative poems and historical chronicles. Her work was very popular in convents all over Europe long after her death.

Elizabeth Gaskell
British (1810–1865)

Mrs Gaskell was the author of one of the great nineteenth-century biographies, one of the best-loved novels of village life, and the first ever factory novel.

Elizabeth Stevenson was born in London, the daughter of a Scotsman who became a civil servant at the Treasury, and was educated at a girls' boarding school in Cheshire. She married William Gaskell, a Unitarian minister, in 1832 and they moved into a house just outside Manchester to be near the cotton operatives of his parish; they lived in it for 40 years. They had three daughters and one son who died as a baby, whereupon Mr Gaskell suggested that his wife should 'write a work of some length to turn her thoughts from the subject of her grief.'

Like Josephine Butler (q.v.), Mrs Gaskell found 'a pain greater than her own' in the 'careworn men who looked as if doomed to struggle through their lives in strange alteration between work and want.' One of them was the model for the father of *Mary Barton* (1848), her novel about the hard industrial life going on around her. Mrs Gaskell liked to write about the places and people she knew best: her famous novel *Cranford* (1851) is about a 'dear delightful oddity of a place' much like a Cheshire village, while *Ruth* (1853) – found shocking by some of her contemporaries – tells the story of a 'fallen' woman and her illegitimate child.

Charlotte Brontë (q.v.) became a friend, and after her death her father, the Reverend Patrick Brontë,

Elizabeth Gaskell: a chalk drawing by George Richmond.

asked Mrs Gaskell to write his daughter's life: 'No quailing, Mrs Gaskell. No drawing back.' The biography, detailed, thorough and sympathetic, was published in 1857. Not entirely free to say all she thought, as Charlotte's father and husband were still living, Mrs Gaskell came in for some criticism at the time; but *The Life of Charlotte Brontë* stands as a model of comprehensiveness and understanding even today.

By the 1850s Mrs Gaskell was rich enough to take her unmarried daughters on long journeys abroad. In Rome she made friends with the young U.S. writer and connoisseur, Charles Eliot Norton (cf. Isabella Stewart Gardner).

She was working on her most personal novel, *Wives and Daughters*, with its vivid portrait of a stepmother remembered from her own youth, when she died.

Ellen Glasgow
American (1874–1945)

Although a true Southerner, Ellen Glasgow wanted her novels to help other Southerners forget the 'moonlight and magnolias' fantasy of the Deep South and bring themselves up to date.

She was born to well-off Scottish-American parents in Richmond, Virginia. She took a degree in Political Economy at the University of Virginia, and then began writing. She burned her first novel, but published *The Descendant* in 1897 and went on to write 21 novels. Her 'Old Dominion' cycle of 11 novels was intended to alleviate the pain Southerners still felt in the aftermath of the Civil War; she urged her readers to look forward, not back.

In 1896 Glasgow went to London where she made friends with Henry James. Back in Virginia, she organized meetings for women's suffrage. She met Hardy and Conrad on return visits to Europe and, despite ill health, kept up a steady flow of novels which culminated in her autobiography, *The Woman Within*, published posthumously in 1954.

Nadine Gordimer
South African (b. 1923)

Nadine Gordimer is a distinguished writer of novels and short stories documenting the life of her native South Africa. As with much writing about Africa, descriptions of the natural beauty of the landscape might dominate were it not that Gordimer's characters are always seen as part of an oppressive regime: 'Society *is* the political situation.' Her most recent novel, *Berger's Daughter* (1978), concerns a girl born into a traditionally Communist Jewish family in South Africa who would like to escape the duty of fighting for the rights of her countrymen but recognizes that she cannot honourably do so. The heroine speaks for the author (who has had her novels banned by the South African Government) when she says 'one must live where one lives, whatever the cost.'

Gordimer is married to a Jewish businessman, a refugee from Nazi persecution in the Germany of the 1930s, and has three children.

Nadine Gordimer, author of the highly acclaimed novel Berger's Daughter *(1978)*.

Edith Hamilton
American (1865–1963)

Edith Hamilton was one of the finest classical scholars of her day in America. Her father, a well-to-do man of leisure in Fort Wayne, Indiana, encouraged her to read Latin and Greek at an early age. She was educated privately and took a degree at Bryn Mawr College, Pennsylvania. In 1895 Hamilton became the first woman admitted to the University of Munich. For more than 15 years she was head of Bryn Mawr College until she retired in 1922 to devote herself to writing. Not until she was 62 did she publish the book that made her famous, *The Greek Way* (1930), in which she expounded the innate superiority of ancient Greek civilization. *The Roman Way* (1933) continued the same theme. In 1957, when she was 90, the Mayor of Athens proclaimed her an honorary Greek citizen.

Lorraine Hansberry
American (1930–1965)

The first black woman to write a play for Broadway, Lorraine Hansberry was the daughter of the founder of the Negro bank in Chicago. Her plays deal with the exploitation of people in slum dwellings (very like those owned by her father), and they try to pinpoint what is wrong with American society in general. *a raisin in the sun* (sic) won the New York Drama Critics' Circle Award in 1959 and *The Sign in Sidney Brustein's Window* was playing on Broadway, directed by her husband Robert Memiroff, when she died of cancer. Hansberry wrote 'social drama about Negroes that will be good art', as she once said of her work. Her autobiography, *To Be Young, Gifted and Black*, was published posthumously in 1969.

Lillian Hellman
American (b. 1907)

One of the most successful and influential playwrights in America, Lillian Hellman was born of Jewish parents in New Orleans: 'I watched my mother's family increase their fortune on the borrowings of poor Negroes.' She achieved fame in 1934 with her play *Children's Hour* about two schoolteachers accused of lesbianism. Always too outspoken for comfort as a writer, she followed *Children's Hour* with *Days to Come*, about the cruelty of strike-breaking in 1936. Hellman cast a cold eye on the decay of the South in *The Little Foxes* (1939), and on Nazi Germany, where she was herself the victim of discrimination, in *Watch on the Rhine* (1941). Family problems inspired the Broadway success, *Toys in the Attic* (1960). A film, *Julia*, was based on her poignant account of a rich young American woman lost in a mysterious political wrangle in Vienna.

In 1936, after the failure of her marriage to Arthur Kober, a Hollywood scriptwriter, she began a dynamic relationship with the socialist detective story

Lillian Hellman, one of America's leading playwrights.

writer Dashiell Hammett. She and Hammett both suffered for their left-wing politics during the McCarthy era. Hellman was subpoenaed in 1952 and questioned by the House Un-American Activities Committee. Hammett was subsequently sent to jail and died in 1966. 'I am angrier now than I hope I ever will be again', she said of those bitter experiences in *Scoundrel Time* (1976). Hellman has written two other autobiographical works: *An Unfinished Woman* (1969) and *Pentimento* (1973).

Héloïse
French (1101?–1163)

'I used to hear of a woman who didst not only excel all women, but surpassed almost the whole race of men', said the philosopher Peter Abelard of his future pupil and mistress, the celebrated Héloïse. Héloïse's uncle, a canon, invited Abelard to live with them in Paris in 1118 as her tutor. They fell in love and their baby son, Astrolabe, was born secretly in Brittany. They married, and when he found out, Héloïse's uncle, enraged, arranged for thugs to enter the house and castrate Abelard. He and Héloïse were forced to part. Abelard became a monk, and Héloïse entered the convent of Argenteuil – 'Why did I, impious, marry thee to make thee wretched, accept the penalties which I gladly pay,' she declared as she took her vows. 'I ought to deplore what we did,' she later wrote, 'but I sigh only for what we have lost.' Her magnificent letters, in which she expresses her own unending sense of loss and Abelard's consoling support, have made the poignant romance of the abbess and the monk famous. Their correspondence lasted from 1128 until the death of Abelard in 1142. Héloïse lived on for 21 years and was buried beside him.

Julia Ward Howe
American (1819–1911)

'*The Battle Hymn of the Republic*', one of America's best loved songs, was written by Julia Ward Howe. She came from a prominent New York family and was married to an enterprising philanthropist, Samuel Gridley Howe, who edited the anti-slavery paper, *Commonwealth*. She was a reformer and abolitionist as well as the author of a volume of poems, *Passion Flowers* (1854).

In 1861 Ward Howe had to sit for hours in her carriage on the way back from a review of troops during the Civil War. She listened to the soldiers singing about John Brown's heroic failure in the raid at Harper's Ferry. That night she could hardly sleep with the rhythm pounding in her head, and got up early next day to write the words of the poem which became *The Battle Hymn of the Republic* – now sung to the tune of *John Brown's Body*.

For the next 50 years Ward Howe was greatly in demand to speak on the rights of women and the oppressed. In 1883 she wrote a biography of Margaret Fuller (q.v.), one of the heroines of the women's movement in America.

Zora Neale Hurston
American (1901?–1960)

A black writer who had trained as an anthropologist, Zora Neale Hurston was determined to write about people as people rather than racial stereotypes. Her father was the Reverend John Hurston, a Baptist preacher and carpenter in Eatonville, Florida, and her mother died when she was nine. She went to school in Baltimore and then to Howard University, Washington DC; her education was partially subsidized by former (domestic) employers. At Howard she decided to study black culture and in 1925 won a scholarship to Barnard to read anthropology. Neale Hurston's books such as *Mule and Men* (1935) and *Tell My Horse* (1938) comprise a mixture of remembrances, pure invention and sensational anthropological discoveries; they deal with Negro life but their subjects are treated as characters in their own right. Hurston also arranged concerts of spirituals and work songs; she wanted to see African lecturers teach Negro culture in America. 'I do not belong to the sobbing school of Negrohood,' she would say.

A woman of great energy and courage, she stuck firmly to her own objectives in writing but made little money out of it. She died, poverty-stricken, in the state welfare home in Florida, but her work has since been accorded new respect; *I Love Myself When I am Laughing*, a Zora Neale Hurston reader, was published in 1979.

Marie de La Fayette.
French (1634–1693)

Marie Madeleine de La Fayette was the author of the first European novel clearly based on personal experience, *La Princesse de Clèves* (1678): realistic in style and content, it was a pioneer work amid a welter of pompous pseudo-historical romances.

A clever girl, Marie Madeleine Poche de la Vergne understood Greek, Latin and Italian. When she was 16, her mother re-married and through her step-father Marie became a cousing and life-long friend of the celebrated Madame de Sévigné (q.v.). In 1655 Marie Madeleine married the Comte de La Fayette and had two sons. He deserted her in 1660 (she believed him dead, although in fact he did not die until 1683) and she returned to Paris. There she fell in love with the writer and wit, La Rochefoucauld, and lived with him until his death in 1680.

Under the pen name J.R. de Segrais, La Fayette published her first novel, *La Princesse de Montpensier*, in 1662, followed by *Zayde* in 1670. Her most provocative novel, *La Princess de Clèves*, was published in 1678. Part of its charm is the clearly autobiographical outline and the elegant and simple style. So greatly did it intrigue the small reading public of the day that La Fayette was glad of authorial anonymity. Indeed she even claimed to have been shocked herself by the bride's declaration in the novel of her love for another man – an announcement that caused her husband to die of a broken heart. A further novel, *La Comtesse de Tende*, was written by way of apology, though published only many years after her death, but by then La Fayette had set a fashion for novels that clearly reflected real life.

Selma Lagerlöf
Swedish (1858–1940)

Selma Lagerlöf was the first woman to win the Nobel Prize for literature. The books she wrote, based on Swedish folklore, swept America. Partially paralysed at the age of four, she spent a great deal of time reading at home in the country. In 1885 she qualified as a teacher, but her first novel, *The Saga of Gösta Börling* (later to be Garbo's (q.v.) first film), shot her to fame in 1891. Lagerlöf had the 'eyes and heart of a child', as one of her admirers put it, and wrote about nature, country people and their traditions. In 1895 she travelled to Italy, Palestine and Egypt on a scholarship, but the subject matter of her books never changed. Two volumes of *The Wonderful Adventures of Nils* appeared in 1906 and 1907. Her books were so popular that she was translated into 34 languages and, when she won the Nobel Prize in 1909, she was at last able to buy back her beloved childhood home. In 1914 she became the first woman director of the Swedish Academy.

Doris Lessing photographed at her London home in 1970.

Doris Lessing
British (b. 1919)

Doris Lessing is a powerful novelist and short story writer, who first made her name writing about Africa. Born Doris Taylor of British parents, she was the daughter of a white farmer and most of her childhood was spent in Zimbabwe. At 20 she married Frank Charles Wisdom, had two children, and divorceed in 1943. Two years later she married Gottfried Lessing, had one child and divorced in 1949. After the success of her novel, *The Grass is Singing* (1950), she settled in London.

Lessing's early writing was influenced by the South African novelist Olive Schreiner (q.v.), but she has since broadened her range considerably. Her African upbringing and her experiences as a woman writer form the basis of her compelling Martha Quest novels, *The Children of Violence* (1952–65). *The Golden Notebook* (1962) has had a great influence on subsequent women's writing. Lessing has tackled a variety of issues; racial, political and personal. *The Summer Before the Dark* (1973) concerns the onset of age, *Memoirs of a Survivor* (1974) discusses the future breakdown of society. *Shikasta* (1979) and *The*

Elizabeth Lynn Linton, the first woman feature writer to be employed on a newspaper.

Marriages Between Zones Three, Four and Five (1980) go further; set outside ordinary time and space – 'space fiction' is the term Lessing uses – they form the beginning of a sequence which views the world's predicament from a vantage point of 30,000 years in the future.

Li Ch'ing-chao
Chinese (1081–1143)

One of the most celebrated of Chinese women poets, Li Ch'ing-chao was the supreme exponent of the short, lyrical poems known as *tz'u* designed to be sung to music – a form as demanding as the European sonnet. She wrote chiefly of the trials and emotions of young women, and was constantly experimenting with unusual rhymes and metres.

Li Ch'ing-chao was born into a wealthy official family in Shantung, and married a man from the same background. The marriage was exceptionally happy: the pair were rich enough to become connoisseurs and collectors of books, paintings and *objets d'art*. Their idyllic existence was ended in 1127, however, by war and invasion, and they were forced to flee southwards, leaving all their possessions behind; two years later, Li Ch'ing-chao's husband died. Thereafter she made her home with her brother and his family at Chiu-hua, in Chekiang.

Here is part of one of the 50-odd pieces which are all that survive:

> The ground is covered with yellow flowers,
> All withered and ruined;
> What else is worth plucking at this moment?
> I stay at the window,
> All alone; how dark it gets!
> Rain drizzling on the *wu-t'ung* tree,
> Drop by drop it falls until dusk.
> All this sequence of things –
> How could it be summed up in just one word:
>   Grief?

Elizabeth Lynn Linton
British (1822–1898)

Elizabeth Lynn Linton was the first woman to be employed as a feature writer on a newspaper in England. Her father was a country parson in the Lake District, and when she was 23 she went to London to work in the British Museum Reading Room. She supported herself for the next 13 years and wrote several novels, notably *Christopher Kirkland* (1845), which is largely autobiographical, and *Azeth, The Egyptian* (1846). In 1848 she was taken on by the *Morning Chronicle*. Ten years later she married an improvident engraver, poet and political writer, W.J. Linton, but she did not enjoy married life and went back to work in London. Her husband emigrated to the U.S.

Linton strongly supported divorce legislation and laws to protect mothers and children. She once said that 'all women should learn to swim, to load and fire a pistol, to climb up a ladder without losing their head – and they need not be "new women" any the more for all those accomplishments'.

Having fought for her own financial independence and with many successful novels behind her, she felt very critical of the 'new woman' image which she thought 'hard and mercenary'. She was trenchant in

The American Imagist poet Amy Lowell.

her attacks on 'The Girl of the Period' in the *Saturday Review* of the 1860s, calling her 'a bad copy of a man . . . immodest, egotistical, self assertive and unwomanly'. Her attacks continued into the 1870s under titles such as *Frisky Matrons* and *Woman's Place in Nature*.

Amy Lowell
American (1874–1925)

Amy Lowell was an important Imagist poet, a generous patron and a great personality of the early twentieth century.

She was born Amory Lowell into one of the grandest Boston families. At 28, she saw Eleonora Duse (q.v.) on the stage and came home, inspired, to write poetry. She did so in the style of the *Imagistes*, for whom the word-picture became the meaning. Her work was published in *Poetry* in the U.S., and the *Egoist* in London – magazines she tried to buy. The editors refused her offer – as did Margaret Anderson (q.v.) on behalf of her *Little Review*. All three feared that Lowell would use their publications to pursue her quarrel with Ezra Pound, who had dubbed her an 'Amygist'.

Two collections of her poems were published, one in 1912 and another in 1914. In 1916 she published her translation of the six French poets who had inspired the Imagist movement as part of her campaign to defend 'free verse' from traditionalists. She went on lecture tours and poetry readings, where her sheer size and penchant for cigars made her an unforgettable speaker. 'The life of a poet is by no means the dreamy aesthetic one people are led to suppose. A mixture of day labourer, travelling salesman and itinerant actress is about what it amounts to', she said.

Thwarted in her desire to be a magazine proprietor, Lowell became a generous patron of struggling writers, notably D.H. Lawrence. The poet Robert Lowell was her great-nephew.

Dame Flora Shaw Lugard
Irish (1852–1929)

Flora Shaw Lugard was the first woman foreign correspondent of a British newspaper.

She was the daughter of a major-general in the British army and was educated at home in Ireland. She became organizer of the first co-operative venture in bulk buying in Woolwich and taught the local poor to read and write. After writing *Castle Blair* (1878), a children's book, she became a regular contributor to the *Pall Mall Gazette* in 1883. By 1890 she was editing French periodicals for Stead's *Review of Reviews* and writing fortnightly articles for *The Times*. Her first article on Egyptian finance was signed F. Shaw 'so that her sex would not go against her'. Flora Shaw was the first woman journalist to be taken on by *The Times* and became head of a department within months. She changed the name of her department from Foreign and Colonial to Overseas News – which it still is today. She covered a slave trade conference, was sent to South Africa, New Zealand and Australia to study labour conditions, and even went to the Klondike.

In 1902 she married Sir Frederick Lugard, then High Commissioner of the Northern Nigerian Protectorate, to which she gave the shortened name Nigeria. She published *A Tropical Dependency* in 1905, but her views on African questions were firmly opposed by Mary Kingsley (q.v.). In 1907 Sir Frederick was made governor of Hong Kong. Together the Lugards were active on behalf of refugees during the First World War. An enthusiastic feminist, she thought women would never be recognized as citizens until they were trained to carry arms.

Mary McCarthy
American (b. 1912)

Even a political 'blue stocking' can write best-sellers, as Mary McCarthy has demonstrated. Her books are both clever and enjoyable, from *The Company She Keeps* (1942) through *The Groves of Academe* (1952) to *Cannibals and Missionaries* (1979). In 1963, she published *The Group*, an account of the lives of eight ex-college girls, which became a major best-seller.

Both her parents died in the influenza epidemic of 1918 and she and her brother Kevin (now a well-known actor) were brought up by resentful poor relations. When Mary won a national essay prize at the age of 11, her guardian beat her so that she wouldn't get 'smart' – all painfully recorded in *Memories of a Catholic Girlhood* (1957).

After graduating from Vassar University in 1933 (a grandfather paid for her education), she first married a disreputable actor, Harold Johnsrud. Working on *Partisan Review* led to a partnership with an editor, Philip Rahv, described in *The Oasis* (1949). After her first husband died in a fire, she married the celebrated critic Edmund Wilson, whom she immortalized in *A Charmed Life* (1955). It was Wilson who persuaded her to write fiction. Thereafter, McCarthy said, 'What I really do is to take real plums and put them into an imaginary cake.' In 1938 she had a son, Reuel, then divorced Wilson. In 1946 she married Bowden Broadwater, but on a visit to Poland in 1961 she left him for her present husband, Jim West, an American information officer.

McCarthy's trenchant style and merciless criticism both of individuals and social evils are what give her writing its power. She was one of the first public figures to attack the U.S. involvement in South East Asia. McCarthy has also written on art, theatre and travel – notably two excellent books on Florence and Venice.

Carson McCullers
American (1917–1967)

Carson McCullers was one of a generation of great American writers who celebrated the Deep South. She had what Edith Sitwell (q.v.) called 'a great poet's eye' and chose to record the anguish of the adolescent, the cripple and the homosexual. She was born in Columbus, Georgia, and originally intended to become a musician. At 20 she married Reeves McCullers, the start of a difficult relationship that ended only with his suicide in 1953. Her first book, *The Heart is a Lonely Hunter* (1940) was written when she was 23, and established her reputation. Further novels, *Reflections in a Golden Eye* (1941) about homosexuality in the army, and *Member of the Wedding* (1946) followed. *The Ballad of the Sad Café* was published in 1951, *The Square Root of Wonderful* in 1958 and *The Clock Without Hands* in 1967.

McCullers was part of an artistic community in New York which included the poet W.H. Auden. Her career was marred by ill health and alcoholism.

Katherine Mansfield
New Zealander (1888–1923)

One of the most gifted and influential of short story writers, Katherine Mansfield was a provincial girl from New Zealand. Born Katherine Beauchamp, she was one of several children of a business man who was sufficiently well-off to send his daughters briefly to school in London. When Katherine returned home, she sold a few stories locally and in Australia, but longed to go back to England. Her parents finally gave her an allowance to settle there in 1908.

Life in England was far from easy, as Mansfield was

still unknown, and she had to tour with an opera company as a member of the chorus to keep herself alive. She married a musician, George Bowden, but left him after a fortnight. Her first book was *In a German Pension*, written in 1909. Middleton Murry, the writer and critic, became her friend and mentor, and eventually, in 1918, her husband. Their relationship was full of difficulties but she never regretted it. *Prelude*, a novella about New Zealand prompted by her brother's death in action, was published by Leonard and Virginia Woolf (q.v.) in 1918, but it was not until a collection of stories, *Bliss*, appeared in 1920 that she won the fame she longed for.

Pleurisy, rheumatism and tuberculosis dogged her and she travelled restlessly all over the south of England, France and Italy in search of health, usually accompanied by a devoted school friend, Ida Baker. In 1922, Mansfield entered the clinic of the faith healer Gurdjieff outside Paris in hope not only of a cure but of becoming 'good' enough, in the spiritual sense, to write as much as she longed to. One evening, just after Middleton Murry arrived however, she had a haemorrhage and died.

The medium of the short story suited Mansfield perfectly. Not quite a miniaturist, she is a writer who marvellously conveys the quality of the evanescent.

Edna St Vincent Millay
American (1892–1950)

Edna St Vincent Millay was idolized in America as the poet of the Jazz Age. She was the middle daughter of parents who soon divorced and was brought up on the coast of Maine. Her mother worked as a nurse to support her family, but there was not enough money for a college education. However, St Vincent Millay won poetry prizes and a Miss Dow paid for her to go to Vassar College in 1914.

After graduating she went to live in Greenwich Village, New York, where she began to be known for her hatred of war and her cynical, flippant style. 'My candle burns at both ends/It will not last the night;/But, ah, my foes, and, oh, my friends,/It gives a lovely light.' She also did a little acting and wrote articles signed 'Nancy Boyd'.

Vanity Fair sent her to Europe as a correspondent for two years in 1921, and in 1922 her collection of poems, *A Few Figs From Thistles*, won the Pulitzer Prize for its outspoken satire and wit. She married a New York-based businessman, Eugen Jan Boissevan, in 1923. St Vincent Millay wrote two further collections of poems and the libretto for a romantic Wagnerian-style opera. Her deep interest in politics and social problems – which inspired her to join those who protested at the execution of Sacco and Vanzetti in 1927 – was the basis of *Observations at Midnight* (1937). Her husband died in 1949, and the following year she herself died of a heart attack brought on by her drinking and poor health.

Marianne Moore
American (1887–1972)

Marianne Moore tossing the first ball to open the 1968 baseball season at the Yankee Stadium.

Marianne Moore was a perfectionist among twentieth-century American poets. She was born in St Louis, Missouri, and was brought up in the house of her grandfather, a Presbyterian minister. She graduated in biology and histology from Bryn Mawr University. When her father died, she moved to Philadelphia with her mother. Forced to choose between writing and her Southern lover, who told her she would have to stop writing poems if she married him, she taught business studies from 1911 to 1915. Her poems were published in the *avant garde* magazine, *Poetry* in America, and *The Egoist* in London. From 1921 she was a librarian in New York and was so modest about her work that her friends had to organize the publication of her *Poems* (1921) for her. After *Observations* was published in 1924 she became editor of the New York magazine, *The Dial*.

As well as producing a steady corpus of poems and essays, Moore translated the fables of La Fontaine. 'Poetry watches life with affection', she once said. Her writing is both fastidious and exciting. The act of writing daily was 'a matter of personal comfort' to her, and she is famous for the catchphrase describing poetry as 'imaginary gardens with real toads in them'.

'Lady Murasaki'
Japanese (c. 978–1026)

The 'Lady' Murasaki is the author of the world's first surviving full-length novel, *The Tale of Genji*, which is read with pleasure to this day. Yet we do not know her real name: Lady Murasaki is the name of her heroine, who loves Prince Genji. We know only that she was born of a leading Japanese family of the Heian period, that her father was a provincial governor, and that she married a cousin in the imperial guard, Fujiwara no Nobutaka. As a child Murasaki was given an education like her brother, but convention demanded that she should hide her intelligence and her love of Chinese literature. She was left a widow very young, and soon after the year 1000 her family connections took her into the service of the Empress Akiko, whom she secretly instructed in Chinese. She wrote a diary of court life, and, around AD 1008, the

long – 54 volumes – and complicated story of Prince Genji's life and loves. It is a novel of jealousy and intrigue, of dissimulation, romance and refinement – and paints a sharp portrait of a small, leisured upper class dedicated to the pursuit of pleasure.

Iris Murdoch
British (b. 1919)

Iris Murdoch is a prolific writer of neo-metaphysical novels characterized by extraordinary events. She was born in Ireland, the daughter of Anglo-Irish parents and educated at boarding school in England and at Oxford. A philosophy graduate, Murdoch has taught philosophy for most of her life and her first book, published in 1953, was a study of Jean-Paul Sartre. She achieved fame with her first novel, *Under the Net* (1954), and has since written more than 20 – all concerned with the psychological conflict between 'the saint and the creative artist', a conflict characteristically enacted in a series of bizarre, often horrifying incidents viewed with an elegant detachment. She is married to an Oxford don, John Bayley.

Walladah al-Mustakfi
Spanish (c. 1001–80)

This brilliant poet presided, like an Islamic George Sand (q.v.), over a literary circle in eleventh-century Andalusia; like Sand too, she was a prolific writer and also dressed as a man. Her father al-Mustakfi, the rascally caliph of Cordova, was finally murdered by his people when she was about 30; her mother was probably an Ethiopian Christian slave. Walladah al-Mustakfi had money of her own and took the revolutionary step, for a Moorish woman, of casting off the veil, and dressing to please herself. The sleeves of her robe were decorated with verses – on the right-hand: 'Here I am, by God, fit for any high position/And I go on my way with pride', on the left: 'To be sure, I will let my love touch my cheek/And I feel free to give my kisses to whoever asks for them'.

It is not possible to say if this freedom of behaviour was typical of any contemporary group or if, like

George Sand, Walladah al-Mustakfi was allowed her eccentricities because of her talent. Certainly, by her personality and her singing she attracted a large circle of followers; the great poet Ibn Zaydun fell in love with her. She never married and late in life she herself fell in love with the beautiful Muhjah al-Tayani al Qurtubiyah, whom she taught and who herself became a fine poet. In later life, Walladah al-Mustakfi was cared for by another admirer, a rich merchant called Ibn Abdus, in whose house she lived to a ripe old age.

Anaïs Nin
French (1903–1977)

The voluminous diaries of Anaïs Nin, full of 'feminine' sensibility, have been a solace to many women. She was born in Paris, the daughter of a famous Cuban pianist, Joachim Nin, and a Danish mother who kept a boarding house in New York. Accustomed to glamorous tours all over the world with her father, she was shattered, at 11, when he left the family for a younger woman. In a desperate attempt to get him back, she began to write a diary as a kind of endless letter to him, and refused ever to be parted from it. During the 1920s, she settled near Paris, where she earned her living as a model and Spanish dancer; Lawrence Durrell and Henry Miller, also struggling young writers, were among her friends. Nin studied psychoanalysis with Otto Rank, but turned out to be insufficiently 'objective'. During the 1940s the *New Yorker* took her up; she lived in Greenwich Village where she attracted a circle of intimates. She never married, but had many lovers. The *Diaries* began to appear in 1966. She called them an account of 'the evolution of woman. I am living it and suffering for all women.' Nin also wrote novels – 'the outcroppings of the diaries' – of which *Winter of Artifice* (1939) and *A Spy in the House of Love* (1954) are the best known.

Flannery O'Connor
American (1925–1964)

Flannery O'Connor was a powerful and original writer of novels and short stories. Her life was cruelly restricted by an inherited disease which crippled her. She spent almost all her short life on her mother's farm in Georgia, although she did take a Master's degree at the University of Iowa. Catholicism, the nature of being a Southerner and her own disease were the raw materials of her writing. 'Everything has to operate first on the literal level', she said of her art, although she often described unimaginable horrors as her way of showing the grace of God. *Wise Blood* was published in 1952 and a collection of short stories, *A Good Man is Hard to Find*, in 1955. She was celebrated in her lifetime for, in particular, *The Violent Bear it Away* (1960) and *Everything That Rises Must Converge* (1965), and has reached an even wider public since her death with the publication of her fascinating *Letters* (1978).

Pan Chao
Chinese (c. 45–115)

The most celebrated woman scholar in Chinese history succeeded her brother Pan Ku as historian to the court of the Emperor Ho at the end of the first century AD. According to the *History of the Han Dynasty*, Pan Chao wrote 'narrative poems, commemorative writings, inscriptions, eulogies, arguments, commentaries, elegies, essays, treatises, expositions, memorials and final instructions, in all 16 books'.

Pan Chao came from a noble family; her great-aunt had been a leading member of the Imperial harem, and her father, Pan Piao, had held various posts at court. At 14 she married Ts'ao Shih-shu and bore him a son and several daughters, before his early death. When her father died, he was in the middle of writing the *History of the Han Dynasty*, which was taken over by Pan Ku, his son, and, when Pan Ku died in 92, was completed by Pan Chao. Thereafter she combined her role of unofficial court historian with being poet laureate, and the teacher of the 15-year-old Empress Teng.

Although she herself was successful and had great influence as an adviser to the Imperial family, and although she claimed to believe that women should be educated – 'to teach sons and not to teach daughters, is this not . . . to discriminate against the latter in favour of the former?' – Pan Chao cannot be described as a feminist *manquée*. Her *Precepts for Women*, written towards the end of her life for her daughters, urges humility, adaptability, and subservience, housewifely duties and the avoidance of lustful intimacy in marriage.

Dorothy Parker
American (1893–1967)

'A blend of Little Nell and Lady Macbeth,' was how the humorist Alexander Woollcott described this most acerbic and witty author. Dorothy Rothschild was half New Yorker and half Scottish, and outrageous from an early age. She was expelled from her convent when she described the Virgin Birth as 'spontaneous combustion'.

She married Edwin Pond Parker in 1917 on the eve of his departure for Europe with the U.S. Army. They divorced in 1928 but she kept the name as she was earning a growing reputation as a writer – having progressed from writing captions for lingerie in *Vogue* to drama criticism in *Vanity Fair*. Her laconic wit was much appreciated at the famous Round Table in the Algonquin Hotel by a group of humorists that included Woollcott, Robert Benchley and Ring Lardner. '*The House Beautiful*,' she wrote of a grossly sentimental drama, 'is the play lousy.' 'Men seldom make passes at girls who wear glasses' is probably her most famous catchphrase. Informed that Clare Booth Luce (q.v.) was always kind to her inferiors, she asked, 'Where does she find them?' When her editor once asked why she was not at work she replied, 'Someone else was using the pencil.'

Parker also wrote short stories and poems – 'I was following in the exquisite footsteps of Edna St Vincent Millay' (q.v.), 'unhappily in my own horrible sneakers.' Her best known poetry is wry and slightly sentimental. Like Millay, she was fined five dollars for keeping watch the night Sacco and Vanzetti were executed in 1927.

Not as frivolous as other contemporary 'destroyers of the Genteel Trend', she went to Spain to report on the Spanish Civil War. In 1933 she married an actor, Alan Campbell, divorced him in 1947 and remarried him in 1950. They lived in Hollywood where she wrote film scripts until her left-wing views became unpopular in the 1940s.

Parker's last years were made wretched by alcoholism. She wanted the words on her gravestone to read, 'If you can read this you've come too close.'

Christine de Pisan
French (1364–1429?)

Christine de Pisan was an important poet in the history of French literature and an early feminist. She wrote a satire, an official biography of the French King Charles V and several hundred poems.

Her father was an Italian astrologer at the French court and at 15 Christine married a French nobleman, Etienne du Castel. Her husband was secretary to the King and the couple had a tiny court of their own with four esquires and three demoiselles. But in 1389 he died and Christine de Pisan was left with a girl of eight, a boy of four, her mother and two brothers to support. Fortune, she said, turned her into a man and made her voice stronger and her body harder. Her daughter went into a convent and her son left to be a page in England. The King's library now satisfied her hunger for education; she read incessantly and wrote ballads and poems. In 1403 she bravely attacked the *Roman de la Rose*, the courtly lovers' bible, on account of its sexism. Philip, Duke of Burgundy, commissioned her to write the life of his brother, Charles V; it was she who called him 'The Wise'. Her most attractive poems, such as the *Dit de Poisey*, are in the true medieval spirit and describe the poet leading a company of beautifully dressed nobles out into the country on a summer morning. She could also be heavily ironic: 'Alas, good Lord, why didst thou not make me to be born into this world in that masculine kind . . . I should not have erred in anything and might have been of so great perfection as they say men are.' In 1418 she retired to a convent and lived long enough to welcome God's choice of a woman, Joan of Arc (q.v.), to lead Charles VII to the throne.

Sylvia Plath
American (1932–1963)

Although only 30 when she committed suicide, Sylvia Plath left behind her two astonishing volumes of poetry – *The Colossus*, 1960, and *Ariel*, published posthumously in 1965; a novel, *The Bell Jar*, largely inspired by her earlier suicide attempt at the age of 19, which was published under a pseudonym a month before her death; and a quantity of short stories and critical pieces. *Letters Home*, edited by her mother, appeared in 1975. In the years since her death she has become a cult figure, particularly among American women.

Sylvia Plath was born in Boston, Massachusetts to parents of German origin: Otto Plath was a professor of entomology, who died of diabetes when she was nine, and her mother Aurelia was a schoolteacher. She was academically brilliant, both at school and at Smith College, Massachusetts, and won a Fulbright scholarship to Newnham College, Cambridge, U.K. There she met the English poet Ted Hughes, whom she married in 1956. After two years (1957–9) in the states, where she taught at Smith and Hughes at the University of Massachusetts, they settled permanently in England, first in London, then in Devon. A daughter, Frieda, was born in 1960, and a son Nicholas, in 1962. When they separated in late 1962, Plath moved with her children back to London, and there, two months later, she committed suicide.

To the outside world, Sylvia Plath seemed to have much of that peculiarly American cheerfulness which her fellow-poet A. Alvarez once called 'instant Doris Day'. She was extremely pretty (at one time she modelled clothes), and very competent – an excellent cook, a devoted and conscientious mother, even a beekeeper. Her inner life, however, was tormented by the memory of her Prussian father, and she was obsessed by the sufferings of the victims of the concentration camps. Death was a major pre-occupation throughout her adult life.

Her gift was there from childhood (her first poem was published when she was eight), and she developed it by intensive hard work. The poems in *The Colossus* (1960) show exceptional technical control and command of the right image in the right place. In *Ariel* her gift had flowered into something more. Most of these poems were written in her last months, after the separation from her husband, when she was rising at four every morning – 'that still blue, almost eternal hour before the baby's cry, before the glassy music of the milkman' – to write one poem, often two, a day. They represent a heroic struggle to face the truth about herself, her past, and the world as she experienced it both in fact and in imagination. That truth was painful, and also dangerous: she risked being driven to act out the death wish she was exploring so ruthlessly in her writing, at a time when she was exhausted trying to look after her children virtually without help, worried about money, weakened by illness and the acute cold of that winter, and deeply unhappy.

Katherine Anne Porter
American (1890–1980)

Katherine Anne Porter was in her seventies when her best-seller, *Ship of Fools*, was published in 1962. Born in Indian Creek, Texas, she was descended from the hunter, Daniel Boone, and distantly related to the writer O. Henry (whose real name was Sidney Porter). Educated at various convents, she subsequently worked as an editor and scriptwriter.

In 1930 Porter's first volume of short stories, *Flowering Judas*, was published and was much admired by the critics. Other collections of short stories and essays, all exquisitely crafted, followed, but it was *Ship of Fools*, her only full-length novel, the fruit of 20 years' writing, which really captured the public imagination. When her collected works came out in 1966 they won the Pullitzer Prize and the National Book Award. She was married and divorced three times.

Beatrix Potter
British (1866–1943)

Peter Rabbit, Jeremy Fisher, Jemima Puddleduck: this gallery of immortals was created in both words and watercolours by Beatrix Potter, whose incompar-

Beatrix Potter photographed at her Lake District farm in 1907.

able drawings and stories have been beloved by generations of children. Barely educated, as was usual for upper middle-class girls of her time, she was allowed by restrictive parents to do very little except 'help' Mamma and visit the museums of London, although she did keep small furry pets in her room and drew them incessantly. Until the tremendous success of her books, she led almost as shy and solitary a life as Mrs Tiggywinkle.

Peter Rabbit began as an illustrated letter sent to a sick child and was published in 1900. Animals were never 'cute' to her, she would enlarge or diminish them in her drawings, dress them in human clothes and give them human speech without ever compromising their essential nature, which she studied with such love and attention. With the proceeds from her books she bought a farm in the English Lake District and in 1913 she married William Heelis, the lawyer who negotiated the sale for her. They settled down contentedly to a life of sheep-breeding in which she could finally deal with real rather than imagined animals. In later life she was prouder of her reputation as a farmer than for her books, and indignantly repudiated any attributions of genius.

Ann Radcliffe
British (1764–1823)

Ann Radcliffe wrote one of the first Gothic novels in English and helped start a literary fashion.

Ann Ward was born in London, the daughter of a shopkeeper, but had rich relations in the country with whom she spent much of her childhood. She read a great deal, but like most girls was not formally educated. In 1787 she married William Radcliffe, who gave up the law to edit the *English Chronicle* – and to publish her novels, the first of which appeared in 1789. Her gift for grotesque melodrama and fine descriptions of scenery developed with every book she wrote, culminating in *The Mysteries of Udolpho* in 1794, which became such a cult that Jane Austen (q.v.) made gentle fun of it and its many imitators in *Northanger Abbey* – knowing her readers would have read it. Such was the popular demand for the tales of mouldering castles and imprisoned nuns created by Radcliffe that she was given huge advances for her novels. *The Italian, or The Confessional of Black Penitents* (1797), on the Inquisition – weak in plot but strong in dark deeds – was her last novel. When no more novels appeared it was generally assumed, with a shudder, that the author had been driven mad by her own horrific creations and had committed suicide. In fact she spent the last 25 years of her life in happy retirement with her husband in the country.

Dorothy Richardson
British (1873–1957)

Dorothy Richardson, the author of *Pilgrimage*, an interesting neglected work of the twentieth century, has not yet received the recognition she deserves.

Her father's lack of success in business meant that Richardson had a nomadic childhood. (Her father became a bankrupt in 1893, and her mother committed suicide in 1895.) After teaching briefly in Germany and in London, she became secretary to a dentist in London, and it was not until 1906 that H. G. Wells, who had become her lover, found her work as a reviewer.

Pilgrimage was based on her own life as a young woman of independent spirit but not independent means. The first five of the 15 volumes were published between 1919 and 1925, the last volume was published in 1938. The work is, as she said, 'religiously plain', like Bunyan's *Pilgrim's Progress*, which inspired the title; and so obsessively detailed that her writing is widely described as 'stream of consciousness'. Richardson disagreed with the description, however, declaring: 'It is not a stream, it's a pool, a sea, an ocean.'

In 1917 she married Alan Odle, an artist, and went with him to Cornwall, where she spent the rest of her life. Richardson's work did not earn her popular success during her lifetime, although she was published in the *Little Review* (cf. Margaret Anderson) and was respected in literary circles – fellow writer Gertrude Stein (q.v.) welcomed her on a visit to Paris in 1923.

Henry Handel Richardson
Australian (1870–1946)

Henry Handel Richardson provides in her novels the best socio-historical record of Australian society in its early days and at the turn of the century. She was born Ethel Richardson in Melbourne, the daughter of a doctor, and brought up by her mother, who became a postmistress after her husband's death. The young Ethel disliked life as a governess but enjoyed writing and music, so in 1887 her mother used all her savings to send her to Leipzig to study the piano. That career was not a success, but by then she had begun to write seriously. In 1895 she married a fellow student, John Robertson, who was appointed Professor of German at London University in 1897. Her first book, *Maurice Guest* (1908) is an account of her student days; her second, *The Getting of Wisdom* (1910), an account of her schooldays (which was turned into a successful film in 1977). *The Fortunes of*

Richard Mahoney (1917–29) is a trilogy about a man who goes out to the goldfields in the 1850s, much as her own father did; it is today widely regarded as an important Australian novel. Her autobiography, *Myself When Young*, was published in 1939.

Christina Rossetti
British (1830–1896)

Christina Rossetti was one of the great poets of the Victorian era – an age well-suited to her fervent expression of deep religious feeling. She was the youngest of five talented children of an Italian patriot who had taken refuge in England – the most celebrated of whom was the Pre-Raphaelite painter Dante Gabriel Rossetti. She and her sister were educated at home.

Rossetti had her first poems printed privately in 1847, and was soon contributing under the name Ellen Alleyne to her brothers' Pre-Raphaelite magazine, *The Germ*, which was founded in 1850. Thereafter she wrote and published steadily, and had acquired a considerable reputation by the time her most famous poem, *Goblin Market*, was published in 1862. Although often melancholy in tone, her work is never sentimental. Rossetti had a perfect musical ear. Her vocabulary is simple, yet her poetry is mysterious and complex. '*In the Bleak Midwinter*' is still a favourite Christmas carol, and her other Christmas carol, '*How Many Miles to Babylon?*' must be known to every English-speaking child.

Rossetti never married; she broke off an engagement because her fiancé lacked her own religious conviction.

George Sand
French (1804–1876)

The history of the nineteenth century is rich in women who defied or ignored the prevailing social conventions, and the career of the writer George Sand is the prime example of a liberated, independent life. Her immense literary output, many lovers, children and grandchildren made her life con-

Christina Rossetti and her mother: a drawing by Dante Gabriel Rossetti, 1877.

tinuously varied and satisfying.

Amandine Aurore Lucile Dupin was brought up at Nohant in central France by a strict, aristocratic grandmother. She would ride and shoot, often dressed up in her dead father's uniform, when not at her convent school in Paris. In 1822 she married Casimir, Baron Dudevant, and had a son and a daughter. The marriage was an unhappy one and, after making sure she would have access to her children, Sand moved to Paris in 1830, where again she dressed as a man, which gave her the freedom to roam the streets as she wished. She soon began to publish short stories and novels, signed George Sand – a *nom de plume* based on the name of her current lover, Jules Sandeau. She was a prolific writer and was emotionally involved with a number of leading writers and composers, notably with the poet Alfred de Musset and the composer Chopin.

Sand wrote more than 80 novels, of which the best known are perhaps her first novel, *Indiana* (1832), and her most ambitious work, *Consuelo* (1842–3). Her books are interesting rather than distinguished, and

A cartoon of George Sand from the Miroir Drolatique, *1842.*

caused a great stir at the time because they recounted the experiences of gifted women and frequently exposed social evils. Sand was an activist in real life: in the Revolution of 1848 she came out on the streets with the workers, full of the blazing zeal which made her books so influential.

For the last three decades of her life she lived at her family house at Nohant in hardworking domesticity; it was there that she wrote her captivating autobiography, the 22-volume *Histoire de ma Vie* (1854–5).

Sappho
Greek (c. 650 BC)

Sappho was one of the great poets of the ancient world, admired both by her contemporaries and by succeeding generations. The ancients regarded her as the tenth Muse.

Not much is now known of her life – except what she herself tells us. She was born on the island of Lesbos, she loved women, in honour of whom most of her poems are written (hence the term lesbianism), she was married and had a daughter Cleis, and three sons. But her love for Phaon (a man) and her suicide by throwing herself off a cliff remain conjectural; so is the possibility that she went briefly into exile in Sicily.

Barely 650 lines of her poetry survive, and only one complete poem. Some of her poems are known in part from Egyptian papyri; others were quoted from by other ancient authors. Her simplicity, directness, and intensity of personal feeling (along with that of her contemporary Alcaeus) herald a completely new mode in Greek poetry, quite different from the Homeric epic which preceded her, and not surpassed by her successors.

'Lady Sarashina'
Japanese (c. 1008–1060)

'Lady Sarashina' is one of the women writers of medieval Japan – like Lady Murasaki and Sei Shonagon (qq.v.) – whose observant, personal writings quite outclass those of their male contemporaries. (One reason is that women of the day wrote in a pure Japanese, where the men used a Sino-Japanese hybrid.) She is usually known as Takasue-no-Musume – 'the daughter of Takasue'. Takasue was a middle class provincial official, and his nameless daughter led a withdrawn, nervous existence on the fringe of court circles; she married in her thirties and had a son and daughter. Her book, *Sarashina Nikki*, is a record, probably written in old age from notes taken over the years, of certain events or experiences important to her – a journey across Japan, her dreams and daydreams, feelings about her father, pilgrimages, exchanges of verses with strangers and acquaintances, evenings spent gazing at the moon, her embarrassment on being required to attend at court, the loneliness of old age. Her own family is barely mentioned. Clearly not the most enlivening of companions, she was none the less able to communicate her thoughts and emotions through her pen with great directness, and her book was already widely read in the thirteenth century. Today *Sarashina Nikki* is known to every Japanese school-child.

Nathalie Sarraute
French (b. 1900)

Nathalie Sarraute has been a key figure in the *nouvel roman* movement in France. She was born in Russia and went to Oxford University and then the Sorbonne. She married in 1925 and practised at the bar until 1941, when her first novel, *Tropismes*, was published in 1957. Seven experimental novels followed. Anxious to get away from the 'uphol-stered' style of the nineteenth-century novel, Sarraute describes her innovative literary style as 'saying it with things'. Her ambition is 'to tackle important issues'; she feels there is 'something dishonourable or even inhuman about the novelist who invents stories in a world full of terrible events'. Sarraute writes her novels in the past continuous tense to suggest time in suspense.

Olive Schreiner
South African (1855–1921)

Olive Schreiner was the author of one of the most remarkable books to come out of Africa in the nineteenth century. Her father was a gentle and idealistic German missionary and her mother an energetic Englishwoman. Their mission station was in Basutoland, then very remote and isolated. Schreiner was a child of the veldt; the surrounding landscape and animals meant more to her than her books, although she read Goethe's *Faust* 'as if I had written it myself'. At the age of nine she declared herself a Free Thinker, a controversial stance which she held to and which later made finding work as a governess – the only job she could do – hard to find. *The Story of an African Farm* (1884) was written during her years of hardship and in 1881 she went to England to find a publisher for it. The book was an

Olive Schreiner, author of the highly successful Story of an African Farm *(1884).*

instant success – and an amazing work for a young author living in isolation. It also raised the controversial issue of the woman's role. While in England she made friends with many progressive thinkers, including the writer and philosopher Havelock Ellis, but their 'soul friendship' did not lead to marriage and she returned to South Africa in 1889.

In 1894 Schreiner married Samuel Cronwright, a farmer and ex-member of the South African Legislature. They campaigned together for many reforms, including female suffrage and the Boer cause. During the Boer War Schreiner was placed under arrest for over six months, her house was sacked and the manuscript of a new book, *Musings*, was burned. She wrote down what she could remember of it, with the British on guard outside; it was later published as *Woman and Labour* in 1911. Schreiner died of a heart attack in England, where she was a popular speaker, but was buried in South Africa, in her native veldt.

Madeleine de Scudéry. Many of her characters were based on acquaintances at court.

Madame de Sevigné: an engraving after a portrait by Goulard.

Anna van Schuurman
Low Countries (1607–1678)

The most celebrated European woman of letters of her day was Anna Maria van Schuurman. A fluent linguist, she could speak French, Italian, English, German, Latin, Greek, Ethiopian and read Hebrew. Schuurman was an exponent of all the fine arts, and was renowned throughout Europe. She wrote, among other things, a *Dissertation on Wives* (1641).

Madeleine de Scudéry
French (1607–1701)

Madeleine de Scudéry was an immensely successful novelist, at first in collaboration with her brother Georges, a soldier and playwright (they were children of an Army officer), and then independently. *Ibrahim, Aratamène, Clélie, Matilde d'Aguilar,* and *Conversations Morales* succeeded each other in several

volumes apiece – all set in exotic times or places, but some of whose characters, at least, were based on Mlle de Scudéry's contemporaries in court circles. These *romans à clef* caused great excitement at the time, and in spite of their turgid prose they also provide information about the manners of the day and offer some description of the characters' inner feelings – thus foreshadowing the masterpiece among seventeenth-century French novels, *La Princesse de Clèves* by Marie de La Fayette (q.v.).

Marie de Sévigné
French (1626–1696)

The Marquise de Sévigné is admired in France for her elegant, sparkling letters. Her parents died when Marie de Rabutin-Chantal was a little girl and her guardian uncle, a young abbé – 'Le Bien Bon', as she called him – found her the best tutors in France. She had a happy childhood, and was brought up with uncles and cousins, but married a feckless aristocrat when she was 18 and went to live in Brittany. The daughter to whom most of the letters were to be written was born in 1646 and her son in 1648.

After the death of her husband in 1651, Madame de Sévigné spent much of the year in Paris, a member, like her friend Madame de La Fayette, of Madame de Rambouillet's (qq.v.) intellectual circle at the Hôtel Rambouillet. Madame de Sévigné was famous for the brilliance of her conversation; and her gift was an ability to write with the spontaneity and freshness of speech. She never married again; her emotional life centred on her daughter, who became Madame de Grignan and lived in Provence. The letters that made Madame de Sévigné famous – a constant stream of entrancing descriptions, character sketches and anecdotes – were mostly addressed to her daughter, who seems to have been sadly unappreciative.

Mary Shelley
British (1797–1851)

Mary Shelley was the author of *Frankenstein*, one of the most famous horror stories ever written – and still, for many people, the best. She was only 18 when she wrote it. Born Mary Godwin, she was the daughter of Mary Wollstonecraft (q.v.) and the philosopher William Godwin. Her mother died a few days after she was born, and Mary was brought up in an atmosphere of free thinking by her father and stepmother. She eloped with the poet Shelley when she was 16, and went with him to Switzerland. Two years later they rented a villa on Lake Geneva, to be near Shelley's friend Byron, at that time living at the villa Diodati.

One day the members of the group decided that each of them would try their hands at a 'tale of the supernatural'. Mary Shelley later described how the idea of *Frankenstein* came to her: 'My imagination, unbidden, possessed and guided me, gifting the successive images that arose in my mind with a vividness far beyond the usual bounds of reverie.' Her unforgettable story of a scientist who created a living being was published in 1818.

Much of her brief married life was taken up with

Mary Shelley, author of Frankenstein, *the first science fiction novel.*

bearing children, all but one of whom died in infancy. After Shelley was drowned in 1822, she wrote several other novels and accounts of journeys taken with the poet to support her child, Percy; there is a portrait of Shelley in *Valperga* (1823). But nothing she wrote is as powerful as the story of her tormented scientist and his alarming creation.

'Sei Shonagon'
Japanese (c. AD 1000)

The Pillow Book, written by the author known as Sei Shonagon c.AD 1000, was one of the earliest and best of the many works of literature by Japanese women of the eleventh century. As with the authors of *The Tale of Genji* (Lady Murasaki) and the *Sarashina Nikki* (qq.v.), we do not know her real name; but *The Pillow Book* makes clear that she had court connections and became a lady-in-waiting around the age of 25. She had many lovers, and much of her *Pillow Book* is devoted to amorous reminiscence. Lady Murasaki (q.v.), a generation younger, complained that Sei Shonagon's principal pleasure was to cause scandal and draw attention to herself.

Dame Edith Sitwell
British (1887–1964)

Edith Sitwell was a poet and member of a flamboyant literary trio with her brothers Osbert and Sacheverell in the London literary world between the wars: 'as cosy as a nest of tigers on the Ganges.' Of her birth and upbringing at Renishaw Hall, Derbyshire – as the eldest of the three children of Sir George and Lady Ida Sitwell – she later wrote, 'I was in disgrace for being female.' A voracious reader from the age of four, she learnt the *Rape of the Lock* by heart when locked up for refusing to recite *The Boy Stood on the Burning Deck*. At 17 she dragged her governess along with her to offer a libation of milk and roses on the poet Swinburne's grave.

In 1914 she set up house in London with her governess Helen Rootham, and published her first book of poems in 1915. In 1923 Edith and Osbert recited 21 of her poems through a 'singerphone' to music especially composed by William Walton; *Façade* was a *succès de scandale* and the young Sitwells' patronage and encouragement of the impoverished young musician, now Sir William Walton, was perhaps their most important single act.

Sitwell's poems appeared in rapid succession: *Bucolic Comedies*, *The Sleeping Beauty* and *Gold Coast Customs* all appeared in 1929, and are a blend of striking images and exotic rhythms. Exotic, too, were the poet's public appearances dressed in medieval turban and robes, her etiolated fingers covered in huge, rock-like rings. Her book *English Eccentrics* (1959) was made into an opera. Her autobiography *Taken Care Of* was published in 1965.

Agnes Smedley
American (1892–1950)

Agnes Smedley was a journalist who devoted much

of her life to fighting injustice, poverty and oppression in China, and wrote *Daughters of Earth* (1929), based on her experiences in Manchuria.

She was born in Missouri and brought up in a strike-ridden mining town in Southern Colorado. She went to night school in New York and married an Indian, Vivendramath Chattopaghyaya. In 1918 they left the States for Britain, where she was arrested briefly while working for the Indian Nationalist Party. The arrest inspired her with a lifelong hatred of colonial administrations – the British in particular.

Smedley was based in Manchuria from 1929 to 1941 and took part in the Chinese resistance to the Japanese invasion in 1931. She fought with the Chinese Communists behind the Japanese lines, and later nursed Chinese wounded in Hankow; she also worked as a correspondent for the *Manchester Guardian*. Her two books, *China's Red Army Marches* (1934) and *China Fights Back* (1938), and hundreds of articles publicized the Chinese struggle in the West.

Smedley returned to the States during the Second World War, and after the war successfully refuted charges of having been a Soviet spy.

Germaine de Staël
Swiss (1766–1817)

The writer Germaine de Staël was the essence of a liberated woman – independent in love, politics and thought. Everything she wrote was on the side of sense. She had considerable influence on the development of the Romantic movement in France.

Her father was the Swiss financier Jacques Necker, who was Louis XVI's finance minister and became Treasurer to the new Republic of France. As a young girl, Germaine played her part in her mother's *salon*, but since she was not pretty, and a Protestant in a Catholic country, she was married off in 1786 to the Swedish Ambassador in Paris, Baron de Staël Holstein, by whom she had three children.

Germaine de Staël was soon holding a *salon* of her own, and in 1788 she published what must be the first work of literary criticism written by a woman on a man, *Lettres sur les ouvrages et le caractère de Jean-Jacques Rousseau*. It generated great excitement, particularly in England. Even after the Revolution of 1789, she was one of the great *salonnières* of Paris, but during the Terror she retreated with her lover Louis de Narbonne to England (where she met and became a friend of Fanny Burney q.v.), and then to Coppet, the Necker home, in Switzerland. Back in Paris, in 1794 she began her famous 14-year liason with the writer Benjamin Constant (who was probably the father of her daughter Albertine).

She was also a fearless critic of Napoleon. When Napoleon rebuffed her plea to allow women to play a larger part in politics, Germaine de Staël retorted: 'In a country where their heads are cut off, it is only natural for them to want to know why.' Napoleon did not care either for her view that 'genius has no sex'. In 1803 he banned her from within 40 miles of the capital. She made her permanent home at Coppet, while making extensive visits to Germany, Italy, Scandinavia and England, besides brief visits to France after the fall of Napoleon.

Germaine de Staël's novel, *Delphine* came out in 1802; it was followed by *Corinne* in 1807. Together these two novels made freer behaviour the fashion for the young women of post-revolutionary France. The welcome which Goëthe and Schiller had extended to her in Weimar prompted her most controversial work, *De l'Allemagne* (1811) in which she maintained that 'enthusiasm' not tradition is the proper guide to action. De Staël's most significant work was her earlier book *De la Littérature considerée dans ses rapports avec les institutions sociales* (1800), which Chateaubriand called 'a prospectus for Romanticism'. In 1811 she married John de Rocca, a young Swiss officer.

Christina Stead
Australian (b. 1902)

The novels of Christina Stead are among the neglected masterpieces of the twentieth century. Stead was born in Australia of English immigrant parents. Her father was a naturalist in the Australian Fisheries Department; her mother died when she was a baby. As she grew up she looked after the children of her father's second marriage and told them stories.

She trained as a teacher – a job she disliked – and changed to business studies as a way of escaping to a job in Europe. She reached Paris on 1929, and started to publish her short stories in the 1930s. In 1935 she married an American banker and author William Blech, who wrote under the name of William Blake and they settled in America.

Her first full-length novel, *The Man Who Loved Children* (1940), is a remarkable semi-autobiographical work about a crazy father who speaks a language of his own invention. Stead has written eight more novels and two collections of short stories rich in social comment and Rabelaisian humour. When her husband died she went back to Australia to live with her brother, a trades union official, in Sydney.

Gertrude Stein
American (1874–1946)

What the Cubists had pioneered in painting, Gertrude Stein wanted to do for writing – break it up and put it together again in a new way. One of three children of Jewish parents, Stein studied medicine at John Hopkins University, Maryland but failed her exams, partly because of the unhappy love triangle which she describes in her book *Q.E.D.* (1903, later re-titled *Things As They Are*, 1950). Since she had a private income, she and her brother Leo were able to settle in Paris in 1903 and collect modern art. Stein particularly admired Picasso, but she and Leo also bought works by Cézanne, Renoir, Matisse, Gauguin and many other modern artists.

Stein's most important relationship was with a fellow American, Alice Toklas. Stein had what Toklas called an 'intellectual luminous quality that shone in her face'. In 1907 the two of them embarked on a loving and harmonious 'marriage'. Toklas did the housekeeping (the *Alice B. Toklas Cookbook* is a delightfully idiosyncratic work) and talked to the ladies after dinner while Stein stayed behind at the table to talk to the men. Stein wrote strange innovative books which met with little popular success – *How to Write* (1931), *Lucy Church Amiably* (1939) – until her *Autobiography of Alice*

B. Toklas, the story of their life together, became a best-seller in 1933. She wrote many plays and operas – including *The Mother of Us All* (1946) about Susan B. Anthony (q.v.).

At least one of her phrases has achieved immortality. Once when Toklas was typing Stein's work she pounced on the phrase, 'A rose is a rose is a rose', and put it on their writing paper and the table linen and 'anywhere that Gertrude Stein would permit it.'

Devoted to France, their country of adoption, the pair spent the Second World War there; Stein died soon afterwards. Toklas survived her by 20 years, and wrote *Staying on Alone* (1973).

Harriet Beecher Stowe
American (1811–1896)

Harriet Beecher Stowe was the author of *Uncle Tom's Cabin*, 'the little book that made the big war,' in Abraham Lincoln's words, and is still one of the most loved American novels. No one has written so eloquently about the institution of slavery before the Civil War.

Harriet Beecher was born in Litchfield, Connecticut, of a long line of Calvinist preachers. Her mother died when she was five and she was sent away to her sister Catherine's school at Hartford, Connecticut. By the age of 10, she had already heard of appalling scenes of degradation in the treatment of slaves in Jamaica, but it was not until Catherine founded a pioneer college for women in Cincinnati and Harriet joined her there as a teacher, that she saw her first advertisement for a runaway slave. For the next 18 years she was divided from the slave-owning South only by the width of the Ohio River.

In 1836 she married one of the teachers at her father's seminary in Cincinnati, a middle-aged widower, Calvin Ellis Stowe. She had seven children over the next 15 years and was often ill and depressed, but her first collection of stories, *The Mayflower*, was published in 1843.

Gertrude Stein and Alice B. Toklas in the 1920s.

In 1850 the Stowes moved to Brunswick, Maine, where one Sunday in 1851 she went into a trance in church and returned home to begin writing *Uncle Tom's Cabin or The Man that was a Thing* at the kitchen table. 'The Lord Himself wrote it,' she later said, 'I was but an instrument in His hands.' Five thousand copies sold on the first day of publication in 1852 and 50,000 within two months. Her mission had succeeded and undoubtedly helped influence both the political leadership of the U.S. and popular attitudes towards slavery. She became famous in America and Europe; she was fêted everywhere. Another anti-slavery novel, *Dred*, appeared in 1856 with a hero modelled on the Negro leader, Nat Turner; and she continued to write novels and stories until her old age.

Dame Rebecca West
British (b. 1892)

Rebecca West photographed at her Oxford home in 1968.

A writer as strong-minded and independent as the Ibsen heroine whose name she took, Rebecca West has written many articles, books and novels. She was born Cecily Fairfield, daughter of an Army officer, and planned to go on the stage. In 1911 she acted in *Rosmersholm* and adopted for good the name of its heroine, Rebecca West. Meanwhile her mother had forbidden her to read *The Freewoman*, a left-wing feminist paper, but in 1912, at the age of 19, West began writing for it, and shortly afterwards joined the editorial staff. She joined the socialist *Clarion* in 1913. In 1914 she had a son (now the writer Anthony West) by H.G. Wells. She married Henry Andrews, a banker, in 1930.

West's distinguished critical work began with a book on Henry James in 1916, and the first of her many novels was *The Return of the Soldier* (1918). An important historical work, *Black Lamb and Grey Falcon*, an account of Balkan politics, was written after an extensive tour of Yugoslavia in 1930.

Edith Wharton
American (1862–1937)

Edith Wharton is increasingly recognized as one of the most original American novelists of the generation of Henry James. She did not publish any novels until she was 40, and since she led a leisured, privileged life it was easy to dismiss her as a dilettante. She was born Edith Jones into the old New York aristocracy, and after publishing some juvenile poetry she married Teddy Wharton, a member of her own social set and they travelled in Europe a great deal.

Wharton's first book was an historical novel about Italy, *The Valley of Decision* (1902), but it was *The House of Mirth* (1905) which made her name – the tragic story of how a rigid society can crush the desire and spirit of an individual. *Ethan Frome* (1911) is about the decline of a rural community – a death of a different kind. She won the Pulitzer Prize in 1921 with *The Age of Innocence*, her account of the power held by a small circle – largely women – who dominated society in the New York of her youth.

Wharton's husband became mentally ill, and she

eventually divorced him in 1913 and went to live in Paris. Her work is often compared with that of her friend Henry James, who greatly admired her; but Wharton had considerably more pace and was sharper in her social observations. Moreover, her novels did not take her 'innocents' abroad, as those of James did, but dissected them on American soil.

Virginia Woolf
British (1882–1941)

Virginia Woolf was one of the most distinguished novelists and critics of twentieth-century Britain. She was born into one of the great families of the Victorian intellectual aristocracy, one of four children of Julia Duckworth, née Jackson, and the scholar, Sir Leslie Stephen, who began his long editorship of the *Dictionary of National Biography* the year she was born. When she was 13 her mother died and Virginia never fully regained emotional stability.

Her emotional imbalance, tenderly treated by her husband Leonard Woolf, who had been at Cambridge University with her brothers and whom she married in 1912, may well have been the inspiration of her richly imaginative and free-wheeling prose. At the same time she was a logical thinker, a resolute feminist, socialist and pacifist, as her essays show. She was also an enchanting friend, witty, understanding and often enjoyably malicious.

The Woolfs' joint venture, the Hogarth Press, was founded in 1917, with Leonard as the driving spirit and Virginia packing parcels – and writing novels – in the basement. Her first two novels, *The Voyage Out* (1915) and *Jacob's Room* (1922), are conventional in form, but in *Mrs Dalloway* (1925) and *To the Lighthouse* (1927), an exorcism of her memories of her parents, she skilfully stops time in its tracks in order to show that emotional experience is more important than the procession of 'gig lamps' – the image she coined for the orderliness of daily life. These earlier novels were succeeded by her innovative masterpiece, *The Waves* (1931), which abandoned all conventional approaches to plot and character, and *The Years* (1937). Her high camp historical *jeu d'esprit, Orlando* (1928), was dedicated to her much loved Vita Sack-

writing is to be found in the many volumes of her *Letters* and *Diaries*, which are still being published.

Dorothy Wordsworth
British (1771–1855)

The poet William Wordsworth's devoted sister is one of the best and least pretentious diarists of the nineteenth century. Her parents died in 1778 when their five children were very young. Dorothy, the only girl, was sent to live with an aunt. In 1787 the children were reunited at their grandparents' and Dorothy became enthralled by her brother William, whom she had hardly known before. By 1795 the brother and sister had set up house together for life. They moved to Dove Cottage in the Lake District in 1800.

As she walked in all weathers over the hills and dales of their beloved Lake District, Dorothy recorded in her diary every sight and sound, intending to help William with his poems. His famous poem which begins 'I wandered lonely as a cloud' relies on her description of the very same scene: 'I never saw daffodils so beautiful. They grew among the mossy stones about and about them, some rested their heads upon these stones as on a pillow for weariness and the rest tossed and reeled and danced and seemed as if they verily laughed with the wind.'

Dorothy Wordsworth never married but stayed on to keep house for William and care for his children when he married. In 1835 she developed arteriosclerosis which eventually affected her brain, and for the last 20 years of her life she was looked after by William's wife Mary.

Virginia Woolf: novelist, essayist, diarist, letter writer and feminist.

ville West, who called it 'the best love letter ever written'. Another *jeu d'esprit* was a biography of Elizabeth Barrett Browning's (q.v.) dog, *Flush* (1933); and she wrote one full-length biography of her friend Roger Fry in 1940. The critical essays collected in the volumes of *The Common Reader* (1925 and 1932) and later, posthumous volumes, testify to her innate good sense as a literary critic.

Woolf became deeply depressed at the beginning of the Second World War, after finishing her last book, *Between the Acts* (1941), and when she found she had lost the ability to concentrate, she put pebbles in her pockets and walked into the river that runs behind the Woolfs' house in Sussex.

Much of her most interesting and uninhibited

Galina Ulanova, star of the Bolshoi Ballet, as Giselle.

THE PERFORMING ARTS

IN EVERY SOCIETY from the most primitive to the most sophisticated, singing and dancing have involved men and women alike. But there have been many times and places where for a woman to earn her living as a performer (as opposed to taking part in village dancing or singing in church) was virtually impossible. A career as a dancer, for example, has been equated with prostitution, in both ancient and modern times; and for a woman in sixteenth-century Europe to sing or act professionally was so unthinkable that women's parts were customarily taken by men. All Shakespeare's female roles were played by boys in his lifetime and for many years after; while for centuries the Italian opera depended on castrated boy singers for its sopranos. But once women had achieved the right to act, dance and sing professionally, they were soon properly recognized as equal to men in ability, and their contribution has been as important as well paid. It is worth noting that those who criticize women for combining motherhood with a full-time career rarely criticize sopranos or actresses – whose roles can no longer be taken by men.

Alongside the performers are women who have excelled as impresarios and innovators – from Okuni in early seventeenth-century Japan, who created Kabuki drama, and Madeleine Béjart, the founder of a successful theatre troupe in seventeenth-century France, to the great twentieth-century dancer-choreographers like Martha Graham and Ninette de Valois. Women musicians have been less numerous, although they clearly follow a long historical tradition – women playing musical instruments appear on Greek vases and Roman mosaics. But even in this more competitive area where male prejudice is known to operate to the detriment of women, there have been several very gifted and influential women musicians and composers in recent years.

Marian Anderson
American (b. 1902)

Marian Anderson was the first black solo singer to appear at the Metropolitan Opera House, New York. As a girl she sang in Baptist Church choirs in Philadelphia and won competitions to pay for her training. In 1930 she made a successful tour of Europe although recognition came more slowly in the U.S. In 1939 she was billed to sing in Constitution Hall, Washington DC, only to have her engagement blocked by the Daughters of the American Revolution because of her colour. Eleanor Roosevelt (q.v.) immediately organized a concert for her at the Lincoln Memorial, which was attended by 75,000 people. In 1949 she won the Bok award and donated the money to the training of young singers. After Anderson visited Finland, Sibelius dedicated *Solitude* to her, and Anderson's singing of *America, the Beautiful* in her deep, velvety contralto during the Eisenhower administration has become a national legend. In 1955 she became the first black soloist when she made her debut as Ulrica in *Un Ballo in Maschera* in New York.

Dame Janet Baker
British (b. 1933)

One of the greatest of contemporary opera singers, Janet Baker was born in Yorkshire. After leaving school, she started work in a bank and joined the Leeds Philharmonic Choir as an amateur singer. The conductor encouraged her to transfer to the London branch of the bank in 1953 and to train her voice with Helene Isepp. In 1956 she won the Kathleen Ferrier Memorial Prize. In 1957 she married Keith Shelley, who gave up his own career in business to manage hers. Baker's fine, warm singing in oratorio and lieder is universally admired. 'I would not know what to do if I couldn't sing', she said, 'it is my life.'

Brigitte Bardot
French (b. 1934)

'The respectable married man's unattainable dream,' as Bardot was described by her first husband, Roger Vadim, is a star whose career might have provided the scenario for one of her films. Born into a rich Parisian family, she first caught the public's eye when she modelled her mother's boutique clothes on the cover of *Elle* magazine at the age of 17. She was spotted by a film director, Marc Allégret, and his assistant, Roger Vadim, married her in 1952. Bardot made 16 films before he directed her in the notorious *And God Created Woman* in 1955, her first major success. Her torrid love scenes with her leading man, Jean Louis Trintignant, shocked even the camera crew.

'B.B.' has had three husbands and many lovers. 'It is not possible to have only one man,' she once said, and the men in her life have included a Swiss barman and a German millionaire (Gunther Sachs, whom she married in 1966). In 1960 she had a son, Nicholas, by her second husband, Jacques Charrier. The highest paid French star ever, she has made 48 films which record her extraordinarily photogenic combination of erotic tomboy and feminine beauty. She made her last film in 1973.

Bardot has been an extremely effective campaigner for the welfare of animals. She joined the protest against seal hunts in Canada in 1977 and in 1980 won a battle in the French courts against the use of pigs and baboons in testing the effects of road accidents on car passengers. On her farm, where she lives with the sculptor and actor Miroslav Brozek, more than 80 animals roam freely.

Lilian Baylis
British (1874–1937)

Lilian Baylis was the most unlikely impresario in theatrical history. She was the daughter of a London musician, and before she was 10 left with her family for South Africa. There she became, she said later, the first dancing teacher on the gold fields of the Rand, and earned a good living. In 1895 she came back to London to live with her aunt, Emma Cons (q.v.), who gave her the job of manager of her temperance music hall – the theatre which Lilian Baylis was to turn into the Old Vic, and which eventually became Britain's celebrated National Theatre.

Lilian Baylis, theatre impresario and manager of the Old Vic, photographed in 1933.

Hitherto lectures had been the staple fare for her aunt's working-class audiences but Baylis started to show 'moving pictures', and having collected £2,000 (at a penny a ticket) she organized a symphony concert. Anxious to raise cultural standards, she procured a dramatic licence in 1913 to put on operas and, in 1914, started a Shakespeare Company with a £1,500 grant from the Carnegie Trust. She later claimed that it was God who had told her what to do to save the Old Vic.

After launching a successful appeal to buy the entire building (half of which was a college) – 'so that the leading lady needn't use my office as a dressing room' – Baylis set about restoring another London theatre, Sadler's Wells, in 1927. She and Ninette de Valois (q.v.) made it the home of opera and ballet, while drama stayed at the Vic, a 'nursery' for many of the greatest names in British theatre. A great character and an obsessive worker, Baylis was also extremely devout; of her success with the Old Vic she once said, 'I had the Almighty in my pocket.'

Madeleine Béjart
French (1618–1672)

It was not until the middle of the seventeenth century in Paris that women were allowed to appear on the European stage, and Madeleine Béjart was one of France's first professional actresses.

Then in her mid-twenties, Madeleine Béjart was the leader of the Béjart family troupe of touring players, which also included two brothers and a younger sister, Geneviève (who used their mother's name, Hervé), when they met the 20-year-old Molière; it is thought to have been Madeleine who persuaded him to become an actor. In 1643 they joined forces to form the Illustre Théâtre. Madeleine was already a successful actress, but the company was soon in debt and for thirteen years the Béjarts and Molière toured the provinces. It was 1658 before they caught the eye of Louis XIV with a performance of Molière's *Le Docteur Amoureux*, and the troupe was adopted by the King's brother. The following year the company presented Molière's *Les Précieuses Ridicules* (cf. Mlle. de Scudéry), and thereafter Molière's company, and his plays, achieved the success they deserved.

Madeleine Béjart was much admired as an actress, particularly in soubrette parts, a number of which Molière wrote specially for her. She remained with him until she died, but details of their relationship are not known.

The youngest Béjart actress, Armande, who was born in 1642, was either Madeleine's much younger sister, or possibly her illegitimate daughter. Armande married Molière in 1662, and bore him two children, but the marriage was unhappy. She too was a star of Molière's company; the witty, flirtatious Célimène in *Le Misanthrope*, a role she was the first to play, is supposed to have been based on her personality.

Sarah Bernhardt
French (1844–1923)

Sarah Bernhardt was one of the *grandes dames* of the nineteenth-century theatre. She was the illegitimate child of a Frenchman and a Dutch-Jewish courtesan,

Popularly known as 'Divine Sarah' Sarah Bernhardt was the grand dame *of nineteenth-century theatre.*

Nadia Boulanger
French (1887–1979)

Nadia Boulanger was the greatest and most influential teacher of composition in twentieth-century music. She 'rediscovered' Monteverdi and promoted Stravinsky.

She was born into a musical family: her father was a teacher of singing at the Paris Conservatory, and she herself was a pupil of Fauré. When her younger sister Lili, a composer who had won the Prix de Rome in 1914, died at the age of 24, Nadia, who had come second in the Prix de Rome in 1908, regarded it as her sacred duty to promote her sister's work.

Her genius as a teacher – 'the tender tyrant' – was not to impose herself on her pupils but to develop their own talent to the full; Aaron Copland, Darius Milhaud, Virgil Thomson, Lennox Berkeley, Thea Musgrave (q.v.) – all learnt from her. Her life was consumed by 'the whole duty' of teaching music. 'It is not sad,' she once said, 'to have to give.'

Anne Bracegirdle
British (1673?–1748)

Anne Bracegirdle was one of the early comediennes of the English stage (women's parts were taken by men until the middle of the seventeenth century). Orphaned young, she went to live with a famous theatrical family, the Bettertons, in London. In 1695 she was one of the actresses who insisted on a share of the takings at Lincoln's Inn Fields along with the men. Bracegirdle was in the theatre for almost 20 years; her greatest success was as Millamant in William Congreve's *The Way of the World*, one of the great Restoration comedies. She left the stage early and spent the last 40 years of her life in retirement after £800 had been collected for her by her enthusiastic public.

Grace Bumbry
American (b. 1937)

Grace Bumbry is one of a distinguished group of black American singers; a mezzo soprano, she trained

and was educated at a convent. She lived to want nothing but the best.

Bernhardt worked from the moment she had been trained at the Paris Conservatoire in 1862 until a few days before she died. Her Phèdre was said to rival the celebrated Rachel's (q.v.), while she was reputed to have suggested Marguerite's agony of choice by the slightest of movements in *La Dame Aux Camélias*. 'Register the thought before the action,' she told her pupils. After a successful season in 1879 on the London stage she chose to spend much of her life there, although she subsequently toured the U.S. and South America – taking prodigious amounts of luggage with her so that she might always be correctly dressed. At 70 Bernhardt had to have her leg amputated, but this did not discourage her and she continued to appear on the stage into her late seventies, even playing Hamlet with her wooden leg.

Bernhardt had many lovers, and was married once, in her late thirties, to a fellow actor, Jacques Damala. But her only real attachment was to her son Maurice, by her first lover.

Clara Butt: according to Sir Thomas Beecham, her voice could be heard across the Channel on a clear day.

under Lotte Lehmann (q.v.) at the Music Academy of the West, California. She made her début in 1959 as Amneris in *Aïda* in Paris, performed Carmen 13 times in Brussels and caused a sensation as the first-ever black Venus in Wagner's *Lohengrin* at the Bayreuth Festival of 1961. In 1968 she starred in the film of *Carmen*. Bumbry continues to play major roles in the opera houses of the world. She has worked hard at consolidating friendship between the generations of black singers and has been awarded a number of medals and honorary degrees.

Dame Clara Butt
British (1873–1936)

Clara Butt was the contralto who could be heard across the Channel on a clear day, according to the conductor, Sir Thomas Beecham. Brought up in the country near Brighton, she won a scholarship to the Royal Academy of Music in London in 1891. Butt had a long and successful professional career. Crowds

gathered to hear her – draped in a Union Jack – sing *Abide With Me* to massed brass bands. During the First World War there was almost no one who did not respond to her thrilling, poignant voice as she sang Kipling's *Have You News of My Boy Jack?* She married another singer, Robert Rumford, and had two sons, both of whom died before her.

Sarah Caldwell
American (b. 1928)

One of the great figures of U.S. opera, director and conductor Sarah Caldwell is a powerhouse of musical ideas.

Her mother was a music teacher and pianist in Maryville, Montana, and at five the young Sarah was playing the violin in chamber music alongside adult musicians; and at the age of six she was giving public concerts in Chicago. After studying psychology for a year (her new stepfather was against a musical career) she then began studying the violin. A scholarship took her to the New England Conservatory of Music in Boston and in 1946 she played the viola at the Tanglewood Summer School, 'a place where gods strode the earth'. Caldwell, not yet 20, was invited to join the Tanglewood faculty in 1947 and had a great success with her first production, a Vaughan Williams opera. In 1952 she developed a fully-fledged opera group out of the Boston Opera Workshop. In 1957, with only 5,000 dollars, she started to turn the Opera Group of Boston into an opera company; it took ten years.

An enthusiast for theatrical effects – Fourth of July firework displays were her passion as a child – Caldwell stages difficult modern music as well as her favourite nineteenth-century melodramas. An indefatigable worker, she rehearses her players tirelessly, 'until the music sails out of them,' as she puts it. In 1975 she became the second woman – Nadia Boulanger (q.v.) was the first – to conduct the New York Philharmonic, but refused to 'take the money and run', as she described the process of repeating the same repertoire all over the States. Caldwell's efforts are currently concentrated on setting up her proposed Baroque Opera House.

163

Maria Callas
American (1923–1977)

Maria Callas was one of the great dramatic singers of all time. She was born to Greek-American parents in New York (her father was a pharmacist), but she and her mother were stranded in Athens by the outbreak of the Second World War. Those years were spent in training her voice. Her operatic debut was in *Cavalleria Rusticana* in Athens in 1940. In 1947 she was acclaimed in Italy. There, two years later, she married a middle-aged business man from Verona, Giovanni Meneghini, who became her manager.

Callas revived the art of *bel canto* (cf. Pauline Viardot) and had such stamina and discipline that she could sing both Bellini and Wagner even in the same week. Great performances in opera require histrionic power as well as a marvellous voice; and that was her strength. Triumphs at La Scala, Milan, in 1953 led to a sensational début in Bellini's *Norma* at the New York Metropolitan in 1956; having shed her excess weight she was now dramatically beautiful and indeed glamorous. Stormy off stage as well as on, heated arguments with Rudolf Bing, the manager, were only resolved in 1958 when she appeared for him as Violetta.

Meanwhile her private life was almost as stormy as her professional life. She left her husband for a well-publicized liaison with the millionaire shipowner Aristotle Onassis, and after almost 20 years in opera she stopped performing. Onassis subsequently left her to marry Jacqueline Kennedy, and Callas turned to teaching in New York. She died at the age of 54 of a heart attack.

Mrs Patrick Campbell
British (1865–1940)

Stella Campbell, always known as Mrs Patrick Campbell, may not have been the greatest actress of her generation, but she was certainly the most spectacular. The daughter of an Italian mother and an Anglo-Indian father, she made her début on the Liverpool stage in 1888. By then she had married the ailing Patrick Campbell and had two children. He left for Africa for health reasons (he died in 1900), throwing the burden of the family on her.

Paula Tanqueray in Pinero's *The Second Mrs Tanqueray* in 1893 was the role that made Mrs Campbell famous. When she subsequently toured the U.S., George Bernard Shaw began to write his famous series of letters addressing her as 'Dear Liar'. She played Hedda Gabler in 1907 and Yeats' *Deirdre* in 1908. Her greatest triumphs were semi-autobiographical parts, as beautiful, witty women with a mysterious past.

Mrs Campbell was famous for her sharp tongue and spared no one, not even herself. 'Isn't age dreadful?' she would say. 'I look at an old photograph of myself as Mrs Tanqueray and now I look in the glass and see a burst paper bag.' In 1914 she married George Cornwallis-West, ex-husband of Lady Randolph (Jenny) Churchill, exclaiming that 'marriage is the deep peace of the double bed after the hurly-burly of the *chaise longue*.'

Susannah Cibber
British (1714–1766)

Susannah Cibber was the most popular English singer and actress of the eighteenth century. She was the sister of the composer, Thomas Arne (who wrote *God Save the Queen*), and made her début in 1732 at the Haymarket Theatre. In 1734 she married the manager's son, Theophilus Cibber, who expropriated her earnings (a wife's earnings were her husband's property until the late nineteenth century). She had two children, both of whom died.

Cibber became the star of Drury Lane. She played Dryden's Cleopatra and Isabella and sang in the first performance of her friend Handel's oratorio, *The Messiah*, in Dublin in 1741. Her husband brought an action of £5,000 against her for adultery, but lost the action and was fined £10 himself. Cibber eventually retired happily to the country with her lover John Sloper, and on her death was buried in Westminster Abbey.

Mrs Patrick Campbell: if she was not the greatest actress, she was certainly the most spectacular.

Susannah Cibber, the star of Drury Lane: an early eighteenth-century cameo by an unknown artist.

Marlene Dietrich setting her own distinctive style in the 1930s.

Kitty Clive
British (1711–1785)

For 40 years Kitty Clive was the first comedienne of the London stage. Her father was an Irish lawyer and early on in life Kitty had to support him and the rest of her large family from her earnings. She had a marvellous voice, and her successes at Drury Lane ranged from playing the *nouveaux riches* married women to the boyish girls of contemporary comedy. A great fighter herself, she was perfect for Garrick's *Catherine and Petruchio*, an adaptation of *The Taming of the Shrew*. Clive excelled as the ingénue Polly in John Gay's phenomenally popular *The Beggar's Opera*. She had a long and successful career and died in the house given to her by the writer Horace Walpole in Twickenham.

Marlene Dietrich
German (b. 1901)

The most enduring of all stage and screen *femmes fatales*, Marlene Dietrich was born in Berlin, the daughter of a German Army officer. She trained to play the violin, but an accident to her arm at 16 led to her entering Max Reinhardt's acting school instead. She set her own style from the beginning. The film director von Sternberg cast her as Lola in *The Blue Angel* in 1930 – and her portrayal of the erotic, sexually ambivalent 'bad' girl singing 'Falling in love again' straddled over a wooden chair had a tremendous dramatic impact.

It was von Sternberg who took Dietrich to Hollywood. There her beautifully groomed hair smooth brow and enormously accentuated eyes –

often contradicted by a man's evening dress, top hat and tails – set a style for many U.S. films of the thirties. Von Sternberg made seven films with her; *Morocco* (1930), *Dishonoured* (1931) and *Shanghai Express* (1932) gave her exotic backgrounds which enhanced her air of mystery. In 1938 she took U.S. citizenship; 'I could not endure the turn my country took,' she said. In 1939 she starred in a spoof cowboy film, *Destry Rides Again*, in which she sang the well-known song 'See what the boys in the back room will have'. During the Second World War she was an indefatigable entertainer of American troops and became famous after the war for her concert tours.

In 1925 she married Rudolph Sieber; they had a daughter, Maria.

Isadora Duncan
American (1878–1927)

Isadora Duncan was a pioneer in the art of expressive dance. She was born in San Francisco, the youngest in a penniless Irish family. She was an enterprising child, however, and she and her sister Elizabeth were soon teaching dancing in wealthy houses. Having decided at the age of 14 to accept any kind of dance and mime engagements from Chicago to New York, Isadora left home, taking her mother and sister with her. In 1899 the family reached London, where society hostesses eagerly engaged her to entertain them in her own special barefoot style, draped in flowing material. In 1903 she went with Loie Fuller (q.v.) to Berlin, then to Budapest, Florence and Athens. She danced for Wagner at Bayreuth, and travelled to St Petersburg where her guiding idea that 'every emotion has its corresponding movement' profoundly influenced the choreographer Fokine, then on the verge of breaking away from the axioms of classical ballet.

Both Duncan's two children, one born of her love affair with the stage designer Gordon Craig (cf. Ellen Terry) and the other by Isaac Singer, the American millionaire, were drowned in the Seine in 1913. The tragedy made her redouble her efforts to found schools – 'children understand that dancing is walking towards the light' and she besieged Singer and

various government heads for financial aid. The Soviets invited her to Moscow in 1921, where she met and married the poet Serge Essenin in 1922. He committed suicide in 1925. In the same year she opened a dance studio in Nice. Two years later she died when her scarf caught in the wheels of her car.

Isadora Duncan and pupils dressed in characteristic neo-Grecian costume.

Katherine Dunham
American (b. 1910)

Under Katherine Dunham's inspiration, black dancers emerged from minstrel entertainment onto the legitimate stage.

Born in Joliet, Illinois, Dunham did well at school and paid her way through college at the University of Chicago by giving dance lessons. Determined to be a choreographer, she won a travelling scholarship to the West Indies where she researched traditional African dances for her Ph.D. in anthropology. In 1939 she formed her own company and created *Tropics* and *Le Jazz Hot*; her choreography for the film *Cabin in the Sky* (1940) established her reputation in New York. Her husband, John Pratt, also designed her revue set.

A highly intelligent and original choreographer of Afro-American dance, Dunham fused rhythms and movements from all over the black world. The dancers shake and shiver to the beat of the drums in brilliant adaptations based on a combination of different Negro traditions – voodoo ritual, the famous Jamaican *danse du ventre* and the native American 'cakewalk' – movements that have now become familiar because of her work in films and Broadway shows. In 1959 she wrote her autobiography, *A Touch of Innocence*. When her company disbanded in the 1960s she taught at the University of Southern Illinois.

Eleonora Duse
Italian (1859–1924)

Eleonora Duse was a great inspirational actress, an 'impassioned pilgrim' as she called herself. She was born into an acting family and was even carried to her christening in a theatrical property box. After creating a memorable Juliet at 14, she quickly became a star in Naples. A woman of great romantic enthusiasms, she had several lovers during her career and married a fellow actor, Tebaldo Checchi; they had a daughter, Enrichetta, in 1882.

Duse always immersed herself totally in every part. 'There are a thousand women within me,' she once said, 'and each one makes me suffer in turn.' Her voice was extremely beautiful and she acted in a style that was realistic but romantic. She was greatly admired by people as different as George Bernard Shaw and Queen Victoria (q.v.).

In 1886, with her lover Rossi, Duse founded her own company and had great success in Paris, London, New York and Moscow. In 1897 she fell passionately in love with the poet Gabriele d'Annunzio, and thereafter she would perform in nothing that was not written by him until they parted in 1902. Ellida in Ibsen's *The Lady From the Sea* then became a favourite part. In 1909 she was obliged to retire because of her asthma, but after 12 years financial worries forced her to return to the stage, and again she took the world by storm. Duse toured the U.S. in 1923 (cf. Amy Lowell), and when she died in Pittsburg the following year hundreds of Italian immigrants knelt on the dockside as her coffin was lowered into a battleship to be taken back to Italy.

Eleonora Duse, the 'impassioned pilgrim' and celebrated nineteenth-century femme fatale.

Ella Fitzgerald
American (b. 1918)

One of the most successful singers of the twentieth century, Ella Fitzgerald has made several different styles her own. She was born in Virginia but was brought up in an orphanage in Yonkers, New York. Chick Webb spotted her in an amateur competition when she was 16. He engaged her to sing with his band, and when he died in 1939 she took over.

Unlike Bessie Smith (q.v.), Ella Fitzgerald taught herself the 'white' music so popular in the 1930s – songs like *My Heart Belongs to Daddy* – and her recordings became best sellers. During the 1940s she developed her own 'scat singing' – a breathless, nonsense syllable style – for songs like *Flying Home* and *Lady Be Good*.

In 1941 she married Bennie Kornegay but divorced him in 1943. In 1949 she married Ray Brown, of the Oscar Peterson Trio, and had a son. They divorced in 1953.

Ella Fitzgerald was the perfect musical partner for her friend the trumpeter, Louis Armstrong, matching him in warmth and artistry. 'I just like music, period,' she has said, 'to me, it's a story. There's only one thing better than singing … it's more singing.'

Dame Margot Fonteyn
British (b. 1919)

Unquestionably Britain's greatest ballerina, Margot Fonteyn dominated Western ballet for 20 years after the Second World War. The diminutive, half-Irish, half-Brazilian dancer with huge eyes and a brilliant smile was born Peggy Hookham. She began to train in London at 14 and danced her first solo role in 1934 for Ninette de Valois' (q.v.) new Vic-Wells Ballet (now the Royal Ballet Company). From the beginning she displayed the beauty and purity of line for which she is famous. Not a great virtuoso dancer technically, Fonteyn thinks herself into a chosen character with all the intensity of an actress.

In 1955 Fonteyn married a diplomat, Roberto de Arias, then Panamanian Ambassador to London. She performed her duties as a diplomatic wife with the punctiliousness and charm characteristic of her dancing. Her husband was badly wounded in a shooting incident in 1964, since when Fonteyn has divided her time between hospital visits and a diminishing number of ballet rôles. Her favourite partner of recent years has been the Russian dancer, Rudolf Nureyev.

Loie Fuller
American (1862–1928)

Loie Fuller was the founder of free expression in dance. The daughter of a farming family which gave its name to her birthplace, Fullersburg, Illinois, her first performance was in a church hall at the age of

One of the many Art Nouveau lamps inspired by Loie Fuller. This bronze lamp is by Raoul Larche.

three. Self-educated, Fuller worked at any theatrical job she could find, and first won public recognition in 1892 at the Folies-Bergères, Paris, for her choreography for the *Serpentine Dance*.

Nature provided the inspiration for Fuller's dance subjects – *Butterfly*, *Clouds*, *Lilies* – and her spectacular stage technique was to whirl hundreds of yards of diaphanous silk around her while coloured lights played on an otherwise darkened stage. The huge delicate shapes thus created appeared to be suspended in space, and her effects were admired by Rodin, Toulouse-Lautrec and W.B. Yeats among others. Fuller choreographed 'for body and silk' in her increasingly elaborate solo dances – she even created a 'radium dance' and became a friend of Marie Curie (q.v.). French scientists awarded her a prize for her innovations in lighting techniques.

A cheerful, generous woman, Fuller founded a school in Paris in 1908 where she welcomed younger dancers such as Isadora Duncan (q.v.). She also painted, sculpted, made films and wrote books. So popular was her style that Art Nouveau lamps and Lalique glass figures were produced to emulate her expressive movements.

Greta Garbo
Swedish (b. 1905)

Probably the most alluring film star of all, Garbo still retains a mysterious attraction 40 years after making her last film. Born Greta Gustafsson, she came from a very poor family in the Stockholm slums. She first worked as a shop assistant and was so pretty that she was chosen to model hats in the spring catalogue when she was 15. She then got several bit parts in films, and in 1922 the director Erik Petschler offered her the lead in *Luffar-Peter*. In 1924 she starred in *The Saga of Gösta Börling*, based on the novel by Selma Lagerlöf (q.v.). Mauritz Stiller, the director, befriended her and masterminded her subsequent success in Berlin in 1924; when Stiller ran out of money, she played the respectable girl turned prostitute in Pabst's *Joyless Street* (1925) along with another newcomer, Marlene Dietrich (q.v.).

Garbo's Hollywood career lasted for 16 years until 1941; she made 23 films for Mayer, Lubitsch and Clarence Brown including *Camille* (1937) and *Ninotchka* (1939). Although she made no films after *Two-Faced Woman* (1941) she was awarded a Special Oscar by the film industry in 1954 for her 'unforgettable screen performances'. In retirement now, Garbo has consistently shunned publicity; she had always claimed that her celebrated catchphrase 'I want to be alone' was 'I want to be left alone'.

Martha Graham
American (b. 1894)

The 'Mother of Modern Dance', Martha Graham is one of the great modern choreographers, and has run her own dance company for half a century.

The daughter of wealthy Presbyterians, she was born in Pittsburgh but the family moved to California when she was a child. Graham's dance career was undertaken in the face of stiff parental opposition, but she eventually managed to train at the Denishawn School (cf. Ruth St Denis). She began to teach there in 1920. In 1926 she appeared in *The Greenwich Village Follies* in New York and in 1929 founded the Martha Graham School of Contemporary Dance, of which she was for decades the principal dancer. Her choreography incorporates oriental dance, Zen philosophy and Greek myth – the celebrated *Clytemnestra* (1958) is one of her most ambitious 'dance plays'. Graham's overall aim is a 'sense of reaffirmation' from the 200 members of her company. Their costumes are individually designed by her, to extend the beauty of each movement and leave the body free. She married once, but later separated.

Billie Holiday
American (1913–1959)

'Lady Day' was the greatest night club singer of them all. She was born Eleanora Fagan, the illegitimate daughter of two teenagers in Baltimore. When she was 10 a woman neighbour held her down while a man raped her, and she was sent off to a reform school for being a prostitute.

Billie Holiday heard her first jazz records in a Baltimore brothel. She danced and sang to support herself and her mother. A runaway success on her first appearance in a New York bar, she signed a record contract with Benny Goodman in 1934 and another with Teddy Wilson in 1935. In 1937 she toured with Count Basie's band but had to wear black face powder in case they got into trouble as a 'mixed' band. She was with Artie Shaw from 1938 and acted in soap opera. 'There's no business like show business,' she would say, 'but you've got to smile to keep from throwing up.' Her 1954 tour of Europe was a high point in her career.

Holiday used her unique voice with meticulous precision in songs that were neither all blues nor true jazz, just highly personal. She was unforgettable in such numbers as *Night and Day* and *The Man I Love*. The man she really loved was her first husband, Jimmy Monroe, who was a heroin addict, and her efforts to cure him ended with her own addiction. Holiday's dazzling stage costume – white gown, white gardenia and white shoes – masked a grim reality. Her life was a pattern of prison and hospital, and her heartbreak voice and world-weary style tragically expressed her own dissolution. As she said, 'Dope never helped anyone to sing better or play music better or do anything better. All dope can do is kill you – the long, slow, hard way.' And it did eventually kill her.

Annie Horniman
British (1860–1937)

Annie Horniman was a patron of the theatre who blew the Victorian theatrical cobwebs away with her dedication to the new realism in playwriting pioneered by the Norwegian dramatist Ibsen. She came from a wealthy family; her Quaker grandfather had made a fortune travelling in the tea business and left a collection of exotic curios, which was turned into London's Horniman Museum by her father.

An illicit visit to the theatre with a governess when she was 14 sparked off Annie Horniman's lifelong passion. During vacations from the Slade School of Art in London she went on bicycle tours of Germany, and it was there that she saw performances of Ibsen's

plays, which inspired her to promote the 'new realism' in England. She financed the production of plays by W. B. Yeats and G. B. Shaw in 1893, at a time when no other management would take them on. Despite their commercial failure, she gave £20,000, a huge sum in those days, to the Abbey Theatre, Dublin, in 1894. She even worked there herself, sweeping floors and making costumes.

But Horniman was determined to found her own repertory theatre. In 1907 she took over the Gaiety in Manchester, and selected modern plays for performance there from the huge numbers of manuscripts sent in. She was notably fair to her actors and devoted herself to the cause of radical change in the British theatre. A dramatic personality, she would appear in magnificent brocade dresses on gala evenings, smoking a cigar and wearing a monocle.

Elisabeth Jacquet de la Guerre
French (1659–1729)

Elisabeth Jacquet was a keyboard performer and composer at the time of Louis XIV. The daughter of a professional musician, she was an infant prodigy, and at an early age was presented to the King, who continued to take an interest in her career. When she was 15, Madame de Maintenon (q.v.) took her education in hand. By the age of 18 she was regularly composing, but her first published book of pieces for the harpsichord, has unfortunately disappeared. She composed a ballet, an opera and, under the influence of Italian music of the day, sonatas and cantatas which are among the best of their period. She also gave harpsichord concerts, and was much admired for her gift for improvisation.

In 1687 Jacquet married Marin de la Guerre, a church organist; he died in 1704, and she survived him by 25 years.

Fanny Kemble
British (1809–1893)

Fanny Kemble was a famous actress and writer – and was one of the first writers to attack the institution of slavery. She was born into a famous acting family, but

The famous nineteenth-century actress Fanny Kemble. She was also an early champion of anti-slavery.

because she had been disfigured by smallpox she did not become a child actress. Instead she was quietly educated in France and Edinburgh. However, in 1829 her father Charles Kemble, her uncle John Kemble and her aunt Sarah Siddons (q.v.) made her take the stage as Juliet in an effort to recoup their losses as theatre managers. She was an instant success and thereafter acted regularly.

In 1832 she went on tour in the U.S. with her father, where she married a rich Southerner, Pierce Butler, in 1834. The marriage was at first passionate, but she soon found her husband's mastery over her and their slaves hard to bear. She expressed her feelings in her *Journal of a Residence on a Georgian Plantation*. When Pierce refused permission to publish the book, Kemble separated from him (they were divorced in 1848), and eventually returned to Europe for good. She was only rarely allowed to see her two daughters until they came of age in the 1850s.

Kemble returned to the stage, and when her father

retired in 1847 she began a series of Shakespeare recitals which were to make her famous (Henry James was a great admirer of them). She wrote plays and numerous books including *Records of a Girlhood* (1878), but the *Journal*, with its account of slaves on a Southern plantation, is by far the most interesting.

Umm Kulthum
Egyptian (1898–1975)

Umm Kulthum was the most phenomenally popular Egyptian singer of the twentieth century. Her concerts attracted gigantic crowds, though her repertoire was traditional, even conservative.

Kulthum was born in a village on the Nile Delta, the youngest daughter of a poor farmer. By the time she was six she was already singing at weddings in return for a dish of yoghurt. She insisted on being educated like her brother and so learnt at an early age the traditional religious chants which were to become the most popular part of her repertoire. Her tremendously successful outdoor concerts would customarily last for four hours or more, her rich, reverential voice almost hypnotizing her audience. She lived quietly with her husband, a doctor, and had no children. Kulthum's death was mourned by millions; the radio broadcast was followed by solemn readings from the Koran, an honour normally reserved for heads of state.

Wanda Landowska
Polish (1877–1959)

Artist, scholar, teacher and performer, Wanda Landowska re-introduced and popularized the music of the double keyboard harpsichord. Landowska was born in Poland; her father was a lawyer, her mother a linguist. She began to play the piano before she learnt to talk. At 14 she graduated from the Conservatoire in Warsaw, and went to Berlin to develop her technique. A passion for Bach inspired further research in museums all over Europe and the discovery of neglected manuscripts and instruments. 'When I study documents thoroughly, they become flesh and blood,' she said, 'they suggest visions that

Wanda Landowska: the celebrated harpsichordist, she re-introduced and popularized the harpsichord.

The great Wagnerian soprano Lotte Lehmann.

haunt me.' Nineteenth-century composers tended to make sentimental concert arrangements of early music; Wanda Landowska reversed this trend and restored the music to its original form. She was much in demand, and in 1909 even went to play for Tolstoy at his home – with one sleigh for her and another for the harpsichord. (Later she took her harpsichord on a gondola, and even once on a camel.) The post of Professor of Harpsichord was created for her in Berlin in 1912.

After the death of her musician husband, Henry Lew, in 1919, she set up her Ecole de Musique Ancienne just outside Paris. In 1940 the advance of the Nazis forced her to abandon 20 years' accumulation of books, manuscripts and instruments (not to mention her dogs, Do, Re, Mi, Fa, Sol and Musette). Landowska settled in the States in 1941 where she recorded her brilliant arrangements of Bach's Goldberg Variations, besides many baroque masterpieces she had rediscovered.

Lotte Lehmann
German (1888–1976)

Lotte Lehmann was the most memorable Marschallin in Strauss's *Der Rosenkavalier*; she was unforgettable as the Austrian noblewoman bidding goodbye to her youth. A graduate of the Royal Academy in Berlin. Lehmann's first operatic role was in a Wagner composition in Hamburg. She then moved to Vienna and made her name, singing both German folk songs and opera. During her career Lehmann sang all three great roles in *Der Rosenkavalier*, and Richard Strauss wrote his comic opera, *Arabella*, for her. In 1927 she was invited to Paris for a performance of *Fidelio* to celebrate Beethoven's centenary, the first performance of German music there since the 1914–18 war. Success at the Metropolitan Opera House, New York, in 1934 encouraged her to seek asylum in the U.S. in 1938, when she became a U.S. citizen.

Lehmann married the singer Otto Krause, who

died in 1939. She taught singing at the Music Academy of the West in Santa Barbara, California, from 1951 to 1961. There her pupils included Grace Bumbry (q.v.).

Lotte Lenya
German (b. 1900)

Associated principally with the Berlin of the Depression years, singing the 'town sparrow' songs of pre-Nazi Germany, Lotte Lenya was to become best known for her promotion of the music of her husband Kurt Weill. She was born Karline Blamauer in Vienna, daughter of a laundress and a coachman, and early demonstrated her creative talent; she was a dancer at the age of six and a tightrope walker at eight. She first achieved success as an actress in Berlin, and married Kurt Weill in 1926.

Lenya made her name as a singer at Baden-Baden in *The Little Mahogany*, the first work written jointly by Weill and Bertolt Brecht. In 1928 she created the famous role of Jenny in the Brecht/Weill version of John Gay's *The Beggar's Opera*, *The Threepenny Opera*; it ran for five years and established her as a popular performer. In 1933 the Nazi administration forced the couple to flee to Paris where they performed Weill's work for two years before leaving for the U.S. Unsuccessful initially as an actress in the U.S., Lotte Lenya became her husband's adviser until his death in 1950. She returned to the stage for several highly successful revivals of *The Threepenny Opera* between 1954 and 1956. In 1951 she married George Davis, an editor.

As Lenya once said, a good performance is like 'walking a tightrope. You either get it right or you don't.' Her husky, gritty voice is integral to the appeal of Weill's music. Her film appearances include parts in *Goldfinger* and *Cabaret*.

Jenny Lind
Swedish (1820–1887)

Jenny Lind, alias the 'Swedish Nightingale', sang her way to fame from a Stockholm slum. She was brought up by a strict, religious grandmother, and by

The 'Swedish Nightingale' Jenny Lind: a portrait by Eduard Magnus.

the time she was nine the very special quality of her voice had already been recognized. She was taken on as an 'actress pupil' by the Swedish Royal Opera House and achieved her first public success at the age of 18 as Agatha in Weber's *Der Freischutz*. Jenny Lind could act as well as sing – her face would light up as she hit top E. After touring the German opera houses for many seasons, she came to England in 1847, where her fans queued for hours for seats – leaving the House of Commons on at least one occasion without a quorum. The impresario Phineas Barnum arranged two years of touring in the U.S. where Lind married her pianist, Otto Goldschmidt, in Boston in 1852.

Lind gave away her earnings from the outset and continued to do so throughout her career. She chose to sing more sacred music as she grew older – and became professor of singing at the Royal College of Music in London in 1883.

Joan Littlewood
British (b. 1914)

Joan Littlewood is the most important director of political theatre in Britain this century. She was brought up in an orphanage in South London and at 16 won a scholarship to the Royal Academy of Dramatic Art. However, she soon ran away from the 'anyone-for-tennis, French-windows' style of acting, as she once called it, and went to study painting in Paris. She married the folk singer, Ewan McColl, and together they founded the Theatre of Action in Manchester with performances given when and where the opportunity arose. After working in radio during the Second World War, she founded a working-class Theatre Workshop in Manchester in 1945, which toured with a programme of classics plus polemical plays – 'Living Newspapers' – written by members of the company.

In 1953 Littlewood and Gerry Raffles, her friend and manager, moved permanently to the disused Theatre Royal in the borough of Stratford in East London. It was the start of her major enterprise. Deeply influenced by Bertolt Brecht, she made the company's name with *Mother Courage* in 1955 and went on to produce both classical and topical plays – notably Brendan Behan's *The Quare Fellow* (1956) and Frank Norman's *Fings Ain't Wot They Used to Be* (1959). In 1963, *Oh What a Lovely War*, a satirical musical about the First World War improvised by the company, made her world-famous.

In 1965 Littlewood became involved with Tunisian theatre and from 1968 to 1975 she organized 'bubble cities' linked to the base theatre in Stratford. Littlewood was made a Director of the University of the Air in 1977.

Marie Lloyd
British (1870–1922)

Marie Lloyd was one of the best loved music hall artists to emerge from London's East End.

Matilda Alice Victoria Wood started her stage career at 14 with the Fairy Bell minstrels singing *Up and down the City Road/In and out the Eagle*. In 1885, at the age of 15, she adopted the stage name 'Marie Lloyd', and within a year she was a star of the music hall stage and already earning £100 a week. With her earnings, she bought boots for 80 children in her native Hoxton. She brought fame to songs like *The boy I love sits up in the gallery*, *Oh Mr Porter*, *A little of what you fancy does you good*, and *I'm one of the ruins that Cromwell knocked about a bit*.

When she was 17 Lloyd married Percy Courtney; by the time she was 18 she owned her own house. She made popular tours of America, South Africa, Australia and the Continent. Photographs of her show endearing 'buck' teeth and a slight figure. Her rabelaisian humour was admired and loved as much by intellectuals as by her working-class fans.

Elisabeth Lutyens
British (b. 1906)

This highly professional and innovative composer introduced atonality to British music, although it was many years before her work was appreciated. The daughter of the famous architect Edwin Lutyens, granddaughter of Lord Lytton, Viceroy of India, and niece of Lady Constance Lytton (q.v.), Elisabeth Lutyens attended the Ecole Normale in Paris to study the viola and composition. There she was deeply influenced by Schoenberg's twelve tone scale and 'serialism'. In 1931 she became co-founder of the MacNaghten-Lemar concerts in London to promote modern music. Her first composition, *The Birthday of the Infanta* (after Oscar Wilde), was performed in 1939.

In 1933 Elisabeth Lutyens married Ian Glennie, a fellow musician. They had five children. In 1943 they were divorced and she married the conductor Edward Clark.

Her music was not much performed in public until the 1950s, but since then she has greatly influenced younger composers like Malcolm Williamson and Richard Rodney Bennett through her professionalism, intelligence and independence. She has

opposite The irrepressible Marie Lloyd, one of the best loved music hall stars.

always been an intellectual composer and has written an unaccompanied motet to a text by the philosopher, Wittgenstein. She has also written more than 100 film scores. Always an individualist, she once said: 'I do not cook musically according to recipe books by others.'

Natalia Makarova
Russian (b. 1940)

Makarova is the greatest contemporary dancer working within the classical tradition. She was born in Leningrad; her father, an engineer, was killed in the Second World War. Makarova trained at the Vaganova Ballet School, and then joined the Kirov Company. She felt the company's work was too limited, however, and defected to join the American Ballet Theatre in New York in 1970.

Makarova's greatest roles are in *Swan Lake* and *The Sleeping Beauty* – both ballets created in her native Russia – which she dances with intense emotion and artistocratic grace. In 1972 she joined the Royal Ballet Company to dance Kenneth Macmillan's modern ballet, *Romeo and Juliet*. Makarova was married twice in Russia before she left for the West. In 1975 she married Edward Karkar, a New York Lebanese electronics expert, who is also a violinist.

Dame Alicia Markova
British (b. 1910)

Britain's first great prima ballerina, Lilian Alice Marks, started her dancing career by changing her real name to a more Russian-sounding one, believing – like her great partner, the Irishman Anton Dolin – that success was impossible with a British name. She was born in North London, one of the three daughters of Alfred Marks, an engineer. It was her weak arches that first sent her to dancing classes and consequently to her first engagement as a child prodigy in 1921. Diaghilev gave her the title role in Balanchine's *Le Rossignol* in 1923; he called her 'his

Alicia Markova, England's first great prima ballerina.

little English girl'. 'He was a second father to me,' she said.

After leaving the Ballets Russes in 1931 Markova spent four years with the Vic-Wells (cf. Ninette de Valois), and was the first British ballerina to dance *Giselle*. In 1935 she and Dolin formed what became the London Festival Ballet Company. From 1938 to 1941 she danced for the Ballets Russes de Monte Carlo, then had seven extremely successful years with the American Ballet Theatre in New York. Markova retired from the stage in 1963. She has been a Professor of Ballet and Performing Arts at the University of Cincinnati since 1970, and has given master classes since 1974.

177

Nellie Melba: her stage name was based on Melbourne, the city of her birth.

Dame Nellie Melba
Australian (1861–1931)

Helen Porter Mitchell was the first of the great Australian opera singers to win world-wide admiration. She was born in Melbourne and went to Europe in 1886, leaving a husband and son behind. She went to Paris first, then to Brussels in 1887. Her début in London in *Lucia di Lammermoor* ensured her succession to Adelina Patti (q.v.) as Covent Garden's prima donna. Melba's high notes reverberated with a haunting beauty and, after the grand opera was over, she would customarily have a piano pushed on stage and sing simple songs like '*Coming Through the Rye*' or '*Home, Sweet Home*' as an encore. Her tombstone reads, 'Addio, senza rancore' (Farewell with no regrets), a line taken from one of her favourite operas, *La Bohème*. Such was her popular success, that both Pêche Melba and Melba toast were named after her.

Agnes de Mille
American (b. 1908)

Agnes de Mille is one of the most distinguished of U.S. choreographers. She was responsible for several legendary dance routines in musical comedy (most notably *Oklahoma* in 1943) and many masterfully choreographed ballets. Agnes de Mille's father was a successful New York playwright, William C. de Mille, and her uncle was Cecil B. de Mille, the Hollywood producer. She saw Pavlova dance when she was a child and knew immediately what she wanted to be. Faced with heavy parental opposition, however, she had to practise secretly in her bedroom, while she enrolled at the Theodore Kosloff Ballet School. She was then forced to go to the University of California for four years, but later she danced in her own compositions before her Broadway début in 1927. She worked for several years in England where she met Marie Rambert (q.v.).

Back in New York, she was influenced by the expressive style pioneered by Martha Graham (q.v.). De Mille choreographed for the American Ballet Theatre and, in 1940, was the first non-Russian to be given the job of choreographer with the Ballets Russes de Monte Carlo; *Rodeo* (1942) was the smash hit that resulted. This was shortly followed by the unforgettable *Oklahoma* (1943), *Brigadoon* (1947) and *Fall River Legend* (1948), all of which owed part of their huge success both on stage and screen to Agnes de Mille's artful blend of zestful 'country style' and disciplined movement.

In 1943 de Mille married Walter Foy Prude, a concert manager, and had one son. *Speak to Me, Dance with Me* (1973) is her autobiography.

Marilyn Monroe
American (1926–1962)

The most celebrated of all Hollywood's screen goddesses, Marilyn Monroe was born Norma Jean Baker, the third child, possibly illegitimate, of a mother who spent much of her life in mental hospital. Her troubled background probably instilled the profound sense of insecurity which, ironically, lent

Marilyn Monroe photo-
graphed by Cecil Beaton in
New York in 1956.

Monroe the air of vulnerable charm which has had such universal box office appeal.

Raised in an orphanage and as a foster child, Norma Jean married a policeman, Jim Dougherty, when she was 16, and worked briefly in a parachute factory before joining a model agency. The agency preferred their models to be unmarried so she divorced Dougherty and, soon after, in 1946, signed a film contract with Fox to play bit parts in half a dozen undistinguished movies. It was not until the 1950s that she was spotted in John Huston's *The Asphalt Jungle*. She had a small part in *All About Eve*, and starred for the first time in the risible *Niagara*. *How to Marry a Millionaire* (1953) and *There's No Business Like Show Business* (1954) at last made her name. In 1954 she married the baseball star Joe DiMaggio, and their honeymoon tour of Korea during the Korean War was the start of the incredible publicity which was to follow her for the rest of her life. However, DiMaggio objected to the sex goddess roles his wife was now playing in films such as *The Seven Year Itch* (1955), her first major part. In 1956, after their divorce, Monroe married the playwright Arthur Miller, but her drinking and dependence on sleeping pills put a heavy strain on the marriage. Yet her best films were made during this period: *Bus Stop* (1956), the one film in which she truly created a character, and *Some Like it Hot* (1959), one of the finest comedies ever made for which Monroe turned in her most engaging performance as a singer with an all-girl

179

band. Although they had separated by then, Miller wrote *The Misfits* (1960) for her; it turned out to be her last film. Though she made several attempts to reach help, Marilyn Monroe was found dead in 1962 still clutching the telephone. Her death was ruled a probable suicide.

Thea Musgrave
British (b. 1928)

Thea Musgrave is a versatile and original composer and conductor. She had her first piano lesson at the age of five, when the teacher stood her on a stool so that she could watch the strings. After boarding school in England, she went to Edinburgh University as a medical student, but she 'didn't like dissecting frogs and as the Music Department was next door …' Two years later Musgrave won the Lili Boulanger prize for composition and studied under Nadia Boulanger (q.v.) in Paris. Seven years of teaching and copy-editing in London gave her time to compose and *The Decision*, an opera about a trapped miner, was first staged in 1967. In 1970 she married a fellow musician, Peter Mark, and wrote and conducted a viola concerto for him in 1973. She has written a romantic ballet, *Beauty and the Beast*, and her two recent operas. *The Voice of Ariadne* and *Mary, Queen of Scots*, were both triumphs in New York. Currently at the height of her popularity, she claims that 'the most valuable thing for a composer is an electric pencil sharpener' and that 'till women realize that they *can* do these things, they just won't.'

Okuni
Japanese (c. 1573–1614)

Kabuki drama, one of the most popular traditions in Japanese theatre (translated roughly, kabuki means 'romantic sketch'), was virtually invented by Okuni. The daughter of an artisan, Nakamura Sanyemon, Okuni was an itinerant dancer from the great Izumo shrine who, in order to raise money for rebuilding the shrine, toured with a company giving performances of religious dance-dramas. In 1601 she teamed up with a popular comedian and together they de-

veloped her idea – a combination of lively mime and religious pantomime. The 'invention' of Kabuki is said to date from 1603, when the pair first performed their new dramas on a stage set up in the dried-up bed of the River Kamo, at Kyoto. Soon after, however Okuni left the comedian for a samurai, Nagoya Sauza, who was well versed in classical drama – and brought another ingredient to the new dramatic genre. By 1604 they had a semi-permanent theatre.

Okuni established the Kabuki tradition of men playing women and women playing men; she herself was famous for her black silk priest's robe and the two swords in her belt. Kabuki was immensely popular both with the people and with the Japanese court. Okuni appeared in Tokyo in 1607.

Adelina Patti
Italian (1843–1919)

Adelina Patti became a world-famous soprano in the Victorian era. Her Italian father and Spanish mother were both singers. She was born in Madrid and made her début at the age of seven in New York. Patti starred as Lucia in *Lucia di Lammermoor* at 14 and was such an attraction that Covent Garden brought her to London to sing *La Sonnambula* in 1861. Her voice was perfect for the famous coloratura roles – Linda, Rosina, Amina, Lucia and Zerlina. She reigned supreme at Covent Garden until she was nearly 50, rivalled only by Jenny Lind (q.v.) who sang a totally different repertoire. In 1868 she married a French marquis, Henri de Caux, but divorced him in 1885 to marry the tenor Nicolini. He died 10 years later and she married the Swedish Baron Cederström, with whom she retired to a castle in Wales in 1899. There she built a private theatre for her own performances.

Anna Pavlova
Russian (1883–1931)

Most legendary of all ballerinas, Pavlova was born in St Petersburg, the daughter of a laundress. When she was eight her mother took her to see *The Sleeping Beauty*, which inspired in her a passion to become a

Adelina Patti, the world-famous Victorian soprano, in Don Giovanni.

dancer. She began training at the Imperial Ballet School at the age of 10. At 13, in 1896, she appeared as a leading ballerina at the festivities of the Tsar's coronation; 10 years later she became a prima ballerina.

Pavlova joined Diaghilev in Western Europe in 1909, but soon broke away to form her own company. For 25 years she toured all over the world – South America, Asia, Australia and Europe. Fokine, who said she seemed to 'fly through the air', created *Les Sylphides* for Pavlova and she is forever associated with her role of the dying swan, so graceful and poignant, yet so full of fire. In 1924 she married her accompanist, André Darmide, and determined to devote herself to domesticity; but she was still dancing when she died.

Mary Pickford
Canadian (1893–1979)

America's Sweetheart, the star who made movies respectable, was born Gladys Marie Smith in Canada. Her father died when she was four and her mother had her acting in the Toronto Stock Company at the age of five. Pickford's favourite part as a child was as Eva in *Uncle Tom's Cabin* (cf. Harriet Beecher Stowe) – 'I counted the handkerchiefs in the audience,' she said later. By 1901, when she was eight, she was on tour, already insisting on roles for her sister Lottie and brother Jack, and channelling all earnings back into the family. On Broadway in 1907 she played the part that earned her her nickname in *America's Sweetheart*.

In 1909 Pickford's film career began, when she went to work with the director D.W. Griffiths in 'flickers' – which were then considered far more disreputable than any theatre. It was he who moulded her as a star. 'I became the little girl I had never been,' she said as her earnings went up playing parts which were so popular with family audiences. In 1916 she formed the Mary Pickford Corporation and filmed Pavlova (q.v.) among other subjects. In 1917 she made her most popular films, *Poor Little Rich Girl* and *Rebecca of Sunnybrook Farm*, still childish, ringleted and pure. She played *Little Lord Fauntleroy* when 27.

Pickford's shrewdest move, however, was to found United Artists with Charlie Chaplin, Douglas Fairbanks Sr and D.W. Griffiths in 1919, the year her unhappy marriage to an alcoholic fellow actor, Owen Moore, ended. In 1920 she married Fairbanks, who gave her a Beverly Hills mansion as a wedding present. They named it Pickfair and reigned as the royalty of Hollywood until their divorce in 1936. She then married Buddy Rogers.

By 1932 Pickford had made 200 silent movies (which she owned); four 'talkies' – and 50 million dollars. She retired early, for, as she said, 'The little girl made me. I wasn't waiting for [her] to kill me.'

Elisa Rachel
French (1821–1858)

Rachel was the most awesome European actress of the nineteenth century. Born Elisa Felix, the second daughter of itinerant Jewish pedlars, she and her sister sang, shivering, in the streets of Paris to earn their living. The tiny dark girl with her guitar was 'spotted' in 1832 and sent to a theatre school. Already versed in Molière – she stole housekeeping money to buy his plays – Rachel studied Racine's and Corneille's great tragic roles; she was to make the role of Phèdre particularly her own.

From her first appearance in 1837, Rachel shone like no other actress. In 1848 she saved the Comédie Française, of which she was made a *sociétaire* in 1842, from the revolutionary mob by her extraordinarily fervent recital of *La Marseillaise*. Her tour of Russia in 1854 left Moscow 'in flames', although a visit to America in 1855 was less successful. Rachel contracted tuberculosis in her thirties. When Charlotte Brontë (q.v.) saw her act in 1855, on her only visit to the theatre in London, she described her as 'pale like twilight, wasted like wax flame', but went on: 'Rachel's acting filled me with horror. That tremendous force with which she expresses the very worst passions in their strongest essence forms an exhibition as exciting as the bullfights of Spain and gladiatorial combats of old Rome.'

Rachel had many lovers. One, a prince, sent a card inscribed 'Ou? Quand? Combien?' to which she replied, 'Chez toi. Ce soir. Pour rien.' She died aged 36, unsurpassed even by Sarah Bernhardt (q.v.).

Dame Marie Rambert
Polish (b. 1888)

Although not a great dancer herself, Marie Rambert has been responsible for the discovery and development of many of the most important talents in British classical ballet. Born Cyvia Ramberg in Warsaw, the daughter of a bookseller, she was sent to Paris to study medicine. However, she had seen Isadora Duncan (q.v.) dance and had resolved on her future career.

She first earned a living as a 'barefoot dancer' in Paris, and then spent three years in Geneva with Jacques Dalcroze, a pioneer in eurythmics, until she was 'spotted' in 1911 by Diaghilev, who took her into his company, then based in Monte Carlo.

Marie Rambert – as she called herself – came to London in 1915; in 1918 she married the playwright and translator, Ashley Dukes, and had two children. In 1920 she founded the highly influential Ballet Rambert School, and gave Frederick Ashton (now Sir Frederick) his first opportunities as a choreographer. In 1930 she and her husband ran a ballet season at the Mercury Theatre, and although it was a commercial failure it has become famous in the annals of ballet. They then formed the Ballet Rambert, still flourishing today. In 1966 the company abandoned the classical repertoire and trained its dancers in innovatory modern dance, many choreographed by its own members. In 1962 she translated Ulanova's autobiography (q.v.) and has written her own autobiography, *Quicksilver* (1972).

Ruth St Denis
American (1878–1968)

Ruth St Denis pioneered modern dance theory in America. As a dancer and choreographer she taught that expressive movement is a spiritual as well as a physical discipline. She was born Ruth Dennis in New Jersey; her mother was a doctor and her father an engineer. At the age of 10 after reading Delsarte's book on body movements she determined to be a dancer and managed to persuade a New York teacher to give her free lessons. Ruth St Denis – the name she adopted – earned a living playing in vaudeville and concerts in the 1890s, then went on a European tour with David Belasco Productions. In Paris she saw Loie Fuller (q.v.) and was inspired to develop her own ideas. *Radha* (1906) – based on Egyptian and Indian philosophy – was the first of many successes; it was followed by *Cobra*, *Nautch* and *Yogi*.

In 1914 Ruth St Denis married the dancer Ted Shawn, and they set up the Denishawn School in Los Angeles; she influenced both Agnes de Mille and Martha Graham (qq.v.). When both the school and her marriage ended in 1931, she founded the Society for Spiritual Art and taught dance at Adelphi College, in New York, until she retired.

Clara Schumann
German (1819–1896)

Clara Schumann was the most famous female musical

Clara Schumann. A brilliant pianist, she was famous for her performances of Bach, Beethoven and Chopin.

Sarah Siddons: acclaimed as 'the greatest tragic actress'. This portrait is by John Downman.

prodigy, and grew up to be an influential and internationally renowned pianist. She was intensively trained by her father, the pianist Frederick Wieck, and first appeared on the concert platform as a tiny child. At 13 her reputation as a performer was established. Exceptionally brilliant technically, she was taught the piano at the Frankfurt conservatory for 15 years. The composer, Robert Schumann, gave up the law to study music with Frederick Wieck, and Clara, much against her father's will, married him in 1839. She was already famous for performing the works of Bach, Beethoven and Chopin, at that time rarely heard; now she became the dedicated champion of her husband's compositions also, and played them all over Europe. At home she gave up her own practising when he wanted to compose.

After her husband's death in 1856 she worked steadily to promote her young friend, Brahms. She

died listening to her husband's *Intermezzi* being played by her grandson.

Sarah Siddons
British (1755–1831)

Mrs Siddons reigned supreme in the English theatre for more than 20 years. She was the eldest of 12 children of the famous Kemble family of actors and was born on tour. Regular school attendance was impossible, but she learnt Milton's *Paradise Lost* by heart at the age of 12. In 1773 she married the actor, William Siddons; they had seven children.

Mrs Siddons' great public career began in Sheridan's *The Rivals* in Bath in 1778. Four years later she was starring at Drury Lane Theatre, London: a majestic figure dressed in flowing robes with her hair streaming down her back. She was much lionized socially, taught the Royal Princesses elocution and had her portrait painted by Gainsborough.

Lady Macbeth was Mrs Siddons' favourite Shakespearean role. She conceived of her as a blue-eyed blonde – 'only such a woman could seduce honourable Macbeth,' she declared. The role was her triumph. Mrs Siddons retired in 1812, but gave memorable readings well into old age.

Bessie Smith
American (1895–1937)

'The Empress of the Blues', as Bessie Smith was popularly known, was the greatest of all blues singers. She was first noticed at the age of 10 in her home town, Chattanooga, Tennessee, and 'Ma' Rainey, another famous blues singer, took her on a tour of cities in the South when she was only 13. In 1923 Bessie's record *Down Hearted Blues* sold two million copies and made her famous; thereafter she sang with Benny Goodman and Louis Armstrong all over America. In 1929 she sang the title song in the film *St Louis Blues*.

Bessie Smith was a true blues singer, full of stoicism and irony, but her traditional idiom went out of fashion in the 1920s when public taste shifted towards more sentimental music; she suffered a decline in popularity, her marriage broke up and she began to drink heavily. The jazz revival of the 1930s had just got under way when she was severely injured in a car crash. As a black woman she was refused admission to a segregated hospital in Mississippi and bled to death, a fate which has since haunted the conscience of America. She had made 159 records.

Dame Ethel Smyth
British (1858–1944)

Ethel Smyth was a fine British composer almost unrecognized in her own country. Her father was an Indian Army General and she was born in Frimley, Southern England, the fourth of eight children. Determined to study music in the face of stiff parental opposition, Ethel Smyth locked herself in her bedroom until her father relented and allowed her to

Dame Ethel Smyth photographed by E. O. Hoppé in 1928.

study in Leipzig. Once there she astonished her German hosts by leaping over tables and by playing tennis, which was in 1877 a very new sport for women. If her social behaviour appeared eccentric at times, her musical ability was at no time in question. She met Clara Schumann (q.v.) and Brahms and had the honour of hearing her own composition for a string quartet performed while she was still a student. She had a Mass performed in 1893 but her strongest work did not readily find an audience: 'I was born 50 years too soon and of the wrong sex,' she said. Sir Thomas Beecham, the great English conductor, eventually brought *The Forest* to Covent Garden in 1906, but her best work, *The Wreckers*, had to have its première in Leipzig in 1906.

Smyth was deeply involved with the Women's Socialist and Political Union with Emmeline Pankhurst (q.v.), to whom she was devoted. She wrote the 'Marseillaise of the Movement', *The March of the Women*. In 1913, she and Mrs Pankhurst were imprisoned along with many other demonstrators in Holloway prison: at one point Smyth, leaning out of a window, conducted her anthem with a toothbrush as it was sung by the suffragettes in the prison's exercise yard below her.

Careless of all save music and friendship, she wore a wig on top of her untidy hair to conduct, put a tricorne hat on top of that, and always wore a tie with her tweeds. Smyth bore her deafness in old age with fortitude. George Bernard Shaw once wrote to her, 'It was your music that cured me of the old delusion that women could not do man's work in art.'

Joan Sutherland
Australian (b. 1926)

'La Stupenda' is only one of the many extravagant names given to this great coloratura soprano. Joan Sutherland's father was a tailor who died when she was six; her mother had always wanted to be singer and Joan was introduced to opera at an early age. At first she worked as a secretary, but in 1944 she won a scholarship for her singing. In 1945 she had won enough money to go to London and embark on an operatic career accompanied by her mother and a fellow musician, the pianist Richard Bonynge, who became her husband and manager. They have one son.

During the early years at Covent Garden, Sutherland relied heavily both on her husband's coaching and his support through various operations for her severe sinusitis. Her triumph came in 1959 with star roles in Handel's *Dido and Aeneas* and Donizetti's *Lucia di Lammermoor* at Covent Garden, soon followed by invitations to perform all over the world. She was acclaimed by everyone, including Callas (q.v.), for her tremendous high notes and her control, which have enabled her to sing certain roles not heard since the last century.

Ellen Terry
British (1848–1928)

Ellen Terry was the most popular actress on the British stage in the nineteenth century. She was one of many daughters from a family of small time actors. She had very little formal education and appeared in

Joan Sutherland photographed in St Marks Square, Venice.

bit parts as fairies and little boys at a very early age. At 16 she married the painter G. F. Watts, but left him shortly afterwards. In 1868 she abandoned the theatre and retired to the country with William Godwin, an architect, and gave birth to two children, Edith and Gordon Craig (cf. Isadora Duncan). Ten years later, abandoned and in debt, Terry returned to the theatre and in 1878 began her long, successful partnership with Sir Henry Irving, the famous actor-manager of the day. They toured the world together. Terry's stage strength lay in her eloquent and graceful expression of charm and humour; she was seen as the ideal of femininity. In 1883 she married a young American actor, James Carew, and subsequently settled in Small Hythe, Kent. Her house is now a museum. Her sister, Kate Gielgud, was the grandmother of Sir John Gielgud.

Twyla Tharp
American (b. 1941)

Twyla Tharp is one of the wittiest and most inventive dance directors and choreographers of the twentieth century. Named after an Indian princess and born in Portland, Indiana, she was dedicated to dance from an early age. She formed her own company in 1965 after working for a short time as a freelance choreographer and following her début with the Paul Taylor Dance Company.

No movement is too bizarre or too comic for Tharp's 'collage' method; she uses jazz, circus clowns' gestures, athletics, even roller skates, and grafts the appropriate movements on to what she has to say. 'Ideas are like chewing gum,' she once said, 'no good when they're old.' Tharp's choreography incorporates all disciplines – including classical ballet – and her company will perform in gyms, out-of-doors, anywhere. Her most recent success was to choreograph for the British Olympic gold medallist skater John Curry. Characteristically, she put on ice skates for the first time ever to do the work. *Eight Jelly Rolls* (1971), *Push Comes to Shove* (1976) and *Mud* (1977) are among her best known works. She was married to Robert Huot, but is now divorced, and has a son, Jesse.

Galina Ulanova
Russian (b. 1910)

The impact of this great *prima ballerina assoluta* in ballet circles when she first appeared in the West after the Second World War was enormous. Ulanova's talent was apparent at an early age, for her mother was a dancer, her father a dance teacher; at nine she was sent to train in an austere boarding school. From her début in 1928 onwards she was entrusted with more and more important roles, particularly such characters as Juliet and Giselle, until she became the most important ballerina in Russia. In retirement now, Ulanova still exercises every day – she feels it is 'the source of the creative process. Talent is work.' Ulanova married the Bolshoi's chief designer, Vadim Rindin, when she left the stage to become a dance teacher. Her autobiography, *Ulanova: Her Childhood and Schooldays*, was translated by Dame Marie Rambert (q.v.) in 1962.

Dame Ninette de Valois
Irish (b. 1898)

The principal architect of Britain's Royal Ballet – one of the world's great ballet companies – Ninette de Valois was born Edris Stannus in Ireland, the daughter of an Army officer who was killed in the First World War. Young Edris Stannus originally wanted to train as an artist, but gave it up in favour of dancing. She danced in opera, pantomime and revue (the name Ninette de Valois was her mother's idea) until Diaghilev made her one of his solo dancers in 1923.

In 1926 she left the Ballets Russes to form her own Academy of Choreographic Art. Badly needing a theatre for her dancers, she joined Lilian Baylis (q.v.) in 1928, and together they founded the Vic-Wells Ballet in 1931. De Valois built up a popular repertoire of classical and contemporary dance for her company which comprised six women and five men, one of whom was Frederick Ashton. De Valois created her own ballets, notably *Job*, *The Rake's Progress* and *Checkmate*. When Alicia Markova (q.v.) left the company in 1935 Margot Fonteyn (q.v.) took her place as the star.

The creative success of the Royal Ballet is the result of de Valois' untiring determination and dedication. She married Dr Arthur Connell in 1935.

Lucia Vestris
British (1797?–1856)

The most successful theatre manager of her day started out as a penniless singer and dancer. Lucia Bartolozzi was born into an Italian family of painters who had settled in England; she married Armand Vestris, a fellow performer, at 16. Her lovely contralto voice and dark curly hair made her a perfect Macheath in *The Beggars' Opera*, one of the many 'breeches' parts which showed her legs off to advantage. She created a sensation as Susanna in *Le Nozze di Figaro* and in the fashionable operetta, *Don Giovanni in London*. By 1830 she had taken over 12 leading operatic roles at Drury Lane and Covent Garden.

Vestris then switched very successfully to theatre management. Her style was distinctly 'French' but she raised the moral tone at the Royal Olympic Theatre during the nine years of her management to a more generally acceptable standard, and in doing so made a fortune. From 1847 onwards she also ran the Lyceum and Covent Garden. So respectable did Vestris become that Queen Victoria (q.v.) invited her to organize a fancy dress ball at Buckingham Palace. Her public successes were undermined however by the drunkenness and bad debts of her second husband, Charles Matthews.

Pauline Viardot
Spanish (1821–1910)

Pauline Viardot was one of the great nineteenth-century teachers and singers and the friend and confidante of many of the writers of the day. Born Pauline Garcia in New York, she was the youngest in a family of singers. Her father was the singer Manuel Garcia; her elder sister, Maria Malibran, was already a famous prima donna by the time she was killed at the age of 29 in a riding accident. After Maria's death, her mother made Pauline give up the piano and concentrate on singing, and she made a successful début as a mezzo-soprano in London, and then in Paris, singing extremely demanding roles in Gluck's *Orphée*, Rossini's *Othello* and Bellini's *La Sonnambula*. In Paris she became a friend of George Sand (q.v.), and in 1840 she married Louis Viardot, at one time the director of the Théâtre Italien in the French capital. They had two daughters and a son.

In 1843 Viardot sang in St Petersburg, a significant event both for Russian music, which she was to promote for the rest of her life, and for her because it led to her long friendship with the Russian novelist Turgenev. Turgenev fell passionately in love with her, and may have been the father of her son Paul; for the next 40 years he was her devoted admirer, and often a member of her household.

The Viardots, after years spent touring, finally settled in Baden-Baden in 1863 where Pauline Viardot presided over a wide social and intellectual circle, and where Brahms wrote the *Alto Rhapsody*

Pauline Viardot, one of the great nineteenth-century music teachers and singers.

for her. But the Franco-Prussian War of 1870 drove the family to take refuge in London where Viardot's brother, Manuel Garcia, was teaching.

By this time Viardot's voice was no longer strong enough for public performances of opera; she taught instead, and composed operettas for her pupils. In 1878 they returned to Paris, accompanied by Turgenev (and his illegitimate daughter Paulinette). But in 1882 both Louis Viardot and Turgenev died – both tenderly nursed by Viardot. She spent the remaining decades of her life teaching.

VISUAL ARTS

THE ELDER PLINY, in his *Natural History* of the first century AD, lists several women artists of the classical world, but sadly we know little of them, with the exception of one Iaia of Cyzicus, an unmarried painter and engraver who was so skilled that 'in the prices she obtained, she far outdid the celebrated portrait painters Sopolis and Dionysius.' After the fall of Rome, Christian monasteries became the repositories of scholarship and art, and one of the main duties of the inhabitants, both men and women, was the copying and illumination of manuscripts. Sometimes the nun-artists name themselves — Guda, Claricia, Maria and Ende are names which have come down to us – and on occasion, drew themselves at work.

One of the earliest identifiable women artists is a sculptor, Sabina von Steinbach, who lived in the early fourteenth century. Thereafter the history of European art is full of women artists, although their names are rarely familiar. If they were lucky enough to be born into an artist's family, women could get a training, and if they had talent they could earn a good living. The fortune earned by Sofonisba Anguissola when she was still quite young gave many a male artist the idea that there was money – and a reputation – to be made out of taking on a gifted daughter as his assistant. Sometimes the assistant's work would be taken for the master's by later generations, and art historical scholarship has scarcely started unravelling the correct attributions even of well-known women artists.

But paint brush and chisel are not the only means of women's artistic expression. The famous Bayeux tapestry, which depicts the Norman conquest of England, was the work of women embroiderers, perhaps attached to the court of Queen Matilda. The nuns of mediaeval Europe were famous for their needlework vestments and altar furnishings, though they remained anonymous, as have the Navajo Indian women of modern times who design and weave their beautiful ceremonial blankets.

The invention of the camera brought women a new way to express their visual gifts: Julia Margaret Cameron was one of the greatest of the early photographers. There have also been some notable women film-makers, such as Leni Riefenstahl, considered by many the greatest of all documentary film-makers.

American film director Dorothy Arzner, on the set of Merrily We Go to Hell, *1932.* 189

Berenice Abbott
American (b. 1898)

Berenice Abbott has had two separate, equally distinguished careers as a photographer – first as the recorder of old New York in the 1930s, and second from the late 1950s as the pioneer of photography to illustrate the laws of physics, for which she designed much of her own equipment.

Abbott was born in Springfield, Ohio, and studied fine art in New York and Europe, where she was a pupil of Bourdelle (cf. Germaine Richier). She turned to photography when she worked in the Paris studio of the artist Man Ray in 1923–5, and subsequently opened her own studio. She took portraits of some of the most famous artists and writers of the day, including James Joyce, Edna St Vincent Millay, Marie Laurençin (q.v.), Jean Cocteau and André Gide.

Back home in New York in the 1930s, Abbott decided to document the city which was gradually being destroyed to make way for rebuilding. *Changing New York* was published in 1937, and this immensely valuable social document made her name. From 1934 to 1958 she taught at the New School of Social Research, and has written several technical books. She has also been responsible for rescuing the work of the great French photographer Eugène Atget from obscurity.

Sofonisba Anguissola
Italian (1532?–1625)

Sofonisba Anguissola was one of the most successful portrait painters of her time, and became famous throughout Europe. She was the eldest of six daughters of a nobleman of Cremona, and in her youth received training from professional painters. In 1559, she became court painter to Philip II of Spain and was showered with presents, paid a high salary, and given a dowry when she married (probably Fabrizio de Moncada) and left Spain to settle in Palermo. When she was widowed she married Orazio Lomellini and settled in Genoa, but returned to Palermo at the end of her life. The painter Anthony van Dyck visited her there a year before her death, when she was in her nineties – blind, but still with her wits about her.

Anguissola was the first European woman painter whose work survives in quantity. Most of it dates from the early part of her life – nearly all her 'Spanish' work has disappeared – so it is not easy to say how good she became. But although she was far from being – as one admirer claimed – the equal of Titian, she was an extremely able portraitist in the tradition of the Italian Renaissance, and, with pictures of her family, particularly an engaging painting of three of her sisters playing chess, was an early exponent of the conversation piece.

Her historical importance is suggested by the fact that in her wake other young Italian women were encouraged to aim for careers in painting (and their fathers were encouraged to pay for their training) – Lavinia Fontana, Barbara Longhi, Fede Galizia, for example, as well as her own sisters. Lucia Anguissola, who died at 25, was thought to have held promise of being even better than Sofonisba.

Diane Arbus
American (1923–1971)

Diane Arbus has been a cult figure ever since her astonishing debut as a serious photographer at the Museum of Modern Art in 1967. She exhibited with two other photographers, but it was to her work that the crowds flocked: haunting studies of outcasts, cripples and deviants, all portrayed with a directness that seemed almost cruel but which was also profoundly sympathetic. 'Her real subject is no less than the unique interior lives of those she photographed,' said the critic John Szarkowski.

Arbus was born in New York into an affluent Jewish family; her father, David Nemerov, was the owner through her mother's family of the Fifth Avenue fashion store Russeks. She married a photographer, Allan Arbus, when she was 18, and had two daughters. For nearly 20 years she worked with her husband as a fashion photographer, and only

---

Manhattan Bridge by Berenice Abbott, 1936. One in her series of photographs of old New York.

when she was 36, after studying with Lisette Model, did she begin to pursue her own painful vision.

In 1972 Arbus became the first American photographer to be exhibited at the Venice Biennale. She once said: 'I've never taken a picture I've intended. They're always better or worse.' As her elder daughter said: 'She was determined to record what others had been taught to turn their backs on.' Arbus committed suicide in 1971.

Dorothy Arzner
American (1900–1979)

Dorothy Arzner is the best known of the few women who became film directors in the heyday of Hollywood. Her German father and her Scottish mother ran the popular Hoffmann's Café in Los Angeles, much frequented by the stars in the early days of the film industry. After graduating from the University of California, Arzner took a job as secretary to Cecil B. de Mille. She went on to work for the director James Cruce, and was given the job of film editor. When her 'home' studio, Paramount, heard she might join their rival Columbia merely to be allowed to direct, they immediately offered her *Fashions for Women* (1927), one of the three films that made her name in the silent era. Arzner subsequently directed Paramount's first sound film, *The Wild Party*, in 1929. To improvize equipment that did not yet exist, she hung microphones over the actors' heads with fishing rods. Over the next 20 years she made 14 films including *Merrily We Go to Hell* (1932), *Christopher Strong* (1933) and *The Bride Wore Red* with Joan Crawford (1937). She also made TV commercials and taught at UCLA.

Hester Bateman
British (c. 1709–1794)

Hester Bateman was one of the great silversmiths of eighteenth-century England. She was a Londoner, daughter of Thomas Needham, and never learned to read or write. She married John Bateman, who was a gold chain maker, and had five children. By the time her husband died in 1760 she was sufficiently skilled as

A silver coffee pot by Hester Bateman, 1773–4.

a smith to be entrusted with the tools of his trade and to acquire her own hallmark. The earliest 'H.B.' dates from 1761. For 30 years, she ran an extremely prosperous family business, and was responsible for some of the most beautiful pieces of domestic silver ever made: teapots, gravy boats, sugar tongs, jugs, porringers, spoons and forks and so on. She also made church plate, and a verger's wand made by her is still in use in St Paul's Cathedral.

Bateman's three sons and one of her daughters-in-law, all worked for her, and after her retirement in 1790 the business passed on to her surviving son Peter and her widowed daughter-in-law Ann. Ann, herself an extremely gifted silversmith, took on her own sons as apprentices, and the business continued in the family until the middle of the nineteenth century.

Vanessa Bell: A portrait by Duncan Grant, 1918.

Vanessa Bell
British (1879–1961)

The painter Vanessa Bell was the eldest child of Sir Leslie Stephen, the sister of Virginia Woolf (q.v.) and the great-niece, through her mother, of the great Victorian photographer Julia Margaret Cameron (q.v.). She was one of the circle of writers, artists and intellectuals who later became known as the Bloomsbury Group. Immensely influenced by the French Post-Impressionists (an exhibition of whose work had been organized in London by her friend Roger Fry in 1910–11), Bell in turn had a considerable influence on the British art of her day, and was particularly associated with the painter Duncan Grant. She painted portraits, still lives and landscapes, and designed screens, textiles and mosaics when she worked in Roger Fry's famous Omega Workshops, besides making embroideries, carpets and pottery.

Vanessa Bell married the art historian and critic Clive Bell, and had two sons, the poet Julian Bell and the art historian Quentin Bell, and a daughter by Duncan Grant. She was deeply affected by her son Julian's death in action in the Spanish Civil War. Her house at Charleston, in Sussex, whose walls she and Duncan Grant decorated with their painting has been preserved as a national monument.

Rosa Bonheur
French (1822–1899)

Rosa Bonheur was the most successful of nineteenth-century women painters – not only in her native country, but in other European countries and across the Atlantic. Her father was a landscape painter from Bordeaux, and from the age of 10 she was already painting the animal studies for which she later became famous. By the time she was 17 her copies of paintings in the Louvre were already earning money.

As a girl and young woman Bonheur dissected animals to learn their anatomy, and regularly visited cattle markets and horse fairs – wearing men's clothing, which she worked in for the rest of her life because it was more practical. Like George Sand (q.v.), whom she greatly admired, she was quite free from the inhibitions of conventional nineteenth-century women. She lived for more than 40 years with another woman artist, Nathalie Micas. At her estate at Bly she kept a menagerie of animals.

Bonheur became widely celebrated for her lively, energetic animal paintings, often set in a broad landscape and based on direct observation from nature. Her best known work is *The Horse Fair*, painted when she was about 30 and now in the Metropolitan Museum of Art in New York. Towards the end of her life, although she never visited America, she also did several paintings of the American Far West. A thorough and dedicated professional, she sent for specimens of the prairie grass of the Far West in order to paint the vegetation as accurately as possible.

Margaret Bourke-White
American (1904–1971)

Margaret Bourke-White was the first woman photo-journalist – and virtually invented the form. She worked for *Life* from its first issue in 1936 until the 1950s, when the Parkinson's disease from which she eventually died prevented her working.

She was born in New York to Minnie Bourke and Joe White. She took up photography to work her way through Cornell University, and was the first U.S. reporter into Russia after the Revolution. Bourke-White is noted for her photographs of the Great Depression and of the Second World War – during which the ship she was travelling in was torpedoed off the North African coast. She was with the American Army invading Europe, and was present at the liberation of Buchenwald concentration camp.

Bourke-White was first married to Everett Chapman and secondly to the writer Erskine Caldwell from 1942 to 1945; together they had published in 1937 *You Have Seen Their Faces*, about the inhabitants of the southern states of the U.S.

Elizabeth Butler
British (1850?–1933)

Elizabeth Butler was an enthusiastic painter of battle scenes – a lifelong interest which started in adolescence, long before she married an army colonel, later General Sir William Francis Butler, in 1877.

Butler was the daughter of Thomas James Thompson, a friend of Dickens, and her mother Christiana Weller was also a painter and musician. Her younger sister was the poet Alice Meynell. In her early 20s she exhibited many military subjects from British history at the Royal Academy – one of which, *The Roll Call*, was so popular that it needed a police guard; the painting subsequently became the property of Queen Victoria. Lady Butler took a great deal of trouble with her research, to the extent of tracking down the correct uniforms and attending army manoeuvres, and she had some influence on military painters who came after her. Her large, crowded canvases are always full of life and interest.

Julia Margaret Cameron, photographed by H.H.H. Cameron.

Julia Margaret Cameron
British (1815–1879)

Julia Cameron is the most famous of Victorian portrait-photographers, although some do not now consider her the equal of her predecessors, David Octavius Hill and Charles Adamson of Edinburgh, whose photographs are less well known. However, her work will always be of immense interest if only because so many famous people of her day sat for her: Charles Darwin, Anthony Trollope, Holman Hunt, Lord Tennyson, Robert Browning, Henry Wadsworth Longfellow, Thomas Carlyle, Ellen Terry and Sir John Herschel (the astronomer, cf. Caroline Herschel) among them. She did everything herself – lighting, developing, printing and even framing – and, more important, secured some remarkable portraits, at once both grand and completely unselfconscious. They were the more remarkable in that her exposure times were usually several minutes. She also did tableaux and 'mythological' portraits, and was very proud to have illustrated Tennyson's *Idylls of the King*; but in these spheres she was less successful.

Cameron's career is exceptional in that she did not begin taking photographs until she was 48, when her daughter gave her a camera and some photographic equipment. Until then she had led the life of a Victorian upper-middle class wife and mother. She grew up in India, the plain one of the seven Pattle sisters (whose progeny included many members of the Victorian intellectual aristocracy), married Charles Hay Cameron, who like her father was in the Indian Civil Service, and had six children. Once back in England, her sisters introduced her to many artists and writers of the day (her great-niece Vanessa Bell, q.v., was born the year she died). Mrs Cameron was overwhelmingly hospitable and generous. She and her husband lived on the Isle of Wight for many years, and her first studio was a converted hen house – with no running water. She appears to have made virtually no money out of her occupation, and remained an inspired amateur.

Rosalba Carriera
Italian (1675–1757)

Not only was Rosalba Carriera a gifted artist, she was also original, influential and extremely successful in two different mediums: miniatures and full-size portraits in pastel. She elevated coloured pastels to a serious medium, and was the first to reveal the subtle and brilliant effects possible. Not only was she a technical innovator but she was also one of the first painters in the rococo style, which was to dominate French and Italian painting during the eighteenth century.

Carriera was born in Venice, the daughter of a clerk and a lace-maker. She may have followed her mother into the lace industry, but by 1700 she was already painting miniatures – possibly having started by decorating the lids of ivory snuff-boxes to sell to tourists (which would explain the fact that she was the first to produce miniatures on ivory rather than vellum). By the time she was in her thirties commissions were flowing in, many of them from the crowned heads of Europe, and her professional career was one of unending success.

In her forties Carriera spent a year in Paris fêted by both the court and her fellow artists (she painted Louis XV and Antoine Watteau), but, apart from brief periods in Modena and Vienna, she spent the rest of her life working at home on the Grand Canal. She never married, and lived with her widowed mother and a sister. Her sight began to fail in her forties, and she became virtually blind in 1746, 11 years before her death at 81.

Carriera was honoured by the Academy of San Luca in Rome, and by the French Academy. Augustus III, Elector of Saxony and King of Poland, had more than 150 of her works in his collection.

Mary Cassatt
American (1844–1926)

Mary Stevenson Cassatt was one of the early 'Americans in Paris'. In spite of the objections of her middle-class family, she studied at the Pennsylvania Academy of the Fine Arts and then, in her twenties, spent most of her time in Europe, learning as much as she could from the Old Masters of Italy, Spain, Holland and France. Her work was much admired by Degas, who invited her to send contributions to the Impressionist Exhibition of 1879. Thereafter she exhibited with the Impressionists regularly.

In 1877 Cassatt's parents and sister came to live with her in Paris (her father had retracted his wish to see her dead rather than studying art in Europe), and she used them, and other visiting relatives, as models. No one has treated the secular subject of mother and child with more truthfulness and less sentimentality. She made etchings and colour prints, and experimented with special techniques inspired by the Japanese prints which had recently become known in Europe. These are now held to be among her best works. Comparing her work to that of Berthe Morisot (q.v.), Paul Gauguin said: 'She has as much charm, and more power.'

Mother and Child *by Mary Cassatt, 1890.*

Cassatt's sphere of activity was not confined solely to Europe. She did an immense mural now lost on 'The Modern Woman' for the 1893 World Columbian Exposition in Chicago, and like the American Impressionist Lilla Cabot Perry (1848–1933) she was instrumental in introducing the work of the Impressionists to the U.S. She advised Mrs Havemeyer Webb of Long Island on building up her famous collection of modern art. When she was 70 Cassatt had to give up painting because of failing eyesight. An extremely private person, she only spoke at length about her life to the art historian, Achille Segard, when she was 69.

Imogen Cunningham
American (1883–1976)

Imogen Cunningham was one of the finest of American photographers, renowned in particular for her exquisite studies of plants. She was also the first woman to photograph male nudes, when she made a series of studies of her husband, the printmaker Roi Partridge, after their marriage in 1915. Cunningham worked to the end of her very long life, and photographed many leading figures in the arts, including Upton Sinclair, Gertrude Stein, Martha Graham (qq.v.) and, for *Vanity Fair*, many Hollywood movie stars.

Cunningham was born in Portland, Oregon, and brought up in Seattle. She resolved to be a photographer in 1901 when she saw the work of the German photographer Gertrude Käsebier. After majoring in chemistry at the University of Washington, she studied photographic printing in Dresden. Her first studio was a converted woodshed. She and her husband were leading members of the f/64 group on the West Coast in the 1930s.

Sonia Delaunay
Russian (1885–1979)

Sonia Delaunay was immensely active and influential all her life working in a variety of pure and applied

Sonia Delaunay, modelling some of her 'simultaneous' fabrics.

arts: painting, collage, book binding, costume and fabric design, interior decoration and tapestry making. She was born in the Ukraine, the daughter of Eli Stern, a factory owner, and was brought up in St Petersburg. She trained first in Karlsruhe and then, in 1905, in Paris, where she soon became a part of the artistic society of the capital.

Delaunay was associated with several movements – Fauvism, Cubism, Orphism, Simultanism – the last two largely initiated by herself and her second husband, the painter Robert Delaunay, whom she had married in 1910, and with whom she had a close working partnership until his death in 1941. Sonia Delaunay painted Simultaneous pictures, designed Simultaneous costumes for herself and her husband, and made Simultaneous bookbindings – art was not merely work, but a part of the very fabric of life. After the First World War she designed costumes for both Diaghilev and Tristan Tzara, and in 1924

La Pittura, *an allegorical self-portrait by Artemisia Gentileschi.*

founded her own fashion and textile house. Delaunay helped create an alliance between modern art, fashion and decoration. In the late 1930s she returned to painting, her first love, but also designed tapestries and did drawings and book illustrations.

Artemisia Gentileschi
Italian (1593–1652)?

Artemisia Gentileschi, daughter of the Roman painter Orazio Gentileschi, has only recently received the recognition she deserves as a substantial artist in the tradition of Caravaggio. Women painters of the period tended to be restricted to portraiture and still life; Gentileschi however worked on major biblical and mythical subjects, often featuring the female nude. Her most celebrated subject is *Judith and Holofernes.*

She was raped at the age of 18 by the artist Agostino Tassi, whom her father had appointed to

teach her the science of perspective. There was a disagreeable trial; Tassi was eventually acquitted, and Artemisia married Pietro Stiattesi and moved to Florence. Later – the marriage appears to have failed – she moved back to Rome, with her daughter Palmira, and then on to Naples for her last 20 years. She made one journey to London, to assist her father who had been commissioned by Charles I to decorate the Queen's House at Greenwich.

Gentileschi lived much of her life as an independent woman. It is clear from her letters that she was well able to stand up for herself – she insisted on getting a proper price for her work. 'As long as I live,' she wrote, 'I will have control over my being.' And later: 'You will find the spirit of Caesar in the soul of this woman.'

Nataila Sergeevna Goncharova
Russian (1881–1962)

Natalia Goncharova was one of a number of gifted and original women artists – others were the abstract artists and theatre designer Alexandra Exter and Sonia Delaunay (q.v.) – who worked in the last decades of the Tsarist regime; they followed in the wake of a whole generation of active Russian women that included many doctors and some of the leading revolutionaries of the day.

Goncharova worked on terms of complete equality with her male contemporaries. She was particularly associated with Mikhail Larionov (they finally married on her seventy-fourth birthday). Together with David Burliuk they were the founders of the Russian Neo-primitivists, who drew their early inspiration from the vigour of native arts and crafts, combining it with the visual discoveries of the French Impressionists and later artists, particularly Gauguin, Matisse and Cézanne. She was also much influenced by the Cubists.

Goncharova was immensely productive: in her second one-woman exhibition in Moscow in 1913, at the age of only 32, she exhibited 761 works. She was particularly inspired by the miracle of electricity, and was one of the first artists to introduce the machine into art.

In 1915 she and Larionov joined Diaghilev to

design sets and costumes for the Ballets Russes, and eventually settled in Paris. Goncharova designed, among other ballets, *Le Coq d'Or*, *Les Noces* and *The Firebird*.

Eileen Gray
Irish (1877–1976)

Eileen Gray was one of the most original and sensitive of 20th-century furniture designers. Already before the First World War she was a precursor of the Art Deco which dominated design in the late 1920s and 1930s. Her particular speciality was lacquer work, but her range was far wider.

She was born at Enniscorthy in Ireland, and studied at the Slade School of Fine Art in London. While there she came across a workshop specializing in lacquer restoration, and 'plucked up my courage and asked the workshop director whether I could work with him.' She started the following Monday.

Gray moved to Paris – as it turned out, for good – in 1902. There she met and worked with the great Japanese lacquer artist, Sougawara. She was almost the first to turn away from the then-popular Art Nouveau, towards a style of uncompromising perfection and plainness. Much of what she then made has disappeared; what survives are now collectors' pieces. She decorated furnished apartments – a boudoir in white lacquer of 1923 caused a sensation – designed functional chairs in leather and steel which predated those of Le Corbusier and the Bauhaus, and was already working in glass and tubular steel when she opened her own gallery in 1926. She also built herself two astonishing houses, one of which belonged to the late Graham Sutherland, and carried out many other architectural schemes. She remained an innovator into her nineties, when she was working with plastics and Perspex.

In her youth Gray had a passion for ballooning and for airplanes: she accompanied Herbert Latham on an unsuccessful Channel Crossing attempt in 1909. She worked as an ambulance driver during the First World War, and was still flying in middle age. Her name suddenly emerged from obscurity in 1972, when a screen she had made almost 60 years earlier

The designer Eileen Gray. She remained an innovator into her nineties.

was put up for auction and was sold for £18,000, then a phenomenal sum. The painter Prunella Clough is her niece.

Kate Greenaway
British (1846–1901)

A much-loved and still very popular illustrator of children's books, Kate Greenaway painted the 'pretty innocents' of a bygone age and was said to have 'dressed two continents'. She was the daughter of a draughtsman, John Greenaway, and his wife Elizabeth, who kept a draper's shop in North London. Kate Greenaway had a scanty formal education, but she had a talent for painting and drawing, and spent 10 years at different London art schools where she and Elizabeth Butler (q.v.) were keen but affectionate rivals.

Kate Greenaway began to sell her drawings in 1871; in 1874 her name was printed on the title page

199

Kate Greenaway, 1880. She was said to have 'dressed two continents' of children.

of a book of fairy stories. Her success was soon assured; she exhibited her watercolours annually (the French novelist, Dumas, bought one, and a royal princess gave one as a wedding present); in 1880 she illustrated Browning's poem *The Pied Piper of Hamelin*; her *Kate Greenaway's Almanack* was published annually, and her *Birthday Book for Children*, still in print, sold 150,000 copies in its first edition. Her illustrations were so popular that it became the fashion to dress daughters in her high-waisted dresses and 'mob' caps after the style of the early nineteenth century.

Edith Head
American (b. 1907)

The person who has received the most nominations for an Oscar – she was nominated for 32 and won eight – is not an actress or a director, but the costume designer Edith Head. The daughter of a mining engineer, she was brought up in mining camps in Nevada and Arizona, where she learnt to love Mexican and Indian costumes. Head studied languages at the University of California and at Stanford, and taught at schools in La Jolla and Hollywood. In her spare time, Head studied art, and in 1923 took some fashion sketches to the head fashion designer at Paramount. She was hired, and was soon designing for cowboy films, spectaculars, costume dramas, and high fashion modern pictures. Her first 'star' client was an elephant in a de Mille movie. Gradually she worked her way up and in 1938 became chief designer at Paramount: the first woman to get such a job with a major studio.

For the next five years Head designed for at least 35 pictures a year. Her first major success was dressing Barbara Stanwyck in *The Lady Eve* in 1941, which launched a fashion for Latin-American clothes. She also introduced her own versions of the Spanish shirt and the poncho to Hollywood. She designed the first sarong for Dorothy Lamour, a mink evening dress for Ginger Rogers in *Lady in the Dark* and Ingrid Bergman's denims in *For Whom the Bell Tolls*. She dressed Mae West in *She Done Him Wrong*, and Olivia de Havilland in *The Heiress* (1949), for which Head was awarded her first Oscar. She won more Oscars for *Samson and Delilah* (1949) and *All About Eve* (both 1950), *A Place in the Sun* (1951) and *Roman Holiday* (1953), and *Sabrina Fair* (1954), both of which starred Audrey Hepburn, and *The Facts of Life* (1960).

Head has designed costumes for most of the major stars, men and women, from the 1930s right up to Robert Redford and Paul Newman in *The Sting* (1974) a film which earned her her eighth Oscar. She married Bill Ihnen during the Second World War.

Dame Barbara Hepworth
British (1903–1975)

Barbara Hepworth was, with Henry Moore, one of the two dominating influences in twentieth-century British sculpture and arguably the best and most original of all Western women sculptors. She represented Britain at the Venice Biennale in 1950.

Barbara Hepworth, photographed through one of her sculptures, Four-square walk through, *in 1966.*

Perhaps her best known monumental sculpture is the Dag Hammarskjoeld memorial at the United Nations in New York.

Like Moore, Hepworth was primarily an abstract and monumental sculptor; like him, she was much honoured (she became a Dame in 1965) and achieved an international reputation. Again like Moore, who was a friend throughout her life, she was born in the industrial West Riding of Yorkshire where her father was an engineer, went to Leeds School of Art and from there went on to the Royal College of Art in London.

Hepworth was a practitioner of direct carving, especially in wood and stone, and highly sensitive to the particular quality of her raw material. She always said she knew what the final shape of the work of art would be before she began carving, and she was an exceptional craftswoman.

Hepworth first married the sculptor John Skeaping, whom she met while working in Italy on a travelling scholarship; they had one son (who was killed in action in the Malaya uprising in 1953). Both were part of a lively group of artists and writers living in Hampstead, London. In the early 1930s Hepworth began to work in association with the abstract painter Ben Nicholson, who was to be her second husband, and her own work became increasingly abstract. In 1939 – now the parents of triplets, a son and two daughters – they moved to St Ives, in Cornwall, which was to become Britain's major art colony after the Second World War. She and Nicholson were divorced in 1951, but she remained there working until her tragic death in a fire in her studio.

Gertrude Jekyll
British (1843–1932)

Gertrude Jekyll had more influence on the style and contents of twentieth-century gardens, in the U.S. as well as in her native England, than any other woman, and at least as much as contemporaries like her friend William Robinson (author of *The English Flower Garden*). An exceptional plantswoman, she championed plants not only for their flowers but for their foliage, their shape and their scent. She introduced the fashion for silver-leaved plants, the woodland garden, the one-colour border, the idea of training roses or clematis up fruit trees, and, with Robinson, helped sweep away the idea of the strictly regimented bedding-out that the Victorians loved. She drew her ideas as much from the cottage gardens and hedgerows of her beloved county of Surrey as from horticulturalists and landscape gardeners.

Gertrude Jekyll had scarcely embarked on her great enterprise before her late forties. Until then, as the unmarried daughter of a prosperous Victorian family, she had lived at home pursuing the accomplishments – considerable in her case – thought suitable for a young lady. She studied art for two years, travelled, made friends in artistic circles, and took up painting, embroidery, interior decoration, photography, carving, gilding, even singing – and a variety of crafts, as well as gardening.

In 1889 Jekyll met the 20-year-old architect Edwin Lutyens – shortly before her eyesight began to

Gertrude Jekyll. A portrait by William Nicholson, 1920.

progressively deteriorate. Lutyens was then on the threshhold of a brilliant career, and the meeting was providential for both of them. Having already created a beautiful and original garden at her family's new home, Jekyll began to design and plant the gardens of the houses Lutyens built. Together with the books she wrote – more than a dozen after the age of 50 – these specially designed gardens made her justly famous. On her tombstone, designed by Lutyens, he had inscribed: 'Artist Gardener Crafts-woman'.

Gwen John
British (1876–1939)

Both as an artist and a person, Gwen John was as different from her notorious younger brother, the almost professionally bohemian painter Augustus John, as it is possible to be. Many people would now rate her a far better painter.

Gwen was one of five children. Her father was a lawyer and her mother died when she was seven, and the children were brought up by relatives in Wales. She trained both at the Slade School in London and in Paris under Whistler, and from 1903 until her death made her home in France. She lived an intensely private life, but appears to have had a love affair with the sculptor Rodin. Her work, which mostly consisted of rather serious, straightforward paintings of women, was greatly admired by the American collector John Quinn, whom she met some time before the First World War, and a good many examples are now in the U.S.

Angelica Kauffman
Swiss (1741–1807)

The daughter of a painter, Angelica Kauffman was already a professional artist by the age of 15. (One of her dozen or so surviving self-portraits was painted when she was only 13.) Father and daughter worked closely together – eventually he virtually stopped painting and became his daughter's manager – and travelled all over Switzerland, Austria and Italy looking for work. In Venice in 1766 Lady Wentworth invited Angelica Kauffman to England, where she was so successful that she became, in 1768, a founder member of Sir Joshua Reynolds' Royal Academy of Art. (One other woman was a founder member, the flower painter Mary Moser; no other women were admitted until 1922.)

Kauffman was not content to confine herself solely to portraiture, or the occasional genre picture and still life – which, with the notable exception of Artemisia Gentileschi (q.v.), had hitherto been the accepted medium for women artists in Europe. As a child, she had helped her father with his church murals; and as an adult she became a full-blown neo-classical painter of historical and mythological subjects. In London she scored an immense success with the pictures she showed in the Academy's annual exhibitions from 1769 onwards, such as *The Interview of Hector and Andromache, Cleopatra at the Tomb of Marc Antony, Vortigern and Rowena* – the latter a medieval subject from English history, one of several which she was the first to tackle. Kauffman worked a great deal with the architect Robert Adam on the decoration of the houses he built for the English aristocracy. In 1778 she was commissioned to paint the large allegorical ovals

*Gwen John: A self-portrait
painted about 1900.*

A self-portrait by Angelica Kauffmann, showing her at work in the studio.

which today decorate the ceiling of the Royal Academy's entrance hall at Burlington House.

Her first marriage to a man named Brandt, who claimed to be a Swedish count, was a disaster. After his death in 1780 she married Antonio Zucchi, another Venetian painter who, like her, had arrived in England in 1766. They returned with her father to Italy, where the elder Kauffman died in 1782. The Zucchis eventually settled in Rome, where Angelica became the most successful artist in the city and a person of considerable social consequence. Goethe called on her frequently when he was in Rome, and she painted commissions for the King and Queen of Naples, the Emperor Joseph II of Austria as well as numerous princes, dukes and counts. She continued to send paintings back to England.

By the time Kauffman died she had painted more than 500 pictures, of which about 200 are known. Her funeral arrangements were modelled on those of Raphael three centuries earlier, and members of academies of several countries followed the cortège.

Käthe Kollwitz
German (1867–1945)

Käthe Kollwitz was an artist and sculptor who worked in black and white – on drawings, etchings, lithographs and woodcuts – and in a traditional style, and is one of the most impressive artists of the early twentieth century. Not for her the sumptuous nudes of her contemporaries in France; she portrayed the poor and the oppressed with a power and sympathy and sense of outrage that evokes Goya or Daumier. Her work was so 'revolutionary' that it was banned both by the Kaiser in 1898, and by the Nazis in 1936. Much of her output was cyclical – *The Weavers' Uprising*, *The Peasant War*, *Proletariat*, *Death*.

Käthe Schmidt was born into a large family in East Prussia. She started her training at 14 and spent much of her adult life in Berlin, where she lived with her husband Dr Karl Kollwitz in a poor working-class quarter. Her life was not happy: she lost her son in the First World War, and her grandson in the Second.

Kollwitz was the first woman member of the Prussian Academy of Arts, and was head of the Department of Graphic Arts from 1928 until 1933, when she resigned in protest against the Nazis. She continued to work until the last year of her life, but was not able to exhibit. Just before the end of the Second World War she was evacuated from Berlin, and died near Dresden shortly afterwards.

Kuan Tao-sheng
Chinese (1262–1319)

One of the finest of Chinese bamboo painters was Kuan Tao-sheng, who lived at the time of the Mongol invasions. She married a fellow-artist, Chao Meng-fu, who was summoned to Peking, at the request of Kublai Khan, as court calligrapher. There Chao Meng-fu became an official in the Office of War, and he and Kuan Tao-sheng moved from place to place as he received further promotions: an adventurous life for a woman in those days. The marriage was clearly a close and happy one: they had three sons and six daughters, and sometimes even worked on paintings together.

Käthe Kollwitz's Self-portrait with a Pencil, *1935.*

Kuan Tao-sheng became celebrated for both her painting and her calligraphy, and the Emperor commissioned from her a copy of the *Thousand Character Classic*. Her paintings of bamboos, too, were greatly admired by the Court, and 'Imperial favours were as abundant as rains,' as her husband wrote in his memoir of her.

Bamboo painting and calligraphy were closely linked, since a bamboo leaf is so similar to the stroke of a Chinese character. But bamboo painting was a fairly late (tenth century) innovation. Its first exponent was probably another gifted woman calligrapher, Li Fu-jen, who began one night by painting on her paper window the shadow of a bamboo cast on to it by the moon.

Adélaïde Labille-Guiard
French (1749–1803)

Adélaïde Labille-Guiard, the daughter of a haberdasher, was an excellent portraitist in both pastels and oils, and, a sturdy champion of the careers of other women artists. She trained with Maurice Quentin de la Tour, greatest exponent of the art of pastel (the possibilities of which had first been shown by Rosalba Carriera, q.v.), and was elected a member of the Académie in 1783 – on the same day as her greatest rival, Elisabeth Vigée-Lebrun (q.v.).

Labille-Guiard had several women pupils, the best known of whom was Marie Gabrielle Capet (1761–1817), and did her best to persuade the Académie to open its doors to more women. When, instead, the Académie restricted its quota of women to four (the others were Anne Vallayer-Coster (q.v.) and Marie Vien), she entered a self-portrait (now in the Metropolitan Museum of Art in New York) to the Salon of 1785 which also included portraits of two of her pupils, Marie Gabrielle Capet and Mlle. Carreaux de Rosemond. It was largely due to her campaigning that the Salon finally accepted the work of women in 1791.

She married twice, first Louis Nicolas Guiard, from whom she separated after 10 years, and second

Portrait of the Artist with two pupils *by Adelaide Labille-Guiard, which was shown at the 1785 Salon.*

one of her teachers, François André Vincent. She had no children, but Mlle. Capet was a member of her household until her death. The whole of Labille-Guiard's life was devoted to becoming a professional artist. In 1787 she showed at the Salon paintings of nine members of the Royal family and the aristocracy; four years later, after the Revolution, she showed eight portraits of Deputies of the National Assembly – but was obliged, to her great distress, after more than two years' work, to destroy a major history painting because of its royalist subject matter.

Dorothea Lange
American (1895–1965)

Dorothea Lange was America's finest documentary photographer, famous in particular for her powerful pictures of the victims of the 1930s Depression: of the hungry, unemployed, the migrant workers and deprived children. Along with Walker Evans and Ben Shahn, she was one of the team of photographers picked by Roy Stryker to record the plight of the inhabitants of the Oklahoma dust-bowl on behalf of the Federal Resettlement Administration during the 1930s; their work spurred the U.S. government into giving aid to impoverished agricultural communities. Many of her pictures are known all over the world. She published *An American Exodus: A Record of Human Erosion* in 1939. During the Second World War she recorded the internment of Japanese Americans.

Lange was born in Hoboken, New Jersey, and, after training with Clarence White, started her career as a society photographer in San Francisco. She worked until the eve of her death from cancer, recording all walks of life from international dignitaries to the Shakers.

Marie Laurençin
French (1885–1956)

Marie Laurençin was a painter of great charm, and a friend of many artists, writers and musicians of her generation. She was born illegitimate in Paris, and lived with her mother until the latter's death. From 1907 until 1913 she had a long relationship with the poet Apollinaire, but finally married a German painter, Otto von Waetjen (whom she divorced in 1920). The outbreak of the First World War made living in France difficult and they settled in Barcelona. While there she wrote *poèmes d'exil* which were later published under the title *Petit Bestiaire*.

In the 1920s, back in Paris, Laurençin became a designer and illustrator. She designed dresses, wallpapers, textiles, and the costumes and sets for Diaghilev's *Les Biches*. She also produced many prints of all kinds, and was a popular portrait painter.

Paula Modersohn-Becker
German (1876–1907)

The first 'post-Impressionist' in Germany, Paula Modersohn-Becker, in spite of her early death, left

Migrant Mother, Nipomo, California *by Dorothea Lange, 1936, shows some of the victims of the Depression.*

behind her 400 paintings and 1,000 drawings. Like her contemporary Kathe Köllwitz (q.v.) she made magnificent studies of peasant women, many of them mothers with children, but the effect was very different. Becker wrote later to a friend, recalling her visit to Paris, that Cézanne had been 'one of the three or four artistic forces which struck me like a thunderstorm and a great experience.' Her late paintings also reveal the powerful influence of van Gogh and Gauguin.

Becker was one of six children of a railway engineer, and studied in Bremen, London and Berlin, where she joined an artists' colony near Berlin. She married one of her fellow artists, Otto Modersohn, in 1891. But her visits to France continued to be very important to her – both for the Old Masters in the museums and 'the very, very moderns' – and 18 months before her death she left her husband in order to work there. It was a time of immense artistic change, experiment and productivity: 'I'm going *to be* something – I am experiencing the most intense, happiest time of my life,' she wrote to her sister. Her husband then persuaded her to return to their home in Germany. There, some months later, she gave birth to her first child, a daughter, and died a few days later at the age of 31 of a heart attack.

Berthe Morisot's Self Portrait, 1885. *She was a leading member of the French Impressionists.*

Berthe Morisot
French (1841–1895)

Berthe Morisot, an important member of the French Impressionist group, was one of four children of a well-off civil servant. She and her two sisters were encouraged to develop their obvious talents, and later she and her sister Edma fell under the influence of Corot, whom they met in 1861. Between 1864 and 1874 Berthe showed regularly in the Salon (Edma married and gave up painting in 1869). She became a friend and associate of Edouard Manet, sat for him, encouraged him to paint out of doors, as she herself did, and in 1874 married his younger brother Eugène. They had one daughter, Julie, born in 1879 – the model for many of her mother's paintings and drawings.

For the rest of her life Morisot was part of the circle of avant-garde artists based in Paris who became known as the Impressionists. They included Degas, Monet, Pissarro, Renoir, Sisley and Mary Cassatt (q.v.). She was a friend too of such men as Mallarmé and Baudelaire, Emile Zola and the composer Rossini – a 'supportive and feminine role' (in the words of a feminist art historian) which has tended to obscure her substantial contribution to the Impressionist vision.

Grandma Moses
American (1860–1961)

Grandma Moses was America's most celebrated 'Primitive' painter and a very gifted one, yet she had barely started painting before she was in her late seventies. As she once said of herself: 'I would never sit back in a rocking chair, waiting for someone to help me'. No one, of either sex, could have had a more productive old age.

She was born Anna Mary Robertson on a farm in New York State, one of five boys and five girls. ('We

Grandma Moses seated beside one of her most popular paintings, Winter Scene *in 1949.*

came in bunches, like radishes.') At 12 she left home and was in domestic service until at 27 she married Thomas Moses, the hired hand of one of her employers. They farmed most of their lives, first in Virginia and then in New York State, at Eaglebridge. She had 10 children, of whom five survived; her husband died in 1927.

Grandma Moses painted a little as a child, and made embroidery pictures as a hobby, but only switched to oils in old age because her hands had become too stiff to sew and she wanted 'to keep busy and pass the time away, but I thought of it no more than of doing fancy work.' Her pictures were first sold at the local drug store and at a fair, and were soon spotted by a dealer, Louis J. Caldor, who bought everything she painted. Three of the pictures were exhibited in the Museum of Modern Art, and in 1940 she had her own first exhibition in New York. Between the 1930s and her death she produced some 2,000 pictures: detailed and lively portrayals of the rural life she had known for so long, with a marvellous sense of colour and form. 'I think real hard till I think of something real pretty, and then I paint it,' she said.

Louise Nevelson
American (b. 1900)

Using leftover scraps of wood or metal – spindles, furniture legs, newel posts, wheels and odds and ends – and spraying them all one colour, black or gold or white – her famous 'no-colour' – Louise Nevelson creates extraordinary tableaux and even total environments of elegant abstract sculpture. She was one of the pioneers of 'environmental art', in her case whole walls of 'boxed reveries' and even entire rooms devoted to low relief wood panels. As she says herself, 'the dips and cracks and detail fascinate me.'

From the age of nine Nevelson knew she wanted to be a sculptor, and said then, 'I don't want colour to help me.' She was born in Kiev, USSR, one of four children of Isaac Berliawsky, and moved to Rockland, Maine, with the family in 1905, where her father became a builder and ran a lumber yard. She married Charles Nevelson, who was in shipping, in 1920, and moved to New York, where her son Myron was born. She has always been immensely interested in all the arts – music, drama, dance, poetry – and became a painter as well as a sculptor after studying at the Arts Students League.

In 1931 she and her husband separated, and Louise Nevelson went to Munich to study under Hans Hofmann, and later to Mexico to study under Diego Rivera. She explored multi-media at the start of her career as a sculptor, and was influenced by European movements such as Cubism and Surrealism, and by the arts of Africa and pre-Columban America. Nevelson had her first abstract show in 1941, but it was many years before her distinctive gifts were fully recognized in the late 1950s. She has held many public positions in the world of art.

Georgia O'Keeffe
American (b. 1887)

One of America's most distinguished artists, Georgia O'Keeffe was brought up on a farm in Wisconsin,

Georgia O'Keeffe in 1966.

and resolved to become a painter as a child. She trained in Chicago and New York, and started her professional career as a commercial artist and then became a teacher. At 30 she destroyed all her work, in which she saw only the influence of other artists, and from then on painted only 'what was in my head'.

The first fruits of this – abstract drawings in charcoal – were shown, without her permission, to the photographer and gallery-owner Alfred Stieglitz, who, again without O'Keeffe's permission, put them on public show. When she demanded that he take them down, he refused. From then on he exhibited her work almost every year, married her in 1924, and took hundreds of photographs of her.

O'Keeffe was introduced to the New Mexican desert, which was to become the major inspiration of her work, by Mabel Dodge Luhan (the friend of Freda and D.H. Lawrence) in 1929. She spent as much time as she could there, and finally settled there after Stieglitz's death in 1946. Much of her art has been abstract, and much reflects the desert she loves. Her 'realist' subjects include barns, shells, pelvic bones and flowers. She has received many honours, and in her nineties has said: 'I have tried to paint what I see.'

Sarah Miriam Peale
American (1800–1885)

Sarah Miriam Peale was the first woman in America to support herself throughout her career by her work as an artist. Like many European women artists, she came from a family of painters. Her father was the portrait painter and miniaturist James Peale; her uncle Charles Willson Peale was also an artist, and a supporter of the education of women (naming all his daughters after woman painters of the past). In 1824, with her sister Anna, Peale became a member of the Pennsylvania Academy, and for nearly 50 years received commissions to paint the portraits of many famous people, including Daniel Webster and General Lafayette.

Clara Peeters
Flemish (1594–1657?)

Clara Peeters was one of the first artists to paint still life, a genre which was to become immensely popular during succeeding centuries. More than 30 of her works survive, the first painted when she was only 14. Little is known of her life – not her parents' profession, nor who taught her, nor even the decade of her death. She is known to have married Hendrick Joossen in 1639, however, when she was 45.

Peeters' technical skill and control were quite exceptional. Most of her paintings were what is known as 'banquet pieces' – that is, depicting fine food and tableware. She enjoyed displaying her skill, particularly in the painting of objects reflected in metals or glass. She made a speciality of portraying her own reflection on the shiny surface of jugs and vases: in one painting her self-portrait appears in this way seven times.

Germaine Richier
French (1904–1959)

One of the finest sculptors of her generation, Richier

Still-Life of Fruit and Flowers by Clara Peeters, probably painted after 1620.

is particularly known for her 'metamorphoses' of human forms – sculptures which combine figures with animal or even mineral elements. She was fascinated by grasshoppers and other insects; and her female nudes are of real women, sturdy and uncompromising, as opposed to the idealized girls of many male sculptors.

Richier was born at Grans, in the south of France, one of four children of a winegrower. She studied at the Ecole des Beaux Arts in Montpelier, against her parents' wishes ('women aren't made for art,' said her father), then moved to Paris to study with Bourdelle, just as Albert Giacometti was finishing as a pupil there. Her early work with Bourdelle is very evocative of Giacometti's standing figures. In 1936, she showed at the Women Artists of Europe exhibition in Paris together with Valadon and Laurençin (qq.v.).

Richier married twice: first a fellow sculptor, Otto Bänninger, in 1929, and then the writer René de Solier, in 1954. She spent the years of the Second World War mostly in Switzerland, Bänninger's native country. She won the sculpture prize at the São Paolo Biennale in 1951. Her last years in the South of France were clouded by the cancer from which she eventually died.

Leni Riefenstahl
German (b. 1902)

Nearly half a century after the celebrated films *Triumph of the Will* and *Olympiad* were made, their director Leni Riefenstahl remains the finest woman film director. She was a protégée of Adolf Hitler and the fact that she made her two major films at his request has hindered her subsequent career.

Riefenstahl was born in Berlin, the daughter of a company director, one of two children (her brother was killed on the Russian front). She became a dancer, creating her own dances, and was spotted by Max Reinhardt; but a knee injury at the age of 24 caused her to switch to acting. She became one of the first stars of the Universum Film Aktiengesellschaft studios when Arnold Fanck offered her roles in five of his 'mountain' films (notably *The White Hell of Pitz Palu*), for which Riefenstahl took up winter sports. In 1931 she founded her own film company, and directed herself in *The Blue Light* (1932), her own romantic version of a mountain film; it was greatly admired by Adolf Hitler and won a gold medal at the 1932 Venice Biennale. Her first documentary, *Victory of Faith*, about the 1933 Nuremberg Rally, was made for Hitler, but no copy of it survives. There followed *Triumph of the Will* (1935), about the 1934 Nazi rally at Nuremberg, and *Olympiad* (1938), about the 1936 Berlin Olympics. They established her as the best documentary film maker of her generation; some would say the best ever.

During the war she shot the remainder of *Tiefland*, a feature film about eighteenth-century peasant life starring herself as a gypsy dancer, which she had begun several years earlier. But because of her association with the Nazis she was not able to finish it until 1954. In 1944 she married Peter Jacob, a major in the Wehrmacht, but they divorced two years later.

In the 1950s Riefenstahl discovered Africa, and found a new career as a photographer. Her colour film on the Nuba tribes has not yet materialized, but her photographic essays *The Last of the Nuba* (1973) and *The People of Kau* (1976) showed that her visual talent was undiminished and have won her a second international reputation.

At 72 (giving her age as 52) she learned aqualung diving, having snorkelled for the first time at the age of 71. She proceeded to photograph wild life underwater in the Red Sea and the Caribbean and produced yet another book, *Coral Gardens* (1978), confirming her mastery of this new medium.

Luisa Roldán
Spanish (1656–1704)

Spain's first celebrated woman sculptor was famous for her religious groups in painted wood and ter-racotta. She was successively court sculptor to both Charles II and Philip V.

Luisa Roldán was born in Seville, and she and her sisters and brothers were trained to paint sculpture in the workshops of their father, the sculptor Pedro Roldán. In 1671 she married another sculptor, Luis Antonio de Los Arcos. By 1687 they were in Cadiz, where she made large statues of angels and patriarchs for the cathedral and, together with her husband, statues of saints. In 1690 they moved to Madrid, and in 1692 Roldán was appointed Sculptor of the Chamber. Her appointment was renewed in 1701, when Philip V succeeded. She executed a St Michael and a Christ Bearing the Cross for Charles II, but received no money for several years as the court was in financial difficulties; she was reduced to begging before she at last received a very modest pension. Her son Thomás worked with his parents as a sculptor.

Rachel Ruysch
Dutch (1664–1750)

Rachel Ruysch was an outstanding exponent of flower and fruit paintings, at a time when many exceptional artists were painting such pictures. One modern art historian, Maurice Grant, claims that she 'is a supreme artist as well as a supreme painter, as great in her line as Rembrandt in his'. She had remarkable technical skill, and a gift for organizing compositions in a marvellously lively way. Her lack of fame today is partly due to the fact that few art historians have ever taken flower paintings seriously, but her prices, high during her lifetime, when she had an international reputation, have been high ever since.

Ruysch was the daughter of a professor who was also an amateur painter, and, like many other women artists, she was extremely precocious: she was apprenticed to the great flower and still life painter Willem van der Aelst when she was 15. She married another painter, Juriaen Pool, in 1693 and they had 10 children; but she remained professionally active for well over 60 years, and produced about 100 pictures after her marriage, possibly more than 200 in all. It is a formidable number for such meticulous work.

Sin Saimdang
Korean (1512–1559)

Sin Saimdang had exceptional talent in many fields but is remembered today as one of Korea's most gifted painters. 32 of her paintings survive; grasshoppers and grapes were her speciality. She was a beautiful calligrapher and embroiderer, and was also known as a poet. A Korean contemporary said, referring to her, 'Who can say that painting is not for women to undertake? Few men could have done better than her.'

Sin Saimdang was one one of seven children of a revered scholar, Sin Myong-hwa, who allowed her to become a scholar herself. She married a government official, Yi Won-su, and had several children. A son and a daughter were also painters, and another son, Yi Yulgok, achieved fame as a statesman. Sin Saimdang was much admired for her great virtue.

Lilly Martin Spencer
American (1822–1902)

An exceptionally popular American artist of her day, both of portraits and genre paintings, Lilly Martin Spencer was born of French parents who emigrated to Ohio. She and her husband, Benjamin Rush Spencer, also have the distinction of having an early 'reversed roles' marriage: it was Benjamin who looked after the household while his wife pursued her career – in spite of the fact that she bore 13 children (of whom seven survived). Her portrait subjects included the poet Ella Wheeler Wilcox and Elizabeth Cady Stanton (q.v.).

Sabina von Steinbach
German (c. 1300)

Some of the most beautiful medieval statues on the cathedral at Strasbourg are the work of a woman mason. It is known from cathedral records that Sabina vonSteinbach received the contract when the previous master builder, Erwin, died, and she herself 'signed' her statue of St John by carving on the scroll he is carrying 'Gratia divinae pietatis adesto Savinae

The Synagogue *(right)* and Ecclesia *(left) by Sabina von Steinbach, from the south portal of Strasbourg Cathedral.*

de petra dura per quam sum facta figura' ('Thanks be to the holy piety of this woman Sabina, through whom I have been given form from the hard stone'). Women masons were probably rare, though not unknown, but other medieval arts were frequently practised by women, such as tapestry, bookbinding, the illumination of manuscripts and above all embroidery, although the names of individuals have not often survived.

Levina Teerlinc
Flemish (c. 1520–1576)

Henry VIII invited Levina Teerlinc or Teerling to his court in 1545 to work as a miniature painter. None of the few portrait miniatures which survive from this period can be certainly identified as being by Teerlinc, but she must have been exceptionally gifted: the king paid her more than he had paid Hans Holbein the Younger (who had died in 1543), and, although Teerlinc was only in her mid-twenties when she left for England, she was already a well known artist.

Like most early women artists, Teerlinc was born into an artistic family: she was the daughter of Simon Benninck of Bruges, a miniature painter and illuminator. When Henry VIII died, she continued to be a court painter to Edward VI, Mary, and Elizabeth I, and remained in England with her husband and son until her death.

Suzanne Valadon
French (1865–1938)

Suzanne Valadon was a notable painter in a notable generation. She had a poor start in life, being the illegitimate daughter of a laundress and virtually uneducated, but from childhood she kept herself by her wits – as a waitress, a circus acrobat, and, after an accident, an artist's model in Montmartre. The young Suzanne sat for Puvis de Chavannes, Toulouse-Lautrec and Renoir, among other artists, and began drawing around 1883 – the year she had an illegitimate child, who was to become, under her guidance, a painter himself – Maurice Utrillo.

As an artist Valadon was immensely successful. The forceful, rather masculine style of her figures owes a good deal to Degas, in whose atelier she worked. But her female subjects, however voluptuous, are not the passive objects often painted by her male contemporaries; her paintings celebrate the independence and equality of women, in a style that is recognizably her own and a reflection of her powerful personality.

In 1896 Valadon married a rich businessman, Paul Moussis, but she left him when she was 44 for the painter André Utter, who was 20 years her junior. They lived together, with Utrillo, for more than two decades, in a ménage of notorious eccentricity and disorderliness.

Anne Vallayer-Coster
French (1744–1818)

Anne Vallayer-Coster became one of the supreme practitioners of still life in the eighteenth century, and the best flower painter in France. Her work has even been compared to that of Manet and Renoir. She was greatly admired by her contemporary Diderot, although, as so often, many critics expressed amazement that a woman could paint so well. She was unanimously voted into the French Académie at her first attempt.

Vallayer-Coster is known to have painted some 450 pictures, in which she celebrated not only beautiful objects and fine food, but also the plainer things of life; her painting of a crust of bread and a steaming bowl of soup is justly famous, one of the masterpieces of the genre. She may also have designed tapestries for the Gobelin works.

She was the daughter of a goldsmith, whose wife took over his workshop when he died and married Jean Pierre Silvestre Coster, a lawyer and member of the French Parlement, in 1781. Industrious to the end, Vallayer-Coster exhibited for the last time in 1817, when she was over 70.

Elisabeth Vigée-Lebrun
French (1755–1842)

Elisabeth Vigée-Lebrun vied with Angelica Kauffman (q.v.) for the distinction of being the most phenomenally successful woman artist of the eighteenth century. Like Kauffman (and Sofonisba Anguissola, q.v., before them), she was prepared to travel in search of fame and fortune, and wherever she went – Russia, Poland, Austria, Italy, Switzerland, England – she was inundated with commissions and invitations from the highest in the land. She painted about 800 pictures, and would have been far richer than she was if her picture-dealer husband, J.B.P. Lebrun, had not gambled so much of her earnings away.

Vigée-Lebrun was, like so many other women artists, the daughter of a painter, and a child prodigy. At 15 she was getting enough work to support not

Suzanne Valadon's forceful Self-Portrait. *She once said: 'I think maybe God has made me France's greatest woman painter.'*

only herself but also her mother, by now a widow, and her younger brother Etienne. Her charm and stylishness, allied to her undoubted talent, soon brought her important commissions from the French Nobility and others. Her portrait of Count Shuvaloff is a work of remarkable skill and assurance for someone barely 20 years old. In the following year she painted the King's brother, and in 1779 Marie Antoinette – the first of many portraits of the Queen. In 1783, when she was 28, she was admitted to the French Academy along with Adélaïde Labille-Guiard (q.v.).

Vigée-Lebrun's association with the monarchy, however, made it difficult for her to remain in Paris after the French Revolution, and in 1789 she fled to

Italy. After three years there she moved to Vienna, then to St Petersburg, then to England, and finally to Switzerland. It was 20 years before she settled in France again. Her last years were clouded. Her only daughter died in 1819, her much-loved brother in 1820. Her autobiography, *Souvenirs*, was published in 1835–7.

Elisabeth Vigée-Lebrun has not yet received her due from art historians. There is no adequate catalogue of her vast output – which included 660 portraits – and too many copies by lesser hands are accepted as her own work. If the quality of her work tended to be variable, her best portraits were very good – far better than the merely flattering and technically skilled likenesses which are too often attributed to her.

Wei Shuo
Chinese (c. AD 272–350)

'Her art was like the breaking of ice in a crystal jar ... graceful as a tree in fragrant blossom, and soothing as a clean breeze.' That is how the ancient *Catalogue of Famous Calligraphy* describes the brushwork of Wei Shuo, wife of Li Chu, a provincial governor. None of her calligraphy survives – but in AD 348 she wrote a manual on the subject, *Diagram of the Battle Array of the Brush*. It became a text book for later calligraphers, and even for painters. Wei Shuo was also the teacher of the greatest of Chinese calligraphers, Wang Hsi-chih.

There were many women calligraphers: Wei Shuo's own master had been taught by a woman, Wen-chi, and another woman, Chu Ching-chien, is also listed as one of the 'teachers of great influence' in the sixth-century *Biographies of Famous Chinese Nuns*.

SCIENCE
AND MEDICINE

WOMEN HAVE ALWAYS PRACTISED the arts of healing. It seems only to have been for three or four centuries, when medicine first became institutionalized, that they were virtually barred from working as doctors or surgeons. Yet there were women doctors in ancient Egypt, in classical Greece and Rome, and in the Middle Ages. The famous medical school at Salerno, near Naples, which was founded in the tenth century, had women students and teachers, of whom the eleventh-century physician Trotula was the most celebrated – indeed, so celebrated that Chaucer's Wyf of Bath mentions her (in the prologue to her Canterbury Tale). In England even as late as the sixteenth century women were permitted to enter the examinations which would allow them to practise medicine, and dozens are known to have passed and been licensed. However, attitudes changed and women became effectively excluded from the profession; indeed they were all too often persecuted as witches if they did try to cure sickness. It was not until the mid-nineteenth century, in the face of considerable opposition, that women once again won the right to train and qualify as doctors.

A similar story is true of the other sciences. Women had more chance of studying mathematics or philosophy in classical times than in seventeenth- or eighteenth-century Europe. Pythagoras was one of several great male teachers who had women pupils, and in the first century AD, the city of Alexandria, Egypt, had many women philosophers, mathematicians and alchemists. Some women in early modern times, such as the mathematicians Maria Agnesi and Mary Somerville, were known and admired far beyond their native countries for their erudition; but these later women scientists never achieved the solid work of their male contemporaries. It was left to Marie Curie, a frail Polish student at the Sorbonne in Paris, who went on to discover radium, to show at last that science was as much the province of women as of men.

Anthropologist Margaret Mead and friend in Samoa, 1925.

Maria Agnesi
Italian (1718–1799)

Maria Gaetana Agnesi was one of the most brilliant Italians of the eighteenth century, and was appointed professor of mathematics at the University of Bologna. She was born in Milan, and at an early age proved herself a gifted linguist. Later, having been persuaded not to enter a nunnery, she turned to mathematics; her father was professor at the University of Bologna and loved to show off her precocious skills. In 1748 she published *Analytical Institutions for the use of Italian Youth*, a mathematics text book on algebra, analytical geometry and calculus which was widely translated. Her name is particularly associated with the curve $x^2y = (a-y)$, which she called in Latin *a versiera*. Since its colloquial meaning is 'witch', it is known in English as the 'witch of Agnesi'.

When Maria Agnesi's father died, the then Pope, Benedict XIV (1740–58), recommended that she should be appointed to succeed to his professorship, but instead she turned to theology, and spent her last years dedicated to good works helping the afflicted, transforming her own home into a hospital.

Elizabeth Garrett Anderson was the first woman to qualify as a doctor in Britain.

Dr Elizabeth Garrett Anderson
British (1836–1917)

Elizabeth Garrett Anderson was the first woman to qualify as a doctor in Britain and have a hospital named after her. She was one of nine children of Newson Garrett, a grain merchant in Aldeburgh, Suffolk (cf. also Millicent Fawcett), and after two years at boarding school lived at home until she was 26. But in 1859 she attended a lecture given by Dr Elizabeth Blackwell (q.v.) which fired her determination to 'open the medical profession to women'. One Harley Street surgeon who subsequently enquired why she should not be a nurse received the reply: 'I should naturally prefer a thousand pounds to twenty pounds a year.'

The long struggle for qualification started with six months' nursing in 1860, which gave her a brief chance to watch operations; but the male students eventually insisted on her leaving. Unsuccessful in her applications for university courses, she studied privately with professors and in 1864 learnt midwifery at the London Hospital. At last in 1865 the Society of Apothecaries gave her a qualification as an apothecary and from 1866 she ran a dispensary for women. But it was only in Paris, in 1870, that she was able to take her final medical exams. That same year she was the first woman to be elected to the new School Board.

In 1871 she married James Anderson, who was in shipping, and had three children (one daughter, Louisa, also became a doctor). In 1872 she opened the New Hospital for women, staffed entirely by women (now called the Elizabeth Garrett Anderson Hospital), where she worked and taught until her retirement. In 1908 she became Mayor of Aldeburgh, the first woman mayor in Britain.

Hertha Ayrton
British (1854–1923)

Hertha Ayrton was a physicist, suffragette and inventor. Born Sarah Marks, she came from a Jewish family in Portsea on the south coast of Britain and at first earned her living by needlework and teaching. In 1874 she was encouraged to take the preliminary examination for Cambridge University and went to Girton College in 1876 to read mathematics (cf. Emily Davies and Barbara Bodichon helped her financially), before becoming a teacher and lecturer. In 1885 she married Professor Ayrton, a lecturer in electricity.

Hertha Ayrton invented a line-divider which is still used by architects, and also worked on the electric arc – solving problems to do with lack of stability and noise – and her book on the subject,· published in 1902, led to defence work for the Admiralty on searchlights. In 1898 she became the first female full member of the Institute of Electrical Engineers. When, in 1903, Madame Curie (q.v.) visited England, they became lifelong friends. An ardent suffragette, Ayrton sheltered the victims of the 'Cat and Mouse' Act – women who were forcefed in prison and let out to recover before being re-arrested. During the First World War she invented the Ayrton Fan for dispersing poisonous gases. In 1920 she became a founder member of the National Union of Scientific Workers. Her stepdaughter, Edith, married Israel Zangwill, the novelist and Zionist; her daughter, Barbara Ayrton Gould, became a Labour Member of Parliament.

Dr James Barry
British (1795?–1865)

James Barry had one of the most astonishing of all careers: born a woman 'he' successfully disguised his sex all his life, and had a long career as a doctor with the British army.

Mystery surrounds Barry's birth in London. She was originally Miranda Stuart, probably the daughter of a General Miranda. The Earl of Buchan seems to have been her patron while she studied at Edinburgh University: already in disguise. Barry qualified in 1811 and passed the Army examination. She was soon promoted to staff surgeon and was sent to the Cape Colony (now South Africa) in 1816. As Colonial Medical Inspector in 1821 she made herself unpopular by insisting on an enquiry into conditions in the public jail, the leper colonies and Robben Prison Island, and her salty letters to the authorities and intransigence on matters of principle led to her eventual removal to Mauritius in 1827 and later Jamaica, in 1831. In 1836, as Principal Medical Officer on St Helena, Barry led a campaign for women (mostly suffering from venereal diseases) to be treated in a building away from the barracks. From 1838 to 1845 she was in Trinidad and had yellow fever so badly that two assistant surgeons penetrated her disguise, but loyally said nothing. In 1858 she was made Inspector General of Hospitals and went to Canada.

Extremely reserved, brusque in manner and irritable, Barry kept people at arm's length and was protected wherever she went by Sambo, a large black man, and a little dog, Psyche. In 1859 she retired to London where she died in 1865. Barry's death created a sensation because her request to be buried without examination was ignored and her true sex, together with the fact that she had had a child, was revealed.

Clara Barton
American (1821–1912)

'The angel of the battlefield', Clara Barton was virtually an unpaid quartermaster to the wounded of the Civil War, and founded the American Red Cross. She was an almost exact contemporary of Florence Nightingale (q.v.), and resembled her not only in her work on the battlefield, but also in her refusal to retire until her nineties despite frail health.

Daughter of a prosperous farmer and sawmill owner of old New England stock, Barton's first experience of nursing was at the age of 11, when she looked after her invalid elder brother David for two years. At 15 she became a teacher, and taught for 18 years. During that time she founded a free school in Bordentown, New Jersey, which was so successful

Clara Barton, founder and first president of the American Red Cross, photographed during the Civil War.

thereafter she ran the American Red Cross. She went to Turkey after the Armenian massacres, Cuba in 1898, the Galveston (Texas) flood in 1900. 'Everybody's business is nobody's business', she once said, 'and nobody's business is my business'. But she was manoeuvred out of the leadership in 1904; she functioned best as an instigator rather than an administrator.

Ruth Benedict
American (1887–1948)

Ruth Benedict introduced the concept of 'patterns of culture' to the discipline of social anthropology. Born Ruth Fulton, she became deaf as a child; her father died when she was two and in childhood she had to manage a grief-stricken mother. Ruth graduated from Vassar in 1909 determined to be a writer; inspired by Walter Pater, she published poems under the pseudonym of Anne Singleton in *Poetry*, Chicago and taught at a school in California for a year. She married Arthur Benedict, later Professor at Cornell Medical School, in 1914.

She was 32 before she began studying anthropology. She took a doctorate at Columbia under Frank Boas, the famous anthropologist, in 1923.

Benedict propounded the idea that cultures had particular personalities, like people, and that the characteristics of one culture communicated themselves to others. Her *Tales of the Cochiti Indians* (1931), based on field work in the South West U.S., was followed by *Zuni Mythology* in 1935. *Patterns of Culture*, her most famous book, came out in 1934 and revolutionized anthropological thought. It was translated into 14 languages. In 1939 Benedict's *Race: Science and Politics* attacked racist arguments while *Chrysanthemum and the Sword: Patterns of Japanese Culture*, written after the Second World War in 1946, was an attempt to unravel the causes of war.

She became the editor of the *American Journal of Folklore* in 1925. She was made Assistant Professor at Columbia in 1931 and full professor in 1948, just before she died.

and expanded to such an extent that a man was appointed principal over her head. She promptly resigned, and suffered a nervous breakdown. In 1854 she began work in the Washington Patent Office, but after the Civil War broke out she advertised for food and medical supplies for the wounded and began to organize their distribution, which took her with her mule-trains into the front line. She refused to allow the Army to have any control over her activities, thus side-stepping bureaucratic delays, and in 1864 acted briefly as an official superintendent of nurses.

After the Civil War Barton organized searches for missing soldiers. Four years later, when she went to Europe for her health, she came across the work of the International Red Cross. It took her 12 years to get the U.S. Government to join the organization;

Dr Elizabeth Blackwell
British (1821–1910)

Elizabeth Blackwell was the first woman in the United States to qualify as a doctor. She was the third daughter of a Bristol merchant who emigrated to New York when she was seven. The family moved to Cincinnati; but her father died, leaving her mother with eight children to support. Three of the sisters ran a school, and Elizabeth was made a headmistress in Kentucky in 1842. She began to study medicine while teaching, convinced she had found her true vocation. In 1844 Philadelphia and New York medical schools turned her down because of her sex but Geneva, New York, admitted her and, after much debate, she was awarded a degree in 1849. In 1850 Blackwell came to England to visit certain hospitals (St Bartholomew's Hospital, London, allowed her into all wards *except* those for women and children) before taking a midwifery training course in Paris. In 1851 she lost the use of one eye from an infection caught in the communal baths at La Maternité and so could not be a surgeon.

With two other women doctors – her sister, Emily, and Marie Zackrzewska – Dr Blackwell opened a dispensary and medical college for women in New York in 1853, and in spite of fierce opposition they managed to found a hospital exclusively for women in 1857. (In 1865 it was granted a charter to set up a four-year training course for women with its own independent examining board.)

In 1858 Blackwell returned to England for good. There she gave a famous series of lectures urging women to qualify in medicine which were attended by, among others, Elizabeth Garrett Anderson and Barbara Bodichon (qq.v.). 'Our duty is loyalty to right, opposition to wrong. Not blind imitation of man or thoughtless imitation of what they teach.' Her name – that of the first woman – was entered on the British Medical Register in 1859.

For the rest of her working life Dr Blackwell was Professor of Gynaecology at what is now the Royal Free Hospital in London. Like her friend, Florence Nightingale (q.v.), she was a strong advocate of common sense and preventive medicine.

Rachel Carson
American (1907–1964)

Rachel Carson was the marine biologist whose analysis of the harm done to the cycle of nature by pesticides led, after her death, to the banning of the use of DDT in the United States, and alerted both scientists and the general public all over the world to the necessity of protecting the environment. *Silent Spring*, which was published in 1962, described the way in which poisons designed to kill the insects which attack crops ended up in the rivers, killing first fish, and then the birds which eat the fish. It is one of the classic ecological studies.

Carson was born into a farming family in Pennsylvania, and after briefly studying English switched to marine biology. From 1935 to 1952 she worked with the U.S. Fish and Wildlife Service, taught at the University of Maryland, and held an appointment with the U.S. Bureau of Fisheries. She wrote five books: *Under the Sea-Wind* (1941), *The Sea Around Us* (1951), which was published in the *New Yorker* and had sold 250,000 copies by the end of 1952, *The Edge of the Sea* (1955), *Silent Spring* (1962) and *The Sense of Wonder* (1965). For the last few years of her life she was in very poor health, and eventually died of cancer, happy only that she had done what she could to publicize the harm mankind has done to nature.

Edith Cavell
British (1865–1915)

Edith Cavell, a famous martyr of the First World War was the heroic British nurse shot by the Germans for obeying the humanitarian principles of her training. Edith Cavell's father was the vicar of Swardeston in Norfolk, and in early adult life she was a governess in East Anglia and Brussels. When she was 30 she went to the London Hospital as a probationer, and subsequently nursed in England for 12 years before deciding to return to Brussels. In 1907 she was appointed matron of the Berkendael Medical Institute in Brussels; she was responsible for transforming it from a small clinic into a teaching hospital.

Edith Cavell with pet dogs. She was shot by the Germans in 1915 for harbouring aliens.

Gabrielle-Emilie du Châtelet. Voltaire christened her Uranie, in honour of her scientific and mathematical knowledge.

In 1914, on the outbreak of the Great War, it became a Red Cross Hospital – and a place of refuge for wounded soldiers of all nationalities. Many of those wounded soldiers were British, French and Belgian, and when they recovered, Cavell helped them to find their way to Holland, from where they could rejoin the Allied Army. For eight months the hospital was a staging post on the escape route for some hundreds of soldiers; its role was impossible to keep secret for long. In August 1915 Cavell was arrested for harbouring aliens and eventually court-martialled, along with 34 other men and women, mostly Belgian. Besides herself, three men and one other woman were condemned to death, although she and only one of the men were executed by firing squad. She met her fate with great courage. Her last message was: 'Standing as I do in view of God and Eternity, I realize that patriotism is not enough. I must have no hatred or bitterness towards anyone.'

Gabrielle-Emilie du Châtelet
French (1706–1749)

Although she is more celebrated for her 16-year liaison with Voltaire, the Marquise du Châtelet was herself a hardworking mathematician and philosopher, who translated Newton's *Principia Mathematica* into French and wrote the introduction, which Voltaire admired; she also introduced the mathematical ideas of the German philosopher Liebniz to France.

Mme du Châtelet was the daughter of the Baron de Breteuil, head of protocol under Louis XIV. She learnt English, Italian and Latin exceptionally well, but especially loved mathematics. At 19 she married the Marquis du Châtelet, an army officer who eventually became a general, and they had two sons and a daughter. As was customary, Mme du Châtelet took lovers. At 27 she met Voltaire, with whom she lived and worked at the Châtelet country house at Cirey in Champagne until her death 16 years later. Neither was faithful: Voltaire fell in love with his widowed niece Madame Denis (with whom he set up house after Mme du Châtelet's death), while she became involved first with another philosopher, Maupertuis, and later with the Marquis de Saint-Lambert, a poet. However, their relationship was for both Voltaire and du Châtelet the most important and stimulating of their lives. Voltaire was grief-stricken when she died shortly after the birth of her fourth child (whose father was Saint-Lambert).

The ménage at Cirey was the most famous of the day. The Marquis du Châtelet accepted it; and the two lovers organized the house – on Voltaire's money – as they wanted it. They talked and worked, read and wrote, entertained and held amateur theatricals of Voltaire's plays.

Madame du Châtelet (whom Voltaire christened Uranie in honour of her scientific and mathematical knowledge, which was greater than his own) brought out *Les Institutions de Physique* in 1740, and her translation of Newton was published in 1756, after her death. She wrote a paper on the nature of fire in 1738, and some *Reflections sur le Bonheur* (1740), which are full of good sense.

Evelyn Cheesman
British (1881–1969)

This distinguished entomologist and collector of insects was largely self-taught. One of four children, she was educated at home by a governess, then sent to school to learn languages. After some years as a governess herself she spent a year teaching in Germany. When she returned she became a 'canine nurse' in Croydon, as women were not admitted to training as veterinary surgeons. During the First World War she became an unpaid typist at the Imperial Institute, spending her lunch hours in the nearby Natural History Museum studying insects. In 1918 she became a secretary in the Insect House at the London Zoo; by 1923 she knew enough about them to be sent on a research expedition to the Galapagos and New Guinea.

Thereafter Cheesman travelled extensively, and in 30 years of solo exploration brought back to London 40,000 insects, and numerous other plants and small mammals, mostly from the tropical island rain forests of South East Asia, aided in her researches by the informed advice of her native guides. She was the author of many books based on her researches. *Things Worth While* particulary communicates her obsessive delight in her work.

Cheesman was eventually appointed Curator of the Insect House. She once said, 'There is nothing I have done that could not be done by others. What were they waiting for? Experience? I bought it. Health? I risked it. Adequate financial aid? I grabbed what I could and went without the remainder.'

Elena Cornaro
Italian (1646–1684)

Born into the Venetian nobility, Elena Cornaro became Europe's first woman doctor of philosophy. Besides her native Italian, she spoke French and Spanish, Greek and Latin, Hebrew and Arabic. At the age of 28 she applied to become a student at the University of Padua, and four years later, having completely won over those who had opposed her, she was unanimously acclaimed a doctor of philosophy when she presented her thesis to an audience of learned men.

Marie Curie
Polish (1867–1934)

Marie Curie was the first world-famous woman scientist and discovered the element radium. She twice won a Nobel Prize, first with her husband Pierre and Henri Becquerel in Physics, then alone in Chemistry. Her work led directly to the treatment of cancer with radium and, by way of the work of her elder daughter Irène and son-in-law Frédéric Joliot, to the splitting of the atom.

She was born Marya Sklodowska in Warsaw, Poland, the youngest of five children of impoverished teachers. Poland at that time was occupied by Russia, and young Poles could only get a university education abroad. Marie spent five unhappy years as a

223

governess financing her sister Bronya's medical studies in Paris; only when she was 23, with pathetically small savings, was Marie able to go to Paris too. After two years of poverty and unremitting work at the Sorbonne, she came top in physics; then, the following year, second in mathematics. The same year, she met a French physicist, Pierre Curie, then 35; after much hesitation, having always intended to return to work in her beloved Poland, she married him in 1895. Thereafter Curie worked full-time at her husband's side, in spite of the birth of two daughters, Irène in 1897 and Eve in 1904.

For her doctorate Curie decided to search for the source of the mysterious rays emitted by uranium salts which had been discovered in 1895 by Henri Becquerel. Her first significant discovery was that the strength of the rays emitted by such salts depended on the amount of uranium present. She also suspected that what she was to christen 'radioactivity' was present in other elements; and soon found that an even more powerful source than uranium was present in pitchblende (the ores left over when uranium has been extracted).

Curie's subsequent years of back-breaking labour in an unheated outhouse in the yard of the Sorbonne School of Physics have become a legend. She submitted some eight tons of pitchblende to chemical analysis – grinding, dissolving, filtering, crystallizing – before she managed to isolate one decigramme of pure radium. She announced its atomic weight in 1902: 225 (later corrected to 226). For this achievement she, Pierre Curie and Henri Becquerel received the Nobel Prize for Physics in 1903.

They were the happiest years of her life. In 1906 her husband, weakened by the radiation which they did not yet know was harmful, fell in front of a horse-drawn cart and was killed. The grief-stricken widow took over his professorship (the first woman to hold such a post), and devoted the rest of her life to her laboratory. She had the satisfaction of knowing that her discoveries were instrumental in curing cancer – but never fully faced the accumulating evidence of the cause of her own poor health and the illness and deaths of others who worked with radium. Always deeply reserved and stiff, she suffered acutely from her fame, particularly when her name was linked in 1911

The last photograph of Marie Curie taken just before her death in 1934.

with that of the physicist Paul Langevin, a married man and former pupil of her husband's. Whatever the relationship, the scandal killed it. Marie Curie spent the Great War touring the front line with her X-ray vans, and later undertook lecture tours in America and Europe, raising funds for her research.

Although she did not live to see Irène and Frédéric Joliot-Curie win the Nobel Prize for Physics in their turn, Marie did witness the researches in artificial radioactivity which earned it, before she finally succumbed to leukaemia brought on by decades of exposure to radium. Irène herself, who had been exposed to radiation since she had toured with her mother in the X-ray vans as an adolescent, died of leukaemia in 1956.

Rosalind Franklin
British (1920–1958)

Rosalind Franklin was the crystallographer whose X-ray photographs of the molecular structure of DNA –

the protein-building 'brick' from which living cells are built up – were a principal clue in the unravelling of DNA's famous 'double helix' in 1953, for which the British scientists Francis Crick and Maurice Wilkins, and the American James Watson, received the Nobel Prize for Medicine in 1962. She herself had died of cancer four years earlier, and was therefore not eligible.

Rosalind Franklin was the second of five children of a distinguished and prosperous Jewish family. Her first important researches were into the molecular structure of coal and coke in Britain, then into graphitic carbons in Paris. Having gained a doctorate from Cambridge, she went to King's College London in January 1951 to work on DNA with Maurice Wilkins. In November she announced her discovery that DNA existed in two forms, and that one form at least was helical, with its 'backbone' – against all expectation – on the outside. By April 1953, when Watson and Crick published their brilliant paper on the model of DNA which they had constructed in the form of a double helix, she herself was, according to Crick, within a very few weeks of reaching the same conclusions. Franklin's invaluable contribution was acknowledged, and subsequently represented, by Wilkins' share of the Nobel Prize. But a bitter row broke out when in 1968 James Watson published his popular book *The Double Helix*. In it he made an ungenerous attack on the personality of Dr Franklin, who had clearly not been on good terms with any of them; many scientists felt that in consequence she did not receive proper recognition.

Jane Goodall
British (b. 1934)

Jane Goodall is virtually the founding mother of ethology – the scientific study of the behaviour of animals in the wild. Brought up in the respectable south coast resort of Bournemouth, she was an ardent naturalist from early childhood – making notes on insects, animals and birds, even opening a 'museum' to the public – and determined to go to Africa when she grew up. She worked as a secretary, a film studio

Jane Goodall at Gombe Stream Research Centre, Tanzania, in 1975.

assistant, even a waitress, and at 23 had saved up her fare to visit a friend in Kenya. Once there, she got a job as secretary to the anthropologist Dr Louis Leakey, and so impressed him with her passion for animals that he encouraged her to study chimpanzees.

After 18 months, finance and permissions were at last organized, and in July 1960 Goodall set off, accompanied by her mother, for the Gombe Stream Reserve in Tanzania on a three-month project. The three months became six years, which were to result in 'the best field study ever done of a mammal', according to her tutor, Professor Robert Hinde. During that time she fitted in six terms at Cambridge University preparing a Ph.D. (though she had no first degree), and marriage in 1964 to a Dutch photographer, equally interested in animals, who had come to do a feature on her in 1962 – Baron Hugo van Lawick. Their son, 'Grub', was born in 1967, and his childhood was spent on safari with his parents. Today the Gombe Stream project is no longer a two-tent encampment, but the Gombe Stream Research

Centre – of which the van Lawicks became the Scientific and Administrative Directors. The van Lawicks have since divorced, and Jane Goodall later married Derek Bryceson, formerly curator of the National Parks of Tanzania and then the only white member of President Nyerere's Government. She continues to spend some time each month at Gombe.

Goodall's great virtues are patience, courage, acute powers of observation and immense determination. It was to take her six months to get near her chosen chimpanzees, but in the following six years she made several discoveries crucial to scientists' understanding of them. Contrary to previous belief, she found that chimpanzees actively hunt meat, use tools – an ability which overlaps with one of the key definitions of Man – and do not necessarily have a formal hierarchy.

Catherine Greene
American (1731–1793?)

Eli Whitney is always given sole credit for the invention of the cotton gin – a piece of machinery which enabled cotton fibre to be separated from the seed quickly and efficiently, instead of laboriously by hand. In fact Whitney owed the idea of the machine to Mrs Catherine Littlefield Greene, widow of General Nathanael Greene, when he was staying in her house in Savannah, Georgia. But since women were not then allowed to apply for patents, the promotion of the scheme was left to him. Several times over the next few months he was on the point of giving up trying to make the machine work, but Greene encouraged him to continue, and in 1794 the cotton gin was patented in Whitney's name. The gin enabled one man to do the work of 200, and had a profound effect on the economy of the Southern States.

Caroline Herschel
German (1750–1848)

Caroline Herschel was the astronomer who discovered three nebulae and 18 comets. She was born in Hanover, the daughter of an Army bandsman, and helped her mother at home until her brother William, an organist and music teacher, summoned her to join

him in Bath, England in 1772. William was also a keen amateur astronomer. His sister both sang in oratorio with him and helped him grind the lenses for the telescopes. He was appointed astronomer to George III in 1782, and Caroline Herschel was given a salary of £50 a year in 1787. With her small Newtonian telescope she independently spotted three remarkable nebulae and eight comets in the years before 1797, five of them particularly important. In 1797 she presented the Royal Society with a list of 561 stars 'accidentally' (as she put it) omitted from Flamsteed's official list. When William Herschel married she went back to Hanover and started work listing 2,500 nebulae in order. In 1828 the Astronomical Society awarded her their Gold Medal – she was 78 – and made her an honorary member in 1833, five years later.

A nineteenth-century artist's impression of Caroline and William Herschel in their observatory.

Dorothy Hodgkin
British (b. 1910)

Dorothy Hodgkin is the X-ray crystallographer who won the Nobel Prize for Chemistry in 1964 for analyzing the structure of Vitamin B12, a vital substance in the fight against pernicious anaemia. Earlier in her career, Hodgkin was the first scientist to determine the chemical structure of any substance solely by X-ray analysis. She successfully analyzed penicillin (for which she became a Fellow of the Royal Society in 1947). In 1965 she became the first woman to be appointed to the Order of Merit since Florence Nightingale (q.v.) in 1907. She became Chancellor of Bristol University in 1970.

Dorothy Crowfoot was born in Egypt, daughter of Dr J.W. Crowfoot of the Egyptian Ministry of Education and his wife Grace, who was an expert on Coptic textiles. Her father later became Director of Education and Antiquities in Khartoum, Sudan, and then Director of the British School of Archaeology in Jerusalem. Her childhood was divided between Norfolk and the Middle East. She studied chemistry at Somerville College, Oxford. She married Thomas Hodgkin, the historian and African scholar, in 1937 and has three children. Dorothy Hodgkin has always been an active worker for peace.

Dorothy Hodgkin, winner of the Nobel Prize for chemistry in 1964.

Karen Horney
American (1885–1952)

Karen Horney was the first Freudian psychoanalyst to reject Freud's view of feminine psychology as a defective version of masculine psychology. Where Freud propounded that 'anatomy is destiny' it occurred to Horney that a male-oriented culture might have something to do with emotional illness in women. For this heresy she was expelled from the New York Psychoanalytic Institute in 1941 – whereupon she founded the Association for the Advancement of Psychoanalysis, the only independent school of psychoanalysis founded by a woman.

Karen Horney was born in Germany, the daughter of a Dutch mother and a Norwegian-born sea captain, Berndt Danielsen, a stern and critical man who tried to prevent her from going on to secondary school and, later, from studying medicine. Only with the support of her mother (who left Danielsen to accompany her daughter) did Karen manage to go to Freiburg University, Germany. In 1909 she married Oscar Horney, a gifted Berlin lawyer, by whom she had three daughters. (She and her husband separated in 1926.)

In 1915 Horney began working in a neurological clinic in Berlin, and underwent analysis with Karl Abraham, one of Freud's closest associates. She shortly joined Abraham's own group, which became the Berlin Psychoanalytic Institute, and taught there until 1932 when she was invited to America as assistant director of the Chicago Institute of Psychoanalysis.

Horney attacked Freud's famous theory of penis envy as early as 1922, and in 1926 was writing 'The psychology of women ... actually represents a deposit of the desires ... of men. Women see themselves in the way that their men's wishes demand of them.' She pointed out that men seemed to need to depreciate women more than vice versa, and postulated the idea of womb envy. Her views were not popular in Hitler's Germany.

Nor were such ideas popular in America. Horney spent only two years at Chicago before going to the Psychoanalytic Institute in New York. There she noticed that Freud's theories, however applicable in Europe, did not work so well in the U.S.; neuroses in America were *different*, and 'only the differences in civilization could account for this.' Anatomy was *not* the sole key to destiny. She also differed from Freud over the importance of the libido and the death wish. *The Neurotic Personality of Our Time* (1937) and *New Ways in Psychoanalysis* (1939) in which she set forth these heretical views, caused a furore which resulted in her expulsion from the New York Psychoanalytic Institute in 1941. To risk losing her livelihood in this way was in fact immensely courageous, since there was plenty of competition for Horney's job from other European immigrants fleeing from the Nazis. Fortunately the Association for the Advancement of Psychoanalysis, which she founded with 20 supporters the following week, prospered, and two further books, *Our Inner Conflicts* (1945) and *Neurosis and Human Growth* (1950) followed. Karen Horney died of cancer in 1952.

Hypatia
Egyptian (c. 370–415)

Hypatia was one of the most popular and admired teachers of the Hellenistic world. She was the daughter and pupil of Theon, professor of mathematics at Alexandria, and also studied under Plutarch the Younger in Athens. She was a mathematician, astronomer and philosopher, and in her turn became a professor at Alexandria, teaching the views of Plato and Aristotle. Her advice was sought by magistrates and others; her most famous and devoted pupil was the Christian bishop Synesius.

Hypatia was murdered during religious disturbances by Christian fanatics, who dragged her into a church, then stripped and butchered her. None of her writings have survived.

Dr Elsie Inglis
British (1864–1917)

'I have two passions in life', said Dr Elsie Inglis, 'suffrage and surgery'. She became famous for the field hospitals she organized in France and Serbia during the First World War without any government support.

Elsie Inglis's father was in the Indian Civil Service and she was born in India; the family went to Tasmania but eventually moved to Edinburgh. Encouraged by her father and inspired by Sophia Jex-Blake (q.v.), Inglis trained as a doctor. She set up in partnership with Jessie Macgregor – 'all the comforts of marriage and none of the disadvantages' she once called it – and founded a Free Hospice for women and children in the Edinburgh slums. She was secretary of the Scottish branch of the National Union of Women's Suffrage Societies and walked and bicycled all over Scotland giving lectures. In 1914 she raised £25,000 within a month and offered her Scottish Field Hospital – 'manned' by all-women teams, from surgeons to chauffeurs and orderlies – to the War Office, but received the response: 'Go and sit quietly at home, dear lady'. The French, however, snapped up her offer; two units were stationed in France and Inglis herself went to Serbia (now part of Yugoslavia), where she dealt with a raging typhus epidemic. When the Austrians overran the camp she refused to leave her Serbian patients and went into captivity with them. In 1916 she took her unit to Odessa to care for the Serbs, who were now part of the Russian Army.

Inglis was a wonderful organizer ('not me, but my team') and an indomitable character – shouting out to her nurses during bombardments: 'Stick by your equipment, dear child.' She became ill towards the

Elsie Inglis at one of her Scottish Field hospitals, in Caramurat, during the retreat.

end of the war and died the day after reaching England when she was being repatriated on her way home. Drinking fountains and a children's home were put up in Yugoslavia as memorials to her: a wing of the Royal Infirmary in Edinburgh also commemorates her achievements.

Barbara Ward Jackson
British (b. 1914)

A brilliant writer on economics and a committed ecologist, Lady Jackson was made one of Britain's few women life peers in 1976. She was brought up in York, went to a convent and to university in Paris and Oxford. She published her first book, *The International Share Out*, in 1938 and subsequently joined the *Economist*. She became a household name in Britain in the 1940s for the part she played in the popular radio programme *The Brains Trust*; later she became a Governor of the BBC. In 1950 she married an Australian diplomat, Sir Robert Jackson; they have one son, and separated in 1973. While teaching at Harvard and Columbia she wrote *The Rich Nations and the Poor Nations* which sold a quarter of a million copies. Then came *Space Ship Earth* (1966) and *The Lopsided World* (1968). She became a professor at Columbia University in 1968. In 1972 the U.N. asked her to write *Only One Earth: The Care and Maintenance of a Small Planet*. As she said: 'They wanted a layman, somebody non-scientific who could write something which other laymen could understand.' A devout Catholic, she was the first woman to address the Vatican in 1971. Barbara Ward Jackson would like to persuade everybody that it only takes common sense to share out the world's natural resources.

Dr Aletta Jacobs
Dutch (1854–1929)

Aletta Jacobs, Holland's first woman physician, opened the world's first birth control clinic in Amsterdam in 1882. The eighth of 11 children, she was determined from the age of six to become a doctor like her father. But she left school at 13 and, in true nineteenth-century middle-class style, the only further education she was permitted was a finishing school – where she stayed for exactly two weeks: 'It was a nightmare,' she wrote in her autobiography. 'I just couldn't understand why, as we were taught, a girl should lower her eyes if she passed a man in the street.' After an unhappy period as a daughter at home, she learnt that another girl had become an apprentice pharmacist and decided to do the same herself. She was awarded her diploma in 1870. She then persuaded her father to write to the Prime Minister for permission to send her to university to read medicine. After much hostility from her fellow-students and from the press, she graduated in 1878 and joined her father's practice.

Thereafter, despite a lifetime of indifferent health and constant opposition, Jacobs devoted herself to many causes: women's suffrage, birth control, pacifism, prison reform, laws to protect children, the rights of women in Asia. She urged frankness between parents and children on the subject of sex, she brought the dangers of venereal disease and prostitution into the open, and, after 20 years of campaigning, she succeeded in making employers legally obliged to provide chairs for shop assistants: she had seen too many gynaecological ailments caused by women having to stand for 10 or 12 hours a day.

Dr Jacobs also stood up for the dignity of women: she always charged the same rates as her male colleagues (though they wanted a woman's fees to be lower), she fought for the right to use a 'men only' reference library and to attend concerts unescorted, she flouted convention by walking the streets alone at night, and constantly protested that the marriage service expected women to promise obedience to their husbands.

In fact, before marrying the radical politician Carel Victor Gerritsen, the couple had seriously considered a 'free' union because of the indignities marriage inflicted on women. When they did marry, in 1891, they shared all household expenses. (Their one child died in infancy.)

In 1882, Jacobs opened a birth control clinic in Amsterdam and was bitterly attacked, often by those who privately made use of the clinic. She advocated the pessary, and she was recognized as an international authority on contraception. Jacobs was a leading campaigner in the suffrage cause. By 1903 she had become president of the Dutch Women's Suffrage Association and was lecturing all over Holland on the importance of giving women the vote. Eventually, after much lobbying and demonstrating, women were permitted to *stand* for election in 1918. The following year they won the right to vote by a large majority.

It was only in the last few years of her life that Dr Jacobs finally won the recognition she deserved.

Dr Sophia Jex-Blake
British (1840–1912)

Sophia Jex-Blake was one of the first women doctors in Britain. Her family was rich – descended from a long line of Norfolk landowners – and her father was a prominent lawyer. Her own struggles to establish herself prompted her to found Scotland's first medical school for women.

After much persuasion, Sophia Jex-Blake's parents eventually allowed her to attend lectures – then considered very unladylike – at Queen's College, London, where she subsequently became a lecturer in mathematics and horrified her father by accepting a salary. Inspired by meeting Dr Elizabeth Blackwell (q.v.) when she visited the U.S. to investigate girls' education there, Jex-Blake applied to enter classes in medicine at Edinburgh University in 1868. But apart from the support of one or two professors, all kinds of difficulties were made for the small group of female medical students of which she became unofficial leader. Finally she sued the university for refusing to award women degrees, but lost the case and had to pay costs of £1,000. At the group's graduation in 1874 some male students let sheep loose in Surgeons' Hall and shouted insults. In 1877 Jex-Blake's name finally appeared on the British Medical Register, after she had qualified in Berne and Dublin. She wrote *Medical Women* (1872), a history of all the early women doctors, began to practise in Edinburgh in 1878 and set up the Edinburgh School of Medicine for Women in 1886. Two of her nieces became heads of women's

colleges in the early twentieth century: Katherine Jex-Blake at Girton College, Cambridge, and Henrietta Jex-Blake at Lady Margaret Hall, Oxford.

Elizabeth Kenny
Australian (1886–1962)

Sister Elizabeth Kenny pioneered physiotherapy treatment for children crippled by poliomyelitis. She was the daughter of a veterinary surgeon in the 'outback' and learnt anatomy in a doctor's household after she had broken her wrist. She then devised exercises for her frail younger brother which were unexpectedly successful, and in 1907 she began training as a nurse.

In 1910 Sister Kenny was called out to treat a child suffering from poliomyelitis, and in desperation applied wrung-out hot cloths to the convulsed limbs. The treatment worked so well that she adopted it as

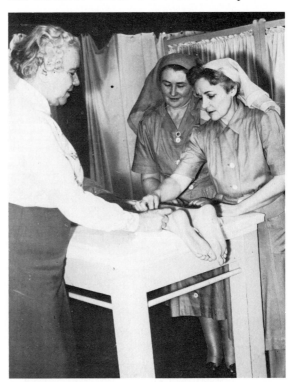

Elizabeth Kenny (left) examining a patient at her clinic in Sydney in 1946.

her method, and she soon opened her own hospital in South Queensland. During the First World War she nursed Australian wounded, but returned to work with disabled children after the War. Derided as a charlatan by orthodox medicine, she was nevertheless invited to the Mayo Clinic, Rochester, in 1940 and her excellent results in combating an epidemic of poliomyelitis in 1942 vindicated her treatment.

Dame Kathleen Kenyon
British (1906–1978)

Kathleen Kenyon made history as the archaeologist who, by digging up Jericho and Jerusalem, re-wrote the prehistory of Middle Eastern townships. Her excavations revealed that the walls of Jericho had indeed tumbled down around 1400 BC – because of an earthquake, rather than Joshua's trumpet.

She was the daughter of Sir Frederic Kenyon, director and principal librarian of the British Museum. After reading history at Oxford, her first archaeological dig was with Dr Gertrude Caton-Thompson's expedition to Zimbabwe, in Africa – legendary site of King Solomon's mines. Thereafter Dr Kenyon dug with Sir Mortimer Wheeler at Verulamium near London (where she uncovered the Roman amphitheatre), in Samaria (in what was then Palestine), all over England, in Libya, and then, most importantly, at Jericho and Jerusalem. She was responsible for bringing the advanced archaeological techniques she had learned from Sir Mortimer to the Middle East. In the 1930s she helped found London's Institute of Archaeology, becoming its acting Director during the Second World War. She was Director of the British School of Archaeology in Jerusalem from 1951 to 1966. From 1962 to 1973 she was Principal of St Hugh's College, Oxford.

Melanie Klein
Austrian (1882–1960)

Melanie Klein was an important figure in the development of the psychoanalytic understanding of children and infants. She was born Melanie Reizes in Vienna, and gave up her ambition to become a doctor

when she became engaged at the age of 17. But after becoming a patient of one of Freud's closest associates, Sandor Ferenczi, she began to study the application of psychoanalysis to young children, and published her first paper in 1919. In 1921 she joined Karl Abraham's Psychoanalytic Institute in Berlin, and finally settled in London with the youngest of her three children in 1926.

Klein's great contribution was the development of a technique for analysing young children's play as an insight into their emotional development, based on her realization that children express themselves more freely in action than in words. Through Klein's analysis of play she also concluded that the Oedipus complex developed early in life, and that aggressive feelings towards the mother were more important than Freud had thought. She propounded these controversial views in *The Psychoanalysis of Children*, published in 1932.

Other important works were *Envy and Gratitude* (1957) – in which Klein discusses how envy affects therapy – and *Narrative of a Child Analysis* (1961), which showed how she worked with a young patient. Melanie Klein's influence has been felt not only by the younger psychoanalysts whom she trained in the 'Kleinian' method, but in infant care and upbringing in general.

Sofya Kovalevskaya
Russian (1850–1891)

Sofya Kovalevskaya was a mathematician whose work on partial differential equations earns her a place as one of the great Russian mathematicians of the nineteenth century.

Sofya Krukovskaya was the younger of two gifted daughters of a liberal-minded general, and grew up on a remote estate near Vitebsk. Her nursery walls were papered, to save money, with mathematical calculations, and by the age of six Sofya was inventing problems herself. In 1866 the family went to Moscow, but General Krakovsky would not allow his daughters to continue their education. To escape, Sofya made a marriage of convenience with a young friend, Vladimir Kovalevsky, and together they went in 1869 to Heidelberg to study. She eventually gained her doctorate at Göttingen. They returned to Russia in 1874, where Kovalevskaya was determined to pursue an academic career. Yet such was the prejudice against women that it was another 10 years before she finally received a professorship – and then only abroad in Stockholm. There her work on the rotation of a solid body round a fixed point won her the French Academy's *Prix Borodin*.

She had one daughter, and wrote a novel, *Vera Barantsova*, in 1880, and a book of *Childhood Memories*. She was greatly admired by young Russian women for the determination with which she had pursued education and a career, and although not a revolutionary her name was anathema to the Russian authorities.

Sofya's elder sister Anna Krukovskaya (1843–1887), a poet and short story writer who had become an intimate friend of Dostoievsky (whose proposal of marriage she had refused), was much more politically minded, and went to Paris in 1869, where she and her medical student husband Victor Jaclard were actively involved in the Paris Commune. General Krukovsky had to use influence to get the young couple – in danger of execution for their political sympathies – safely back to Russia.

Dr Dorothée Leporin
German (1715?–1762)

It took the support of King Frederick II of Prussia for this eighteenth-century woman doctor to be allowed to study. Her father was a Dr Erxleben, and she learnt from him and his colleagues before applying – with the King's permission – to the University of Halle for the degree of Doctor of Medicine. She was granted it in 1754. Inspired by her experiences, she subsequently published a pamphlet, *On the Reasons which Keep Women Back from Higher Education*, and practised as a midwife and obstetrician.

Dame Kathleen Lonsdale
British (1903–1971)

The finest X-ray crystallographer of her generation, Kathleen Lonsdale was one of the first two women to

be elected to the Royal Society in 1945. Fifteen years after winning this most coveted of honours in Britain's scientific community she became its vice-President. She was also the British Association's first woman president in 1967–8, and was Professor of Chemistry at London University from 1949 to 1968).

Kathleen Yardley was born into a Baptist family, but with her husband Dr Thomas Lonsdale became a Quaker. A woman of conviction, she was an ardent pacifist, and accompanied a peace mission to Russia in 1951. She spent a month in prison during the Second World War for refusing to register for civil defence duties (although she took her share of firewatching). Lonsdale was the author of *Is Peace Possible?* as well as many distinguished scientific publications, and lectured all over the world. She always said that scientific careers were ideal for women with children (she had three), but that having the right husband obviously helped: her own shared their household chores, from baking bread to washing clothes.

When offered funds for research by a military organization, which asked her, when she needed to apply for an entry visa, if she belonged to any peace societies, she replied: 'As many as I can afford.' When asked her race, she said: 'Human'.

Ada Lovelace
British (1815–1852)

The young Ada Byron, the poet Byron's only legitimate child, grew up to be an exceptionally gifted mathematician, and as Lady Lovelace became a close friend and supporter of Charles Babbage, inventor of the calculating machine. She foresaw, over a century ahead of her time, how a digital computer would work, and that any calculating machine could only 'do whatever we know how to order it to perform'.

Augusta Ada Byron was born shortly before Lord and Lady Byron (formerly Annabella Milbanke) separated for ever: Byron never saw his daughter after she was a few months old. By the time she was 15 she had taught herself part of Paisley's *Geometry*, and was soon learning astronomy. At 18 she first saw Charles Babbage's 'difference engine'; she was one of the few people to understand it, and thereafter she and the middle-aged widower were lifelong friends. She also began a friendship with the mathematician Mary Somerville (q.v.).

At 19 she married Lord King, subsequently Lord Lovelace, and bore him two sons and a daughter (Lady Anne Blunt, q.v.). They lived in the country (where her mother, Lady Byron, a keen educationalist, persuaded Lord Lovelace to let her found a 'classless' school for working-class children). Charles Babbage was a frequent visitor, and with his and her husband's encouragement, Ada Lovelace pursued her mathematical studies. In 1843 she published, with extensive mathematical notes, her translation of L.F. Menabrea's *Sketch of the Analytical Engine invented by Charles Babbage*.

Lovelace not only understood the analytical engine, but grasped the principles of symbolic logic. In 1844 Professor Augustus de Morgan was writing secretly to Lady Byron that her daughter (already a married woman of 29) had the makings of an original mathematical investigator, which was dangerous in a woman, he believed, because the necessary tension of mind would be beyond a woman's physical strength: he left it to Lady Byron to do what she thought fit.

However, Lovelace had another possibly more Byronic weakness. Inspired by an early paper of Charles Babbage, *Some Questions connected with Games of Chance*, she resolved to devote the remainder of her short life to the quest for an infallible gambling system (the mathematician Gabrielle du Châtelet, q.v., was another inveterate gambler). By the time Lovelace died of cancer at the age of 36 she was hopelessly entangled in debt, and had published nothing more.

Anna Manzolini
Italian (1716–1774?)

Anna Manzolini was celebrated throughout Europe for the wax models she made of different organs of the body, and became a professor of anatomy at the University of Bologna. Originally she made the models as a teaching aid for her husband, who was himself professor of anatomy; she overcame her revulsion for dead bodies in order to study corpses to ensure that her models were anatomically correct. When her husband became ill, she took over his lectures and undertook dissections, and after his death she was appointed lecturer and then, in 1766, professor of anatomy at Bologna. Her particular contribution to learning was her discovery of the correct termination of the oblique muscle of the eye.

Jane Marcet
Swiss (1769–1858)

Jane Marcet refused to believe that science was beyond the understanding of ordinary people and set an educational fashion with her *Conversations on . . .* series. She was born Jane Hardimond in Switzerland and married a rich English merchant. Her first book, *Conversations on Chemistry*, dealt with a subject her husband gave lectures on, and was followed by others tackling Political Economy, Natural Philosophy and Vegetable Physiology. Marcet's approach was very successful; 160,000 copies of her books were sold in America and the series was also to be found in nearly every schoolroom in Britain. *Conversations on Different Kinds of Government* and *Stories for Very Little Children* were written for her son, Willy. Inspired by Marcet's success, Harriet Martineau (q.v.) modelled her own educational handbooks along similar lines.

Mary the Jewess
Egyptian (c. AD 50)

The water-bath, or *bain-marie*, is said to have been invented by (and called after) Mary the Jewess. Her full name is not known, but she was one of the early alchemists who at that time were working in Alexandria on the chemistry of metals (the word chemistry was probably based on the local word for Egypt). Mary devised experiments and invented other apparatus for distillation and sublimation. The *bain-marie*, known to every domestic cook, is a dish of hot water in which pans containing the substance to be heated are placed. This method ensures moist, even, gentle heat, from which some authorities deduce that *marie* derives from the Virgin Mary. But in fact women scientists were not unknown in Egypt at that date (cf. Hypatia).

Margaret Mead
American (1901–1978)

Margaret Mead was the first person to make anthropology comprehensible to ordinary people. Her pioneer studies in the Pacific islands (she learnt seven Pacific languages, and lived as an accepted member of the communities she studied) are a model of their kind; one of them, *Coming of Age in Samoa* (1928), became a best-seller, and *Growing Up in New Guinea* (1930) was not far behind. Her great contributions were to show that societies existed where adolescence was not a traumatic, rebellious phase; and that 'human nature' and 'sex roles' are not the same the world over, but incredibly varied.

After the Second World War Mead turned her attention to her own society, notably in *Male and Female* (1949), using the insights gained from her work with primitive peoples. She vividly showed that progress is paid for by cultural loss. She wrote some 30 books, including *A Rap on Race* (1971) with James Baldwin and *Blackberry Winter* (1972), a memoir of her early years.

Mead was the daughter of an economics professor and was brought up in Philadelphia. As a child she was taught to observe and make notes on her younger brother and sisters: invaluable training for a future anthropologist. She graduated from Barnard College, then moved to Columbia were she was trained and immensely influenced by Frank Boas and Ruth Benedict (q.v.). She was married (and divorced) three times: first in 1923 to the archaeologist Luther Cressman, second in 1928 to the New Zealand anthropologist Reo Fortune, third in 1936 to the English biologist and anthropologist Gregory Bateson, by whom she had a daughter (and with whom she did a pioneer photographic study of the Balinese, *Balinese Character*, published in 1942. Margaret Mead kept her own name throughout. She held several professorships and other academic appointments. She was a brilliant teacher and lecturer, always ready to involve herself in the issues of the day, from teenage marriage to the legislation of marijuana.

Lise Meitner, who pioneered the splitting of the atom, but dissociated herself from the bomb.

Lise Meitner
Austrian (1878–1968)

Lise Meitner was an eminent physicist who pioneered the splitting of the atom, but refused to help make the atom bomb. Her father was a Jewish lawyer in Vienna although the family was brought up as Protestants. She was one of the first women to receive a doctorate in Vienna in 1906 with a dissertation on radioactivity. In 1907 she went to work with the great physicist Max Planck, inventor of the quantum theory, and subsequently continued her radioactive researches with Otto Hahn at the Kaiser Wilhelm Institute in Berlin, where she was appointed head of the department of radioactive physics. Meitner and Hahn's experiments with beta and gamma rays at the Institute were the first attempts to release latent energy from the atom's nucleus. Nazi persecution drove Meitner first to Holland and then to the Nobel Institute in Stockholm – and it was there that she successfully pioneered nuclear fission. Disassociating herself entirely from further American research into the discovery's warlike potential, Lise Meitner only came to Washington DC in 1946 as a visiting professor. She was made head of the Royal Institute of Technology in Sweden and became a Swedish citizen in 1949. Meitner retired to Cambridge, England in 1960 where she later died.

Maria Sibylla Merian
German (1647–1717)

Maria Sibylla Merian can be said to have shown the way to the proper classification of species which Linnaeus eventually undertook in the mid-eighteenth century. An exceptionally gifted entomologist and botanical illustrator, she was the daughter of a Swiss father and a Dutch mother, and was born and brought up in Frankfurt. Her father was an engraver and publisher who died when she was small; her mother then married a Flemish flower painter, one of whose pupils, Johann Andreas Graff, she herself married in 1665, when she was 18. They had two daughters, Johanna Helena and Dorothea Maria.

Merian's first publication (in three volumes, 1675–1680) was *The New Flower Book*, a catalogue of flower engravings. It was followed by *The Wonderful Transformation of Caterpillars and Their Singular Plant Nourishment* (also three volumes, 1679–1717), a catalogue of 186 European moths, butterflies and other insects. She claimed, rightly, that her method of research for this remarkable publication was 'a completely new discovery', for she was the first entomologist to collect eggs and caterpillars and rear them herself; other entomologists studied only dead specimens. Each insect was then shown on a single page in all its life stages, with its preferred food, and depicted in an admirably clear and lively style.

In 1699 (having divorced her husband), accompanied by her younger daughter, Merian set off on the long journey to the Dutch colony of Surinam, in South America, to visit her elder daughter, who had married a Dutch merchant. The result of her two years' stay was *Metamorphosis of the Insects of Surinam*, published in 1705. The 60 plates show not only the

insects themselves, but also the many tropical fruits – bananas, papayas, pomegranates – on which they feed; the text covers local recipes and medicinal cures as well as the life-cycle of the insects (she was indefatigable in interviewing the native inhabitants of Surinam). This work alone demonstrates that, in the words of one art historian, 'Merian . . . deserves to be as famous as Redouté and Audubon'.

No complete catalogue of Merian's original watercolours, which are now dispersed all over the world, yet exists.

Maria Mitchell
American (1818–1889)

One of the great scientists and teachers of the nineteenth century, the astronomer Maria Mitchell was the first woman to be elected to the American Academy of Arts and Sciences. She was born in Nantucket, the daughter of Quaker parents, and first began to interest herself in astronomy at an early age. From the age of 18 to 42 she worked as a librarian at the Nantucket Athenaeum but, together with her father, made observations every evening from the roof of his bank and in 1847 sighted a comet which was subsequently named after her, a discovery which won her a medal from the King of Denmark. On a trip to Europe in 1857 she met many other scientists, including Mary Somerville (q.v.). In 1865 she was invited to take charge of an observatory and telescope built by Matthew Vassar for the women's college.

A brilliant teacher, Mitchell somewhat unconventionally refused to report student absences or grade their work: 'You cannot mark a human mind because there is no intellectual unit', as she once said. Instead, she relied on curiosity and keen observation as her educational yardsticks. By taking daily photographs of the sun Mitchell was able to report on solar eclipses and on the planets Jupiter and Saturn in particular. Of her career, she once said: 'I was born of only ordinary capacity but of extraordinary per-

A banana plant, one of Maria Sybilla Merian's illustrations from Metamorphosis of the Insects of Surinam, *1705.*

J. Miller Sculp

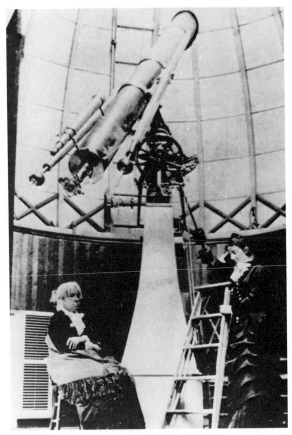

Maria Mitchell (left), America's first woman astronomer, in her observatory.

Lady Mary Wortley Montagu, who pioneered smallpox vaccine in England.

sistence.' When she died her students raised money for an association to be founded in her memory.

Lady Mary Wortley Montagu
British (1689–1762)

Lady Mary Wortley Montagu introduced vaccination against smallpox to England, but became famous throughout Europe for her 'Turkish Embassy' letters. Voltaire thought these superior to the letters of Madame de Sévigné or Madame de Maintenon (qq.v.), because in his view they could 'instruct all nations'.

Not all aristocratic girls of the time were educated, but Lady Mary Pierrepoint was the daughter of the Duke of Kingston and had the run of her father's library. She eloped with the future Ambassador to Turkey in 1712; they lived in Constantinople from 1716 to 1718. There she discovered that the Turks practised vaccination; she had her own children treated and said: 'I am patriot enough to take pains to bring this useful invention into fashion in England.'

She eventually separated from her husband and went to live in France and Italy.

Florence Nightingale
British (1820–1910)

Florence Nightingale was the founder of modern nursing and the famous 'Lady of the Lamp' in the

Crimean War. Yet important as that is, her achievements were even wider.

She and her younger sister Parthenope were born into the English upper classes, and although taught Latin and Greek by their scholar father, they were brought up primarily to be ladies of leisure. Unlike 'Parthe', Florence keenly resented her upbringing, and her book *Cassandra* is one of the most eloquent expressions of the frustration experienced by able women in a society which forbade so many of them to work. Nightingale felt she had been called by God to a life of service; she tried to meet that call by doing charity work in the local village, but it was not enough. Only when she was 24 was it clear to her that her destiny lay in nursing. Her family forbade it – hospitals at that time were little better than brothels – and Nightingale, in despair, studied as best she could from books. But gradually she turned herself into an expert on hospitals, and began to break free from her family. Having finally refused her suitor Richard Monckton Milnes (later Lord Houghton), and this time ignoring her family's disapproval, she trained briefly in Germany and in 1853 was recommended by a friend, Mrs Sidney Herbert, to be superintendent of the Institution for the Care of Sick Gentlewomen in Distressed Circumstances in Harley Street, London. There her talents for organization at last had full scope.

A year later, *The Times* reported how large numbers of British soldiers were dying like flies in the Crimea because of the lack of adequate medical treatment. Sidney Herbert, then Secretary of State for War, asked Nightingale to take a party of British nurses to the Crimea. Within a month she was in Constantinople with 38 nurses, and had moved into the hospital barracks at Scutari. During the next two years, in spite of the hostility of the Army authorities, she somehow made friends with the medical men, organized supplies, arranged for mattresses to be made from sacks stuffed with straw, supervized the nurses, provided warm food and drink – all the time writing letters and reports to Sidney Herbert, and every night touring the wards, bringing comfort and hope to the injured, sick and dying. She also went backwards and forwards between Scutari and the hospitals in the Crimea, on the other side of the Black Sea; she opened a reading room; fought for the soldiers to have the right to send money home, organized classes, schools, even plays. Yet although famous on the home front, she failed to win her battles against the Army establishment.

Florence Nightingale became seriously ill, and came home in 1956. She was in despair. She believed it essential to overhaul the whole Army system to prevent another such calamity, and asked for a Royal Commission on barracks, military hospitals and the Army Medical Department; this was eventually set up under the chairmanship of Sidney Herbert. Queen Victoria (q.v.) wrote in admiration of her efforts: 'I wish she were at the War Office.'

A year later, in spite of weakness caused by her illness, Nightingale had written *Notes on Matters Affecting the Health, Efficiency and Hospital Administration of the British Army*, which when published amounted to nearly 1,000 closely printed pages. (Its first words were: 'It may seem a strange principle to enunciate as the very first requirement in a Hospital that it should do the sick no harm.') Once more she was near to collapse – so near that her obituary notice was prepared. She did not die; but from then on she constantly believed herself on the point of death, and was constantly driving herself on to finish her work. She scarcely ever left her bed again. Yet she was to live more than half a century longer, working almost to the end.

She was a one-woman survey team, constantly demanding reports and answers to questionnaires she sent out. In 1860, from her sickbed, she finally set up a school for nurses at St Thomas's Hospital, with the help of the matron Mrs Wardroper and £45,000 raised by public subscription; every detail of the nurses' training was supervized by her. She became an expert on the British Army in India, which she never visited, and even on the welfare of the Indians themselves. Her example inspired Henri Dunant to found the International Red Cross. At home, she worked on Poor Law reform and district nursing, and collected statistics on childbirth. She continued to campaign for ventilation and good drainage, and kept up lively contacts with the nurses at the Nightingale School.

Nightingale later became reconciled with her

Florence Nightingale, with nurses from the Nightingale School, in 1887.

family. She went blind in 1901, and received the Order of Merit in 1907, the first woman to do so.

Marguerite Perey
French (1909–1975)

Marguerite Perey discovered the element actinium K – which she called francium, in honour of her native country. She originally wanted to become a doctor, but family poverty, occasioned by the death of her industrialist father Emile Perey, made that impossible, and at the age of 20 she joined the staff of Marie Curie (q.v.) at the French Radium Institute, as a junior laboratory assistant. A brilliant chemist, she became professor of nuclear chemistry at Strasbourg University and a director of the Nuclear Research Centre there. She was also the first woman to become a member of the Académie des Sciences, in 1962. Like Marie Curie before her, she died of a long illness caused by radiation.

Dixy Lee Ray
American (b. 1914)

The United States has had several women State Governors (cf. Ella Grasso), but Dixy Lee Ray, elected first woman Governor of Washington in 1977, has also had a distinguished career as a scientist.

Second of five daughters of a commercial printer, she was born and brought up in Washington, studied zoology at Mills College, and spent the next three decades as a teacher in schools and at the University of Washington. Her main area of study was the crustacea, and the organisms which attack wood underwater. She became an expert in the damage done to wharves, dry docks and boats, and constantly warned of the dangers of pesticides and radioactive materials in the ocean. From 1945 she held several public appointments, including special consultant in biological oceanography for the National Science Foundation and visiting professor aboard the Stanford University Research ship in the Indian Ocean.

In 1963 Ray became director of the Pacific Science Center in Seattle, which in the following 10 years she developed into an important scientific institution. In 1972 President Nixon appointed her a member of the Atomic Energy Commission, and she applied such vitality and good sense to her job that she was appointed Chairman the following year. Always a great believer in the public's right to know, she brought atomic energy matters to public attention. In 1974 she was switched to Assistant Secretary for Oceans and International Environmental Matters, but resigned two years later.

Ray's eccentric lifestyle – wearing knee socks, living in a caravan – may not have gone down so well in Washington DC, but it was well received in Washington State: already a well-known figure there, she entered the 1976 election for governor, without political experience or an adequate organization behind her, and on barely half what her opponent spent, managed to beat him by 129,000 votes.

Margaret Sanger
American (1883–1966)

The pioneer of birth control in the U.S., Margaret Sanger was one of 11 children of a stonemason. The young Margaret Higgins campaigned for women's suffrage, and gave up her plans to act when a drama school asked her to send them her measurements. She became a nurse instead, married an architect called William Sanger and had three children. She lectured

Dixie Lee Ray, America's second woman governor, after her election to office in 1977.

on health to young mothers and was soon writing articles for the left-wing newspaper *Call* (one of which was suppressed for using the words gonorrhoea and syphilis; it was later reprinted for American troops).

Distressed and angry at the sufferings of poor women overburdened with children or resorting to backstreet abortions, Sanger resolved to find out how to limit births safely. She went to Europe for information, which she published in her pamphlet *Family Limitation* (1914), advising on the use of condoms and pessaries. (One printer said: 'That can never be printed, Margaret. It's a Sing Sing job.') Her main obstacles were Comstock's Law of 1873, which forbade such information being sent through the mail, and the medical profession, which considered attempts to prevent conception both harmful and wicked. Sanger's own publication, *Woman Rebel*, was suppressed several times and when she was indicted for breaking the law she fled to Europe. In England she was able to advise Marie Stopes (q.v.) on the French pessary (and fell in love with Havelock Ellis); in Holland she learnt about the Dutch cap, but, as a non-doctor, was told to keep away from such medical matters by Dr Aletta Jacobs (q.v.), whose birth control clinic of 1882 was the first in the world.

William Sanger went to jail in the U.S. for distributing a copy of *Family Limitation*. When Margaret returned from Europe, she opened a birth control clinic in Brooklyn and she too was arrested; out on bail, she returned at once to reopen the clinic. It was to be a hard struggle before help could be given to the hundreds of women who needed it, and another ten years before birth control got a fair hearing in the U.S. The campaign was not helped by the hostility between Mrs Sanger and other campaigners for birth control. But the illegal practices of some of those hostile to birth control – medical records were seized, women patients arrested – eventually swung both medical and public opinion round. By 1932 there were nearly 80 clinics in the U.S.

Meanwhile Sanger – from 1922 Mrs Slee, after her second marriage to an oilman – had been campaigning internationally for birth control, and was eventually one of the founders of the International Planned Parenthood Federation. She believed the whole world must have 'the same benefits that are now accorded to the more fortunate'.

Dr Regina von Siebold
German (1771–1849)

Regina von Siebold was one of the first European women to be granted an academic degree in gynaecology. She studied under her husband, Dr Damien von Siebold, from 1806 and in 1815 was finally awarded the title of Doctor only two years before the same title was earned by her daughter, Charlotte, at

the age of 25. Mother and daughter both practised in Darmstadt for the rest of their lives. A hundred years were to pass, however, before more women were to be officially recognized by orthodox medicine.

Mary Somerville
British (1780–1872)

Although lacking any formal education, Mary Somerville established herself as a mathematician and astronomer of international standing. She was the fifth of seven children of Admiral Fairfax of the Royal Navy. Her one year of schooling ended at 11 and thereafter she was entirely self-taught – gazing at the stars, she said later, for her real education. The discovery of the word 'algebra' in a magazine led her to her brothers' Euclid, which her horrified father forbade her to read. Deprived of even a candle at nights, she forced herself to memorize the hardest possible problems and worked them out in her head in the dark.

It was only when her first husband, Samuel Greig, Russia's minister to London, died in 1807 that Mary had enough money to study seriously. She returned to Scotland with her young son and was greatly encouraged by the Edinburgh scholars she met. In 1812 she married William Somerville, an army doctor, who encouraged her studies. They had two daughters and in 1816 moved to London where they moved in a circle of writers, poets and scientists from all over Europe (she made a friend of the young Ada Lovelace, q.v.).

Somerville's paper on the magnetizing effects of sunlight appeared in 1826 and she continued to write and translate for the next 45 years. She was so successful that the Royal Society commissioned a bust of her, and she and Caroline Herschel (q.v.) were the first women to be elected to the Royal Astronomical Society in 1835. Her book *Physical Geography* (1848) went into seven editions and won her a gold medal from the Royal Geographic Society.

The last 40 years of Somerville's life were spent in Italy where her husband had settled for health reasons. After her death her library went to the

Mary Somerville, author of
Physical Geography, *1848,*
which won her a gold medal.

students of Emily Davies (q.v.) at Hitchin, which later became Girton College, and she left money for an Oxford women's college, which was founded in 1879 and named Somerville after her.

Marie Stopes
British (1880–1958)

Marie Stopes was a pioneer in the long struggle to make contraception available to women in Britain. The daughter of highly educated parents, she was herself precocious both as a child and a young adult: she got her degree in botany and zoology at London University in two years instead of three, and her

doctorate in Germany the following year with a thesis written in German. She became the first woman lecturer at Manchester University; her academic career was studded with grants and prizes, including a research trip to Japan in 1907.

Stopes's first book was not on her subject, palaeobotany, but *Love Letters of a Japanese* – a record, published under a pseudonym in 1911, of a long, unconsummated love affair with a Japanese professor. In the same year, she met and married Dr Reginald Ruggles Gates – another unsuccessful sexual relationship: but, for a former student of zoology, so little did she know of sex at the age of 27 that she only found out what was wrong by reading books in the

243

Marie Stopes, photographed at her home in 1932.

British Museum. This first marriage was annulled in 1916, but led Marie Stopes to write – in her words – 'a book on marriage and sex [which] would teach a man and a woman how to understand each other's sexual problems'. This was *Married Love*, published in 1918, a rather flowery encouragement of sensuous enjoyment (with barely a hint on contraceptive practices) which at once became a best-seller. It had a very mixed reception but Stopes received hundreds of enquiring letters from readers, and for them she wrote *Wise Parenthood* (1918), which contained more practical information on caps, pessaries, condoms, coitus interruptus, douching and the 'safe' period. Stopes had by now married Humphrey Verdon Roe, an aircraft manufacturer who had financed the publication of *Married Love*. Her first baby was still-born but in 1924 she had another son, Harry.

In 1921 she and her husband opened Britain's first birth control clinic, in Islington, London; it was specifically for poor women, and its advice was free. Needless to say, the medical profession was hostile – Stopes's lack of a medical degree was frequently jeered at – and the Roman Catholics attacked her

even more fiercely. Halliday Sutherland, a Roman Catholic doctor, accused her of 'serious crime' in setting up the clinic, whereupon Stopes sued him for libel. A famous trial ensued, which she eventually won in the Court of Appeal, only to lose once again in the House of Lords. It was the first of many legal battles in the cause, some of which she won, some of which she lost, but all of which spread her fame – and with her fame, the knowledge that contraception was possible – to the millions of women she wished to reach.

Stopes was a born propagandist, and by the time she died birth control had become not only respectable but available to nearly everyone who wanted it. This was at least in part due to her own strenuous efforts. Stopes' immense energy also expressed itself in several volumes of poetry, plays, a novel and a volume of fairy stories.

Trotula
Italian (c. AD 1100)

Most famous of the women teachers of medicine at Europe's first university at Salerno, near Naples, was Trotula Platearius. Her speciality was gynaecology and obstetrics, and her book on *Diseases of Women* remained a major textbook for seven centuries. She also studied dermatology and epilepsy, and was a brilliant diagnostician – observing the patient's pulse, testing the urine and carefully noting other clinical signs. Most unusually in the light of medical practice in succeeding centuries, she understood the need for cleanliness and exercise, and she stressed the importance of making sure that the patient was comfortable.

Trotula was married to a fellow-physician, and her two sons both became physicians. She was greatly respected in her day and when she died her funeral cortège is said to have been two miles long.

Dr Mary Walker
American (1832–1919)

Mary Walker became an army surgeon and won the Congressional Medal of Honour for her care of the

Army surgeon Dr Mary Walker in characteristic if unconventional dress.

wounded during the American Civil War. She was born in Oswego, New York, and went to medical school in Syracuse and New York City. She married Albert Miller, a fellow graduate, but did not take his name and practised medicine jointly with him in Rome, New York. Dr Walker was also a keen campaigner for dress reform – 'corsets are coffins,' she declared – and wore trousers and a long tunic like Frances Wright and Amelia Bloomer (qq.v.). At the outbreak of the Civil War she went to Washington DC and worked in tent hospitals in Virginia, and in 1863 she was appointed an official army surgeon – a role for which she wore officers' uniform. Dr Walker continually crossed Confederate lines to look after civilians and was taken prisoner for four months in 1864. Always an unconventional dresser, after the war she wore a man's full evening dress and silk hat for her many lectures on women's rights.

Chien-shiung Wu
Chinese (b. 1912)

Chien-shiung Wu became professor of physics at Columbia University in 1944. Her most important contribution in the field is her experimental proof of the theory advanced by two Chinese scientists working in the U.S., Dr Tsung Dao Lee and Dr Chen Ning Yang, that, contrary to accepted theory, similar nuclear particles do not always act similarly. Lee and Yang received the Nobel Prize for Physics in 1957 for their theoretical work in thus overturning the 'law of parity'. In 1975 Chien-shiung Wu became President of the American Physical Society, and has received many other degrees and honours.

Chien-shiung Wu was born in Shanghai and studied at China's National Central University and the University of California at Berkeley. She married Dr Luke Chia-lin Yuan and has one son. She became an American citizen in 1954.

MONEY
AND MANAGEMENT

THERE ARE FEW SOCIETIES in which women have not played some sort of commercial role, even if it is little more than taking butter and eggs to the market. The 'mammies' of twentieth-century Nigeria control much of the country's internal trade through their marketing enterprise and through running the local buses, popularly known as mammy-wagons. But the laws of the western world were extremely restrictive at least until a hundred years ago, and although individual women could earn a great deal of money in certain fields, such as literature or the stage, and a few enjoyed enormous fortunes left to them by fathers or husbands, only rarely did they have complete control of their earnings.

Many of the women here did indeed inherit money or property and thus were able to build their own very real achievements on a solid financial base. Others, such as Chanel, Sarah Walker or Margery Hurst, have risen to riches through their own efforts. No doubt significantly, most have made their money in what is still considered 'women's work': fashion, cosmetics, catering, the retail trade. Others have been entrepreneurs in the media: in newspapers, advertising, the theatre. Madame Tussaud, whose story is perhaps one of the most extraordinary in this book, was in a branch of show business, while the stockbroker Victoria Woodhull, started her career in a travelling medicine show.

It is worth adding, in passing, that just as women were beginning to make their mark as entrepreneurs and business women, even bigger fortunes were being made in the oldest profession of all by *les grandes horizontales* – the great courtesans of nineteenth-century France.

Helena Rubinstein. A painting by Graham Sutherland, 1957.

Elizabeth Arden founder of a cosmetics company that spread round the world.

Margaret Anderson
(see Sylvia Beach)

Elizabeth Arden
Canadian (1884?–1966)

Elizabeth Arden revolutionized the modern cosmetics industry and made herself a multi-millionaire in the process.

Florence Nightingale Graham was the youngest of five children of a Scottish grocer in Ontario. After training as a nurse in Toronto she worked in a beauty parlour and developed considerable talent at body massage. Make-up was so crude and coarse at the time that she began to prepare her own products and when

she opened her New York salon in 1912 it was an instant success. She learnt everything she could from doctors and chemists. The name of her company was inspired by a favourite book and poem, *Elizabeth and her German Garden* and *Enoch Arden*. Fanatical attention to detail and a drive for perfectionism were the hallmarks of her business, which soon had branches all over the world decorated in her favourite pinks and red. The first branch in Europe opened on the Place Vendôme in 1914.

Arden's three great rules were 'cleanse, tone and nourish'. Her pioneering work not only made make-up respectable but also encouraged women to lead healthier lives and to wear any colour – but always with a matching make-up.

In 1931 she took up horse racing, and it soon became a passion; her most famous perfume, Blue Grass, was the name of her Kentucky stables. In 1935 she divorced Thomas Jenkins, her business manager, after 17 years of marriage (he moved to Helena Rubinstein (q.v.).) She subsequently married Prince Michael Evlanoff, but divorced him in 1944. A peppery conservative, always dressed in shades of pink, she refused to divulge her true age and was still in complete control of her empire when she died (no employee could marry without Arden's consent).

Sylvia Beach
American (1887–1962)
Margaret Anderson
American (1893–1973)
Harriet Weaver
American (1876–1961)

These were the editors – all women – who had the courage to publish the Irish writer James Joyce when no one else would do so. Sylvia Beach and her beautiful sister Cyprian had gone from America to Belgrade with the Red Cross in 1917 during the First World War. After the war Sylvia used her mother's savings to open her famous shop in Paris, Shakespeare and Company, which was both a bookshop and a lending library. She decorated the walls with paintings by William Blake and photographs of

Oscar Wilde. Her stock was very *avant garde* – she had two circulating copies of *Tender Buttons* by Gertrude Stein (q.v.) – and Joyce persuaded her to turn herself into a publishing company for the sole purpose of publishing *Ulysses*. Joyce's slow working methods created many difficulties and it was largely due to Beach's faith, that the masterpiece was published in 1922.

Months of negotiating with the printer, however, left the company short of money and it was another woman, Harriet Weaver, who came to the rescue. Weaver, the daughter of an evangelical English doctor, had been left a considerable private income. She had worked as an editor of the advanced London magazine, *The Egoist*, since 1913 and in 1918 she, too, had published Joyce although it meant daily fear of police raids. She not only bailed out Shakespeare and Company in its one publishing venture but continued to support Joyce and his family for many years. 'I shall think of her when I think of goodness,' said writer Samuel Beckett, Joyce's disciple. Weaver gave her manuscript of *Ulysses* to the National Library of Dublin on St Patrick's Day 1952, 30 years after it was published – with a fine sense of irony, as the book is still banned in Ireland.

Another brave woman who published Joyce was Margaret Anderson. She had launched the *Little Review* in 1914 in Chicago when she was only 21. Extracts from *Ulysses* were printed in 1918 in the magazine and the U.S. Post Office burned the four issues which carried it on an obscenity charge. Thus support and encouragement for the most innovative twentieth-century writer came from three independent-minded, generous women. Samuel Beckett, another 'difficult' writer, was also first published by a woman – Nancy Cunard.

Angela Burdett-Coutts
British (1814–1906)

'The most remarkable woman in the kingdom', said King Edward VII of Angela Burdett-Coutts, 'after my mother' (cf. Queen Victoria). A multi-millionaire at the age of 23, she was the most influential benefactor of the Victorian era.

Angela Burdett-Coutts was the daughter of the

Angela Burdett-Coutts, popularly known as 'The Queen of the Poor': a painting by W.C. Ross.

radical MP, Sir Francis Burdett, and granddaughter of the banker Thomas Coutts. During her long life her inherited money was spent on a wide range of social improvements. She supported actors and built churches; she housed students and 'fallen women'; she instituted training for sailors and markets for barrow-boys; she organized stables for donkeys – 'Life whether in man or beast is sacred', she said – and model housing; she even founded a bishopric in New Zealand in 1847. Although her benevolence was all-embracing, each separate project was considered with deep seriousness and concern; she thought of herself as 'married' to the responsibility of her enormous wealth.

Burdett-Coutts was a friend of Dickens and of Queen Victoria. She lived most of her life just outside London in Highgate with Mrs Meredith, her former governess and a lifelong friend. In 1871 she was made a peeress in her own right, and in 1872 became the first woman to be made a Freeman of the City of London. In 1881 she married a young American, William Ashmead Bartlett, who later became a Member of Parliament. Upon her death, thousands lined the streets to watch her funeral, in grateful tribute to 'The Queen of the Poor'.

Gabrielle Chanel
French (c. 1883–1971)

'Coco' Chanel was the dress designer who put rich women into simple clothes – cardigan suits, jerseys, trousers, the little black dress – and gave them proper pockets, sling-back shoes and costume jewellery; she made a suntan chic. 'Nothing makes a woman look older than obvious expensiveness, ornateness, complication', she once said. 'I still dress as I always did, like a schoolgirl.' Millions followed her example. She even put perfume – the famous NO. 5 – into an utterly simple square bottle. Her success brought her immense wealth.

Born into a peasant background about which she was always secretive, she started her career as a small-town cabaret singer. Chanel's first shop, in Deauville, was financed by an English lover. She moved to Paris in 1914. A friend of the rich and famous (she was the Duke of Westminster's mistress for 14 years), she lived in great splendour – her apartment was full of ornate treasures.

In 1938 Chanel left *haute couture*, and went into retirement for 16 years. In 1954, when she was 70, she made what seemed at first a disastrous comeback: it was still the heyday of Dior, swirling skirts, pinched waists. But her instinct was right, and within a couple of years, her braided cardigan suit, gilt chain bag, black and beige sling-back shoes and obviously false pearls became the uniform of the decade.

Nicole-Barbe Clicquot
French (1777–1866)

Veuve Clicquot is famous wherever champagne is drunk, and deservedly so, not merely for the quality

Coco Chanel: a painting by Peter Blake, 1962.

of the wine which bears her name, but because it was she who devised the *remuage* and *dégorgement* which are, to this day, the means by which the champagne in the bottle is freed from its impurities without losing the gas which gives it its sparkle, *la méthode champenoise*. Clicquot's method involved keeping the bottles upside down (*sur pointe*) on a big table with holes in it so that the debris in the champagne collected on the corks and in the couple of inches of liquid in the bottle neck. To prevent the sediment from sticking to the neck, the bottles were turned (*remuage*) every day with a gentle knock. The rapid removal of the dirty corks, with an inch or two of wine, from the upended bottles was the *dégorgement* (today the necks of the bottles are frozen to make it easier). The wine was then topped up with a drop or two of brandy and a little sugar, because Clicquot's most enthusiastic customers were the Russian officers

Nicole-Barbe Clicquot, inventor of la méthode champenoise.

Emily Faithfull, the founder of Victoria Press, one of the earliest all-woman printing firms.

whose army, then Napoleon's ally, was quartered in Rheims shortly before Waterloo, and they liked their champagne on the sweet side. The officers continued to order her champagne once they had returned to Russia – and Madame Clicquot became even more successful.

Mme Clicquot was the daughter of Monsieur Ponsardin of Rheims, who represented his city in the Parlement of Paris in 1789, and later became Mayor of Rheims. She married François Clicquot in 1799, and like many women she came into the wine business through her husband, whose family were in banking and textiles but made wine on the side. Early widowhood (her husband died in 1805) obliged her to take command, which she did with immense efficiency. Through her only child, Clementine, who married the Comte de Chévigné, she became the ancestress of three dukes.

Emily Faithfull
British (1835–1895)

Emily Faithfull believed that the printing trade should provide jobs for women. She was an Anglican clergyman's daughter who wanted to find a solution to the problem of 'so many idle working-class women'. She knew that there had been women compositors soon after printing was invented in the fifteenth century, so she set up her own all-women printing firm in Edinburgh in 1857. She went to London in 1860 and founded another all-female printing firm, the Victoria Press. She began to print the *Victoria Magazine* in 1863 and also the *Englishwoman's Journal*, an important suffrage paper, besides the reports of the Social Science Congresses. Faithfull's business came under attack both for undercutting prices and for its emancipated working conditions: 'the mixture of sexes in a printing office tends very much to injure the morals and minds of the innocent female and aggravates all the baser passions of humanity', thundered the *Printers' Register* in 1869. But by 1899 over 500 women were employed as printers in Edinburgh alone. Continuing the pioneer spirit, the Victoria Press printed *The Herald* for the newly formed Independent Labour Party after Faithfull's death.

Isabella Stewart Gardner
American (1840?–1924)

Barely a hundred years ago the great American art collections scarcely existed; but within two generations many rich and determined collectors had laid the foundations of America's present wealth of European art masterpieces in both private and public collections. These great collectors included almost as many women as men, for example Mrs Potter Palmer of Chicago, Mrs Henry Havemeyer and her husband, who bought widely among the French Post-Impressionists following the advice of Mary Cassatt (q.v.), and most notably Isabella Stewart Gardner. Mrs Gardner, pursuing what her friend Henry James, another Bostonian, called 'a preposterously pleasant career', collected Old Masters.

Isabella Stewart was born into a rich New York family and married John L. Gardner of Boston in 1860. After the death of her son in 1865, she went to Europe in a state of collapse and on her return pursued two vocations: the first as a patron of music and the outrageous and witty star of Boston society – she was once dubbed 'the risqué Mrs Gardner' – and the second, in middle age, as an art collector. She was inspired by the example of Harvard's first professor of the history of art, Charles Eliot Norton, whose passion was the Renaissance; and from 1894 she relied on the advice of Bernard Berenson.

Mrs Gardner began to collect art seriously in 1891, when her father died and left her 2.75 million dollars. She first bought a Vermeer and a painting attributed to Fra Filippo Lippi. It was Berenson, however, who steered her towards Giotto. Guardi, Rembrandt, Holbein, Botticelli, and her most celebrated acquisition, Titian's *Rape of Europa*. To house her collection,

which also included works by Bronzino, Correggio, Raphael, Velasquez, Simone Martini, Piero della Francesca and Giorgione, Gardner built Fenway Court in Boston, a sensational Venetian palace which at her behest incorporated architectural features from all over Europe. To this day, Fenway Court with its fabulous contents forms a permanent memorial to one woman's taste.

Katharine Graham
American (b. 1917)

Both spectacularly successful and greatly admired for her courage, Katharine Graham is one of the twentieth century's leading newspaper proprietors. It was in her newspaper, *The Washington Post*, that the Pentagon Papers were published in 1971 and that the drama of Watergate was unfolded between 1972 and 1974. She has always fought staunchly for freedom of the press, and been prepared to resist political pressure. The *Post*'s decision to publish the Pentagon Papers against the wishes of the Pentagon in 1971 was upheld by the U.S. Supreme Court. She has a reputation for hiring the best people, paying them properly, and then giving them the encouragement and backing to do their job as they think fit. Her company also owns *Newsweek* and a half-share in the *International Herald Tribune*, as well as other news-

Katherine Graham celebrating the Supreme Court decision to let the Washington Post *cover secret U.S. Vietnam involvement.*

paper and TV properties. Although the core of this empire was inherited from her father and husband, Mrs Graham has substantially increased its value as well as its prestige. It is now a public corporation, and one of *Fortune*'s top 500 companies.

Katharine Graham was born in New York, the daughter of the banker Eugene Mayer, who bought *The Washington Post* for well under one million dollars in 1933. She went to Vassar and the University of Chicago, and became a reporter on the *San Francisco News* in 1938, moving in 1939 to the *Post*. She married lawyer Philip Graham in 1940; they subsequently had three sons and a daughter. When he went on war service in the Pacific, she returned briefly to the *Post*.

At the end of the war her husband became assistant publisher of the *Washington Post*, then publisher, and in 1948 Eugene Mayer sold the paper to the young couple for one dollar. Philip Graham was responsible for turning it into a successful newspaper, and also for buying *Newsweek* in 1961. But when, in 1963, Mayer committed suicide, Graham, although heartbroken, stepped into his shoes. Since then she has vastly increased both budgets and profits.

Lady Charlotte Guest
British (1812–1895)

A daughter of the ninth Earl of Lindsey, Lady Charlotte Bertie married in 1833 Sir Josiah John Guest, the Welsh ironmaster who had succeeded to the control and ownership of the Dowlais ironworks in Wales which pioneered many of the advances in the production of steel. Throughout their married life – she bore ten children – she took a close interest in the ironworks, eventually working alongside her husband in the running of the firm, and when he died in 1852 she assumed control. Thereafter she effectively ran the Dowlais ironworks, and took a close interest in the firm's workpeople and their families.

Guest was also a writer – she translated and edited the ancient Welsh saga *The Mabinogion* – and was an enthusiastic collector of fans, china, and playing cards. Her china was of exceptional quality: she donated it to the Victoria and Albert Museum in London. In 1855 she married as her second husband Charles Schreiber, a former Member of Parliament.

Peggy Guggenheim
American (1898–1980)

Peggy Guggenheim was one of this century's most enterprising patrons of modern art. She was the niece of Solomon Guggenheim, founder of New York's Guggenheim Museum, and after an unhappy childhood – her father was drowned in the Titanic disaster – settled in Paris. She married the bohemian writer and artist Laurence Vail, and had two children. She then lived with John Holms, and it was after his death in 1934 that she embarked on her career as a patron, backed by a million-dollar inheritance from the family copper-smelting interests, and with the advice of experts such as Marcel Duchamp and Herbert Read.

In 1934 she opened a gallery, Guggenheim Jeune, in London; in 1942 she opened another, Art of This Century, in New York. Among the artists whose work she showed were Cocteau, Kandinsky, Brancusi, Tanguy, Motherwell and Jackson Pollock – most of them at a time when their work still met with hostility and incomprehension. She was able to buy much of her own collection in Paris early in the Second World War, when prices were exceptionally low, before leaving for America just before the Germans reached Paris.

In 1942 Guggenheim married the painter Max Ernst, but they divorced soon afterwards. Her private life was notoriously tangled: her many lovers included Samuel Beckett, Yves Tanguy and Jackson Pollock. After the war she returned to Europe and bought a palazzo, Venier dei Leoni, on the Grand Canal in Venice to house her collection, which she subsequently donated to the city. *Out of This Century*, an autobiography, was published in 1946, and *Confessions of an Art Addict* in 1960.

Margery Hurst
British (b. 1914)

Margery Hurst is one of Britain's most successful women. Starting with nothing except her own

Margery Hurst, who founded the highly successful international Brook Street Bureaux chain.

in London's Mayfair where she first set up shop in one room), in Britain, the US, Australia and Hong Kong, which together have found employment for more than two million men and women. Her company went public in 1965 and has a valuation of several million pounds.

Margery Hurst was born in Southsea, Hampshire, daughter of Sam Berney, who built cinemas; she worked for her father until the war. She then served in the Auxiliary Territorial Service, and after the war married Eric Hurst, who is joint chairman of the company with her. She has two daughters, both now married. Mrs Hurst was one of the first women members of Lloyds of London.

Juanita M. Kreps
American (b. 1921)

Juanita Kreps has achieved several 'firsts': as a public director of the New York Stock Exchange, as a vice-president of Duke University, and (although there have been four other women members of U.S. Presidents' Cabinets) as Secretary of Commerce.

She was born Juanita Morris, daughter of a coalmine operator in Kentucky, and trained as an economist. She married a fellow economist, Clifton Kreps Jr., in 1944 and has two daughters and a son. Kreps specializes in the problems of women at work and the economics of old age, and has several publications to her name; she moved into academic administration, and thence to public appointments.

Mary Quant
British (b. 1934)

Mary Quant revolutionized British fashion in the 1960s, when 'swinging London' had a world-wide influence. She put not only the young but also the middle-aged into mini-skirts, and her off-beat, casually chic clothes spelt the end of more formal, *haute couture*-based fashion.

Quant was educated at 13 schools, and went to Goldsmiths' College of Art, although not to study fashion there. In 1955, with two male partners, she

secretarial skill after the Second World War, within ten years she had become a millionaire and is now one of the richest business women in the country. She did it by supplying a service – shorthand typists by the day – but on a larger scale than anyone had thought of previously. From her first days, when she had to send herself out on emergency jobs when she had no one else she could trust to do the job properly, she soon diversified into the whole field of finding permanent office jobs. Her memorable advertising slogan has been: 'We got big by bothering', and her aim has been by proper pre-selection to fit the right person to the right job. There are now more than 200 branches of her Brook Street Bureaux (named after the street

opened a shop in Chelsea called Bazaar, and began to design for it. Bazaar was a great success, and she was soon selling all over the world. She married Alexander Plunket Greene, one of her partners, in 1957 and they have one son.

Quant has since switched her interest from clothes to cosmetics, now a global industry, worth millions and part of Max Factor. She was the first to produce make-up for 'contouring' the face; camel silver and white nail polish; gloss for eyes and lips; eyelash strips; waterproof make-up—at prices the young could afford. In 1966 she received the OBE.

Armi Ratia
Finnish (1912–1979)

One of the most influential women in modern design, Armi Ratia inspired the fresh, lively clothes and fabrics which are associated with the name Marimekko (literally, 'a little dress for Mary'), and put Finland on the fashion map. By the time she died, Marimekko designs had become international big business.

She was born in Karelia, part of which has now been ceded to the Soviet Union, and trained as a textile designer. When she and her husband Viljo Ratia, an army officer, fled to Helsinki from the Russians, she had with her 'nothing but a raincoat and a gas mask that leaked'; her three brothers were to be killed in the fighting. Between 1942 and 1949 she worked for the Swedish office of the American advertising company Erwin Wasey, left to write a novel, but ended up helping her husband to restore the fortunes of an oilcloth company he had acquired; it was to become the launching-pad for Marimekko.

Armi Ratia gradually left the designing to others, particularly to Maija Isola, who was responsible for many of the most celebrated Marimekko patterns. Marimekko went public in 1974; and by 1978 exported to 28 countries and had sales amounting to about 15 million dollars.

Armi and Viljo Ratia had three children – one of whom now runs the North American operation – but subsequently separated.

Mary Reibey
Australian (c. 1777–1855)

Mary Reibey, a lively and enerprising orphan from Lancashire, England, became Australia's first woman tycoon. The young Mary Haydock first attracted notice at the age of 13, when she was tried for stealing a horse and sentenced to seven years' transportation to Australia. She arrived in Sydney in 1792 and after a brief spell as a convict, became a nanny. In 1794 she married Thomas Reibey, a ship's officer.

When Thomas started an import business Mary opened a shop in which to sell the goods – which ranged from essentials like rice and sugar to luxuries like velvet waistcoats and tortoiseshell combs. When Thomas died in 1811, leaving her with a large family of three sons and four daughters, he was a shipowner as well. Mary took the business over, running coastal ships, building, buying and managing property, and becoming a very rich woman in her own right. She was both kind and eccentric and did a great deal for charity. One of her grandchildren became Prime Minister of Tasmania.

Helena Rubinstein
Polish (1872?–1965)

Helena Rubinstein turned an old wives' recipe into a multi-million dollar cosmetics empire. She was born in Poland and went to medical school. In 1902 she emigrated to Australia. The women there enthusiastically welcomed her jars of Crème Valeze, made from an old Hungarian herbal recipe, for which Helena Rubinstein's own creamy complexion was the perfect advertisement.

As her business flourished Rubinstein took university courses in dermatology. In 1904 she left the Melbourne business with two of her younger sisters, and opened a London branch in 1908 and another in 1912 in Paris, where she made her home; a chain of beauty shops across the states shortly followed, with her seven sisters acting as managers. Rubinstein's face powders were the first in the world to be tinted and use real silk. Later she launched cosmetics for men.

Rubinstein's first husband was Edward Titus, an American journalist, by whom she had two sons; her second husband was Prince Artchil Gourielli Tchkonia. 'I am a great gambler,' she once said. Her collection of modern art was formed in her early days in Paris. It included works by Picasso, Kandinsky and Léger as well as the world's largest collection of African sculpture. She wrote her autobiography, *My Life for Beauty*, and set up the Helena Rubinstein Foundation to help organizations involved in education, health, community services and the arts.

Margaret Rudkin
American (1897–1967)

Margaret Rudkin was the founder of one of the most successful bakery businesses in the world, Pepperidge Farm Inc. She did not embark on her business until she was 40, yet ended up a multi-millionaire. Pepperidge Farm rarely advertised, relying entirely on its reputation for using only the best ingredients – stone-ground, unbleached flour, real butter, fresh yeast – and for employing no short cuts (dough was kneaded by hand) or additives.

Margaret Fogarty was born in New York City, one of five children. She first worked for a bank in Flushing and then for a brokerage firm, where she married one of the partners, Henry Rudkin, in 1923. They had three sons, and when one of them developed asthma the doctor asked her to bake him some special bread. 'I had never baked bread in my life', she said. She made it the way she remembered her grandmother baking it. Soon the doctor was asking her to bake bread for other patients; one day she had some left over and asked her grocer to sell it for her. Within a year, she was employing women to help her, had converted the family farm's stables and garage, and was baking 4,000 loaves a week. Her husband organized the finances and marketing, and the firm eventually expanded to include melba toast, cakes, cookies, frozen pastries and other products.

By the time Rudkin died, Pepperidge Farm was synonymous with pure food all over the United States and abroad. *The Margaret Rudkin Pepperidge Farm Cookbook* appeared in 1963.

Elsa Schiaparelli
Italian (1890–1973)

Elsa Schiaparelli was one of the great Paris fashion designers between the wars; her main competitor was Chanel (q.v.). For a time she, too, had a salon in London. In 1931 Schiaparelli introduced the built-up shoulder, which remained the fashionable outline until Dior's 'new look' of 1947.

Schiaparelli introduced the idea of boutiques and made aggressive, strong colours chic. She invented shocking pink, sportswear, evening sweaters and was the first designer to use zips and man-made fabrics for *haute couture*. She also made a speciality of outrageous hats, and firmly believed that fashion should be fun.

Like Chanel, Schiaparelli knew many artists; Dali created the décor of her 1935 boutique, and Jean Cocteau and Christian Bérard designed fabrics for her. The daughter of a professor in Rome, she had an early, unhappy marriage and after spending a period of great poverty living with her infant daughter Gogo in New York, finally settled in Paris in 1920. She had innate talent, but no training, and became a couturière by chance. She designed herself a sweater with a butterfly bow knitted into it and wore it to a lunch; a New York buyer saw it, and immediately ordered 40. Anita Loos (who wrote *Gentleman Prefer Blondes*) was her first private customer. The actress Marisa Berenson is one of her granddaughters. Her autobiography, *My Shocking Life*, was published in 1954.

Dorothy Schiff
American (b. 1903)

The *New York Post* was personally owned and managed for nearly 40 years, from 1939–76, by Dorothy Schiff. For some years she also wrote a weekly column.

Although Dorothy Schiff inherited money from her family, who were in banking, it was her own decision to become in 1939 the majority stockholder of the *New York Post*. She was a very active

Elsa Schiaparelli, photographed by Cecil Beaton in the 1930s.

proprietor, and her newspaper had become New York City's only crusading liberal newspaper, with a circulation of around 375,000 daily, when it was acquired by Rupert Murdoch in 1977.

Dorothy Schiff was born in New York City, the daughter of Mortimer and Adele Schiff. She dropped out of Bryn Mawr because, she says, her grades were too low, and became a debutante. She has been married four times: to Richard Hall in 1923 (div. 1932), to George Backer in 1932, who became the *Post*'s publisher and president (div. 1943), to Theodore Olin Thackrey in 1943, who was then the *Post*'s executive editor but was replaced in 1949, and to Rudolf G. Sonneborn, a petroleum executive, in 1953. She has one son and two daughters. Her interest in politics began during the Depression. She became a keen admirer of Roosevelt's New Deal and took a very active part in social welfare, with many appointments on different boards and committees.

Marie Tussaud
French (1761–1850)

Wax-modeller and businesswoman, Marie Tussaud founded the famous London waxworks museum Madame Tussaud's, which is still, 150 years later, a major tourist attraction.

Madame Tussaud herself had a youth at once fascinating and macabre. Born in Alsace, the (posthumous) daughter of a German soldier called Grosholtz, she and her mother moved shortly to Berne, where her widowed mother became housekeeper to a Dr Curtius. Curtius was a wax-modeller who had discovered his skill making models of anatomical organs and had turned to portraiture. He was invited to Paris, where his *salon de cire*, or wax museum, soon became one of the sights of the city and Marie and her mother eventually joined him there. Curtius meanwhile had done miniatures of the King and Queen, and a full-size figure of the young Madame du Barry – still on show at Madame Tussaud's. He also had a profitable sideline in making erotic tableaux in wax.

Marie received her training from her 'uncle', and by the time she was 17 had modelled heads of Rousseau and Voltaire among others. In her twenties she spent eight years at Versailles as art tutor to Princess Elisabeth, King Louis XV's sister. Marie's tableau *The Royal Family at Dinner* still survives from those early years.

With the French Revolution, uncle and niece adroitly switched sides – Curtius was among those who stormed the Bastille. During the Terror Marie was in almost daily attendance among the dead, taking death masks of the victims for her uncle's exhibition, including those of Louis XV, Queen Marie Antoinette, and also Marat, Charlotte Corday and Robespierre. The *salon de cire* made Curtius a fortune, and when he died in 1794 he left it and other properties to Marie – along with substantial debts. Earlier that year, however, a brief spell in prison had brought Marie the acquaintance of a fellow-prisoner, Josephine Beauharnais, who was shortly to marry Napoleon, and so she was well placed to find work with the new regime. Both Josephine and Napoleon subsequently sat for her.

Shortly after Curtius' death Marie Grosholtz was married to an engineer called François Tussaud; they had a daughter who died at six months, and two sons, Joseph and François. But the *salon de cire* was no longer so popular, and Marie decided to try her luck in England, leaving her affairs and her younger son in the care of her husband and her mother. She was never to see France again – nor her husband.

For Marie Tussaud there followed more than half a century of unremitting hard work and enormous success, all achieved single-handed. For 30 years she travelled all over the British Isles with her exhibition; on one occasion she was shipwrecked in the Irish Sea, and lost nearly everything. All the time she was adding models (including a second head of Napoleon made in 1815 when he was a prisoner of the British) and collecting Napoleana, pictures and scenery. Madame Tussaud's particular gift was an exceptional journalistic sense: she realized that people wanted to know what famous people looked like, and enjoyed the sensation of 'mingling' with the famous, as they still do in her rooms. The Chamber of Horrors was a special feature from the beginning.

In 1834, the popular success of her travelling exhibition had enabled her to set up a permanent

Marie Tussaud. A drawing attributed to her son, François Tussaud.

waxwork museum in London. Madame Tussaud worked until the final decade of her life; her last self-portrait was modelled when she was 81.

Madeleine Vionnet
French (1876–1975)

Madeleine Vionnet was the first couturier to cut women's clothes on the bias (diagonally across the fabric), a revolution in fashion, as it made possible the clinging, seductive styles of the 1920s and 1930s. Her father was a plumber and her mother founded a *café concert* in Paris called Le Petit Casino. At 14 Madeleine was apprenticed to a local dressmaker, and at 16 began a two year training in various fashion houses in London and Paris. She became famous for her lingerie in the first decade of the twentieth century, but was 30 before she created her own models, for the Doucet fashion house.

In 1914 Vionnet opened her own house, which for the two decades between the World Wars was the most important in Paris. Her famous bias cut gave her dresses a distinctive line and she used crepe, satin and velvet as they had never been used before. Vionnet was also largely responsible for liberating women from the corseted line of preceding centuries. She closed her fashion house in 1939.

Sarah Breedlove Walker
American (1867–1919)

Few people have risen so dramatically from rags to riches as Sarah Breedlove, who was not only a woman, but a black woman at that. She was born a sharecropper's daughter in the Deep South and first earned her living as a washerwoman at $1.50 a day. She was 34, long widowed with a young daughter, before she hit on the idea of special hair preparations for black women, particularly for those who wanted to straighten their hair. After many experiments mixing up salves and soaps in her washtubs, she demonstrated her first products door-to-door, insisting on the importance of health and cleanliness, although the actual straightening agent was the use of hot iron combs. Her immediate success in St Louis enabled her to move to Denver, Colorado, to manufacture her products. There she married C.J. Walker, a newspaper man, and as Madame C.J. Walker she trained many of her enthusiastic clients in her sales methods. Her Walker Agents, dressed in black skirts and white shirts, had such success all over the U.S. and the Caribbean that she became the first black woman millionaire, and lived in a 'coloured woman's palace' on the Hudson River. She founded several factories and beauty colleges, and supported many good causes – including the National Association for the Advancement of Coloured People, scholarships, old people's homes, the YMCA and other charities. After her death her daughter A'Lelia ran a salon in New York which was a meeting place for white and black musicians, authors and artists.

Harriet Weaver
(see Sylvia Beach)

Mary Wells
American (b. 1928)

The success story of the 1960s was that of Mary Wells, the advertising chief, who became the highest paid woman executive in the United States.

She was born Mary Berg in Youngstown, Ohio, the daughter of a furniture salesman; at 17 she enrolled in New York's Neighbourhood Playhouse School of the Theater, then moved to the Carnegie Institute of Technology. There she met and married Burt Wells; they subsequently adopted two daughters.

Wells' career was meteoric: at 23 she was fashion advertising manager of Macy's department store, at 24 copy group head for McCann Erickson. At 35 she had been promoted to copy chief and vice president of Doyle Dane Bernbach earning 40 thousand dollars a year. She then joined Jack Tinker & Partners, where her work with Richard Rich and Stewart Greene on the Braniff Airlines account brought her a wider fame. The trio did not merely sell their product, they transformed it – redecorating the exteriors of the aircraft in bright colours, and restyling both the interiors (by Alexander Girard) and the stewardesses' uniforms (by Emilio Pucci). This inventive campaign, 'The End of the Plain Plane', provided an enormous boost for Braniff. By now Wells was earning 80 thousand dollars a year.

In 1966 Wells, Rich and Greene opened their own agency, with Wells as president and chief administrator. It has been the most spectacularly successful advertising agency of the last 20 years.

In 1965 Mary Wells was divorced from Burt Wells and two years later married Braniff's chairman, Harding L. Lawrence.

Victoria Claflin Woodhull
American (1838–1927)

'All talk of women's rights is moonshine', said Victoria Woodhull, who was the first woman to be nominated for the Presidency of the United States; 'women have every right. They have only to exercise them.' Mrs Woodhull and her sister Tennessee spent all their lives not only exercising their rights but doing exactly as they thought fit, and showing the world what could be done without money or education, relying on looks, personality, guts, energy and native intelligence. Both sisters were quite uninhibited by Victorian morality.

Victoria was the seventh and Tennessee the ninth of the 10 children of Buck and Roxanna Claflin of Ohio. When the Claflins' mill was burnt down and arson suspected, the Claflin family took to the road. They were soon living by their wits in a travelling medicine show which toured the Middle West: a special feature was to be the 'spiritualism' practised by Victoria and Tennessee. At 15 Victoria married a Dr Canning Woodhull, an alcoholic, and bore him a son and daughter. The marriage was soon ended and Victoria rejoined the disreputable family circus.

In 1868 – after a vision of the ancient Greek orator Demosthenes appeared to Victoria – the whole tribe moved to New York, together with her lover Colonel Blood. The two sisters secured an introduction to the multi-millionaire railway promoter Commodore Cornelius Vanderbilt, whose wife had just died, on the promise of arranging psychic messages from beyond the grave. In no time, with Vanderbilt's help, the two sisters had set up shop as the first professional women stockbrokers. Woodhull, Claflin & Co was so successful that for several years the pair kept the Claflin clan in great style in a mansion on Murray Hill, New York, and were able to turn their energies elsewhere: in Victoria's case to Stephen Andrews, an anarchic thinker who converted her without much difficulty to free love, and by extension to women's rights, legalized prostitution and reforms of all sorts. *Woodhull & Claflin's Weekly* appeared between 1870–76; it was a mouthpiece for their own views and also the journal in which the *Communist Manifesto* was first made available in English to American readers.

Woodhull then adopted – and was adopted by – the women's movement, to its subsequent embarrassment, for her vigorous views caused a severe difference of opinion between Susan B. Anthony and Elizabeth Cady Stanton (qq.v.) of the National Woman Suffrage Association, and Lucy Stone (q.v.)

of the American Woman Suffrage Association. In the space of a year she had become a rousing orator, and nearly wrested the leadership of the NWSA from Anthony. When defeated by Anthony, Woodhull announced a convention of her own for the Presidential election of 1872, for which she was nominated as a candidate.

But by Election Day Woodhull was in jail, and her career was subsiding in a blaze of scandal and bad debts. *Woodhull & Claflin's Weekly*, ever ready to expose sexual hypocrisy, (especially since she had been attacked for having her former husband, Dr Woodhull, and her second husband, Colonel Blood, living together in her house), revealed the adultery of the famous preacher Henry Ward Beecher (brother of Harriet Beecher Stowe, q.v.) with one of his parishioners. Many refused to believe the charges (although they were true), and the moralist Anthony Comstock ingeniously suggested that the sisters should be jailed for sending obscenity through the mails (the same charge that Margaret Sanger, q.v., had to endure from the same quarter some years later). Eventually the sisters were acquitted and, having had to sell the Murray Hill mansion, tried their hand at respectability. In 1877, possibly at the financial prompting of Commodore Vanderbilt's family, they retired to England, where Victoria took up lecturing once more. Tennessee married Francis Cook, shortly to become Sir Francis Cook, and in 1883 Victoria married John Biddulph Martin of the banking family, who had fallen in love with her when he heard her lecture on 'The Human Body the Temple of God'. Woodhull remained immensely energetic, publishing a journal on eugenics and working for women's suffrage with the Pankhursts (q.v.). But the sisters' life in Britain was an anticlimax after the irrepressible splendour of their American career.

TRAVEL AND EXPLORATION

WOMEN HAVE ALWAYS done their share of travelling, albeit much of it involuntarily. They have packed up and left home as brides, refugees, emigrants and colonizers, or as pilgrims, teachers and missionaries. But some women, particularly in the last two hundred years, have deliberately chosen to travel – independently of male protectors – as explorers of and commentators on the wider world.

It was the Christian Church which first set individual women on the move. In the fourth century, St Jerome drew several Roman widows to a life of prayer in the Holy Land, and in the eighth century English nuns were in the vanguard of the missionary movement to pagan Germany. Much later, in the nineteenth and twentieth centuries, missionaries such as Mary Slessor and Gladys Aylward penetrated West Africa and China.

The secular travellers covered here belong mostly to the last two or three centuries. Many of these women, such as Celia Fiennes at the end of the seventeenth century, kept diaries or wrote books about their experiences. Some, notably Marianne North, studied the flora and fauna of distant countries. Osa Johnson pioneered the wildlife nature film. Mary Kingsley, on behalf of the British Museum, travelled up the unknown Ogowe River in Gabon, West Africa, collecting rare specimens, while Olga Fedchenko explored remote areas of Turkestan and the Crimea in search of plants. Many women have simply travelled for the sense of freedom and adventure, as lone yachtswomen, pilots, even bicyclists. If women travellers have not, like men, led great expeditions of exploration, they have certainly not lacked courage or initiative.

Amy Johnson about to board her Tiger Moth biplane for her epic solo flight to Australia in 1930.

Isabella Bird, author of The Englishwoman in America *and* A Lady's Life in the Rocky Mountains.

Isabella Bird Bishop
British (1832–1904)

Isabella Bird was an independent-minded Victorian lady who found health in travelling and wrote a great many popular books. She was the daughter of an English clergyman and in 1854 set off alone for the Hawaiian Islands, with the sum of £100. Her accounts of her adventures in America were originally letters to a beloved sister at home but proved so popular when they appeared in magazines that they were published in book form: *The Englishwoman in America* appeared in 1856. Thereafter she travelled indefatigably until the end of the century, specializing in remote places such as Japan, Korea, Persia and Tibet. Back in Edinburgh between trips, poor health obliged her to lie on her day-bed where she wrote articles on social evils and sewed clothes for emigrants

to Canada. Once abroad again, however, she had 'the appetite of a tiger and the digestion of an ostrich'. *A Lady's Life in the Rocky Mountains* (1879) describes her meeting with a Wild West character called 'Mountain' Jim Nugent who fell in love with her, but could not persuade her to marry him. *Unbeaten Tracks in Japan* (1880) recorded one of several visits to the Far East. Bird married a patient admirer called Bishop in 1880, but was widowed soon afterwards. She is buried on the Island of Mull among the fisherfolk who became her primary interest in old age.

Lady Anne Blunt
British (1837–1917)

The first Englishwoman to travel in and write about the Arabian peninsula, Lady Anne Blunt was as fearless and enquiring as her grandfather, the poet Lord Byron. Her mother was Lady Lovelace (q.v.), Byron's only surviving child, but she had an erratic education. She married the eccentric diplomat, poet, explorer and political activist Wilfred Scawen Blunt in 1869. They had a daughter, Judith, in 1873 and in the same year travelled through Turkey on a second honeymoon. Lady Anne was an excellent linguist and they both spoke Arabic. In 1874 they went to Algiers and in 1875–6 to Egypt, reaching the Sinai peninsula at the end of that year. In 1877 they embarked on a desert trek through Syria from Aleppo to Baghdad, following the Euphrates. 'Gloomy thoughts vanish once one sets foot in Asia,' Lady Anne wrote in *The Bedouin Tribes of the Euphrates* (1878). On these desert travels, she wore a kaffiya – an Arab headdress – over her tweed Ulster and once narrowly escaped being speared to death in a desert raid, but remained undaunted: 'She was afraid of nothing but the sea,' said her husband. Describing their journey across the dangerous red sands of the Nafud, she wrote: 'There is something in the air which would exhilarate even a condemned man' (*A Pilgrimage to Nedj* (1881)).In 1881 they bought an estate in Egypt, Sheikh Obeyd, where Lady Anne Blunt largely lived from 1906 until she died. Her husband returned to England and bred from the horses they bought in Arabia - the foundations of the famous Crabbet stud.

Mildred Cable
British (1878–1952)

Evangeline French
British (1869–1960)

Francesca French
British (1871–1960)

The 'Trio' were Christian missionaries who travelled for many years over the hostile Gobi Desert preaching the Gospel. Evangeline French was born in Algiers and her sister Francesca in Belgium. They went to school in Geneva, then the family moved to England. Eva French had become a nihilist and a communist when she was at Geneva University but in 1893, after hearing the China Inland Mission lectures, she was converted to Christianity. She sailed to Shanghai to become a missionary in China.

Mildred Cable was born in Guildford. She, too, was inspired by the China Inland Mission and, after studying science at London University, sailed to China in 1901. She met Eva French there in 1902 and they became lifelong companions.

Francesca French joined her sister and Mildred Cable in China when her mother died, and together the three women ran a school for girls. In 1923 the 'Trio' applied to the China Inland Mission for permission to travel in the sparsely inhabited region of the Gobi desert. 'If no more could be done for these people certainly no less was owed to them than to place a Gospel in each man's hand written in his mother tongue.' They set off from the City of the Prodigals (Suchow) to the City of the Seagulls (Chuguchak) across the immense desert wastes armed only with a stock of Bibles, three sleeping bags, a kettle and a frying pan. Their 'combination of grey hairs, celibate state and pilgrim life', however, appears to have ensured them a safe passage and enabled them to talk to lamas, bandits and finally revolutionary generals. *The Gobi Desert* (1942) is a personal account of their experiences.

Alexandra David-Neel
French (1868–1969)

Alexandra David-Neel was the first European woman known to have reached the forbidden city of

Mildred Cable and Evangeline French in the Gobi desert, 1934, part of their caption reads:
'*at midnight the alarm was given and we had to move on!*'

Lhasa in Tibet (but cf. Helena Blavatsky), and her books are an important historical source on Tibetan religious practices. The only child of an unhappy marriage between a French schoolteacher and a Belgian, she constantly ran away from home. At 18, following her researches at the Musée Guimet in Paris, Alexandra David determined to travel to the East. She was over 20 before she had enough money – which she inherited – to visit India and Ceylon; thereafter, she toured the Far East, Middle East and North Africa as a singer with the Opéra Comique.

In Tunis in 1904 she married an engineer, Philippe François Neel. He financed expeditions to Europe, China and, in 1911, India, where Alexandra enrolled at the Calcutta College of Sanskrit. In 1912 she was the first woman to interview the Dalai Lama, who suggested that she learn Tibetan. She subsequently graduated as a lama and adopted a boy companion called Yongden. David-Neel was deeply impressed by Tibetan anchorite nuns; determined, like them, to learn endurance, she spent the winter of 1914 with Yongden in a cave at 13,000 feet, dressed only in a cotton garment and studying Buddhist teaching. She then spent three years in a Peking monastery.

In 1923 she disguised herself and Yongden as an old woman and her son to go to Lhasa. 'I had sworn that a woman would pass, and I *would*.' They succeeded, although it took great courage to face hunger and cold and the suspicion of officials. 'Luck has a cause,' she said, 'and I believe there exists a mental attitude capable of shaping circumstances according to one's wishes.' In *My Journey to Lhasa*, the book that made her name in 1927, she recorded 'magic' feats done by monks and holy men – such as making fire without flint and 'flying', the Tibetan art of fast walking. In 1936 she returned to France and settled in Digne. 'Travel not only stirs the blood,' she wrote, 'it also gives strength to the spirit.'

Amelia Earhart
American (1898–1937)

The first woman to fly solo across the Atlantic, Amelia Earhart was the daughter of an unsuccessful American lawyer who took to drink. After nursing First World War victims in Toronto she began medical training, but in the meantime had had a trial flight at a California air show. Thereafter she was determined to become a pilot, and at the age of 23 flew solo for the first time. She became a social worker in Boston, but the 'flying fever' which hit America in the 1920s gave her her chance: a publisher was on the look-out for someone to become the first woman to cross the Atlantic by air and write her story.

In June 1928, accompanied by a male pilot and navigator, Earhart flew from Newfoundland to Wales as a passenger. She became an immediate celebrity, with a ticker-tape reception in New York and hundreds of requests to lecture, broadcast, write, and meet other celebrities. She married the publisher, George Putnam, who 'promoted' her flying in order to make money. Finally on 20 May 1932, she became the first woman to fly solo across the Atlantic, a feat which brought her extraordinary adulation. In an attempt to fly round the world in July 1937, she disappeared with her navigator Fred Noonan on the last leg home across the Pacific.

Amelia Edwards
British (1831–1892)

Amelia Edwards was one of the first British people to travel widely in Egypt. The daughter of an Army officer, she began her writing career with novels and elementary history books. In 1873 she learned as much Egyptology as she could – it was not then a recognized academic subject - in preparation for her visit to Egypt in 1877. *A Thousand Miles up the Nile* (1877) was the record of her extremely adventurous journey, and her *Pharaohs, Fellahs and Explorers* was published in 1891.

Edwards was a co-founder of the Egypt Exploration Fund in 1882 and she left her vast specialized library to London University together with enough money to found a Chair in Egyptology.

Olga Alexandrovna Fedchenko
Russian (1845–1921)

Olga Fedchenko was an important nineteenth-century plant collector, almost completely unknown

record of seventeenth- and eighteenth-century England. She was the granddaughter of Viscount Saye and Sele, one of the anti-Royalist leaders of the English Civil War, who was made a peer by Cromwell. In pursuit of health she set off round England on horseback in 1685 with a few servants. She was still making trips many years later, and in 1698 she travelled more than a thousand miles in a year, 'not above a hundred of them in a coach'. She was delighted to see the crafts and trades of the country, and to meet Dissenters, for whose right to worship freely her grandfather had fought in the Civil War. She visited grand houses and beer tastings, descended into coal mines and explored caves, and even had to face highwaymen – all the time recording her adventures in her fascinating diary.

Clare Francis
British (b. 1946)

In 1976 Clare Francis became the fastest solo yachtswoman across the Atlantic, when she sailed from Falmouth, England, to Newport, Rhode Island, in 29 days in the *Observer* Royal Western Single-handed Transatlantic Race. Two years later she skippered 11 other men and women in the Whitbread Round the World yacht race, in which they came fifth (cf. Dame Naomi James).

Clare Francis began sailing because her family had a holiday house on the Isle of Wight. She was educated at the Royal Ballet School, but gave up dancing to take a degree in economics at London University. She spent six years in marketing, first with Beechams and then with Robertsons, but gave it up in 1973 to make her first solo trip (in 37 days) across the Atlantic in a 32-footer bought for £7,000. In 1974 Reckitt & Colman sponsored her and a friend in the Round Britain race, in which they finished third on handicap; for the Transatlantic Race two years later she was sponsored by her former employers Robertsons.

In 1977 Francis married another yachtsman and former teacher, Jacques Redon. She published *Come Hell and High Water* in 1977.

Amelia Edwards, who co-founded the Egyptian Exploration Fund in 1882.

in the West. Trained as a botanist, she travelled to very remote areas to collect plants for the herbarium she founded in Moscow in 1861. On a two-year journey to Turkestan and the Crimea in 1868 with her husband, she discovered more than 1,800 new varieties of plants.

Celia Fiennes
British (1662–1741)

First in a long line of vigorous, eccentric English women travellers, Celia Fiennes was also one of the first travel writers. In her diary she has left a vivid

267

Evangelina and Francesca French
(see Mildred Cable)

Constance Gordon-Cumming
British (1837–1934)

Constance Gordon-Cumming was an enterprising Victorian traveller who made her exotic journeys sound cheerful and even domestic. She was born into a large landowning family in the north of Scotland, the youngest of many children – one brother, Roualeyn, became a famous lion hunter in Africa. A happy, devout woman, she lived in Sri Lanka for two years and then spent another two years in Fiji; *At Home in Fiji* (1881) is typical of her many other books about her years in Hawaii, China, Japan, California, New Zealand and Austria. *A Lady's Cruise in a French Man-of-War* (1882) is also based on personal experience.

Dame Naomi James
New Zealander (b. 1949)

In 1977–8, Naomi James became the first woman to sail alone around the world. She also set the record for the fastest round the world trip, making the journey in just under 272 days, breaking Sir Francis Chichester's record of 274 days. Just as Chichester became a Knight of the British Empire, so James was made a Dame of the British Empire in 1979, and she held the record until May 1980. It was her first solo trip ever, and she had only learned to sail two years earlier, after marrying Rob James, a director of lone yachtsman Chay Blyth's charter company. Rob James was skipper of *Great Britain II* in the round-the-world Whitbread Trophy race of 1977 (in which Clare Francis, q.v., also competed), and Naomi decided to follow him in a boat which she was lent by Chay Blyth – the 53–ft *Express Crusader*.

Dame Naomi was born Naomi Power in New Zealand and brought up on a farm. When she left school she was a hairdresser for five years. She moved to Britain in 1970, and was a language teacher before switching to a yacht charter crew.

Amy Johnson
British (1903–1941)

One of the most famous of all the solo pilots of the 1920s and 1930s, Amy Johnson was the daughter of a fish merchant in Hull on the East coast of England. After studying at Sheffield University, she found a job in London as a secretary and took lodgings where she could hear the sound of the planes from the London Aeroplane Club. In 1928 she started flying lessons which cost her nearly as much as she earned, but soon qualified as a pilot and an engineer. She called herself 'Johnnie' and was treated as one of the boys.

In 1930 Johnson flew solo from London to Australia, the first woman to do so. She was fêted everywhere and was soon a world celebrity. In 1932 she married Jim Mollison, a fellow pilot, and for a while they shared the limelight for their daring flights, but they divorced in 1938. At the outbreak of war, Johnson worked for Air Transport, ferrying planes all over England. She disappeared over the Thames Estuary in mysterious circumstances in 1941.

Osa Johnson
American (1894–1953)

Osa Johnson pioneered the fashion for 'shooting' wild life with the camera, not the gun. She and her husband were the first to make successful films of cannibals and gibbons. Born in Chanute, Kansas, the daughter of a railway worker called William Leighty, she married Martin Johnson, an itinerant photographer, when she was 16. The author Jack London took on the young couple as crew on his yacht in the South Seas. Enterprising and fearless, the Johnsons earned a living by dancing and singing, and then spent their savings on exploring islands in the New Hebrides. In 1917 they had made enough money to photograph the wild life – and wild men – of North Borneo, pictures which made their name in the States.

From 1921 onwards the Johnsons made five expeditions to Africa. *Simba*, *Congorill* and *Baboona* were filmed from their two small planes, which Osa piloted herself; they also discovered Lake Paradise.

Martin Johnson was killed in a plane crash in 1937 and his widow was left in charge of the Twentieth Century Fox team (the largest crew ever sent overseas at that time) to make *Stanley and Livingstone*. In 1940 she wrote a successful autobiography, *I Married Adventure*; she also wrote children's books and made many films – determined to do all she could for the scientific conservation of the natural world.

Mary Kingsley
British (1862–1900)

Mary Kingsley was the cleverest of the famous Victorian women travellers. Her father was a restless, inquisitive doctor who travelled the world looking for curiosities of all kinds, and her uncle was Charles Kingsley, author of *The Water Babies*. Mary was educated at home and, advanced though her father's biological theories may have been, she was only allowed to teach herself German when she had demonstrated that she could starch and iron a shirt properly. Later, she learnt mathematics from a neighbour and when the family moved to Cambridge she got to know Charles Darwin and T. H. Huxley. All through her youth Kingsley was expected to be the dutiful daughter; she was only free to travel in 1892, following her parents' death. Her first voyage, on behalf of the British Museum, was to West Africa, to complete her father's collections.

In 1894 she eagerly accepted a commission from the Natural History Museum to go up the unknown Ogowe River in search of more fish and plants.

Extremely impatient with the attitudes of the various Christian churches, Kingsley always chose to travel as a trader rather than as a teacher or missionary. 'Africa should send *us* missionaries instead of our sending them to her,' she said. She was overwhelmed by the great natural beauty of the forests and rivers. She was also deeply impressed by African cultures and – well ahead of her time – hated the 'thin veneer of rubbishy white culture' imposed by British officials and missionaries (although she approved of Mary Slessor, q.v.). Her *Travels in West Africa* was published in 1897 and made her famous. It is a serious account of her journeys, and extremely

'Few of you know the blessings of a good thick skirt,' wrote the intrepid Mary Kingsley in one of her travel books.

readable: 'Few of you know the blessing of a good thick skirt. Here I was with the fullness of my skirt sitting on nine ebony spikes some twelve inches long in comparative comfort, howling lustily to be hauled out,' she wrote of her fall into an elephant trap. So distressed was she at the maltreatment of 'natives' at the hands of the colonial government that she launched a vigorous campaign of lectures, later published as *West African Studies*. Speaking engagements and writing articles kept Kingsley away from her beloved Africa until she went to nurse Boer prisoners in the South African War in 1900; there she caught enteric fever and died.

Dervla Murphy
Irish (b. 1931)

Dervla Murphy has shown that even in the second half of the twentieth century the age of the classic traveller

is not dead. At the age of ten she received a bicycle as a Christmas present, and almost at once determined that one day she would travel to India. From adolescence to the age of 30 she was tied to her home by family circumstances (about which she has written unforgettably in *Wheels Within Wheels* (1979)), for her mother was totally crippled by rheumatoid arthritis; she got no further on her bicycle than England, Spain and Germany. But when she was 30 Murphy's journeys began: overland to India (celebrated in her first book *Full Tilt* (1964) and in four further books) long before the 'hippy trail' made it a cliché; Tibet; Nepal; Ethiopia (for once on a mule); the Andes; and Northern Ireland. The sympathy and understanding she displayed for that unhappy province in *A Place Apart*, (1978), won her the Christopher Ewart-Biggs Memorial Prize. Her daughter Rachel was born in 1968, and at the age of five was already travelling with her mother in India.

Marianne North
British (1830–1890)

Marianne North was a Victorian lady traveller who became famous for her botanical paintings. She was the eldest daughter of the then MP for Hastings. After a short time at boarding school, she went for three years to the continent, accompanied by her family, to train as a singer. Her plans to become a singer came to nothing – perhaps because her adored father could not 'stand' music – and instead she developed her skill as a painter of flowers.

In 1855 Marianne North and her father, now a widower, went on a leisurely journey through Turkey, Syria and Egypt. Her sister married in 1864, and their father's death in 1869 left Marianne free to 'realize her ambition of painting the flora of distant countries.' In 1871 she left for Canada and the U.S., and came home by way of Jamaica and the Brazilian jungle. Everywhere she painted. In 1874 she travelled round the world; then almost at once was off again to California, Borneo, Java, Sarawak, Ceylon and India. She exhibited her paintings in London in 1879, and

A rare photograph showing Marianne North's working methods during her travels.

Lady Hester Stanhope, 'Queen of the Arabs', enjoying a hookah.

launched plans for a gallery to house her work at the Royal Botanic Gardens at Kew. Charles Darwin suggested that she should go to Brisbane, Australia, where she could paint 'twenty-five different flowers without moving from the spot'; she went there also. The North Gallery at Kew opened on her return in 1882. Then she was off again to the Seychelles, Chile and South Africa, painting to the last. Her work can be seen at Kew in the gallery named after her.

Lady Hester Stanhope
British (1776–1839)

Lady Hester Stanhope fulfilled a gypsy's prophecy that she would be 'Queen of the Arabs'. The high-spirited daugher of Citizen Stanhope (as her father, Lord Stanhope, insisted on calling himself), Lady

Freya Stark, traveller in the Middle East, photographed in 1956.

Dame Freya Stark
British (b. 1892)

Freya Stark's much-admired travel books have made her many expeditions in the Middle East famous. The daughter of a sculptor, she spent most of her childhood in Devon, England. In 1902 the family moved to Asolo in Italy, where her mother helped to run a silk factory. Soon after, Freya Stark's hair caught in the machinery and half her scalp was torn away, the beginning of a series of physical misadventures which Freya Stark has never allowed to interfere with her active life. During the First World War she worked as a nurse.

In 1921 Stark began to learn Arabic from an Italian monk and subsequently took a degree in Arabic at London University. In 1928 she made her first journey, to the Lebanon, and went further and further east each year – first to Baghdad, then into the interior of Iraq and Iran. In 1931 she undertook a pioneer expedition to the mountains of Luristan in Iran, and wrote a best-seller about her experiences, *The Valley of the Assassins* (1934). Her travels in the Hadramaut in Southern Arabia during the 1930s resulted in *The Southern Gates of Arabia* (1938) and *A Winter in Arabia* (1940). Her knowledge of Arabic and of the desert peoples made her a valuable source of intelligence to the British government during the Second World War.

Besides her many travel books, Stark has also written a three-volume autobiography. Active well into her eighties, she made a journey to Afghanistan in 1972 – the year she was made a Dame – and travelled down the Euphrates in 1976. She married the historian and writer Stewart Perowne in 1943, but they were subsequently divorced.

Valentina Tereshkova
Russian (b. 1937)

Valentina Tereshkova was the first and is so far the only woman to have travelled in space. In 1963 she orbited the earth 49 times in three days in Vostok 6.

Born on a farm 250 miles from Moscow, Tereshkova is the daughter of a tractor driver who was

Hester was orphaned young. At 27 she joined the household of her uncle, the Prime Minister William Pitt, acting as his hostess until he died in 1806. She was then granted a substantial royal pension. In 1810 she moved to Constantinople, ostensibly for her health. She lost her luggage in a shipwreck off Rhodes, and thereafter always wore Turkish dress 'for its splendour and convenience'. Lady Hester was one of the first English travellers to Egypt, but finally settled in a castle at Djoun on Mount Lebanon in 1814. Her generosity and courage became a legend; she would feed and clothe hundreds of the local Druses (a religious sect) during periods of Ottoman oppression and refused to be intimidated even when Emir Buchir, the tyrannical local governor, left dead bodies as a warning at her castle gates. She was revered as a queen by the neighbouring tribes and was proud of her gifts as a healer and astrologer. Left alone and penniless towards the end of her life, she appealed in vain for Queen Victoria to restore her pension, and died in possession of her castle, but little more.

Valentina Tereshkova, first woman cosmonaut.

Fanny Workman in mountaineering dress, with her 'treasured topie' hat and ice-axe.

killed in the war and a textile worker. She too went into the textile trade, and qualified as a cotton technologist in 1962.

Tereshkova took up parachute-jumping as a sport in 1959 at the Yaroslav Aero Club, and by the time of her space flight had made 126 drops. She was a keen member of the Young Communist League, and applied to be trained for space after Yuri Gagarin had become the first man in space in 1961. After her own orbit, she married another cosmonaut, Andrian Nikolayev, and they have a daugher. Since then she has become a member of the Soviet Praesidium, and travelled abroad to lecture about her epic voyage. Tereshkova became chairwoman of the Soviet Women's Committee in 1977 and is a committee member of the Communist Party.

Fanny Workman
American (1859–1925)

Fanny Workman was a pioneer of mountain climbing and bicycling for women. She was the youngest of the three children of Governor Bullock of Massachusetts, and was educated privately. In 1881 she married a doctor and had a daughter in 1884. Her husband gave up his practice in 1888 because of 'ill health' (in the event, he lived to the age of 91), and together they toured Europe to listen to Wagner and climb the Alps. In 1895 the Workmans went round Spain on bicycles; in 1897 they embarked on a bicycle tour of India, Burma, Ceylon and Java – armed with revolvers and dog whips. The sight of the Himalayas spurred Fanny to make an attempt on the height record for women climbers, and in 1902, in the days before oxygen masks, she climbed the 22,000-foot Mount Lunga – a remarkable feat. In 1912 she mapped the Great Rose Glacier, and there is a photograph of her, taken at 21,000 feet, which shows her reading a newspaper headline announcing 'Votes for Women'. The Workmans gave many lectures and wrote eight books on their exploits in the 'ice wilds'. Fanny Workman left money for fellowships at four American women's colleges.

273

SPORT

WOMEN'S SPORT as we know it is a very modern phenomenon. It was not until 1924 that women were allowed to compete in a fairly full range of events in the Olympic Games. They first competed professionally in tennis and golf in 1900.

Although in ancient Greece women were barred from the Olympic Games, even as spectators, the classical legend of Atalanta – who could run faster than any of her suitors and who was only distracted from winning the famous race because of the golden apples dropped in her path – and the worship of Diana, a hunter whose weapon was the bow, suggest that the Greeks appreciated that women could enjoy and excel in athletic sports and exercises. Certainly, the women of Sparta were trained in running, wrestling and throwing the discus and javelin, and had Games of their own. The bull-jumpers of Crete included young women, and the famous Roman mosaics at Piazza Armerina, Sicily, show women gymnasts dressed in bikinis.

There are few sports in which women do not compete. Mary Queen of Scots was one of the first women to take up golf; the first woman bullfighter was mentioned in Spain in 1654; and nowadays there are women jockeys, lone yachtswomen, even motor racers. Some of the greatest all-rounders of either sex have been women, notably 'Babe' Didrikson and Lottie Dod, and several women hold more records in a single sport than their male contemporaries, for instance Judy Hashman in badminton. Women compete on a level with men in show-jumping, in ice-dancing and (although they do different exercises) in gymnastics: indeed, the first perfect scores in Olympic gymnastics, a full 10 marks, were achieved in 1976, by a girl of fourteen, Nadia Comaneci. Women may lack strength and speed compared with men but, interestingly, in the late 1970s their record times in, for instance, swimming and running, were increasing at a faster rate.

Suzanne Lenglen: her bandeau became a personal trademark and her tennis clothes set the modern style.

275

Sophie Blanchard
French (1778–1819)

The most intrepid of all women balloonists was Madame Blanchard, born Sophie Armant near La Rochelle. She dominated this spectator sport, although she had been married to the balloonist Jean-Pierre Blanchard for 10 years before she nerved herself for her first ascent. In 1805 she went up alone for the first time in her gas-powered balloon; night flights were her speciality, because it was quieter and more people could watch, and she would sleep in the 'car', as it was then called. A very popular performer, Madame Blanchard entertained public and royalty with her dramatic ascents to the accompaniment of 'brilliant music' from the Tivoli Gardens in Paris. In a fatal accident in 1819, a firework ignited her balloon. Madame Blanchard bravely remained calm, threw out the ballast as the balloon lost height, and crash-landed on the roof of a building. Unfortunately the car then slid down to the pavement and she was killed.

Fanny Blankers-Koen
Dutch (b. 1918)

Fanny Blankers-Koen was the star of the 1948 Olympics, held in Britain. Already 30, with two children, she became the first woman to win four gold medals – setting three Olympic and one world record. At home in Amsterdam, there was a public holiday in her honour and she was given a triumphal reception. One of the great all-round athletes of all time – she already held five world records for running, hurdling, high jump and long jump – the crowds warmed to her exceptionally sympathetic personality.

Koen was born at Baarn in the Netherlands into a family of four brothers. Her father was a keen shot-putter and discus-thrower. She did not take up athletics herself until she was 16, when she met Jan Blankers, a trainer, who was later to become her husband. The 1948 Olympics was the peak of a phenomenal career, but for some years afterwards she continued to break records all over the world. Although she competed in the Helsinki Olympics in 1952, it was clear she had lost her edge; she retired shortly afterwards.

Fanny Blankers-Koen (left) after winning the 1948 Olympic 80 metres hurdles event.

Beryl Burton
British (b. 1937)

Beryl Burton has had a 20-year unbroken reign as British women's cycling champion, winning the British Best All-Rounder every year since 1959. In 1967 she became the only woman athlete ever to break a man's record when she achieved 277.25 miles in 12 hours, beating the men's record, made earlier the same day, of 276.52 miles. By 1977 she had won seven world championships and more than sixty British titles.

Beryl Burton came from a poor Yorkshire family, and was introduced to cycling by her future husband, Charles Burton, when they both worked as clerks with the local Electricity Board. They have one daughter, Denise, also a cycling champion. Beryl Burton works on a farm, and lives near Leeds.

Beryl Burton at the World Cycling Championships in 1970.

Nadia Comaneci on the uneven bars at the Champions All event at Wembley in 1978.

Vera Caslavska
Czechoslovakian (b. 1942)

In many people's opinion Vera Caslavska is the greatest woman gymnast ever, having won 22 World, Olympic and European titles between 1959 and 1980 – including seven Olympic gold medals. At the Tokyo Olympics in 1964 she won gold medals for beam and vault plus the combined individual title. At the Mexican Olympics four years later – in spite of having to train while in hiding during the 1968 Soviet invasion of Czechoslovakia – she achieved the highest score ever in the all-round championship, this time winning three golds and a silver. She retired during the Games and married a fellow Czech, Josef Odlozil, the 1500-metres runner. They now have two daughters.

Caslavska had real star quality – not just for her

brilliance but also for her beauty and glamour. Only she and Larissa Latynina (q.v.) have won both the floor and the individual combined Olympic championships. She now works as a coach in Prague.

Nadia Comaneci
Romanian (b. 1961)

The first athlete ever to achieve a perfect score of 10, hitherto thought impossible, was Nadia Comaneci, then aged 14. In fact she achieved *seven* full scores of 10 in the 1976 Olympics gymnastic event, after achieving 10 *sixteen* times in the qualifying events. She won three individual gold medals, a silver medal in a team event and an individual bronze.

Nadia Comaneci was born in Onesti, Romania,

277

daughter of a garage mechanic and a hospital caretaker. She was spotted at the age of six by the great Romanian coach Bela Karolyi, who has described his first sight of her jumping around in her school playground as 'the most important moment' in his life. Comaneci is particularly famous for an incredible dismount from the uneven parallel bars which involves a twisting back somersault.

In the 1980 Moscow Olympics Comaneci tied for a gold medal with the Russian Natalia Shaposhnikova in the individual compulsory exercises.

Maureen Connolly
American (1934–1969)

'Little Mo' was the great prodigy of lawn tennis. By the age of 20 (when a riding accident which injured her leg forced her to retire from active competition) she had already dominated world tennis for three years, and had become the first woman to win, in one year, the four great singles championships – Forest Hills, Wimbledon, France and Australia.

Connolly was born in San Diego, California, in 1934, daughter of a naval officer and a musical mother who divorced when she was four. At 14 she became the youngest player to win the U.S. junior title. At 16, in 1951, she won the U.S. senior championship at Forest Hills, and in 1952 won the Wimbledon singles at her first attempt. She won both the British and the U.S. titles three times running, and the Australian singles in 1953 and the French in 1953 and 1954. She won the Grand Slam – all four major championships – in the year she was 19.

Blessed with immense energy and confidence in her game, 'Little Mo' was famous for her steady, accurate forehand and backhand drives and her dedication to constant practice. She was a competitive player with a considerable 'killer' instinct.

A year after her retirement, she married the Olympic rider Norman Brinker, and they had two daughters. She continued in tennis as a coach and commentator, but became ill with cancer in 1966 and died, after three operations, in 1969.

Lorraine Crapp
Australian (b. 1938)

Lorraine Crapp was the first of the great superswimmers. In August 1956, she became the first woman swimmer to break the five-minute barrier for 400 metres freestyle, with nearly 10 seconds to spare. From the age of 15, Lorraine Crapp broke a total of 16 world freestyle records – including five on the same day. In 1960 she married a Sydney doctor, Bill Thurlow.

In Lorraine's wake Australian teenagers became the great record-breakers of the swimming world (cf. Dawn Fraser).

Mildred 'Babe' Didrikson
American (1914–1956)

The most prodigious woman in the history of sport, 'Babe' Didrikson not only won gold medals in very different events at the 1932 Olympics – javelin throwing, 80-metre hurdles, and high jump (in which she tied), all of which set new world records –

Lorraine Crapp at the Townsville (Queensland) Baths in 1960.

'Babe' Didrikson driving down the fairway at the Doherty Tournament, Miami, in 1947.

Lottie Dod, still the youngest tennis player ever to win the Women's Singles title at Wimbledon.

but was also a national baseball player, basketball player, golfer, and even billiards player.

Didrikson was one of seven children brought up in Beaumont, Texas; her father set up a gymnasium in the back yard where she did work-outs. The family was also musical, and at the age of seven Mildred performed on local radio as a harmonica soloist. She could also tap dance. In 1930, when she was 16, she was spotted as a basketball player, and played for two years for a nationally known company team in Dallas – at the same time winning medals in swimming and skating, and breaking athletics records for every track and field event she entered. The 1932 Olympics established her as the world's finest athlete.

Didrikson's greatest love was golf, which she began learning when she was 18. She spent some years as a professional athlete, golfer and games player to put her nieces and nephews through school, but eventually reverted to amateur status for golf. In

the 1940s she won every available golf title, and in 1947 became the first American to win the British Women's Amateur Championship – one of 17 major tournaments she won that year, a record not likely to be beaten by anyone.

'Babe' Didrikson had great courage: she made a dramatic comeback after being operated on for cancer, and continued to play in spite of intense pain. She won the U.S. National Open and the All American Open golf tournaments in 1953 after a major operation. She was married to the wrestler George Zaharias.

Charlotte Dod
British (1871–1960)

Lottie Dod won the fourth women's Wimbledon tennis championship in 1887, when she was still two

Dawn Fraser at the Olympic Games in 1956.

Judy Hashman (right) with her trophy for the All-England Badminton championships, 1967.

months short of her sixteenth birthday – the youngest winner then, and still the youngest nearly a century later. She went on to win again in 1888, 1891, 1892 and 1893. She was never defeated at Wimbledon – she did not play in 1889 or 1890.

It is difficult to know how Lottie Dod would have stood up to Maureen Connolly or Suzanne Lenglen (qq.v.), but she was one of the first women to volley and smash – at which she was very good – and her anticipation of her opponents' shots struck onlookers as uncanny. No doubt her game was not as fast or as hard as that of modern players since tennis was much less competitive then, but she was nevertheless the outstanding woman games player of the nineteenth century. Her all-round abilities encompassed archery, skating, hockey and golf. She played hockey for England in 1889–90, and was British Ladies' Golf Champion in 1904.

Dawn Fraser
Australian (b. 1937)

Dawn Fraser is the only woman swimmer ever to have won gold medals in three successive Olympic Games for the same event – the 100 metres freestyle in 1956, 1960 and 1964. She achieved 40 world records in all. Born into a large, poor family in Sydney's dockland, Fraser has been all her life a controversial, rumbustious character; with three other girl swimmers she was barred from competititive swimming in 1965 for indiscipline. In the same year she married a bookmaker, Gary Ware, from whom she later separated, after the birth of a daughter. The swimming ban was lifted in 1968.

Judy Hashman
American (b. 1935)

Judy Hashman is one of the famous Irish-American Devlins who virtually created the game of badminton as a modern spectator sport. Judy, her elder sister Sue Peard and her father J.F. Devlin have together won 40 championships between them including, for Judy, 10 world singles titles.

Judy Devlin was born in Winnipeg, Canada, but

moved with her family to the U.S. in 1936, eventually becoming a U.S. citizen. She grew up a first-class all-rounder. She could have been a great player in hockey, lacrosse or tennis, but her father's influence meant that the final choice was badminton. She won the United States junior title for the first of six times in 1949, and for the next two decades she dominated the game.

In 1960 she married a fellow player, Dick Hashman of Britain, and they had two sons. She has been a British citizen since 1971.

Sonja Henie
Norwegian (1912–1969)

Three times Olympic figure skating champion, a record 10 consecutive years women's world champion, the biggest sporting fortune (£17m or $37.5m), and still, 40 years after her greatest successes, considered the finest figure skater ever, Sonja Henie created an art from what had hitherto been only a sport. She also introduced the short skating skirt.

Sonja Henie was born in Oslo, Norway, daughter of a former cycling champion and furrier, Wilhelm Henie, and became Norwegian women's skating champion at the age of 11. When she turned professional after her third Olympic gold medal in 1936, she moved to Hollywood, where she made 11 films and ranked with Clark Gable and Shirley Temple in box office appeal. She became a U.S. citizen in 1941.

She was married three times: first to sportsman Dan Topping from 1939 to 1946, second to socialite Winthrop Gardiner, Jr. from 1949 to 1956, and finally to the Norwegian shipping magnate Niels Oustad in 1956. Her great wealth enabled her to indulge her passion for modern art; she formed an important collection, particularly of abstracts, and founded a museum for modern art in Oslo.

Billie Jean King
American (b. 1943)

Billie Jean King, née Moffitt, was the most redoubtable U.S. tennis player of the 1960s, not only as a player, but as a campaigner for women in sport. She was brought up in a non-tennis playing family (her father was a fire department engineer in Long Beach, California) but, having first learnt to play tennis in a local park, was lucky enough, when she was 16, to meet the former U.S. champion Alice Marble who offered to coach her. By 1970 King had won 18 singles titles in Australia, France, Britain and the U.S.A., including the Wimbledon singles three times running in 1966, 1967 and 1968, and six times altogether. She was also a highly successful doubles player, winning nine times in all at Wimbledon. King has won a grand total of 20 Wimbledon titles, a higher score than any other competitor. Her service and volleying were outstanding.

In 1962, when she was majoring in history at Los Angeles State College, she met law student Larry King, whom she married in 1965. Together they have done a great deal of voluntary work for underprivileged children, and Mrs King has mounted a tough campaign against the professional lawn tennis bodies to equalize women and men's tennis prizes. In 1973 she beat the former men's champion Bobby Riggs in straight sets in a famous 'Battle of the Sexes' to add weight to her campaign.

Olga Korbut
Russian (b. 1955)

Olga Korbut is the tiny gymnast whose dazzling performance and exuberant personality at the 1972 Munich Olympics astonished and delighted the world's television audiences. Within six months of her success there, amateur clubs throughout the world had doubled or even tripled their membership: gymnastics had become popular, and it was Korbut, almost single-handed, who was responsible.

The youngest of four daughters of a retired engineer in Grodno (formerly in Poland), she enrolled at the local gymnastics school at the age of nine. Before she was 15 she came fifth overall in the Soviet National Championships. By the time she was 16 she had become a Master of Sports in gymnastics, the youngest in Russia, and had come fourth overall in the National Championships. After a brief period

Olga Korbut on the balance beam at the World Student Games, 1973.

gold medals – more than any other woman athlete, and her nine Olympic gold medals set a new record. She also won five silver and four bronze Olympic medals. Latynina is the only gymnast, male or female, to win medals in every event in two Olympics (1956 and 1960) and to be the supreme champion of both. In the 20 years since then, women's gymnastics have become much more competitive; she might find such an achievement less easy today. But Latynina's sheer success remains unique. She also gave birth to two children during her active career. As a coach, she was instrumental in ensuring that Korbut (q.v.) was allowed to compete in adult events while still very young. She still coaches for Russia.

Suzanne Lenglen
French (1899–1938)

The first superstar of lawn tennis, Suzanne Lenglen was renowned not only for her impeccable playing – her accuracy was such that she was said to be able to hit a handkerchief anywhere on the court – but for her glamour, her temperament and her tantrums. Her famous bandeau was her trademark, and her bare arms and short, unhampering skirts set the style for women's tennis for decades to come. She liberated tennis from the fustian and amateurism of the early years of the century.

Lenglen's parents were extremely ambitious for her – and for themselves – and her father coached her ruthlessly. Although it was the first time she had ever played on grass, she defeated the reigning Wimbledon champion (the British Mrs Lambert Chambers) in 1919. Lenglen dominated women's tennis for the next seven years. In those seven years she lost only one match. She won the women's singles at Wimbledon six times, and all three events in the French championship seven times.

In 1926 she retreated into professional tennis, and spent her last decade running a coaching school in Paris. Her poor health caught up with her and in 1938, already a legend, she died of pernicious anaemia. Lenglen was posthumously awarded the Cross of the Legion of Honour, and thousands attended her funeral.

when her successes proved too much for her to cope with and she did less well, she helped the Russian team win their gold medal at the Munich Olympics, and in the individual events won two golds and a silver. Her back somersault on the balance beam, which no one else offered (but which is now virtually a standard exercise for young female gymnasts), and her breathtaking virtuosity and originality in the optional floor exercises – a routine that was changed at the last moment at her insistence, and which she learnt perfectly in only one week – were decisive. Yet she has never won a major overall title and all her accomplishments as an all-round gymnast in the 1970s were always well below those of her compatriot Ludmila Tourischeva. Korbut retired from competition in 1977 and from gymnastics in 1978.

Larissa Latynina
Russian (b. 1934)

Larissa Latynina, the first of the great women gymnasts, won 24 Olympic, World and European

Heather McKay
Australian (b. 1941)

A squash champion whose unbroken run of success has scarcely been matched by anyone, man or woman, in any sport, Heather McKay was Australian champion 14 years running, from 1960 to 1973 and British champion 16 years running, from 1962 to 1977. When she retired from competitive squash in 1979, she had lost only two matches in two decades and none between 1962 and 1979.

Heather Blundell was one of 11 children of a baker and keen rugby footballer living near Canberra, all of whom were brought up to play a variety of games. Heather, in her youth both a tennis champion and a noted hockey player, took up squash at 17, and two years later won the Australian championship. In 1965 she married a professional coach, Brian McKay, and herself turned professional in 1974. She and her husband have been coaches at the Toronto Squash Club since 1975. McKay has done an immense amount for squash – and has now taken on the challenge of turning herself into a first-class racquetball player.

Maria Mednyanszky
Hungarian (b. 1907)

A legendary sportswoman of the 1920s and early 1930s, Maria Mednyanszky was the star of women's table tennis for nearly a decade. She won 18 world titles between 1927 and 1935: seven in doubles, six in mixed doubles – the highest number ever in each class – and five in singles.

In singles championships, the leading winner, with six consecutive wins from 1950 to 1955, also hails from Eastern Europe – Angelica Rozeanu of Romania.

Annie Oakley
American (1860–1926)

Phoebe Anne Oakley Mozee, better known as Annie Oakley, was one of the crack shots of all time. 'The

Annie Oakley, also known as 'Lady Sure Shot'. She toured in Buffalo Bill's Wild West Show.

Girl of the Western Plains', 'Lady Sure Shot', was born in Ohio, where she shot game to help her family pay off their debts. By the time she was 12 she could hit anything that moved, though she did not learn to read until her husband taught her.

In her teens she won a shooting match in Cincinnati against the well-known marksman Frank E. Butler; they were later married, and toured the circuses and vaudeville halls before joining Buffalo Bill's Wild West Show in 1885. Audiences loved her and she soon had top billing, and the Butlers remained with Buffalo Bill for 17 years.

Her skill was phenomenal. She could hit a playing card at 30 paces *end on*, or knock the ash off a cigarette held in her husband's lips, or anyone else's – she performed the same trick in Berlin on Crown Prince

ИНАР...НЫЕ СОРЕВНОВАНИЯ ПО ФИГУРНО
...РИЗ ГАЗЕТЫ...НУВЕЛЬ ДЕ МОС...

Irina Rodnina with her husband and partner Alexander
Zaitser training for the 1979 Winter Games, Lake Placid.

William of Germany ('I wish I'd missed,' she said during World War I, when he had become the Kaiser). She could shoot the flames off a revolving wheel of candles, and even perform when lying on the back of a galloping horse.

Annie Oakley was badly injured in a train crash in 1901, but recovered sufficiently to continue touring. She was deservedly immortalized in one of the great post-war Broadway musicals, Irving Berlin's *Annie Get Your Gun.*

Irina Rodnina
Russian (b. 1949)

Irina Rodnina has won the Olympic Pairs skating gold medal three times, in 1972 with Alexei Ulanov and in 1976 and 1980 with her husband Alexander Zaitsev, and the World Pairs skating title ten times in succession from 1969 to 1978 – four times with Ulanov and six times with Zaitsev. Pregnancy

prevented her competing in 1979, and she retired just before the 1980 world championships.

Rodnina and Ulanov displaced the great Protopopovs as world champions. It was at the Winter Olympics in 1972, where they won the gold, that their partnership began to break up in the face of a love affair between Ulanov and Ludmila Smirnova, member of the runner-up pair, and the partnership was ended by Ulanov's sudden marriage to Smirnova. Alexander Zaitsev was picked out as a replacement partner for Rodnina after a nation-wide search – and was said to be 'terrified' when he was first paired with her on ice. However, in the 1973 world championships he and Rodnina achieved together the unprecedented total of 12 full scores, and went on to become Olympic gold medallists in 1976 and 1980.

Rodnina has undertaken skating of exceptional difficulty and daring, and has always been the dominant skater in her partnerships, a rare quality for the woman in pairs skating. Her three successive gold medals have been matched by only two other skaters, Sonja Henie (q.v.) and Gillis Grafstrom.

Wilma Rudolph
American (b. 1940)

Wilma Rudolph was the star of the 1960 Rome Olympics, and the first American girl to win three gold medals in the track and field events. She was the seventeenth of 19 children of a porter in Tennessee. At the age of four she was crippled by a severe attack of polio, and could not walk properly until she was eight. However, she became an excellent basketball player, was spotted by a coach, and began to train. By the time she was 16 she was a good enough runner to join the U.S. Olympic team, and helped them earn their bronze in the 1956 4 × 100 metre relay.

Pat Smythe
British (b. 1934)

Pat Smythe grew up horse-crazy, like many British girls. She was determined to get to the top in show-jumping – and did, without money, influence or a horsy background. Along the way, she and the horses she rode – Finality, Prince Hall, Tosca, Flanagan – helped make show-jumping the immensely popular spectator sport it is today.

Smythe was born in London and first rode at local stables, but during the war the family moved to the country. After the war she helped her widowed mother run a guest house. When she was 13, her mother gave her a three-year-old, offspring of a work horse, whom they called Finality. Smythe trained her herself, and was soon doing so well in local competitions, in spite of many setbacks – illness and accident – that she was urged to enter for the International at the White City. She was at once invited – aged only 19 – to join the British team. She was soon beating Olympic riders, although women were not then allowed to enter. There was a famous jump-off in the 1950 Horse of the Year Show, when she tied equal first on Finality with Colonel Harry

Pat Smythe on Tosca at the International Horse Show, White City in 1953.

Llewellyn on his famous Foxhunter. Finally she became the first woman show-jumper in the Olympic Games when she was a member of the British team which won a bronze in Stockholm in 1956. She retired soon after the Rome Olympics of 1960 (the British team was eliminated), and went to live in Switzerland with her husband Sam Koechlin, whom she married in 1963. They have two daughters.

Smythe has an unerring eye for a horse – Tosca and Prince Hal were each bought for only £150 – and an exceptional gift for both training and riding. She has written many books, including stories for children.

Dorothy Steel
British (1884–1965)

Only three women have won the Open Croquet Championship – and one of them, Dorothy Steel, won it four times, in 1925, 1933, 1935 and 1936. She was the supreme woman croquet player, without doubt the equal of any man, and dominated the game for 20 years between 1919 and 1939. She also won the Women's Championship 15 times, and five doubles and seven mixed doubles titles. In all, she won 31 titles, and played with a handicap of minus 5 – the lowest ever for a woman.

PICTURE ACKNOWLEDGMENTS

The illustrations in this book were supplied or are reproduced by kind permission of the following:

By gracious permission of HM the Queen 198
All-Sport 277 (right)
American Museum of Natural History 216
American Red Cross 220
Arden, Elizabeth, (UK) Ltd 248
Ashmolean Museum, Oxford 211
Associated Press 15
Australian Information Service, London 232

Beaton, Cecil, (photograph courtesy of Sotheby's Belgravia 129, 179, 210
Bettman Archive Inc. 119
Bibliothèque Nationale, Paris 110, 148
Brook Street Bureau (photo: Godfrey Argent) 254
Bulloz 222

Camera Press 38, 50 (right), 224
Cape, Jonathan, Ltd (photo: Gerry Bauer) 133
Chicago Art Institute 208
Church of Scotland Overseas Council 92
Controller of HM Stationery Office and Director, Royal

Botanic Gardens, Kew; Crown Copyright 237, 270
Evans, Mary, Picture Library 200
Fawcett Library, City of London Polytechnic (photos: Geoff Goode) 36, 37
Gerson, Mark 136, 157
Giraudon (SPADEM) 105, 215
Girton College Cambridge, Mistress and Fellows 68
Hamiltons (photo: Geoff Goode) 197
Imperial War Museum, London 229
Japan Information Centre, London 107
Kansas State Historical Society 82 (top)
Keystone Press 12, 43, 48, 50 (left), 51, 55, 90, 112, 185, 201, 262, 274, 277 (left), 278, 280 (top), 285
Kinley, Monika 199
Library of the Chemical Society (photo Geoff Goode) 227
Library of Congress 58, 245
Mansell Collection 20, 23, 53, 61 (right), 74, 78, 89, 91, 100, 104, 125 (left), 164, 167, 168, 181, 184, 222 (left), 244, 252, 269

Metropolitan Museum of Art. Gift of Julia A. Berwind, 1953 206
Mother Jones (photo Geoff Goode) 33
National Film Archives 134, 188
National Gallery of Art, Washington. Rosenwald Collection 205
National Galleries of Scotland (photo Tom Scott) 243
National Portrait Gallery, London 25, 62, 65, 72, 80, 121, 123, 130, 132, 147, 155, 166 (left), 174, 183 (right), 193, 202, 203, 204, 259, 267
National Trust 75
Novosti Press Agency 35 (left), 57, 114, 158, 273 (left), 282, 284
Oakland Museum. Gift of Dr Paul Schuster Taylor 207
Observer Magazine (photo Geoff Goode) 22
Popperfoto 71 (left), 79, 95, 166 (right)
Press Association 24, 111, 225, 280 (bottom)
Radio Times Hulton Picture Library 14, 27, 31, 40, 60, 70, 82 (bottom), 115, 138, 149, 150, 161, 162, 172, 176, 273 (right), 276, 279 (right)
Richmond Fellowship 76

Rijkvoorlichtinsdienst 131
Ronan, Anne, Picture Library 226
Royal College Music 163, 173, 178, 183 (left), 187
Royal Geographic Society 17, 264, 265, 271, 272
Royal Photographic Society of Great Britain 194
Rubinstein, Helena, Foundation Collection 246

Salvation Army 97
San Francisco Museum of Modern Art. Mrs Ferdinand C. Smith Fund Purchase 191
Sotheby's Belgravia 169
Strasbourg Cathedral 213

United Press International 21, 30, 35 (right), 83, 99, 116, 140, 209, 235, 238 (left), 241, 251 (right), 279 (left), 283

Veuve Clicquot Champagne 251 (left)

Warne, Frederick, & Co Ltd 145
Weidenfeld & Nicolson Archive 28, 41, 44, 61 (left), 69, 96, 124, 126, 137, 151, 154, 177, 240, 250, 257
Whitworth Art Gallery, University of Manchester 56
Wichita Art Museum. The Roland P. Murdoch Collection 196

INDEX